T0326277

UNDEAD UPRISING

Finally an authoritative book on that weird, complex figure of the zombie that delves deep into the dark heart of the matter rather than skating the surface.—Roger Luckhurst

This comprehensive work is a must read for anyone wishing to understand more about the destinies of African-based religions in the Americas, and especially concerning the uses and abuses of Haitian cultural phenomena by outside interests.— LeGrace Benson

In 1929 the explorer William Seabrook published *The Magic Island,* a questionable travelogue that portrayed the Caribbean state of Haiti as a menacing hinterland of ecstatic ritual, voodoo possession, zombie labourers and meddling spirits.

Despite the sensational nature of Seabrook's book, the image of Haiti as a mysterious domain stricken by dark forces has come to characterise western pop-cultural impressions of the country ever since, from Graham Greene's novelistic evocation of state-terrorism *The Comedians,* to the lurid depictions of 'voodoo nations' in Ian Fleming's *Live and Let Die* and Wes Craven's visceral adaptation of Wade Davis's anthropological memoir *The Serpent and the Rainbow.*

Pursuing the figure of the zombie from folk bogey to cinematic icon, artist and writer John Cussans asks how myth and reality have come to find themselves so entangled in Haitian history, and how Vodou beliefs have informed both Haitian politics and the superstitious diplomacy of foreign nations.

Cussans' book is a richly researched and original exploration of the mythical life of Haiti, tracing its stories through mesmerism, Surrealism, imaginative literature and the nightmare images of Hollywood. At once a thorough survey of colonial racism and a philosophical provocation, *Undead Uprising* traces the feedback loops that occur between fantasy and reality, and asks how a vibrant mythology has worked both for and against this fascinating country in its quest for independence.

Undead Uprising by John Cussans
Published by Strange Attractor Press 2016
This print on demand edition 2023
ISBN: 978-1-907222-47-4

Original cover art and design by Graham Humphreys

Strange Attractor Press
BM SAP, London, WC1N 3XX, UK www.strangeattractor.co.uk

UNDEAD UPRISING

HAITI, HORROR AND THE ZOMBIE COMPLEX

JOHN CUSSANS

CONTENTS

PART TWO

THE ZOMBIE COMPLEX

> The aim by itself is a lifeless universal, just as the guiding
> tendency is a mere drive that as yet lacks an actual
> existence; and the bare result is the corpse which has left
> the guiding tendency behind it.
>
> - G. W. F. Hegel[1]

In its passage from myth-figure to metaphor the zombie has come to
perform a vast range of allegorical functions, its meanings as diverse
as a displaced person eking out a precarious existence at the bio-
political limits of late capitalist society or the unfeeling advocates of
free-market fundamentalism who oversee it. The "zombie apocalypse"
has been used as a metaphor for climate change advocacy, its denial,
and as a blueprint for national disaster preparedness. In contemporary
journalism "zombie-the-adjective" is attached to objects as diverse
as banks, businesses, computer programmes, sociological categories
and tweets. As a myth-figure the zombie has been used to reflect
upon the destiny of souls and the meaning of the body after death, to
denigrate African religious and cultural presence in the Americas, as a
covert theme within neo-colonial propaganda and as a representation
of collective guilt and trauma about the colonial slavery system.
As a popular sociological allegory it has represented the effects of

---

1 Hegel (1952) 3

industrialisation and mass media on modern societies, the psychology of contemporary consumerism and changes in global labour practices. And as a philosophical thought-figure it has helped think the construction and critique of the category of the human, the nature of consciousness and sentience, the existence of the soul, distinctions between the living and the dead and material and immaterial modes of existence. But in whatever form they are imagined or whatever masters they are made to serve, zombies rarely speak for or about *themselves*. They are, in almost every case, dumb and mortally compromised *agents-without-autonomy*. In this sense zombies share the historical fate of the dead described by Stephan Palmié in *Wizards and Scientists*:

> They are denizens of a world that no longer exists, and, even though we may concede that our world reverberates with the consequences – intended or not – of the actions that the dead once took, the choice whether we want to see matters this way must remain ours. Paraphrasing Marx, one might say that, given this particular structuring of the past in the Western historical imagination, the dead have to be represented because they can no longer represent themselves.[2]

The zombie-figure, beginning its popular *un*life as a ghastly allegory for the horrors of colonial slavery and the potential of humans to be reduced, by sorcery and commerce, to soul-less, living-dead cadavers in the 1920s, has developed into the most ubiquitous figure for the end of humanity as we know it at the end of history. In the process the figure has evolved two very distinct behavioural characteristics: one entirely passive, docile and manipulable, governed by the will of a sinister external agent, the other utterly ungovernable, massively insurrectionary and driven only by a relentless "need to feed". The extreme behavioural ambivalence of the modern zombie figure, at times entirely subordinate to an external authority, at others totally devoid of any "human" restraint, can be traced back to representations of the insurrectionary African slave armies of Saint-Domingue, who began a revolutionary war against slavery in 1791. It was widely

2 Palmié (2002) 5

believed at the time that these armies were in thrall to a diabolical serpent cult called "Vaudoux", whose priests they were entirely devoted to and under whose influence they would commit acts of the utmost barbarity. In 1804 the victorious military leader of these slave armies - Jean-Jacques Dessalines - founded the Republic of Haiti, the first slave-free nation in the world, and the birthplace of the modern *zombi*, a figure whose mystical roots lie in the displaced African religion secretly forged by slaves under the execrable conditions of the colonial, plantation economy.

The multiple and often contradictory metaphorical meanings associated with the figure, and its ubiquity and resilience in contemporary popular culture, are the chief components of what I refer to here as The Zombie Complex. It is a nod in the general direction of Carl Jung's formulation of "psychological complexes": a core pattern of emotions, fantasies, fears and ideas *clustered around a central motif.* Unlike Jung I am not interested in the notion of personal or individual complexes but in more broadly cultural and social ones. The idea is more directly indebted to Stephan Palmié's formulation of an "Afro-Cuban *nganga* Complex", a concept modelled upon the ritual cauldrons of the Afro-Cuban *Palo Monte* tradition in which spirits of the dead are housed. Within this religion a man-made artefact (the *nganga*) takes on characteristics of a living *being*, one which must be continually fed to prevent it running out of control and killing its master, maker or owner. This magical giving of predatory sentience to an inanimate thing is imagined by Palmié as a kind of allegorical reversal of the processes by which a human being was made into a "mere tool" within the slavery system. As such the *nganga* "dissolves the distinction between objects and persons" while at the same time speaking of the violent history of "dehumanization under slave-labor-driven forms of plantation-production":

> Thinking with *ngangas* (or *zonbis*, for that matter) allows us access to an analytic dimension that radically exposes, rather than merely metaphorises, a dimension of the now globalised moral dis-order that first emerged, in stunningly drastic form, on those New World production sites where a novel regime of value made it possible to productively merge depersonalised humans

with machines, treat their bodies as sheer sources of extractable value, and terminate their lives solely in regards to considerations of utility.[3]

The Zombie Complex then refers to a range of ethical, psychological and political thought-problems clustered around the central figure of the "living-corpse" which, though ostensibly fictional, stubbornly reminds us of the horribly actual limits (or lack of limits) of "humanity", "the individual" and "the human". Ultimately at stake in the Zombie Complex are a series of questions about consciousness, violence, morality and economics, and a dialectic of remembering and forgetting, awareness and oblivion about the *un-being*'s historical origins and the conditions which have accelerated and propagated its spectacular ubiquity at the dawn of a new millennium. In this sense the zombies that concern *Undead Uprising* are all, in one form or another, *zombies of historical consciousness*.

In order to untangle the diverse range of things and meanings the term zombie has been applied to, and to temporarily suspend its collapse into the semantic abyss of endlessly proliferating metaphoricity, I have traced the figure's path from its ancestral roots in Haitian folklore, its migration into "Western" popular culture, its transformation into a literary, cinematic and popular allegory for a range of social ills, to its becoming a generalised figure of speech in popular parlance for anything that refuses to die properly. In the process I ask what useful correlations might be drawn between contemporary metaphorical uses of the zombie figure and its folkloric and "possessed" revolutionary ancestors, and what this might tell us about the way Haiti has been imagined since the revolution that brought it into existence. As I trace the zombie's mindless path through Anglo-American popular culture, I make readings of some of the best known literary and cinematic examples of Voodoo-horror, asking how their chimerical optics have distorted the realities of Haiti and how the magic of cinema and media spectacle raise questions for consciousness, autonomy and agency in their historical, political and individualistic modes. I also question the ways in which Voodoo-horror can be seen in reverse as it were, as a kind of "modern magic", used on its users to keep the historical

---

3 Palmié (2006) 877

and political realities of Haiti obscured and "occulted". Although the zombie plays a leading role in *Undead Uprising* it is only one of several themes through which Haiti has been viewed "from the outside" in overtly *diabolical* terms: "demonic possession", "cannibalism" "human sacrifice" and "insurrectionary barbarism" form an essential cluster of "Black practices" imagined to be at the dark heart of "chimerical" Haiti. As such they are the central themes in the "horror" of the book's title. All the examples of Voodoo-horror discussed here are subsequently contextualised in terms of the political realities of Haiti at the time of their dissemination elsewhere.

I am aware that bringing the Haitian folkloric *zombi* into critical proximity with its flesh-eating, apocalyptic and philosophical cousins might well be taken as an example of what Donald Cosentino and others have called "Vodou Chic", something scholars within the Haitian Studies community look upon disdainfully. Their disapproval is understandable given the historical role of sensationalistic and distorted representations of Vodou and the popularly associated *zombi* figure in hostile, foreign propaganda. I have tried to avoid making any unsupported claims or inferences about an assumed "authentic" Haiti beyond the distortions of Voodoo-horror or about the practices of "actual" Haitian Vodou. This is not to deny the reality of either. It is rather to insist that "undead uprisings" happen primarily in the realm of fiction and myth and that, because my focus has been on representations of Voodoo-horror and zombies which have had wide and popular circulation in the English-speaking world, the Haiti of which I write is, first and foremost, the mist-enveloped one they point to with osseous fingers.

In his book *Haiti: State Against Nation* the historian Michel-Rolph Trouillot wasted no time dismissing reductive explanations for the peculiarities of Haitian political life to what he called "the myth of Haitian exceptionalism" (the idea that there is something fundamentally irrational about the Haitian mind that makes a reasoned analysis of its political history impossible). I agree wholeheartedly with Trouillot's criticism. Both the *zombi*-myth and the cult of Vodou have been dominant themes in the perpetuation of the idea of Haiti's "irreducible particularity" and as such they have been used to render its place in modern, global history "unthinkable". But it is precisely at the intersection of the general unthinkability of horror and the particular unthinkability of Haiti's role in modern, "universal" history that the thinking of *Undead Uprising* operates. In order to bring a serious account of Haiti into the analysis of the sensationalist tropes discussed here I have re-situated them in relation to contemporaneous accounts of the political and social realities of Haiti at the time that Voodoo-horror was entertaining audiences elsewhere. In other words I have attempted to look through the refracted image of a "diabolical Haiti" to the real Haiti that ostensibly lies beyond them. To do so I make reference to a history of the politics of Haiti drawn from a range of scholarly works. It is important to emphasise however that I am an armchair historian and my personal experience of Haiti is far too limited to draw upon in any empirical way. As such the "real" Haiti beyond the sensational distortions is still an "imaginary" one, the product of a different kind of discourse, more academic, trustworthy and respectable no doubt, but no less "immaterial" for that.

THESE PEOPLE, THOSE THINGS

So what can the zombie swarms that lay spectacular waste to human civilisation in films like *World War Z* possibly tell us about the representation of Haitian history and culture? Surely even proposing a correlation is to perpetuate the profoundly prejudicial vision that has viewed Haiti as a place of savage barbarism and unthinkable horror for two centuries? Yes, of course the contemporary zombie figure has its cultural roots in Haitian folklore, but today's zombies have nothing to do with that history. To propose as much will only perpetuate the racist and xenophobic stereotypes that have distorted western perceptions of the country since colonial times, undermining its struggle for international legitimacy, political recognition and independent self-governance ever since. And I agree, very much so. But still I think the task may prove valuable for our understandings of the real and historical Haiti as well as offering new ways of tackling and countering the mediums of misrepresentation it has been subject to. There is no doubt that zombies and other broadly Vodou tropes in modern and contemporary horror films have been detrimental to Haiti's image to the outside world and have at times coincided directly with international foreign policy towards the country. By entering more deeply into their chimerical optics, exposing and analysing their

PREFACE

narratives and effects, correcting, replacing or "détourning" them if necessary, and comparing the images that horrify us with those from other, less sensational or emotive representations, I believe we might eventually arrive at a more realistic, sober and politically pragmatic view of the country (and "our" views of it) without altogether negating the intoxicating powers of horror that make the films, novels and travelogues I write about here so alluring and grimly affecting.

With this in mind there are three relatively distinct ways in which a film like *World War Z*, a popular example of the contemporary zombie genre from 2013 (based on Max Brooks's best selling novel of the same name), could be read in relation to Haiti. The first is the simplest: a history of the zombie trope. From this perspective we could trace a history of the figure from its roots in Haitian folklore, through the major phases of its figurative and metaphorical transformation, pointing out the most important shifts in this evolution from which the constitutive features and meanings associated with each particular version emerge. Zack, the personal name Max Brooks gave the "mass-being" of the zombie apocalypse in the original novel, for instance, is clearly an apocalyptic cannibal-type zombie, which began its cinematic *un*-life in George A. Romero's *Night of the Living Dead* in 1968. Insurrectionary, predatory and insatiable, this new form of zombie brought its folkloric and classic cinematic ancestors to the brink of spectacular extinction. We could reflect upon the meanings of this flesh-eating transformation, why it became such a popular trope in the latter half of the 20th century (and even more so at the turn of the new millennium), the sudden increase in the speed and appetite of zombies, the central theme of a zombie plague in these narratives and their circumstantial and metaphorical meanings for representations of contemporary and historical Haiti. But again, it could reasonably be argued that the flesh-eating zombie marks such a radical species break in the zombie-continuum that any reference back to Haiti is now even more unwarranted than it already was. In response we might cite Phillip Mahoney who has argued that prescient fears about contagious mass-zombie uprisings in contemporary horror films were expressed by crowd psychologists of the late 19th century, who advanced explicitly racial and clinical theories of susceptibility to violent, insurrectionary and collective behaviour in ways that echo those of the colonial authorities of 18th century Saint-Domingue shortly after the Haitian Revolution. Still a stretch? OK. Let's try another angle.[4]

The second approach we might call "theoretical". It examines the scholarship on particular Haiti-related horror tropes and films, the theoretical concepts and analytical tools it uses, asking how these might help us to understand and interpret the broader cultural politics of representation within which Haiti has been framed.[5] Gerry Canavan for instance, drawing on a range of social theorists and political philosophers (notably Michel Foucault and Achille Mbembe), has proposed that incarnations of the zombie figure in popular culture constitute "a hyperbolic re-enactment of the imaginary racial demarcation into life and anti-life that is crucial to the construction of the contemporary biopolitical state".[6]

> Although not every modern state reaches a final moment of unbounded extermination – most staying instead within regimens of legal and customary segregation, ideological norms, imprisonment and unjust practices of labour exploitation – we nonetheless find the terrible exterminative potential of biopolitical logic lying in wait for us in all temporal directions: such terrors as colonialism, imperial warfare and the Holocaust in the past; the militarised American inner city, post-invasion Iraq and Afghanistan, genocides in Rwanda and the Sudan, post-earthquake Haiti, post-Katrina New Orleans and any number of similar horrors in the present; and

---

4 Philip Mahoney 'Mass Psychology and the Analysis of the Zombie: From Suggestion to Contagion' in Boluk and Lenz.

5 See Boluk and Lenz *Generation Zombie: Essays on the Living Dead in Modern Culture* (2011), Bishop *American Zombie Gothic: The Rise and Fall (and Rise) of the Walking Dead in Popular Culture* (2010) and Christie and Lauro *Better off Dead: The Evolution of the Zombie as Post-Human* (2010).

6 Canavan 173

PREFACE

finally the fantasy of social breakdown that dominates the contemporary imagination of the future, the zombie apocalypse.[7]

From this perspective the apocalyptic flesh-eating zombie represents a kind of zero-degree race figure, the ultimate expression of the *race-which-is-not-one*, an "undivided" and literally *in*human race that must be eradicated before it contaminates and annihilates the very foundation of the body-politic (i.e. "us" living humans). As such it clearly has characteristics in common with the depiction of the revolting slaves of Saint-Domingue, who, within the dominant reasoning of 18th century European race theory, were hereditarily predisposed to subhuman savagery and consequently, to reasoned, colonial domination. With this in mind one could point to the ethnic and cultural characteristics of *World War Z*'s hero-figure Gerry Lane, an Anglo-American, former UN investigator, and friendly, loyal, caring, Caucasian father-figure, played by Brad Pitt. Known outside his film roles for humanitarian work against poverty and AIDS in the developing world, and for his support of embryonic stem-cell research, his character's entire nuclear family, including their zombie-orphaned, newly-adopted, Latino son manage to survive the global apocalypse completely intact. "If you want to help your family," the Army General in charge of the military response to the epidemic tells him early in the film, "you better help us stop this thing". Having survived the fall of fortress Jerusalem and an airplane crash in which all the passengers except himself and a newfound female compatriot from the Israel Defence Force die, Lane makes his way to the World Health Organisation Research Facility in Wales. When asked by the scientists why he had come there and what he needs from them, Lane tells them bluntly "Your worst disease". The camera cuts to a close-up of a leering, Black, dreadlocked zombie, bashing its grimacing face against the glass wall of the lab. "You want a what?" a doctor asks. "A deadly pathogen. With a high mortality rate. But curable," he explains. The doctors tell him that he would need a bacteria not a virus. But that has been tried before and failed. Zombies don't have circulatory systems. "You can't make a dead person sick". "I believe these things have a weakness," Lane responds. Cut to full-

---

7 Canavan 175

screen shot of the zombie-doctor looking suddenly scared. "And this weakness *is* weakness. It's *our* weakness". Cut back to a close-up of the leering zombie snarling against the glass.

Scenes such as these suggest that barely-concealed racial meanings are still embedded in contemporary zombie narratives, even if the figure has been ostensibly deracinated since 1968. But again one could argue that drawing inferences about Haiti from such an optic simply repeats accusations, made since the beginning of the 20th century, that western representations of Haiti in popular fiction often have covert (and at times overtly) racist implications. So what's new? The contemporary paradox of the zombie, as many commentators have noted, has to do with their being just like "us" but not "us" at all. And although this difference is absolute and universal for all humans within apocalyptic zombie narratives (i.e. it is technically "anthropological" rather than "ethnological") the residual traces of racial and cultural differences are clearly inferred within them. But to reduce the politics of Haiti to those of race and its representation is not only to grossly simplify Haitian culture, history and society but also to perpetuate racist myths about Haiti that have been used to denigrate the Republic since its independence in 1804. Once again, we are in agreement.

Shortly after the bifurcation of the zombie-continuum in 1968, the figure found its way into the philosophical field of Consciousness Studies when the so-called "zombie problem" was introduced to debates about the nature of consciousness. The general schema of the problem, first outlined by Robert Kirk in an article for the journal *Mind* in 1974, was the conceivability of a being that looked and acted exactly like a human being but lacked sentience (i.e. reportable conscious awareness of its own sensations and reactions). Although "zombie" was perhaps not the most appropriate name for this hypothetically insentient being, as with Romero's flesh-eating "ghouls", the living-corpse moniker stuck, perhaps because of something stubbornly abject at the core of the "difference that makes a difference". The general form of the zombie problem can be traced back to philosophical debates between materialists and idealists in the 18th century, a period in which moral justifications for slavery were bound up with an emergent philosophy of the enlightened, autonomous, self-conscious human being, distinguished by higher, universal and progressive purposes from the mere brute, automaton or machine. Following this line of reasoning one can draw a critical-theoretic arc that connects beings like Zack to the *thing-like* status of slaves in the colonial plantation system.[8] The Haitian Revolution coincides with one of the most influential statements in the philosophy of human self-consciousness and difference, Hegel's 'Dialectic of Lordship and Bondage' in his *The Phenomenology of Spirit* (1807). Despite being concerned explicitly with how humans can be reduced to the status of mere things, and the struggle to the death they must engage in to win true freedom, Hegel chose not to mention the Haitian Revolution, which he would have been familiar with from reports in German newspapers at the time (as Susan Buck-Morss has convincingly shown).[9] Within Hegel's philosophical schema the zombie coincides with the figure of the slave, a mere "human thing", spiritually unenlightened and unable to achieve self-consciousness, political subjecthood or autonomy, who must wage a war of extermination in order to win its liberty.

Anthropological debates about what constitutes the "properly human", forged in the historical milieu of the trans-Atlantic slave trade, still haunt the zombie figure in its spectacular slave-like, insurrectionary and "actual" modalities, all of which fundamentally challenge Enlightenment claims about the agency and autonomy of thinking, self-conscious and fully individuated human beings. From the perspective of a bio-politically inflected cultural theory then, historical and political meanings can be read off the flesh-eating zombie trope that have relevance for both contemporary and historical representations of Haiti and the revolutionary subjects who founded it, which have contributed to myths of Haitian exceptionalism ever since. The issue of "zombic-difference", as articulated in contemporary culture and philosophical thought, might therefore hold up an uncanny historical mirror to the constructions of racial, cultural and human difference upon which these myths have been constructed since the colonial era. Furthermore, in the expanded media-sphere of contemporary, global mass culture, celebrity humanitarians like Brad Pitt, fighting world poverty one day and the zombie apocalypse the next, explicitly draw

---

8 See Markus and Žižek (2009), *Žižek* (2006)

9 Buck-Morss *Hegel, Haiti and Universal History* (2009) 21-65, 87-107

the real politics of post-disaster Haiti into the spectacular orbit of Hollywood blockbusters. Fictional zombie killer one day and actual human suffering eradicator the next, Pitt draws our attention to the more abstract and extended systems of meaning, knowledge and value production that are constituted by, and constitutive of, a spectacular global society in which Haiti has had a momentous but largely occluded role.

A final way to connect Haiti to *World War Z* is to compare it with contemporary pictures of Haiti like that represented by Raoul Peck's film *Assistance mortelle,* released the same year. Peck's documentary takes an inside view on the international and government effort to reconstruct Haiti after the earthquake of 2010, exposing the calamitous involvement of thousands of multinational aid agencies and their collective incapacity to respond in any practical or constructive way to the massive human catastrophe taking place there. Peck, a Haitian-born film-maker who served for a period as minister of culture for the first government of René Préval (1996-97), was able to gain (almost) unrestricted access to the international disaster relief operation, including the visits by Hollywood celebrity humanitarians like Brad Pitt, Angelina Jolie, George Clooney, Sean Penn and their patron saint Bill Clinton. The film exposes the debacle that ensued in the wake of a disaster that caused the deaths of as many as 300,000 people and in which billions of dollars of international aid money was almost entirely redirected back to the coffers of the donor nations.[10] Even though the

---

10 The estimated number of deaths has been a contested issue in the five years since the disaster. Several factors have contributed to this, not least the human scale of the catastrophe. They include the necessity to deal immediately with the tens of thousands of injured and homeless, the fact that many people buried their dead in informal graves and that many more "uncounted" bodies were dumped into local landfill sites. The official Haitian government figure in 2013 was 316,000 deaths. A U.S. government report, published one year after the disaster for USAID (the US Agency for International Development), put the figure between 46,000 and 85,000. According to the UN Haiti Humanitarian Action Plan of 2013 the number was estimated at 217,300. Claims were made at the time that the Haitian government was deliberately inflating the figure in order to receive more international aid, an accusation, as we will see,

Haitian government was largely excluded from the IHRC (Interim Haiti Recovery Commission), ostensibly because of corruption fears, most of the money still managed to evaporate before any concrete re-construction projects could be realised. Peck's conclusion is that foreign aid has done more harm than good in Haiti and that if well-meaning foreigners want Haiti to flourish they should stop supporting the NGOs and their disaster-amplifying involvement in the country. Although *World War Z* and *Fatal Assistance* are poles apart cinematically there are clear discernible threads, already suggested by cultural theorists like Canavan and the symbolic involvement of celebrity humanitarians like Pitt and Angelina Jolie, that have to do with global disaster response, the philosophical concepts of bio-power and bare life, and the international politics of humanitarianism, "celebrity" or otherwise.

Throughout *Undead Uprising* I use all three approaches, but not in a systematic or methodical way. I have relied primarily on textual sources – both written and visual – and the images, claims and argumentation contained within them. These have tended to fall broadly into four main areas: i) popular, sensationalist and documentary representations of Haiti, Vodou and zombies in literature, television and film, ii) scholarly critiques of said representations, iii) academic studies about the cultural significance of the zombie figure and iv) scholarly accounts of Haitian history and Vodou. Moving between four fields my thinking has taken on a broadly philosophical character responding to prompts from the contexts themselves. I have adopted a general structure that begins in 1929 with the publication of William S. Seabrook's notorious *The Magic Island*, the book that introduced the *zombi* and Haitian Vodou to popular international audiences, then, following a generally historical path, I discuss some the most popular and widely recognised depictions of Voodoo-horror from then to the present. In each chapter I situate these representations in the context of the actual politics of Haiti at the time of their making, asking what if any impact they may have had on foreign policy towards the country and how Haitian writers and politicians attempted to counter them. With each "case

---

that was probably a consequence of the enduring legacy of Duvalierism in Haiti, a regime that tactically exploited international aid under the pretext of being a "bulwark against Communism" in the Caribbean.

study" I focus on the nature of the Vodou knowledge upon which the particular representations were based, mapping their mythical, popular, cultural evolution. One exception to the general pattern is Chapter Three – 'The Romance of Revolutionary Vodou' – in which I discuss the ethnographic reclamation of Vodou by Haitian scholars in the 1920s and '30s, attempts to counter sensationalist accounts of the religion in Anglo-American popular culture, and the consequences of these for the emergent *Noiriste* politics of Duvalierism in the 1950s. Ultimately the aim of *Undead Uprising* is to explore how Voodoo horror and zombie films, staples of Anglo-American popular culture since the 1920s, have contributed to a fantastical, diabolically exotic, and racist optic on Haiti that has served the interests of "foreign powers" ever since the world changing events that began on the northern plains of Saint-Domingue in August 1791.

DEMONS THROUGH THE ETHER

I was born at the height of the terror. Conspiracies were rife, invasions and popular uprisings, real or imagined, were swiftly and ruthlessly dealt with, as they had been since the election eight years ago. Crippled by chronic heart disease, diabetes, degenerative arthritis, its veins swollen with phlebitis, the stricken body of the president limped through the palace that had become his private prison. A student of Vodou since the 1920s, friend and confidant to many *houngans* (Vodou priests) and *mambos* (Vodou priestesses), François "Papa Doc" Duvalier, so named because of the esteem and admiration in which he was held by the thousands of poor Haitian peasants he had, as a dedicated country doctor, cured of yaws before his Machiavellian rise to power, was now a world famous "Voodoo Dictator". His sunglasses-wearing private army of Tonton Macoute, named after the bogeyman of Haitian folklore who prowled the night looking for bad little boys and girls to put in his straw bag, had been given the power to enact summary justice against anyone who might conceivably pose a threat to the leader's absolute authority.

In the early days of his presidency the small, bespectacled and infirm, but always impeccably well-dressed Duvalier said that he wanted to kill three hundred people a year. His regime was now executing the same number every month, many reputedly dispatched by the president's own hand.[1] Those whom he did not kill himself he observed through

---

1 Most of the "facts" in this section are taken from Elizabeth Abbott's *Haiti: The Duvaliers and their Legacy* (1991). It should be noted that many

a peephole in the palace's private torture room, its walls painted rust-brown to camouflage the blood smeared over them. The palace even had a coffin-shaped iron maiden for particularly special cases. Never completely convinced that known conspirators were truly dead unless he was present himself, he demanded their heads be delivered to him at the palace. An estimated 3,000 prisoners were murdered at the "Dungeon of Death", Fort Dimanche, a former U.S. military base that had become the main facility for incarcerating, torturing and killing political prisoners during his reign. Many prisoners were placed in *cachots*, coffin-like cells with no room to move, until they died. Those not beaten or tortured to death died of dysentery, tuberculosis or "having their blood sucked from them by scores of vermin", as one journalist at the time put it.

There were hundreds of other prisons in Duvalier's Haiti where torture was routine. Like their leader, many powerful Macoutes had private cells in their own homes. The bloated corpse of one murdered conspirator, Yvan Laraque, a member of the U.S.-based resistance group *Jeune Haiti*, who had launched an heroic but ill-fated invasion against the regime in 1964, was propped up for ten days in an armchair at a major intersection in the capital Port-au-Prince under a Coca-Cola sign saying "Welcome to Haiti!"

It was believed by some Haitians that shortly after becoming president Papa Doc had made a pilgrimage to the great cave of Trou Foban, known since the time of slavery as the dwelling place of notoriously powerful and evil spirits. The president, aided by a group of powerful *houngans*, had ceremonially invited the spirits to a new home in the presidential palace. Rumours had been circulating since a major heart attack in 1959 that the president had been taken over by the very demons he had made a pact with. They had eaten his soul, leaving only the living carcass behind. In short "Papa Doc" was now a *zombi*. To consolidate his image as a man dedicated to the spirit of death he donned the bowler hat, funeral coat, dark glasses, white gloves and distinct nasal tone of Baron Samedi, keeper of the cemeteries and master of the dead.

When, finally, the Organisation of American States decided to act

---

of them are derived from private conversations and newspapers and that her sources are not cited in the book. As we will see, some of Abbott's claims depart markedly from "objective" journalistic reporting, especially when it comes to the purportedly "darker" practices of the Duvaliers.

on reports about the widespread, systematic political repression and the hundreds of deaths in police custody, Duvalier announced to an apparently adoring nation: "Bullets and machine guns capable of daunting Duvalier do not exist. They cannot touch me... I am already an immaterial being". Should any Haitian schoolchild doubt that he was indeed a living incarnation of the historical founders of the Haitian nation, he penned his *Catechism of the Revolution* to be read out loud before classes:

> "Our Doc, who are in the National Palace, hallowed be thy name in the present and future generations. Thy will be done at Port-au-Prince as it is in the Provinces. Give us this day our new Haiti and never forgive the trespasses of the anti-patriots who spit every day on our country. Let them succumb to temptation, and under the weight of their venom, deliver them not from any evil".

None of these "horrors" I knew anything about until twenty years after the death of the Great Voodoo Dictator. Intimations of the terror of Haiti under his rule had however made circuitous inroads to our semi-detached family home in Acomb, on the outskirts of York (an historical city in the north of England) where, a decade later, my sister and I would enjoy regular Friday night "Appointments with Fear", horror film double-bills emanating from the suddenly sinister television set in the corner of our otherwise safe and cozy living room. Our first encounter with the dark powers of Voodoo-horror came through *Dr. Terror's House of Horrors*, a portmanteau film, made in 1965, that tells the stories of five men brought together by chance on an outbound commuter train from London to the suburbs. Through the mysterious power of his tarot deck the sinister Dr. Schreck reveals to each of his fellow passengers their terrible fates. The third to have his story read is Biff Bailey, a chipper, happy-go-lucky jazz trumpeter. When Schreck turns over his fourth card, The Devil, Biff quips "That's my mother-in-law!" "Do not jest at the image of a god", Schreck warns, especially not "the powerful and malign god of Voo-doo!"

And so the fable of Biff Bailey begins: Biff has a regular gig playing jazz standards at the Caravel club in London until he is offered a new booking in the West Indies, at the Flamingo club in Dupont on the island of "Paiti". Biff is more than happy with this arrangement, especially when the women of the island flashed their "white smiles at him from dark lips – from mouths that were sometimes Negro, sometimes Spanish, and sometimes tantalizingly both".[2] While chatting with outgoing resident trumpeter Sammy Coin about where the "real action" is, Biff notices that the cigarette girl at their table is wearing a medallion depicting a grotesque, gaping-mouthed face. When he tries to make a gag about it the girl rushes away and the diners fall suddenly silent in glaring condemnation. Sammy explains quietly that the "monster" is the Voodoo god Damballa, and Voodoo is the one thing you don't make cracks about.[3] "Not round here. Look around man". He does. "All the chicks are wearing them!" Biff observes. Unperturbed by Sammy's warning to stay clear of the Vodou ceremonies that take place at night, deep in the jungle, Biff, drawn by the alluring rhythms that permeate his sleep, makes his way to a clearing where a ceremony is in full swing. Keen to capture some authentic "Paitian" beats to stir up the nightclub crowd back home, Biff excitedly scribbles down the drum patterns on a sketchy musical stave. But before he can finish the transcription he is discovered by four shirtless and face-painted members of the Vodou congregation, who manhandle him into the centre of the proceedings, and he is brought before high-priest. Outraged that Biff would try to steal the music of the gods, the priest rips his notebook to shreds and warns him that Damballa is a jealous god, and wherever Biff goes, the god will be avenged.

Back in London, paying no heed to the warning, Biff plays his own version of the "Voodoo" tune with the image of the god decorating the stage behind him. Half way through the number the doors of the club blow open and a powerful wind tears through the building blowing the score around the room, ripping up tablecloths and over-turning chairs. The punters rush for the exits in panic but the band plays on. Unshaken by the wrecked nightclub and Sammy's insistence that he destroy the score, Biff chooses instead to take it home to perfect the middle section. As he walks the empty streets he feels like he is being

---

2 The quote is from John Burke's novelisation of the film (Burke 78). Thanks to Andy Sharp (English Heretic) for the loan of the book.

3 Within the Vodou pantheon of deities (or *lwa*) Damballa is the great sky serpent that encircles the universe. A primordial father figure, patron of waters and heavens and a major *lwa* within the tradition, he is syncretised in with the Catholic St. Patrick.

followed. He bumps into a tall Black man who asks him for a light. Safely back in his apartment Biff pours himself a stiff drink as the windows and doors slam shut around him. Then the main lights go out. He fumbles in the dark for a table lamp. When the room is once more illuminated he is face to face with another Black man whose face and chest are painted with the telltale markings of the Vodou devotees. As the man reaches toward his throat Biff faints in terror. Taking the score from Biff's jacket pocket the man slowly leaves the unconscious trumpeter's apartment. The film dissolves back into the train carriage, Biff Bailey wide-eyed in fear. "That'll teach me not to steal tunes" he jokes. "Well, how do I get out of this?" he asks. Schreck turns over the final card. As with all the others, it is the Death card.

It was not however Biff Bailey's nocturnal forays into the "Voodoo nights" of Paiti that led to my interest in the revolutionary history of Haiti, the role of Vodou therein, and their representations in popular culture, but a labyrinthine path that owed more to another story in *Dr. Terror's House of Horrors*, that of Franklyn Marsh, snooty art critic and ardent sceptic about all things "mumbo jumbo". The story tells of a third-rate painter called Eric Landor who publicly tricks the famous critic, in front of an entourage of obsequious, sycophant collectors, into evaluating the work of a young artist that the gallery is allegedly thinking of exhibiting in the future. Upon examination of a canvas Marsh announces that it was "clearly the work of a creative artist of considerable promise. Notice the wide sweep of colour, the balance, the brushwork, together with a certain denial of the accepted standards, the mock critical humour of the entire composition. You could learn a great deal about painting from this young artist Mr. Landor". "Then I should very much like to meet him" Landor replies. "Would that be possible?" he asks the gallerist. "He's here now, as a matter of fact" she replies. The camera pans down to reveal that she is holding the hand of a dungaree-clad chimpanzee. Marsh's entourage erupt with affected hilarity as the humiliated but indignant critic makes a hasty exit. Over the coming weeks Landor torments Marsh at a number of high-profile art world events. Marsh begins his speech to The City of London Council for the Preservation of Painting: "My Lords, Ladies and Gentlemen, I am extremely honoured to have been asked to address this fine organisation which has done so much to foster an interest in the arts". Landor, unnoticed by the critic, holds up a paper napkin folded and cut into a string of dancing monkeys. "The world of art today..." Marsh continues before registering the offending item. "The... world... of art... today", he falters, "of art... today". But it's no good. He holds a napkin to his forehead and, to the great concern of the toastmaster and dignitaries, sits back down in his chair, unable to carry on. Eventually the humiliations prove too much and Marsh decides to act. From his parked car he watches Landor lock up and leave the gallery. It is late and the streets are empty. As Landor crosses the road, Marsh starts up his car, steps on the accelerator and mows the painter down, severing his hand in the process. When the artist finally comes round, realising he will never be able to paint again, he returns to his gallery with a revolver and blows his brains out in front of the mirror. The last shot we see as he falls to the ground is his remaining hand clutching at the air. The shot of the dying hand cuts directly to one of a "living hand" emerging from the back of Marsh's car as he drives home in the rain. But this hand has no body attached to it, just a stump, blood congealed around the wrist. For the next two days and nights Marsh is tormented by this revolting, disembodied thing: reaching for his collar, crawling up his trouser leg, clambering on his writing desk and throttling him while mid-flow in his writing. But nothing he does – throwing it in the fire, stabbing it with a letter opener, locking it in the petty cash box or dumping it in a river – seems to stop it. Finally, driving home after a drink with his work colleagues, and smugly contemplating his assumed triumph over Landor's severed extremity, the hand appears on the windscreen, grabbing the wiper. Marsh veers off the road in terror and crashes into a ravine. "Is he hurt bad?" a detective at the scene asks as Marsh is being lifted into the ambulance the following morning. "He'll live" the medic reassures him, "but he'll be blind for the rest of his life poor guy". Screams from inside the ambulance. "Still, there's lots of things a blind man *can* do".

That "zombie" hand haunted me too. For nights after watching the film I couldn't sleep without the lights turned on, convinced that the severed appendage was hiding under my bed, behind the curtain, in the cupboard... somewhere. That horrible *un*-thing had crawled from the television set and into my mind. That it was "only in my head" was no reassurance. Presumably it had only been in Franklyn Marsh's head too. Now it was in mine. Everyone knows dead hands can't walk. But when your mind is *damaged* they can. On those nights that the infernal thing plagued my sullied brain, my dad would sit at my bedside until I was asleep.

INTRODUCTION

Eventually, of course, I forgot about the hand. Until, that was, a decade later, while studying Art History at university, when I was directed by my supervisor to an article on 'Base Materialism and Gnosticism' in a recently published collection of essays by the French writer and philosopher Georges Bataille. The book was called *Visions of Excess* and the encounter was to prove a lasting one. What I found there was a "philosophy" of the kind of things I had assumed to be far below the proper remit of such a distinguished discipline as Art History. Bataille's thinking set the experience of horror, mental delirium and abject matter against dignity, civility and academic propriety, undermining the worthy principles upon which sensible philosophy and the cultural hierarchies it served propped themselves up. For a residually angry and discomfited "working class" young man from "the North", having found himself somewhat unexpectedly in what felt like a very upper-middle class environment, Bataille's writing had quite an appeal. Not only did Bataille evoke the dark eroticism and dizzying excesses of the horror films I had been watching since childhood, long since relegated to the annals of crass cultural kitsch, but the critical legitimacy of Bataille in 1980s academic circles gave me an unexpected license to make "the powers of horror" the subject of what was to become a long-term project, one for which a certain latchkey subcultural capital had an unexpected and welcome cachet.

INTIMATIONS OF A PHANTOM HAITI

By the early 1990s I had begun a PhD in Cultural History, investigating the so-called Video Nasty controversy in the U.K. from a critical perspective extracted from the unruly and anti-methodical writings of Bataille. Video Nasty was a popular term, coined by the Conservative, Christian, moral crusader Mary Whitehouse and quickly picked up by the British tabloid press, to identify a number of low-budget, very violent horror films available in rentable video formats from local retailers in the 1980s. The films were considered to be in breach of the Obscene Publications Act of 1959, which was being surreptitiously circumvented by the new media format. It was at the end of this project that several threads of the research formed themselves into a supplementary appendix: 'Demons Through the Ether: Magnetism, Mediation and Sacred Contagion'. To summarise drastically,

Bataille's theory of sacred revolution, articulated in several essays and collaborative projects written and realised during the 1920s and '30s, proposed a contagious, *Acephalic* (or "headless") and collective expenditure of social wealth, a kind of exponential, revolutionary *potlatch*, triggered by a sacred and explicitly sacrificial ritual.[4] It was precisely the forces of base materialism, intimately encountered in the ritual of sacrifice, that Bataille believed had the potential to ignite "real revolution". Although such ideas were a long way from the concerns of the largely unwitting producers of Video Nasties or their censors, there was in the rhetoric of the latter a recurrent appeal to fears of imitative violence – the so-called "copycat effect" – and intimations about the sinister, hypnotic characteristics of such films which, they proposed, could set young people with suggestible minds down the slippery slopes of video-addiction towards violent, sadistic and imitative psychopathology. At the extreme and overtly propagandistic end of the censorial spectrum some critics, closer to Bataille in spirit than their academic sociologist detractors, proposed that "the Nasties", as they came to be called, posed an unprecedented mental and moral health risk that could bring society to a point where "left-wing revolutions occur or right-wing dictators after the pattern of Hitler may arise and pose as social saviours".[5]

The notion of a copycat effect was a recurrent idea in media censorship and criminality debates throughout the 20th century. By the mid 1960s the term had come to describe crimes allegedly committed in imitation of those read about in books or newspapers, heard about on the radio or seen in plays or films. It was, effectively, a new term for "post-hypnotic suggestion", a phenomenon that had been discussed widely in academic circles and the popular press since the late 19th century. An earlier name for the effect was The Werther Syndrome, after a spate of "emulation suicides" that followed the publication of Goethe's *The Sorrows of Young Werther* in 1774. The basic formula goes something like this: certain individuals from particular

---

4 For the most overt expressions of Bataille's revolutionary fervour at this time see his 'The Use Value of D.A.F. De Sade' (1930), 'The Psychological Structure of Fascism' (1933), 'The Notion of Expenditure' (1933) and 'Popular Front in the Street' (1936) (all in *Visions of Excess*) and 'Toward Real Revolution' (1936) published in *October 36*.

5 Barlow and Hill *Video Violence and Children* (170)

social groups or of specific psychological types are so susceptible to the effects of dramatic representations that they will tend to act out the things they have seen in "real life" (a theme addressed directly, and controversially, in films like Stanley Kubrick's *A Clockwork Orange* in 1971 and David Cronenberg's *Videodrome* of 1983). The notion of contagious, imitative behaviour, triggered by contact with virulently sacred forms of base matter-energy, was central to Bataille's theory of revolution, and his thinking on this matter was directly informed by ethnographer colleagues like Michel Leiris and Alfred Métraux (the person who first introduced Bataille to the work of Marcel Mauss, and who would go on to write one of the most important books about Haitian Vodou – *Voodoo In Haiti* – in 1959). Bataille was also influenced by contemporary psychological theories which were shaped by the history of hypnosis and concerned particularly with the mechanisms of imitative behaviour. Pierre Janet, who during the 1930s outlined a psychology of the *socius* that emphasised the inter-subjective and imitative foundations of the self, was an important influence on Bataille's theory of "contagious subjectivity".[6]

For Bataille, contagious, inter-subjective behaviour like laughing, yawning, sexual excitement, crying or anger, evidenced the porousness of individual boundaries and suggested that the "other" with whom one communicates is already, in some way, interior to the self. Janet's theory of the imitative subject was itself indebted to debates about hypnosis and hypnotic suggestion in the 19th century, which in turn find their historical roots in the practice of "animal magnetism", invented by Anton Mesmer at the end of the 18th century, on the eve of the French Revolution, under whose influence patients would fall into convulsive and contagious emotional crises.

One of the most thorough accounts of Mesmer's role in the development of 20th century dynamic psychiatry is Henri Ellenberger's classic *The Discovery of the Unconscious*, which also contains an important chapter on Janet. As we will see, Mesmer's theory of animal magnetism was based on the assumption of a vital, ethereal fluid permeating all physical bodies, from planets to molecules, which, when blocked, caused ailments of all kinds in humans and animals. Cures were exercised with the aid of specially prepared tubs, called *baquets,* which contained magnetised water and iron-filings connected

---

6 See Lawtoo.

together with wooden and metal rods. Mesmer's system combined physical theories of magnetic conduction between material bodies with an interpersonal therapeutic technique that involved the induction of physical and emotional crises in patients through the use of "passes" (the movement of the magnetiser's hands or wand over the patients' bodies). Mesmer's theories and techniques were to become hugely popular in late 18th century Europe and, importantly, in France's colonial territory of Saint-Domingue. It would also prove to be very important for the development of modern, clinical psychology in the 20th century, while at the same time leading to a "Mesmeric" occult revival, as "artificial somnambulism" became associated with Spirit communication, telepathy and clairvoyance. The "ethereal medium" through which the magnetic will of the Mesmerists was allegedly channelled would also become equated, by the mid 19th century, with new forms of technological communication and emergent "mass mediums".[7]

From the debate about Video Nasties and the copycat effect, through Bataille's theory of sacred revolution and mimetic contagion, to the influence of Mesmerism on modern psychology's recurrent pre-occupation with hypnotic suggestion, possession trance and dissociated personality disorders, a complex of parallel themes emerged suggesting that these aberrant and disturbing behavioural propensities were "survivals" of psycho-social states that modern society and culture had not yet managed to fully transcend, propensities which, for the ethnographic Surrealists of Bataille's circle in the 1930s, might be channelled into the practice of revolutionary ecstasy. For the British censors of the 1980s such "black arts" were being given a new potential for anti-social expression through the influence of the unrestricted, unlicensed and, importantly, privately "reproducible" new form of mass media (i.e. video player-recorder). This complex of concerns was intimately associated with ideas about the return of "archaic" or "primitive" subject formations that had the potential to bring about uncontrolled and unpredictable social change if unchecked.

---

7 See Erik Davis's *Techgnosis: Myth, Magic and Mysticism in the Age of Information* (1999) and Jeffrey Sconce's *Haunted Media: Electronic Presence from Telegraphy to Television* (2000) for historical accounts of this general trend.

Unsurprisingly such fears found their expression in modern horror films themselves (most notoriously perhaps William Friedkin and William Peter Blatty's *The Exorcist* of 1973) where the themes of demonic possession, Satanic rites, voodoo sorcery, criminal hypnotism and zombiedom characteristically exploited semi-conscious collective fantasies about the return of "savage" non-western, non-White and pre-modern cultures "mired in primitive superstition". But even though a certain "Phantom Haiti" was already hovering on the horizons of my thinking I was still caught off guard by the following claim I stumbled across in Ellenberger:

> In Saint Domingue, magnetism degenerated into a psychic epidemic amongst the Negro slaves, increasing their agitation, and the French domination ended in a bloodbath. Later Mesmer boasted that the new Republic – now called Haiti – owed its independence to him.[8]

This audacious claim seemed utterly fantastical and not a little delusional. It was, I assumed, the product of Mesmer's notoriously egomaniacal personality. But digging a little deeper into the revolutionary history of Haiti one soon encounters the story of Bois Caïman, the legendary Vodou ceremony that reputedly inaugurated the Haitian Revolution. This signal event in the history of Haitian national independence took place in the Alligator Woods on the northern plains of Saint-Domingue in August 1791 where, as legend has it, during a torrential rain storm, a secret gathering of Maroons and rebellious slaves participated in an austere ceremony presided over by the priest and former slave-driver Dutty Boukman and the priestess Cécile Fatiman. During the ceremony a black pig was sacrificed, its blood drunk, and an oath sworn to the God of the Blacks and the Spirit of Liberty that would bind the participants in a pact to the overthrow of their White masters and the plantation-slave system. A week later hundreds of sugar plantations lay in smouldering ruins, thousands of White slave-owners had been killed, and a thirteen-year revolutionary war of independence from colonial slavery had begun. Although there was, as yet, no suggestion that Mesmerism (or animal magnetism, as it was called at the time) had a role to play in the Bois Caïman ceremony,

---

8 Ellenberger 73

the coincidence of a conspiratorial religious ritual, involving blood sacrifice, and setting in motion a violent, insurrectionary uprising, which in turn led to massive expenditures of social wealth, was about as Bataillean as a revolutionary event could be. And so, intermittently, over the next few years, I gave a number of public lectures exploring the relationship between Bataille's religious and revolutionary theories, the "ethnographic Surrealism" of his contemporaries, and the relationship between sensationalist misrepresentations of Haitian Vodou in horror films and the actualities of Haitian history and culture. And as I dug deeper into Mesmer's claim about the role that magnetism had played in the Haitian Revolution, it began to appear much more plausible than it had at first seemed.

KLINIK ZONBI

It was largely because of these interests that in December 2009 I was invited to speak at an academic symposium at the Ghetto Biennale in Port-au-Prince, Haiti. The Ghetto Biennale was conceived and curated by the artist photographer Leah Gordon and Atis Rezistans, a group of sculptors who had been making work in an area on the Grand Rue in Port-au-Prince, called Lakou Cheri, since the 1990s. The founding members of the group André Eugène, Jean Hérard Celeur and Frantz Jacques (aka Guyodo), and other core members (including Ronald Bazin (aka Cheby), Jean Claude Saintillus and Evel Romain) all live and work in the lakou, making Vodou-themed figurative sculptures that combine wood, metal, waste materials, discarded objects and human bones in a rough-edged, unpolished and often grotesque manner, usually containing sexual, religious and death-related symbolism that owes much to the guiding influence of the Guede family of spirits within the local community. At this, the first of several Ghetto Biennales to take place in their neighbourhood, artists from around the world were invited to make and show work in the same environment as their hosts. The symposium organised to compliment the event was called 'Of Revolution and Revelation', a title taken from a three-volume work on Christianity, colonialism and modernity in South Africa by the anthropologist couple John and Jean Comaroff, and it was there that I first presented my thesis about Bataille and Bois Caïman to a largely Haitian audience.

INTRODUCTION

In the hotel where the attendees were staying I met Cameron Brohman. Cameron is a social entrepreneur who was at the Biennale to promote Slum Toys, one of his "Brandaid" micro-marketing projects that was attempting to establish a community of young artisans in the Cité Soleil, a notoriously poor and historically conflict-ridden district of Port-au-Prince, who would produce toy tap-taps, the brightly decorated local buses in Haiti, made with materials gleaned from local landfills. Cameron had spent many years living in Haiti working as the secretary for legendary choreographer, dancer and ethnographer Katherine Dunham, who, in the 1990s, created a botanical garden in the grounds of Habitation Leclerc, the former residence of Pauline Bonaparte, Napoleon's sister. Dunham had acquired the property in the 1940s and converted into a school of dance and Vodou. Cameron had managed Dunham's botanical garden project for several years. Over the course of several conversations I had with him while visiting Grand Rue, Habitation Leclerc and the garbage dump close to Cité Soleil, I explained to Cameron why I was in Haiti and the questions driving my research. In one of these conversations we struck on the idea of creating a comic-book project called *Klinik Zonbi* based on 1950s horror comics, using the archetypical tropes of zombie narratives from Haitian folklore and popular culture that would tell the story of Vodou in Haitian history and the way it had been manipulated by foreign interests who wanted to represent the country in a negative light. The general idea was of an artistic and educational, anti-imperialist de-programmeming project that would be designed and drawn by young artists in Port-au-Prince, produced locally and distributed via art-related markets in Europe and the U.S. The idea of *Klinik Zonbi* had parallels with the *Goute Sel* ("a taste of salt") literacy programmeme established by the *Ti Legliz* (little church) movement in the 1980s that was instrumental in bringing down the dictatorship of Jean-Claude Duvalier. Eating salt, as people in Haiti know, is the only known cure for zombiedom, the state that many observers felt the country had collectively fallen into after thirty years of intolerable dictatorial oppression.

Although plans for *Klinik Zonbi* drifted out of focus over the years that followed the 2010 earthquake, it is still part of the long-term goal of *Undead Uprising* which, like *Klinik Zonbi*, seeks to connect the story of popular misrepresentations of Haiti and its culture back to the historical, political and social realities of the country in ways that will be of educational and artistic value for audiences on both sides of the "chimerical optic" with which Haiti has often been viewed from outside. So, although on the surface *Undead Uprising* may look like a "Weird Stories" version of Haitian history, the intention is to explore the ways in which these misrepresentations have influenced and shaped foreign perceptions of Haiti and, by extension, foreign policy perspectives and attitudes both inside and outside the country. In so doing I hope to re-connect and re-think the psychological, cultural and political anxieties subtending xenophobic tropes within horror cinema back to the actual political contexts that their chimerical optics often overtly distort and occult. I ask if popular representations of the mythical monsters derived from the real horrors of colonial violence in Saint-Domingue are still implicated in those histories? Are there ways to resurrect the repressed or occulted histories of colonial, race and class violence from these massively popular forms of horror narrative? What are the implications of such narratives for our understanding of the contemporary geopolitics in which Haiti is involved? And how do the mechanisms of imaginary psychic communication with an abjectly configured "otherness within" relate to wider mechanisms of political ideology and propaganda?

In Bataillean terms one could say that I enjoy thinking about the imaginary encounter with an appalling and unbearable otherness that is at once both within and without, an idea indebted to my reading of ethnographic Surrealists like Michel Leiris and Michael Taussig. In this sense I am still invested in the primitivist cultural stereotypes and reactionary subject formations that Voodoo-horror films perpetuate and exploit. I don't want to make apologies for this, nor do I want to find a rational justification for it. That is not my intention. But the language of "interest" and "investment" point in imprecise and multivalent ways to the nebulous mechanism I am trying to expose the workings of. That mechanism, if this is indeed the right term, is the cultural construction of subjectivities on two ends of a mediated network of imaginary and symbolic relations: on one side European, English-speaking subjects like myself, encountering sensational, salacious and unsettling representations of fantastical "otherness" in popular and mass culture, and on the other side the actual people and culture that these fictions ostensibly, and in a generally far-fetched way, refer to. What is much harder and less palatable than offering a sober corrective to sensational misrepresentations of Haitian culture is to propose that the vicarious pleasures of horror may share characteristics with an outsider's understanding of Vodou rites and ritual. While being conscious not to perpetuate the Anglo-American demonization of Vodou that has been ongoing for several centuries, I also recognise the disingenuousness of a politically correct "care-bearization" (Leah Gordon's term) of a religion for which animal sacrifice and possession by discarnate spiritual beings are fundamental to its ritual practice. Obviously Vodou is a religion for which the "other within" constitutes a fundamental metaphysical foundation. To be ridden by a deity, to be dispossessed of one's self, to undergo a prolonged and arduous ritual of initiation or to be present at the sacrifice of living creatures are not experiences a person is likely to remain unchanged by. And they do, in practice and in fact, pose profound existential and moral problems for what we might broadly call "the Western mind". Furthermore fears of Vodou amongst the colonial authorities of Saint-Domingue were not unwarranted. Far from it. Vodou seems to have been a religion of resistance since before the revolution, one in which it played a vital role. From this perspective there seems little doubt that Vodou has had an intentionally "scary" dimension to it, particularly as a practice which evolved secretly under the auspices of a terrible and incredibly sadistic system of colonial violence, inspiring conspiracies and insurrectionary strategies of counter-terrorism against that very system. Furthermore Vodou continues to have a role in anti-imperialist struggles for Haitian nationhood and collective identity as the Haitian authors and artists continue to affirm. I am thinking specifically here of people like Rachel Beauvoir-Dominique, her father, the *houngan*, Max Beauvoir, others involved in the KNVA (National Confederation of Haitian Vodou) and the scholars of KOSANBA (The Congress of Santa Barbara), a number of whom the book in hand is deeply indebted to. Although I am not suggesting that the "other within" we encounter vicariously through horror films has any direct relationship with the workings of the *lwa* or the spiritual beliefs of *Vodouisants*, I do want to suggest that, from the particular place from which I write, there is something in common between vicarious, cinematic encounters with that which is "absolutely other" but inside us still, and an imaginary encounter with supernatural intelligences like those of the *lwa*. I have tried to leave this speculative channel of occult communication between the two kinds of encounter as open as possible throughout the writing of *Undead Uprising*.

PART ONE

fig. i AXIS OF LIVING-DEAD

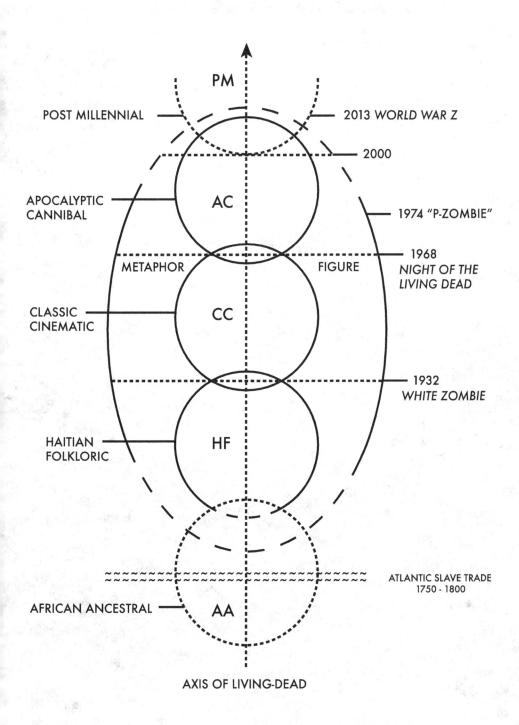

PM

POST MILLENNIAL

2013 WORLD WAR Z

2000

APOCALYPTIC
CANNIBAL

AC

1974 "P-ZOMBIE"

1968
NIGHT OF THE
LIVING DEAD

METAPHOR

FIGURE

CLASSIC
CINEMATIC

CC

1932
WHITE ZOMBIE

HAITIAN
FOLKLORIC

HF

AFRICAN ANCESTRAL

AA

ATLANTIC SLAVE TRADE
1750 - 1800

AXIS OF LIVING-DEAD

"...blood-maddened, sex-maddened, god-maddened..."
Alexander King's original illustration for *The Magic Island*, 1929

LEAVING THE MAGIC ISLAND

"THE WAY IS OPEN AND CLOSED"

"May Papa Legba, Maitresse Ezilée and the Serpent protect me from misrepresenting these people, and give me the power to write honestly about their mysterious religion, for all living faiths are sacred."

- Words spoken by the Mambo Maman Célie to William Seabrook on the completion of his ouanga charm in *The Magic Island* (1929)

And now the literary traditional white stranger who spied from hiding in the forest, had such one lurked near by, would have seen all the wildest tales of Voodoo fiction justified: in the red light of torches which made the moon turn pale, leaping, screaming, writhing black bodies, blood maddened, sex-maddened, god-maddened, drunken, whirled and danced their dark saturnalia, heads thrown weirdly back as if their necks were broken, white teeth and eyeballs gleaming, while couples seizing one another from time to time fled from the circle, into the forest to share and slake their ecstasy.

- William Seabrook *The Magic Island* (1929)

Much maligned by serious scholars of Haitian history and culture at the time of its publication, and still considered by many the principle source of clichéd and xenophobic conceptions of Haitian Vodou, *The Magic Island,* the book that introduced the folkloric Haitian *zonbi* to Anglo-American popular culture is, for that reason, a foundational text for *Undead Uprising.* The foreword to this sensationalist travelogue into the Vodou heart of Haitian darkness reminds us that *Undead Uprising* approaches the country from the outside, taking what Franck Degoul has called an "exogenous" perspective on its history and customs.[1] Observing the magic island from a mail boat anchored in the bay of Cap-Haïtian at sunset, Seabrook invokes a picturesque image of fallen, colonial grandeur, Black insurrection, the massacre of Whites and the triumph of Black, national sovereignty. But as the sun fades and the image of history falls into darkness, only the jungle mountains remain, from whose slopes comes "the steady boom of Voodoo drums".

The Magic Island's main selling point, and sell it did, was its sensational accounts of blood sacrifice, orgiastic rites, "ouanga" charms, the *culte des morts* and the dreaded *zombi.* But within its pages one also finds stories about life in Haiti under U.S. occupation, the recent political history of the republic, descriptions of life and culture in rural Haiti and some of the first detailed and reasonably sober accounts for English speaking audiences of the gods (*lwa*), ceremonies, rituals and cosmology of Vodou (including plans of the *hounfo* (Vodou temple) at which Seabrook was initiated, a sketch of a *vévé* (sacred drawing) that protected the threshold, samples of Vodou musical notation and his personal photographic documentation of Vodou *sociétés, houmforts,* altars, *vévés,* temple paintings and members of a Gede cult, probably the first to be seen by a popular readership). The appendix – *From the Author's Notebook* – includes notes on Kreyòl phonetics; an orthography of the term 'Vodou'; its cultural origins and that of the major gods; details of the Haitian criminal codes used against the religion; a description of Vodou drums; and a translation of the preface to a moral and philosophical defence of the religion by Arthur C. Holly, *Les Daïmons du Culte Voudo* (1918). The third and fourth parts of the book – 'The Tragic Comedy' and 'Trails Winding' – give us a picture of the complex cultural politics of Haiti from the perspectives of various characters that Seabrook met and socialised

---

1 Christie and Lauro 24-38

with during his time there. In this sense *The Magic Island*, to paraphrase the author, simultaneously "opens and closes the way" to a real Haiti beyond the more lurid and insalubrious representations of its culture that Seabrook exploited with such lusty enthusiasm.

Seabrook was both a fantasist and unapologetic self-publicist, the weave of sensational fiction blending awkwardly into biographical fact until his untimely death by his own hand in 1945. Born the son of a Lutheran minister and a "proud but impoverished gentlewoman Myra" in Maryland in 1886, Seabrook moved with his family to the Kansas prairie town of Abilene at the age of nine. In his autobiography *No Hiding Place* he claimed to have had "deep Black roots" because his White grandmother had been wet-nursed by a Black Obeah slave-girl from Cuba. Since her plantation childhood Piny, as she had been christened by her Black nanny, had experienced "illuminations". Later in life she discovered that she had special powers, enhanced by the use of laudanum. It was Piny who introduced young William to the subtle power of inter-subjective fantasies that would lead him into her "other world", as if by hypnotism (that "dangerous and sometimes evil power") which, no matter how "radiantly beautiful, illuminating and heaven-sent some of its prolonged moments may seem in their nick of time", may have "deeper and more evil occult roots". It was during one such escape from reality with Grandma Piny that Seabrook encountered the "supreme evocation" of his "deepest wish fantasy" and the "key to his locked need". In an enchanted castle in the depths of a local wood in which he and Piny would take regular walks, he found at the end of a red velvet carpet, and seated on a great chair, a girl "robed in green with red-gold braided hair", whose high golden heels rested on a leather foot stool, her ankles bound by shining metal circlets connected by a gleaming chain. The chains tinkled like soft bells as she smiled to welcome them into her chamber. Stroking his hair as he knelt before her, the girl-in-chains led Willy's hands down the soft silk folds to her chained feet and pressed them tightly there until his hands drew the chains tighter. Young William trembled with happiness.

At sixteen Seabrook taught himself Pitman shorthand, escaping into "mysterious, beautiful, secret, hieratic" curlicues as into "war, to jungles, to deserts, and ultimately to drink". Later, working for a local newspaper in Augusta, Georgia, he reported on "wonderful" Negro murders like that by old Tom Hendon who, after having had a practical joke played on him by a local dockworker, slashed the stevedore to ribbons with a razor, and another, about a Black man who killed his entire family with a chop-ax. It was at this time that he first came to know an abject physical fear that he connected with killing and ("in a totally different way") with Negroes. The feeling involved a sense of guilt "that all white Southerners shared", one that stopped him making coloured friends. To illustrate the point he described passing a small Black man in overalls on the sidewalk of a wide Augusta street who, as he approached the young Seabrook, said quietly, in a gentle, "almost pleading" voice: "Git out of my way, white man". Never before had Seabrook felt that he was in the presence of death. He stepped aside and let "the little Negro man" walk quietly on. The next man on the path had sobviously not been so accommodating: newspapers the following morning reported that a White man "lay slashed to death in a welter of blood" on the same Augusta street.

Later, after tramping his way across Europe, Seabrook studied philosophy and metaphysics at the University of Geneva, before serving as a volunteer ambulance driver in the American Field Service (AFS) during WWI. Seabrook wrote about his experiences in *History of the American Field Service "Friends of France"* (1920), a collection of accounts originally intended to be published in the *Atlantic Monthly* in 1915, but published privately instead in a free booklet, made to garner funds for the service. In diaristic accounts of his time at the front he described encounters with mass roadside grave sites, holding ground in the face of shell fire close to the front line, driving ambulances through artillery bombardments over the bodies of dead horses, and men mangled by shells on the road before them. It was evidently a traumatic and formative experience that, as with so many writers of the interwar period, profoundly shaped the course of his later writing career. In *No Hiding Place*, which includes an account of him being chlorine-gassed, he concluded of the war that "it had not made the world any safer for democracy, or from future wars... but it had helped me escape for a time into something bigger than myself". This notion of "escaping into something bigger than himself" would form a fundamental subtext for the adventures he would find himself pursuing in the coming decades. During his time at Verdun Seabrook had a premonition of his own death in a car crash that, he was certain, would happen a few hours later. Having read a little Freud, as he put it, Seabrook asked himself, as he lay on his bunk, whether this was not precisely why he had come to France. After recounting the tale of several dead and dying bodies that he had encountered in his life – the first being a young Negro, shot with a pistol in Augusta "writhing, screaming, naked to the waist in the hot sunshine, his eyeballs rolling, with a tiny, pink, puckered hole in his distended belly" – he explained how, when he drove to the front that day, expecting to die, nothing happened. This put an end, he claimed, to all mystical premonitions about his own mortality or the idea of him harbouring a secret death wish.

After returning from France Seabrook and his first wife Katherine Edmondson were gifted a farm in Atlanta by her father as a token of respect for their services during the war. It was at this time that he met the English occultist Aleister Crowley, an encounter that led to his first published fiction – 'Wow!' – in 1921 (a story he would recount in *Witchcraft: Its Power in the World Today* in 1940). The short story grew out of an experiment he conducted with Crowley mimicking the silent practices of Trappist monks. For a week the only expression the two men could use to communicate was the word "wow". His Negro servants at the time were convinced, he wrote, that the two men had either joined, or were founding, a branch of some new religion. Twenty years later Seabrook would limit the speech of his "research workers" too, the women with whom he performed sado-masochistic parapsychology experiments at his estate in Rhinebeck, New York. Maya Deren, the pioneering American artist, dancer and film-maker, who would later author one of the most important ethnographic accounts of Vodou – *Divine Horsemen: The Living Gods of Haiti* (1953) – was offered the job of literary secretary to Seabrook while he was conducting these experiments. It was there that he invited her to be one of his research subjects, an offer which she politely but firmly declined. In letters written at the time Deren explained how the contract he asked her to sign included detailed descriptions of the experiments to be performed on his research assistants. There were three conditions which governed all of them: i) the condition of nudity, ii) the condition of punishment by whipping if the person violated the agreement and iii) the person could not utter an intelligible word but only animal sounds. After declining Seabrook's offer Deren became secretary to Katherine Dunham, legendary anthropologist, dancer, choreographer and author of *Island Possessed*.[2] It seems very likely, therefore, that Deren's interest in Vodou, and witchcraft in general, was informed by her encounter with Seabrook and his earlier work.

Around the time of Seabrook's encounter with Crowley, on an impulsive whim inspired by a chance reading of a passage by Heinrich Heine in a neighbour's house, Seabrook followed the dream of the "lady-in-chains" to New York where, in the figure of a woman he'd met briefly on his way back from Europe, he realised for the first time his childhood fantasy. Not long afterwards William and Katherine Seabrook moved to New York where he worked for several years as a journalist for the *New York Times* and William Randolph Hearst's *King Features Syndicate,* writing "crime-and-horror" features. Katie Seabrook opened a cafe in Greenwich Village where, after meeting a young Arab sheikh called Daoud Izzeden, her husband began to cultivate the persona of an intrepid adventurer, "willing to try anything and committed to reporting it objectively", as Susan Zieger has put it.[3] Six weeks after the meeting he was in the deserts of Arabia in search of whirling dervishes and Yezidi devil worshippers. Later, speaking to his friend Hamilton Smith from the publishers Harcourt Brace, Seabrook said that he was going to "write a book about voodoo", boasting that for *Adventures in Arabia* he had "turned Arab and liked it" and that now he'd like to "go down to Haiti or somewhere and turn Negro".

---

2 See Vévé Clark *The Legend of Maya Deren Vol.1* 411-416.

3 Susan Zieger 'The Case of William Seabrook: *Documents*, Haiti and the Working Dead', *Modernism/modernity*, Volume 19, Number 4, November 2012, 737-754

DARK WOMB OF TERRIBLE ECSTASIES

Archaic man was mainly taken up with what is sovereign, marvellous, with what goes beyond the useful, but that is precisely what a consciousness enlightened by the advancement of learning relegated to a dubious and condemnable semidarkness, which psychoanalysis named the unconscious.

- Georges Bataille 'The Historical Development of the Knowledge of Sovereignty' from *The Accursed Share: Volume II*[4]

Continuous crime committed in broad daylight for the mere satisfaction of deified nightmares, terrifying phantasms, priests' cannibalistic meals, ceremonial corpses, and streams of blood evoke not so much the historical adventure, but rather the blinding debauches described by the illustrious Marquis de Sade.

- Georges Bataille 'Extinct America' (1928)

The Magic Island is a complicated and ambiguous work, written with a distinctly sceptical voice, full of classical, literary and biblical allusions, that combines sensationalist adventure narrative, travel literature, journalism and popular ethnography in ways which are at times disparaging and at others full of praise for the life, people and culture of Haiti. On the whole, and particularly in relation to works by earlier foreign authors like Spenser St. John or Stephen Bonsal, Seabrook is sympathetic to Vodou, dispelling many popular misconceptions about it, praising it as a vibrant, living religion beside which modern rituals and reasoning pale. "I believe in such ceremonies" Seabrook wrote:

I hope that they will never die out or be abolished. I believe that in some form or another they answer a deep need of

---

4 Bataille (1993) 226

the universal human soul. I, who in a sense believe in no religion, believe yet in them all, asking only that they be alive – as religions. Codes of rational ethics and human brotherly love are useful, but they do not touch on this thing underneath.[5]

Less sympathetically, and in ways which perpetuated popular, xenophobic myths about Black African atavism, the book is illustrated by Alexander King's expressionistic caricatures of various Black and Mulatto characters, including an image of an obese cloven-hoofed and horned demon, observed by a tall, sinister figure draped in a long black coat and wearing a wide-brimmed hat, which is feeding milk to a child-like man and a woman from hulking breasts. The image illustrates the following lines:

Haitian people [...] are habitually a little comic, a little childish, a little ludicrous, they are easily vulnerable to a certain sort of caricature [...] then suddenly from time to time something that is essential in the colour and texture of their skins - something more than atavistic savagery, but which may trace none the less to their ancestral Africa, dark mother of mysteries – some quality surges to the surface of a group or individual; and when this happens, we others are in the presence of a thing shorn of all that can provoke superior smiles or scorn, a living thing that strikes terror and sometimes awe.[6]

This image of something "shorn of all that can provoke superior smiles or scorn, a living thing that strikes terror and sometimes awe" is clearly reminiscent of the Negro murder stories that so affected Seabrook as a young journalist. But it also evokes historical depictions of the Haitian Revolution that saw it as an act of racial barbarism. That this sublime and terrible "thing underneath" which, when it erupts, exceeds "atavistic savagery" is *essential* in "the colour and texture of their skins" suggests, despite his ostensibly anti-racist perspective, that Seabrook assumed black-skinned people to have a particular

5 Seabrook (1929) 61-62

6 Seabrook (1929) 277

"... dark mother of mysteries." Alexander King's original illustration for William Seabrook's *The Magic Island*, 1929

propensity for excessive and murderous violence, a myth which has been, and continues to be used in xenophobic condemnations of the Haitian Republic and its capacity for self-governance. In the immediate aftermath of the Haitian Revolution the imperial powers of France and the United States created an image of the new republic as a "monstrous anomaly" in the proper course of history. According to Nick Nesbitt, Haiti came to represent a void at the heart of 18th century myths about democracy and independence, a void that took the place of the disavowed structural violence that made the American and French republics possible (i.e. the violence of plantation slavery).

In distinctly Žižekian terms, Nesbitt describes this "disavowed void of violence" thus:

> Haiti, that dysfunctional, barbaric, undemocratic, and undemocratisable Haiti fatally prone to ever-renewed disasters, is a fantasy. It remains and returns endlessly, however, because this site has the misfortune of constituting an essential fantasy of Haiti's big Other: the fantasy of an eminently democratic, developed, and civilised nation. Haiti is the fantasy projection, the negative kernel of the real that so effectively sustains North American misunderstanding and disavowal [of itself] ... Haiti is the impossible truth, the inadmissible real, of North Atlantic democratic self-identity.[7]

From this perspective Seabrook's admiration for the awesome, innate violence of Black Haitians is a kind of ideological reversal of this disavowal, turning it into a positive affirmation of the "inadmissible real" that civilised, democratic self-identity denies. As we will see, the extent to which the practice and beliefs of Vodou were *essentially* African or *archaic* in a universal, *anthropological* sense, has shaped political and ideological differences within Haiti that continue today. In his *The Equality of Human Races (Positivist Anthropology)*, first published in 1885, Anténor Firmin, the Haitian anthropologist, historian and statesman, argued strongly that "human sacrifice", "barbarism", "cannibalism", "possession" and "fetishism" (in short, all the "deviations" from modern reason and civilisation of which Haiti and Vodou had been accused by foreigners) were characteristics common to all races in different places at different times. Haitian writers associated with the ethnological and *Noiriste* movements of the 1930s and '40s, like J. C. Dorsainvil, Lorimer Denis, François Duvalier, tended, on the other hand, to emphasise the essentially African character of Vodou and its associated practices, placing it firmly at the centre of the republic's revolutionary struggle for independence against slavery and European imperialism, which by then had come to be associated explicitly with White supremacism.[8]

---

7 Nick Nesbitt 'Haiti, the Monstrous Anomaly' in Millery Polyné (ed) *The Idea of Haiti: Rethinking Crisis and Development* (2013) 5-6

8 See Chapter Three, 'The Romance of Revolutionary Vodou'.

For Nesbitt, when colonial and imperialist violence was met by revolutionary violence (or, in his words, when the nascent subjects of universal emancipation responded to terror *with* terror) the effect was a transference of the identification of *inhuman* violence from the (White) slave masters to the (Black) slave revolutionaries. The consequence of this symbolic reversal for the history of Atlantic modernity was that Haiti, rather than being seen as the most advanced (i.e. slavery-free) society in the world, was cast as a monstrous anomaly in the proper course of Universal History. And it was in this context that established myths about essential African primitivism were used to condemn the Haitian Revolution as barbaric and to protect the rest of the slave-holding world from its "contagious consequences".[9] At the same time, and in service of the same ends "Vaudoux", as it was then called, became, in Kate Ramsey's words, an exemplary trope in the service of broader claims about the unfitness of peoples of African descent for liberation from the slave and colonial regimes against which they were then struggling across the Americas.[10] Nesbitt (following Jean-Paul Sartre's description of the "wild voluntarism and youthful barbarism" of Russian peasants during the Soviet Revolution) uses the word *bossale* to describe the former slaves of Haiti, those "uncivilized marginals of time" who "actually and actively subordinated the so-called enlightened Western intellectuals".[11] His use of the term is significant for the discussions that follow. A Creole term used in pre-revolutionary Saint-Domingue to describe slaves newly debarked from Africa and not yet Creolized or Christened, it carried the connotations of being uncivilised, uncultured, wild, uncouth and unclean. It is also used in Vodou to describe a new initiate into the cult (*Hounsi Bossale*) and a person who is not used to being possessed by the *lwa* and therefore *wilder* and in need of more careful control by the *houngan* or *mambo*.[12]

---

9 On the subject of the contagiousness of the Haitian Revolution in other slave-holding colonies at the time see Ashli White *Encountering Revolution*, Chapter Four 'The Contagion of Rebellion'.

10 Kate Ramsey 'Legislating "Civilisation" in Postrevolutionary Haiti' (Goldschmidt and McAlister 231-258).

11 Nesbitt 17

12 See Dunham for a detailed account of her *hounsi* initiation (1929).

After recounting the many obstacles in the "tropical-upheaved, tumbled-towering, madland of paradises and infernos" that stood between him and the "Voodoo Holy of Holies", Seabrook described his initiation into one of the two main *nanchons* (nations) of Vodou: the Petro cult.[13] During the ceremony in which a number of animals were sacrificed, he notes an impression so vivid that, should he live for twenty more years, it would be "acid-etched so deeply that it will leave some lines [...] when my brain lies rotting". It was the sound of the bleating he-goats, tethered in the shadows, piercing through the "symphonic female howling choral of the women" and striking something elementally male in him that "shivered with icy terror". This, he claims, had nothing to do with the fact that he was a White man kneeling amongst "swaying blacks" who would shortly become "blood frenzied". They were, after all, his friends. It was a terror of something "blacker and more implacable than they – a terror of the dark, all-engulfing womb". Although Seabrook immediately dismissed this subjective excursion into the elemental nightmares of his own soul as an unwarranted interruption of his properly ethnographic task-at-hand, such excursions, as Mary A. Renda has suggested, were an essential part of the literary fabric of *The Magic Island* and the fantasy Haiti into which the author had "escaped".[14] For Renda, Seabrook's "fantasy island" was a literalised spatial representation of the Freudian

---

13 Petro (or Petwo) refers to one of the two main branches of Vodou, the other being Rada. It also refers to a separate group of *lwa* deriving from Congo rather than Dahomey (Rada) (Métraux 86-89). The Petro deities have a reputation for being *"plus raide"* (more hard) than the Rada, and are generally associated with aggressive action. Several of the major deities within the Vodou pantheon have personalities on both sides of the Petro/Rada division. According to Maya Deren, in times of Vodou's suppression the Petro deities come to the fore. As such it was the violent Petro deities of Ogoun Ferraille and Erzulie Ge-Rouge who were reputedly invoked at Bois Caïman (Deren, 61-71). As Jean Price-Mars and others have noted it seems very unlikely that what Seabrook experienced was an authentic Vodou initiation rite, which ordinarily take several days or weeks of fasting and preparation and involve several levels or degrees. See Price-Mars (1929).

14 Mary Renda *Taking Haiti: Military Occupation and the Culture of US Imperialism 1915-1940* (2001), 253

unconscious, a place where the family romance and earlier experiences of polymorphous sexuality could be revisited and unshackled.[15] It was simultaneously something like a war. The metaphor of the all-engulfing womb is made all the more appropriate, and complicated by Seabrook's *ur*-fantasy of the woman-in-chains to which his writing career was literally bound. For him there really seemed to be no hiding place from the dark womb of the primal mother to which we all must ultimately return. As Worthington has written, and Seabrook confirmed in his autobiography, the author had a very difficult relationship with his own mother. According to his second wife and biographer "Willie liked women in spite of a deep-rooted hostility to his mother Myra, that compelled him to make them miserable".[16] Seabrook's adventures beyond the shackles of himself therefore, often involved the binding of the women he simultaneously desired, feared and depended upon for his ultimate ecstasies.

Typically Seabrook's description of his initiation into Vodou equates female sexuality with this "terrible darkness". Moreover the "dark mother of mysteries", that awesome "living thing underneath", is configured explicitly as Black, female, of African heredity and the primal source of Haitian people's awesome potential for violence. His relationship with Maman Célie, the *mambo* who takes him under her wing and organises his initiation, is clearly a maternal, fantasmatic and incestuous one, recalling Seabrook's love for Piny, who, wet-nursed by a Black slave, had introduced him to the mysteries of his deeper self. As Zieger has noted, this fantasy of surrogate Black motherhood, initiating him, via a rite of blood and milk into the mysteries of the Vodou cult, "magically" transforms the social realities of chattel slavery into a personal fantasy of intimate, familial nourishment that was used as proof of a mystical, Black birthright. "Psychoanalysis" she writes "redirected the Victorian ideal of imperial exploration inward", a claim, as we will see, that could also be applied to Michel Leiris, Seabrook's former acolyte.[17] Between him and Maman Célie, Seabrook wrote, there was a bond which he could neither analyse nor make others understand because its roots went beyond analysis and conscious reasoning. It was as if they had known each other always,

---

15 Renda 249

16 Worthington 10

17 Zieger 739-744

joined by "the mystical equivalent of an umbilical cord" he had "suckled in infancy at her dark breasts, had wandered far, and was now returning home".[18] It is no surprise then, that animal sacrifice would be depicted by Seabrook in similarly erotic ways and that the violence he felt in his own soul should be associated with the traces of Black blood in the milk on which he was nurtured.

In the description of his own blood baptism, a chapter entitled 'Goat-Cry Girl-Cry', he describes in distinctly Bataillean tones how Maman Célie sacrificed a white turkey in a "swanlike simulacra of the deed which for the male is always like a little death". When a he-goat that Seabrook had developed an affectionate interest in was being mystically substituted before the altar for Maman Célie's youngest, unmarried daughter Catherine, he heard the voice of Jephtha's daughter "doomed to die by her own father as a sacrifice to Javeh, going up to bewail her virginity on Israel's lonely mountain".

> The smell of blood was in the air, but there was more than that hovering; it was the eternal, mysterious odor of death itself which both animals and human beings always sense, but not through nostrils. Yet now the two who were about to die mysteriously merged, the girl symbolically and the beast with a knife in its throat, were docile and entranced, were like automatons [...] the girl began a low, piteous bleating in which there was nothing, absolutely nothing, human; and soon a thing infinitely more unnatural occurred; the goat was moaning and crying like a human child [...] Other signs and wonders became manifest. Into this little temple lost among the mountains came in answer to goat-cry girl-cry the Shaggy Immortal One of a thousand names whom the Greeks called Pan. The goat's lingam became erect and rigid, the points of the girls breasts visibly hardened and were outlined sharply pressing against the coarse, thin, tight-drawn shift that was her only garment. Thus they faced each other motionless as two marble figures on the frieze of some ancient phallic temple.[19]

---

18 Seabrook (1929) 28 and (1942) 280. Seabrook repeats the lines from *The Magic Island* verbatim in *No Hiding Place*.

19 Seabrook (1929) 64-65

When the final sacrificial cut is made into the goat's throat the girl, "with a shrill, piercing, then strangled bleat of agony [...] leaped, shuddered, and fell senseless before the altar". As the newly initiated author drinks the goat's clean, warm and salty blood, he feels that he is actually drinking the blood of Catherine who, in the body of the goat, "had mysteriously died for me and for all the miserable humanity from Léogane to Guinea" (or, in other words, Africans brought to Haiti by the slave trade). In a footnote to this passage Seabrook comments that, according to Maman Célie, actual human sacrifice is occasionally an integral part of the Vodou ritual in Haiti but "only under stress of seeming dire necessity". He goes on to tell the story of Cadeus Bellegarde, a reputed *papaloi* (Vodou priest), notorious mass murderer and cannibal who allegedly killed and ate a number of victims between 1916 and 1918 during the American occupation. By establishing similarities between Vodou, cannibalism and the pagan-Christian traditions of European and Middle Eastern antiquity, Seabrook's ultra-subjective, fantasy-island version of Haiti helped perpetuate an image of the country as a preserve of archaic primitivism, a land where "adventurous white men could revisit the savage childhood of their own race" and there commune with the dark, metaphysical roots of civilisation and empire.[20] For the blood of Christ Catherine's Black blood is sacrificially transubstantiated – "the symbol of free-flowing primitive energy" – "liquidating an ossified white modernity", as Zieger has put it, into a mystical blood-marriage between a White man and Black Haitian *femme-enfant*.[21]

As we will see, essentialist myths of Black people's propensity to extreme, ecstatic violence, such as those indulged by Seabrook in his fantasies about Vodou, are highly ambivalent politically: in the hands of White supremacists they have been used to support arguments that people of African heredity are beyond the realm of reasonable governance and liable to sink, without severe discipline, to the state of primitive tribes, while, in the hands of pan-African Black nationalists, they have been used as a source of racial pride, revolutionary prowess and the inspirational means to overthrow intolerable tyranny. They were also fundamental to arguments supporting the decision of the

---

20 Renda 247

21 Zieger 741

United States government to occupy Haiti in 1915, after then President Guillaume Sam, who had ordered the execution of 167 Mulatto prisoners from the elite classes of Haitian society, was murdered in the Embassy where he had sought refuge, his body thrown over the embassy wall and then ripped to pieces by the crowd outside. An act of such barbarous, popular savagery signalled to its concerned neighbour that the country was on the brink of descending into an irrevocable and bloody anarchy from which it needed to be saved by force.

SEABROOK AND THE OCCUPATION

"'Should the future resemble the past," wrote Mr. Adams... "and the conditions of competition remain unchanged, the Caribbean archipelago must either be absorbed into the economic system of the United States or lapse into barbarism"

- Stephen Bonsal *The American Mediterranean* (1913)[22]

The experience of Liberia and Haiti show that the African races are devoid of any capacity for political organisation and lack genius for government. Unquestionably there is in them an inherent tendency to revert to savagery and to cast aside the shackles of civilisation which are irksome to their physical nature. Of course there are many exceptions to this racial weakness but it is true of the mass, as we know from experience in this country. It is that which makes the Negro problem practically unsolvable.

- Robert Lansing, U.S. Secretary of State at the time of the U.S. intervention in Haiti.[23]

Popular books about Haiti that focused on the most sensational aspects of Vodou rites, the grisly practices of animal and child sacrifice, orgiastic excess and cannibalism, helped create an image of Haiti as a country in desperate need of a neocolonial civilising mission that would rid the nation of the scourges of African tribalism, prevent its descent into wholesale barbarism and bring it back up to speed with Anglo-American modernity.[24] As such they can be considered to be part of an overarching ideological strategy that helped to manufacture consent at home for U.S. intervention in the "Black Republic" in the "American Mediterranean". Carl Van Doren, professor of literature at

---

22 Bonsal 20

23 Schmidt 62-63

24 Dash (1997) 22 - 23

Columbia University, friend of William Seabrook and member of the literary guild that awarded *it* book of the month prize in January 1929, described *The Magic Island* as a significant work in the literature of the American empire.[25] That empire was imagined to be a core federalist republic made up of the United States and a peripheral empire made up of countries like Puerto Rico, the Philippines, Nicaragua and Haiti, places that may well seem, in the words of Van Doren, like the remotest corner of the world "despite being only six hundred miles from the Florida coast".[26] At the time of Seabrook's journey to Haiti it was twelve years into the grip of a U.S. occupation that would not come to an official end for another six. During the occupation the U.S. marines installed a puppet president, dissolved the legislature at gunpoint, denied freedom of speech and imposed a new constitution on the Republic that was more favourable to foreign investment and foreign land ownership.[27]

While waging war against Haitian rebel insurgents (the Cacos), the occupation took control of Haitian finances, re-introduced forced labour (the *corvée* system) and re-organised the Haitian military in ways that would have long-term consequences for Haitian civil society.[28] *Corvée*, a form of forced labour imposed by the state on certain classes of people, and originally practiced by the French state, was introduced into Haiti by the President, and later King of Haiti, Henri Christophe in 1811, in order to build fortifications against a French invasion. It was revived during the occupation in order to build roads for the development of (foreign owned) industry in Haiti. Peasants would be forced to work for free or pay a road-building tax. As we will see, Victor and Edward Halperin, directors of the first zombie film, *White Zombie,* rather than drawing a correlation with the building of a road network during the U.S. occupation, drew one with Henri Christophe's use of forced labour to build Citadelle Laferrière, his famous mountaintop fortress in the north of Haiti (obliquely referred to as the castle of Murder Legendre in their 1932 film). It is one of several symbolic

---

25 Van Doren quoted in Renda 6

26 Van Doren quoted in Renda 8

27 Renda 10

28 See Michel-Rolph Trouillot, *Haiti: State Against Nation – The Origins and Legacy of Duvalierism* (1990)

evasions of the role of America in Haiti, displacing the sources of the kinds of violence and sorcery that can reduce living beings to mindless zombies on to "foreign influences".

Despite believing that Haiti would ultimately benefit from an imposed political order, Seabrook's evaluation of the occupation was mixed, praising the construction of infrastructure, the stabilisation of the currency, economic prosperity and the political peace that it had brought about, while criticising attempts on the part of the Americans to instil "race-consciousness" amongst the Haitian elites.[29] Even Jean Price-Mars, father of the Haitian *Indigéniste* movement, acknowledged that *The Magic Island* made an important contribution to the critique of racism and Europhilia amongst the Haitian ruling classes. But despite his avowed intention to defend the integrity of African-derived Haitian culture against its xenophobic and racist detractors, Seabrook, who claimed to have no interest in politics, still ultimately supported White, militaristic paternalism over the child-like innocence and potential savagery of Black Haitians. Recounting the trouble he had trying to attend a Vodou ceremony that was blocked because of political intrigues in the region of Croix de Bouquet, Seabrook wrote: "If I had ever read the newspapers, or taken any interest in politics, I might have already known this and guessed the rest".[30]

In the final chapter of *The Magic Island*, 'The Soul of Haiti', Seabrook likens the late President Guillaume Sam – whose dismembered body had been the ultimate pretext for the occupation – to the mythical president of Nicaragua who appears in the prologue to G. K. Chesterton's 1904 *The Napoleon of Notting Hill*, a novel set in an imaginary London where nothing has changed for a hundred years. The figure popped into Seabrook's head, he tells us, because he found himself standing in front of the late president's palace. Echoing Stephen Bonsal, whose scathing description of Haiti in *The American Mediterranean* he was familiar with, Seabrook describes the *opéra bouffe* that led up to the events as proceeding habitually by fixed rules "like a game of checkers" and unfolding in predictable fashion with villages liberated, cities surrendering and generals of

---

29 Seabrook (1929) 127. Such race consciousness did not have to be instilled. It had been an enduring one in the political and intellectual life of Haiti since the revolution.

30 Seabrook (1929) 26

the defensive armies retreating to Port-au-Prince, after grabbing what funds they can to maintain the government, and then sailing to Jamaica. When the "Liberator of the People" arrives in the capital he finds the palace empty, swept, ready and waiting for his occupancy. Sometimes this oft-repeated comedy gets out of hand and turns into a blood bath, an inevitability, Seabrook writes, in a land where the mass of the populace possess naïve, lovable and laughable child-like traits while also having a "powerful underlying streak of primitive, atavistic savagery".

Perhaps the most overt expression of Seabrook's tacit support for the occupation is the chapter he dedicates to Lieutenant Faustin E. Wirkus, the so-called "White King of La Gonâve", a U.S. Marine, whose story, "like a strangely potent dream", held an intoxicating fascination for the American adventurer. Wirkus was a Polish-American soldier from Pennsylvania who volunteered to be posted on the island of La Gonâve during the occupation. Shortly after taking up his post he went to meet Ti Meminne, the "Black Queen" of the island, and, after consulting with her and her followers for a day and eventually being introduced to "the old, blind soothsayer", he was crowned King Faustin II. Seabrook spent several weeks with Wirkus on the island and wrote an introduction to the marine's own account of his time there. A photograph taken by Seabrook of Wirkus and Ti Meminne (though interestingly cropped to cut Wirkus out) is included in the plates of *The Magic Island*. The fantasy of a White, American male holding sway over an island of devoted Black subjects seems to have been something that realised a deep-seated one for Seabrook, a fantasy he assumed would appeal to many of his U.S. readers too. "To hold undisputed sway in some remote tropical island set like a green jewel amid the coral reefs of summer seas" he wrote "how many boys have dreamed it, and how many grown men, civilisation tired?" He even included a postal address for Wirkus in Haiti so that any fellow dreamers who wanted to amuse themselves could write to a king. In *Taking Haiti* Mary A. Renda discusses a cache of such letters written to Wirkus by U.S. schoolboys.[31]

Michael Dash has identified *The Magic Island* as one of several books written during the occupation which, regardless of its literary merits, builds upon the work of Spenser St. John, Bonsal

31 Renda 5

and others that use such stories as a moral justification for the occupation.[32] At the same time these books profitably exploited a popular taste for the theatrical, exotic and sensational images of "Black savagery" and orgiastic sexuality that guaranteed their commercial appeal back home. More sober works like Edward Beach's unpublished *The Last Haitian Revolution* (1920) were too reasonable, Dash argues, to meet with commercial success. Dash divided American literary accounts of Haiti during the occupation into two categories: apologists for the occupation and defenders of Negro primitivism. Although Seabrook's work falls much more towards the second camp it does so not because of an implicit opposition to U.S. imperialism, but because the occupation threatened to eliminate the "pure soul" of the Negro race that he had gone there to immerse his waning Whiteness in. But no matter how much Seabrook revelled in this "thing of darkness underneath", it was still White Americans who would have, for better or for worse, the natural, if burdensome, right to rule there. The "benevolent despotism" of a White U.S. marine married (for convenience's sake) to a Black, native, queen, seems to be the kind of political model that Seabrook, less expediently and reluctantly perhaps than Wirkus, offered as a remedy for Haiti's ills.

---

32 Dash (1997) 22-23. Other examples include John Houston Craige's *Black Bagdad* (1933) and *Cannibal Cousins* (1934), and Wirkus's *The White King of La Gonave* (1931).

THE GOAT WITHOUT HORNS

> My own impression, after personally knowing the
> country above twenty years is, that it is a country in a
> state of rapid decadence. The revolution of 1843 that
> upset President Boyer commenced the year of troubles
> that have continued to the present day. The country
> has since been steadily falling to the rear in the race of
> civilisation... In spite of all the civilising elements around
> them, there is a distinct tendency to sink into the state of
> an African tribe.

- Spenser St. John *Hayti, or the Black Republic* (1884)

In his preface to *Life in a Haitian Valley*, one of the first modern ethnographic accounts of Haitian peasant life and Vodou culture, the American anthropologist Melville Herskovits comments on how badly Haiti had fared at the hands of occupation era writers like John Houston Craige and Seabrook who had subjected it to "the greatest distortion of facts, the most striking misrepresentations, and the largest measure of misplaced emphasis".[33] This tone of sensationalist distortion, Herskovits notes, was largely absent from earlier writers on Haiti, for whom the importance of Vodou lay in the fact that it was a rallying point for the Haitian Revolution. The tone had changed decisively since the publication of Spenser St. John's *Hayti or the Black Republic* in 1884, a book described by Bob Corbett as "singly the most negative book ever written about Haiti.[34] That Seabrook's fantastical description of the sacrificial and erotic transubstantiation of the Goat-Girl should include the symbolic drinking of human blood is entirely in keeping with one of the dominant myths of Haitian atavism during the 19th century: the association of Vodou with cannibalism. This association, which has been present since the earliest accounts of "Vaudoux" in Saint-Domingue, was consolidated by several works during the 19th and early 20th centuries, but most notoriously by Spenser St. John.

---

33 Herskovits vii

34 Bob Corbett, review on the Corbett List, April 1993.
http://www2.webster.edu/~corbetre/haiti/notes/stjohn.htm

The British government's *chargé d'affaires* in Haiti from 1863 to 1871, St. John was the writer who introduced readers to both the "goat without horns" (human sacrifice) and "Congo Bean Stew" (a cannibal meal made with the flesh of a sacrificed child and reputedly widely eaten during Vodou rites in Haiti at Easter, Christmas and other annual festivities). In two chapters on the subject of "Vaudoux" and cannibalism he insisted that, despite the systematic and concerted efforts of the Haitian elites to suppress evidence of their fellow countrymen's barbarism to the outside world, cannibalism was widespread throughout the country. His purpose, therefore, in dedicating so many pages to the topic, was to "fix attention on this frightful blot, and thus induce Enlightened Haitians to take measures for its extirpation, if that be possible". Such evidence included a story told to Monseigneur Guilloux, Archbishop of Port-au-Prince, by a Catholic curé who was present when the story was re-told about his first-hand experience of the sacrifice of a "goat without horns". What could be more direct, St. John asks, than the testimony of this curé whom was sitting opposite them and listening to the Archbishop during the whole recital? What indeed?[35] Another piece of "irrefutable" evidence comes from an article written by an anonymous author for *The New York World* on December 5, 1886, who St. John had latterly made the acquaintance of. It tells of how an American businessman and his Dominican friend managed to get themselves invited to a human sacrifice ceremony at

---

35 It is worth noting here that the Catholic Church in Haiti has often been at the forefront of campaigns against Vodou and has, at times, actively promoted "black propaganda" against it. It is also interesting to note that the myth of human sacrifice continues to exist amongst contemporary Vodouists. Former Salesian priest and Haitian president Jean-Bertrand Aristide, the first to decriminalize and publicly endorse Vodou as a national religion, claimed, in his doctoral thesis, written while in exile in South Africa, that during the Bois Caïman ceremony a slave named Jean Viksamar was substituted for the sacrificial pig (Aristide 304). The reference to Viksamar is part of a glossary entry on the term Sanpwèl, a Haitian secret society of African origin, lending weight to the myth that the ceremony of Bois Caïman was organised by such a sect. Markel Thylefors, who did fieldwork amongst Haitian *Vodouisants* between 1996 and 2007, also reports stories told to him by a *Vodouisant* in Croix-de-Bouquets in 2004 that it was a French soldier who was sacrificed (Thylefors 79).

which, disguised in black face, they witnessed a young boy, bound in ropes, being made to ask for the possession of a young virgin – "That object above all other objects in the world which he most desired" – before having his throat slashed. Typical of such stories, at the site of the atrocity, the horrified secret witness revealed himself by crying out loud and had to flee hastily for his life. His Dominican colleague decided to stay however, explaining later that the young girl had eventually been sacrificed too, and that both were cut up, cooked and eaten in an "awful orgy" that lasted all night. The chapter continues with several more examples of irrefutable, second-hand information from "entirely trustworthy" European and American sources.

The myth of Congo Bean Stew also seems to have been introduced by St. John, who makes reference to it in his discussion of the so-called *Affaire de Bizoton* of 1864. The story involves a man named Congo Pellé from the village of Bizoton, close to Port-au-Prince, who, seeking to improve his station in Haitian society ("without any exertion on his own part"), sought the services of his sister Jeanne, a "Mamanloi" and "true African priestess", who prepared for him a meal containing the sacrificed body of their niece Claircine whom they killed, cooked and ate on New Year's Eve. Later that night neighbours, roused by the noise of Claircine's murder, spied the family eating the meat with congo beans shortly before the New Year was welcomed in, along with much drinking, dancing and debauchery. St. John recounts both the court proceedings, which he purportedly attended, and the ingredients of the stew in great detail, noting how the boiled head of the young girl and a jar of the stew were placed on a table at the centre of the courtroom throughout the trial, and how the defendants were brutally beaten into confessing their crimes. Dash has noted how the *Affaire de Bizoton* became a national news story in 1864 consolidating popular myths of Haitian savagery to an international audience at a time when President Fabre Geffrard was trying to present an image of Haiti to the outside world that was intolerant of, and intent upon eradicating, the blight of Vodou from the nation. The strategy, with hindsight, seems to have backfired, not least because of the detailed and lurid reporting of the court proceedings by St. John.

In a second chapter, dealing specifically with cannibalism, St. John argues that the barbaric practice had been present on the island since the time of Moreau de Saint-Méry, who had spoken about the Mondongoes, an African people whose depravity had reached "the most execrable of excesses" of eating their fellow creatures. Surprisingly perhaps, from our contemporary perspective, the chapter opens with accounts of children being miraculously risen from the dead by the application of magical potions, and of people being buried alive in cemeteries with the aid of a mysterious sleeping potion that creates the semblance of death. In a historical reversal of the apocalyptic cannibal formula, familiar from contemporary zombie films, something like zombification (though the term was not used by St. John) was allegedly used to deceptively procure "undead" bodies for the cannibalistic rites of the living (or more prosaically, in the author's words, "to be used as food").[36] After citing numerous claims about the widespread practice of eating corpses, St. John concludes the chapter by quoting the eminent British historian, novelist and vehement racial separatist, James Anthony Froude, who, having been incredulous at first, concluded that:

> behind the immorality, behind the religiosity, there lies active and alive the horrible revival of the West African superstitions: the serpent-worship and the child sacrifice and the cannibalism. *There is no room to doubt it.*[37]

Almost fifty years later, towards the end of the U.S. occupation, Richard A. Loederer would use 'Congo Bean Stew' as the title of the first chapter of his *Voodoo Fire in Haiti*, which begins, emblematically, with a contrast between Haiti's white beaches and dark mountains beyond at the dawn of Hispaniola's colonisation. In ways clearly shaped by the writings of St. John and Seabrook, it goes on to describe the "bloodstained face" that separates the arrival of Columbus in the 15th century from present-day Haiti, a "dark chapter" in history that saw "the foul butchery of the entire population by the frenzied Negroes" (a reference, presumably, to Jean-Jacques Dessalines' 1804 post-revolutionary genocide of the remaining *White* population of Haiti). At

---

36 St. John 240

37 James Anthony Froude, the biographer of Thomas Carlyle and a historian of England, argued for the Enlightened Despotism of the English in Ireland, for a White separatist party in South Africa and the forced labour of the indigenous Xhosa there. His comments come from his 1888 record of his travels in the West Indies *The English in the West Indie*s.

that time "the clean white beaches ran red with blood... in a holocaust of murder and primeval madness".

Amongst Loederer's traveling companions on the Dutch West Indian Steamer from New York were two "pure-blooded Negroes" whose astonishing elegance and education (they had recently graduated as doctors from the Louis Pasteur Institute in Paris) could not fully conceal a "primitive African layer" which broke through the shell of civilised convention when someone onboard played a gramophone record. Suddenly their "consciousness of rhythm submerged the veneer of civilisation" and, surrendering to the throbbing beat, their bodies were completely transformed. Later in the journey, as the author sits down for dinner, a fellow passenger orders from the menu the Congo Bean Stew, a concoction much favoured by the Dutch, Loederer explains. A British traveller, Sir Joshua Higginbotham, is so disgusted by the presence of the lamb casserole that he is compelled to leave the table. Meeting Higginbotham later on the upper deck the Englishman explains that he left the table to avoid insulting the two Black passengers. He goes on to tell the author about how "the curse of voodoo" was brought to Haiti along with the slave caravans from Africa and there the old rites and orgies were recommenced in the virgin forests. Out of the demoniacal dances, mad drinking orgies and sexual frenzies overseen by the *Papaloi* and *Mamaloi*, there grew an atavistic impulse towards cannibalism which culminated in the ritual slaughter of children and grown men, followed by a meal of roast flesh. Sir Joshua then recounts the story of the *Affaire de Bizoton* explaining how he had also attended the trial, alongside Spenser St. John, and had seen with his own eyes the remains of what looked to him like a Lancashire hot-pot, the sight of which compelled him to rush out of the courtroom to vomit. The following day, Higginbotham claimed, after the priests had been executed by firing squad, their bodies had vanished and in their place were found the carcasses of goats.

Unsurprisingly, given Seabrook's later creation of a personal cannibal legend for himself, the eating of human flesh figures repeatedly in *The Magic Island*, if less overtly than in its predecessors. In *Jungle Ways* (1931), which recounted his journey to French West Africa in search of real-life cannibals, Seabrook deceptively represented his own act of cannibalism as a traditional practice of the Guéré people there. A variety of recipes were described to Seabrook by the Guéré cook to a Cannibal King in the forests of the Ivory Coast, the meat's subtle texture and flavour described with great delectation by the gastronomic adventurer. The actual meal however, it turns out, took place in Paris after Seabrook, unable to satisfy his curiosity in Africa, managed to procure the dead body of a 30 year old male factory worker, from whom he took a cut of flesh to eat like a steak, with a bottle of red wine.[38] For Seabrook cannibalism was assumed to be an archaic, if rare and exceptional aspect of Vodou rites, which, by inference, was framed as an essentially African practice. The sources upon which Seabrook supports his claims are, like those of St. John, largely the product of hearsay and questionable official sources. In footnotes to the chapter which tells the story of Célestine Antoine-Simon, daughter of the President François Antoine-Simon and allegedly the *grand mamaloi* of all Haiti, for instance, Seabrook claimed that she had a soldier's heart ripped out in the grounds of the National Palace, taken away on a silver platter and presumably eaten. Seabrook's source is Stephen Bonsal's *The American Mediterranean* (1913), a book which contains numerous dubiously supported claims about the prevalence of cannibalism in Haiti, most gleaned directly from Spenser St. John. Like so many of the more sinister myths associated with Haiti and Vodou by foreign writers, they often seem to be the product of their authors' vivid imaginations, and the appropriation of hearsay reported as fact by their literary precursors, rather than first-hand experience. Even Seabrook, who prided himself on doing what others only dreamed of, had to resort to subterfuge when it came to the practice reputedly endemic to the Black Republic.

Stephen Bonsal, like Seabrook, was a journalist and world traveller, who spent several weeks in Haiti during the ousting of President Nord Alexis by Antoine-Simon in 1908. His book seems to be the principle source of stories about human sacrifice at the National Palace, which would continue into the 1990s. In her book *Haiti: The Duvaliers and their Legacy* from 1991 for instance, Elizabeth Abbott claimed that on the eve of their departure from the National Palace, Jean-Claude and Michèle Duvalier had two unbaptised babies ritually sacrificed by a *houngan* in order to curse the presidential bed.[39] Throughout the

---

38 For an account of the circumstances of Seabrook's cannibal meal in Paris see Worthington 50-57. For Seabrook's own account see *Jungle Ways* (1931), 169-173.

39 Abbott 324-325

chapter on Haiti, Bonsal refers to the National Palace as the Black House, a term allegedly used contemptuously by the White residents of the capital. He describes Vodou as an anti-White religion that "occasionally relapses into cannibalism". It is a taint on the nation that president Alexis Nord, like Fabre Geffrard before him, had tried to fight before succumbing to the power of his wife, "the red-mitred priestess of their sect", at the end of his life. In a chapter entitled 'The Truth about Voodoo' Bonsal proposes that Haiti is the best country in the world to satisfy a cannibalistic craving and that, if it were not for the check and control upon native practices by foreign residents, the "African darkness" of cannibalism, serpent worship and child sacrifice would become rampant throughout the land. Despite admitting never having seen the dark frenzy of cannibal feasts into which the "voodoo" ceremonies regularly descended, he claimed to have absolutely unimpeachable evidence, corroborated by thousands of witnesses, regarding two stories of children stolen from their parents, murdered and eaten at such ceremonies. More damning for the Haitian political establishment, which Bonsal claimed to be almost irrevocably corrupted by these scourges, Haitian officials protected the kidnappers and frequently took part in the cannibal rites themselves. Any president who attempted to rule independently of the consent of the priests would find their government coming to a disastrous and bloody end (a claim we will hear repeated in 1985 by members of the Bizango secret societies consulted by Wade Davis in his ethnobotanical study of the Haitian *zombi, The Serpent and the Rainbow*).

As with St. John before him, and Seabrook later, Bonsal claims that the abominations of human sacrifice and cannibalism are always shrouded in mystery and carefully guarded from interlopers. Such precautions, he claims, restating St. John's accusations almost to the letter, have led the Haitian government to all but bankrupt itself printing books for foreign audiences denying the existence of cannibalistic rites there (a reference to Jacques Nicolas Léger's defence of Haiti entitled *Haiti: Her History and Her Detractors* of 1907).[40] And like St. John, he had only written at length on the topic as a corrective to such "black propaganda".[41]

---

40 Leger was a Haitian lawyer, politician and the Haitian Diplomat in Washington from 1896-1909, who Bonsal targets directly in *The American Mediterranean*.

41 Bonsal was also critical of Anténor Firmin, a pioneer of Haitian

Stories of "voodoo" cannibalism, promoted by the works of St. John, Bonsal and Seabrook, flourished as powerful myths amongst U.S. marines during the occupation of Haiti.[42] One of the most sensational stories, discussed at some length by Seabrook, concerned one Sergeant Lawrence Muth, a U.S. marine who was captured and murdered by the Cacos rebels after a skirmish in the mountains. The story of his death and subsequent mutilation was to become part of marine lore at the time. Kate Ramsey notes that such stories had a significant role in testimony given at U.S. senate hearings that questioned the reasons for the occupation in November 1921.[43] Seabrook's account, reputedly based on an unofficial report kept at Marine Corps headquarters in Port-au-Prince, itself based on testimony given by a captured rebel some days later, told of how, before he was dead, Muth was partially decapitated by the rebel commander Benoît Batraville, who then ordered his men to rub their sights with part of the head to assure the accuracy of their fire against Muth's comrades. Afterwards the soldier's heart and liver were cooked and eaten so that the rebels would not be hit by the Americans' bullets or cut by their bayonets.[44] Seabrook concludes his account of the Muth case with a story about how, when Batraville was killed by marines in 1920, they found in his possession a book of spells with instructions how to call up spirits and the dead, create an invisible face and other spells, thirty three of which Seabrook translates in their entirety in *The Magic Island*.[45]

---

anthropology, staunch defender of the equality of races, critic of the U.S. intervention in Haiti and, for a period, Haitian foreign secretary, who was eventually driven into exile by President Alexis Nord.

42 Ramsey (2011) 137

43 Renda 66

44 In a second account, given on oath by Lieutenant Colonel R. S. Hooker, the rebels reputedly castrated Muth before disembowelling him and cutting two large strips of flesh from his thighs (Heinl and Heinl 424). As we will see in Chapter Three, the general structure of the Muth case is remarkably similar to the first accounts of the Bois Caïman ceremony which were also extracted from captured rebels under duress who claimed to be using ritual magic to protect themselves from harm.

45 The book of spells was probably a popular grimoire like the *Grand Albert, Petit Albert* or *La Poule Noir* which had been in popular circulation

Batraville, a descendent of Joseph Benedict Batraville who fought the French alongside Dessalines in the revolutionary war of independence, was the most prominent leader of the Cacos rebels after Charlemagne Péralte, whose murdered body was famously photographed tied to a police station door by the U.S. marines and used in the propaganda war against the Cacos in 1919.[46]

Another popular story used to underscore the marines' moral campaign against Vodou during the occupation was that of Cadeus Bellegarde, a wealthy Haitian landowner, reputed *houngan* and sometime informant for the marines who, in February 1920, was charged with arson, aiding and abetting an armed uprising against U.S. forces, murder and cannibalism. During his trial, which was handled by the U.S. military rather than the Haitian judicial authorities, the prosecution focused on the threat that Vodou posed to the occupation, accusing it of being "the foundation of the present uprising".[47] Bellegarde himself testified that he supported the U.S. struggle against the insurgents, a claim dismissed by the prosecution as ridiculous because the U.S. forces were working explicitly *against* the "barbaric and inhuman perversion" of Vodou, which Bellegarde was purportedly a priest of. Seabrook, never one to miss a cannibal sensation, discussed the Bellegarde case in the footnotes to *The Magic Island*, including it in a short section about "actual human sacrifice" in Haiti, where he describes Bellegarde as a *"papaloi* turned criminal, a pathological monster comparable religiously to Gilles de

---

in the French-speaking Caribbean since the 1880s (see Davies 160 and Herskovits 238). Katherine Dunham, who may have encountered a *Petit Albert* on the altar of Congo *hounfo* (Vodou temple) dedicated to the reputedly human-flesh-eating Moundong, notes that at the time of her visit in 1936 the *Petit Albert* was banned in Haiti (Dunham 208).

46 How Seabrook gained access to official Marine documents was a topic of correspondence between Melville Herskovits and John Houston Craige, author of *Cannibal Cousins,* and the publication of *The Magic Island* led to an official enquiry about how he came to be in possession of the classified information. See Ramsey (2011) 326 n199. Batraville would re-appear in fictional guise in Ishmael Reed's 1972 novel *Mumbo Jumbo* as a "VoodDoo General" who arrived in New York in the 1930s to teach the Harlem Renaissance about Haiti and the Cacos rebellion.

47 Ramsey (2011) 146

Rais, criminally to Landru and the 'Hamburg Butcher'". According to Seabrook twenty-seven peasants testified that between 1916 and 1918 they had been present at human sacrifices made by Bellegarde at which the blood of the victims was drunk and their flesh eaten. Such acts, Seabrook claimed, represented a throwback to an ancient "Voodoo blood-sacrificial cult" that even old *houngans* had themselves participated in "and perhaps would do so again". Whether or not Bellegarde was guilty of such atrocities was no matter of concern for the U.S. Navy's Judge Advocate General however, who, reviewing the case back in Washington, concluded that military courts should be convened only for offences which affected the exercise of military authority. Because none of Bellegarde's alleged victims were military personnel, and none of the properties he allegedly damaged owned by the U.S., the conviction was judged illegitimate and Bellegarde was released without charge.[48]

DEAD MEN WORKING

In the second chapter of the 'Black Sorcery' section of *The Magic Island* – "...Dead Men Working in the Cane Fields" – Seabrook introduced his readers to the *zombi*, a figure that for the first few decades of the 20th century would be directly associated with Haiti and Vodou. Seabrook's *zombi* story begins when a local, trusted informant from La Gonâve, a Haitian farmer called Constant Polynice, was talking to him under a full moon about fire-hags, demons, werewolves and vampires. Presently they hit upon a subject that "lies in a baffling category on the ragged edge of things which are beyond either superstition or reason", a creature which sounded to Seabrook exclusively local. Neither ghost nor person, a *zombi* was a thing that had been raised like Lazarus, a "soulless human corpse, still dead, but taken from the grave and endowed by sorcery with a mechanical semblance of life". When Seabrook asked to hear more about this local superstition Polynice puts his hand on the American's knee, astonished that he should consider it a mere *superstition*: at that very moment, he said, there were *zombis* labouring in the moonlight on the same island. He promised to take Seabrook the following day to see the *zombis* working in the cane fields.

---

48 Ramsey (2011) 146

Perhaps he had heard of those that worked at HASCO, the Haitian-American Sugar Company.

And so Polynice's tale began. During the spring of 1918, following a big sugar cane season, HASCO had offered a wage bonus to new workers on their plantations that attracted many people from the surrounding areas looking for work. Shortly afterwards a man called Ti Joseph arrived at the plantation from the nearby mountains with a band of ragged creatures shuffling along behind him, "staring dumbly, like people walking in a daze". Polynice claimed that these people were in fact *zombis* and that Ti Joseph and his wife Croyance had raised them from their graves in order to work. Ti Joseph, however, insisted that they were simply ignorant peasants from the slopes of Morne-au-Diable, close to the Dominican border, who were frightened by the noise and smoke from the great factory. For several weeks the *zombis* laboured silently in the fields until one day, feeling pity for them, and hoping to cheer them up a little, Croyance decided to take them to the Mardi Gras in nearby Croix de Bouquet. At a market stall Croyance mistakenly fed the *zombis* salted peanut cakes and, suddenly aware of their miserable fate, they marched in single file back to their mountain villages, where, to the horrified amazement of their relatives, they tried to crawl back into their graves. Realising what had been done to their loved ones, the families arranged for another local *bokor* to make a deadly *wanga* to kill Ti Joseph. And, just to be on the safe side, they also sent men down to the plain who hacked his head off with a machete.

Unconvinced by Polynice's *zombi* story, Seabrook was eventually introduced to a group of them working in broad daylight on a rough terraced slope on the island, chopping earth with machetes. Polynice goes to speak to Lamercie, the *zombi* gang-master, before Seabrook has made it up the hill. As he clambers up the slope Seabrook senses something unnatural about them, something brute-like and robotic. Polynice taps one of them on the shoulder and asks him to get up, which he does, "obediently, like an animal". The face of the *zombi* came as a sickening shock to Seabrook:

> The eyes were the worst. It was not my imagination. They were in truth like the eyes of a dead man, not blind, but staring, unfocussed, unseeing. The whole face, for that matter, was bad enough. It was vacant, as if there was nothing behind it. It seemed not only expressionless, but

incapable of expression... Then I suddenly remembered
– and my mind seized the memory as a man sinking in
water clutches a solid plank – the face of a dog I had
once seen in the histological laboratory in Columbia. Its
entire front brain had been removed in an experimental
operation weeks before: it moved about, it was alive, but
its eyes were like the eyes I now saw staring.[49]

When recovered from this moment of mental panic, Seabrook
reached out to grasp the *zombi*'s dangling, calloused hand. "Bonjour,
compere" he says. But Lamercie pushed Seabrook away yelling at him
that Negro affairs were not for Whites! Suddenly the word "keeper"
jumped into Seabrook's mind, and reflecting on it, he concluded
that *zombis* were nothing more than poor, ordinary demented human
beings, idiots, forced to toil in the fields. Later, still reeling at the
memory of the *zombi*'s dead eyes, Seabrook found himself grasping
for a rational explanation for their abject condition, explaining to
Polynice that "it is a fixed rule of reasoning in America that we will
never accept the possibility of things being 'supernatural' so long as
any natural explanation, even far fetched, seems adequate". Perhaps
his involuntary association with the lobotomised dog held a clue to the
mystery. Later, speaking to his colleague Dr. Antoine Villiers, a man
of exemplary reason and a pragmatic, scientific mind, about the doubt
that still persisted within him, Seabrook was offered an interpretation
of zombiedom that was to prove influential in later formulations of
the condition. Villiers explained that it was likely that some of the
victims may indeed have been taken from their graves. "It is then
something like suspended animation?" Seabrook asked.[50] In response

---

49 Seabrook (1929) 101

50 The notion of zombiedom as suspended animation is one repeated by
Zora Neale Hurston in a radio interview in 1943. The concept of suspended
animation seems to have first been used around 1800 in reference to an
intermediate phase just before death in which life exists in a liminal state,
without vital signs, as can happen after drowning. The source of the idea
seems to be Samuel Jackson's *An Essay on Suspended Animation* (1808). As
we will see in Chapter Six, 'The Return of the Haitian Zombi', medical
interest in zombification in the 1980s was based on its potential use in
"artificial hibernation" during voyages into space.

Villiers showed him an article from the contemporary criminal code in Haiti:

> Also shall be qualified as attempted murder the employment which may be made against any person of substances which, without causing actual death, produce lethargic coma more or less prolonged. If, after the administering of such substances the person has been buried, the act shall be considered murder no matter what result follows.[51]

This piece of judicial evidence, with which the chapter closes, performs a pivotal function in the modern myth of Haitian *zombis*: on the one hand it gives rational credence to the myth by suggesting a *natural* or scientific explanation for the condition, while at the same time preserving the mysterious secrets of the *zombi*-creating potion in the hands of the sorcerous *bokor* (or evil magician). The so-called *zombi* potion (or powder) would become one of the enduring components of the myth of Haitian *zombi* creation both within and without Haiti. In his essay '"We are the mirror of your fears": Haitian Identity and Zombification', Franck Degoul has shown how *zombi* powder became part of the "witchcraft arsenal" that contemporary Haitian culture has re-appropriated from exogenous visions of Haitian Voodoo-horror, an example of how foreign fears of Vodou are turned against foreigners by Haitians.[52] As we will see, the evidence of the Haitian penal code will be transferred directly to the first zombie film, *White Zombie*, three years after Seabrook's book, and the notion of a powerful *zombi* narcotic will be revived by Wade Davis in *The Serpent and the Rainbow* (1985) in which he claims that the secrets of the *zombi* powder are held by *bizangos* (secret societies) with a direct lineage to West African sects, who use zombification as a form of punishment.

Seabrook's need to find a naturalistic explanation for zombiedom is oddly out of character for a man who considered himself "half-black" and largely unshackled from the reasonable constraints of civilisation.[53]

---

51 Seabrook (1929) 103

52 Degoul in Christie and Lauro 32

53 In *Jungle Ways* Seabrook claimed that the natives he met on his journeys with the forest people of the ivory coast called him Mogo-Dieman "the-

Why would he find zombification so "irrational" when he accepted the mysteries of possession as a subjective truth, and the realities of human sacrifice and cannibalism on such flimsy evidential supports? Perhaps, as Zieger has suggested, it was because the *zombi* represented for him the antithesis of what he had come to Haiti to seek: a tonic for his waning Whiteness, the rejuvenating and mystical essence of Black blood, Black bodies and that *living* thing underneath – the great life-giving womb. For him the *zombi* was too much a reminder of the modern, laboriously secularised White world.

> Of what use is any life without its emotional moments or hours of ecstasy? They [the Vodouists] were reaching collective ecstasy by paths that were not intrinsically peculiar to their jungle ancestors, but which have been followed by many peoples, some highly civilised, from the earliest ages, and will be followed to the end of time or until we all become mechanical, soulless robots.[54]

But it is still difficult to understand why Seabrook didn't make the obvious connection between the figure of the *zombi* and the history of slavery. That humans can be reduced to the level of "labouring brutes" or "mere automatons" should have come as no surprise to Seabrook, especially since the American military had re-introduced forced-labour there during the occupation. Furthermore it was in the production of sugar, the principle crop produced during the plantation slavery era, that the *zombis* toiled like mindless and soulless robots. A clue to this omission may be the "American-commercial-synthetic" name HASCO, which, for Seabrook, was the last name anyone would think of connecting with either sorcery or superstition.

The HASCO plant, situated in the eastern suburbs of Port-au-Prince, and at the time of Seabrook's sojourn, the largest industrial sugar manufactory in the country, was founded in 1912 by three American businessmen to produce sugar and other goods for markets in Haiti, and the U.S. HASCO's sugar production methods differed from the traditional system which had involved landholders controlling large numbers of tenant farmers. Instead they employed

---

black-man-who-has-a-white-face" (Seabrook (1931) 19).

54 Seabrook (1929) 42

wage-labourers and industrial production techniques that eventually eroded the traditional agricultural economy and forced thousands of newly landless peasants into the cities looking for work. Between 1912 and 1915 many of them were employed to build the HASCO plantations and refineries, making them the targets of political opposition and Cacos resistance. In 1915 HASCO's operations were threatened by anti-American unrest which, along with the murder of President Guillaume Sam, was one of the principle reasons for the U.S. government's decision to invade Haiti. The main HASCO plant in Port-au-Prince, whose plantations Ti Joseph's *zombis* were allegedly sub-contracted for, was constructed between 1916 and 1918 under the protection of the U.S. military, the same period in which the *corveé* system was reintroduced to the country.[55] Furthermore, as Kate Ramsey astutely pointed out, the particular article of the Haitian Penal Code (actually Article 246 rather than 249) that gave legitimacy to the myth of the *bokor*'s mysterious *zombi* potion, was one of only three penal laws translated into English for U.S. marines during the first seven years of the occupation, the other two being articles against spell-making and vagrancy. All three laws were used to justify the suppression of Vodou which was considered by the occupying forces, the Catholic church and the Haitian elite, to be a source of rebel resistance. So under the guise of the suppression of the cult the occupying authorities compelled unemployed and landless peasants into civil engineering projects at gunpoint.[56]

Although Seabrook found it hard to imagine supernatural beings and modern, American capitalism being part of the same world, contemporary readings of the zombie metaphor explicitly associate the figure with transformations of labour practices within modern and contemporary capitalism.[57] Stephan Palmié for instance, reflecting on the relationship between stories of *zombis* and actual labour practices in Haiti at the time of the occupation, has written:

---

55 Ramsey notes that it was largely in response to the forced labour regime that the Cacos resistance resurfaced in Haiti (Ramsey (2011), 127). According to her it is not at all incongruous that the Haitian peasants should associate HASCO with sorcery (Ramsey (2011) 173).

56 Ramsey (2011) 128

57 See Comaroff and Comaroff (2002) and Palmié (2002 and 2006)

The loss of control over one's selfhood and individual volition characteristic of the notion of the soulless "living dead" at work in the cane fields quite clearly indexes the fundamental alienation of labour power "which is abstract, exists merely in the physical body of the worker, and is separated from its own means of objectification and realization" (Marx 1977, 1:716). Far from representing a mistaken interpolation of archaic fantasy into the rational script of agroindustrial labour relations, the image of the *zonbi* and the reduction of humans to commodified embodiments of labour power to which it speaks are cut from the same cloth of a single social reality long in the making, a reality deeply riven with a sense of moral crisis unleashed by a predatory modernity and experienced, chronicled and analyzed by its victims in the form of phantasmagoric narratives about how even the bodies of the dead, bereft of their souls, do not escape conscription into capitalist relations of production.[58]

Seabrook's general disinterest in the local and national politics of Haiti seems to have prevented him from making connections between the U.S. occupation, the racial aspects of the plantation slavery system and the history of anti-imperialist struggle in Haiti in which Vodou, and armed slave resistance, had played a combined role since before the revolution. Despite acknowledging the *zombi*'s distinctly local nature, Seabrook himself did not seem to recognise, in the broken, shuffling gait, expressionless faces, dead eyes and mindless labour of these poor, brute, idiot-automatons (or "kept" beings, as he called them), a spectre of slavery enduring within modernity, one that fantasmatically embodied an explicitly Black history of alienated labour, and loss of individual and collective freedom all the way "from Guinea to Léogane". As Zieger has put it, the *zombi*'s capacity for labour was key to its modernity – "the replication of the plantation in the factory field" – and the "soul-draining, monotonous work in a place of industrial terror" made it *newly* modern.[59] To encounter in the face

58 Palmié (2002) 66

59 Zieger 748

of the *zombi* the historical consciousness of the systematic horrors and brutality of the plantation slavery system would have been something more terrible and exorbitantly sadistic than animal sacrifice, spirit possession and black-skinned orgiastic frenzy, something deeper, colder and "Whiter" upon which the modern, industrial and lifeless order he so disdained was built. From this perspective the *zombi* is not so much *beyond either superstition or reason* but traverses the ostensibly distinct realms that Seabrook's world view required keeping apart: the sacred realm of mystical excess, sorcery and "Black Magic" and the deadening, soul-eating labour practices of modern and pre-modern capitalism. Seabrook had gone to Haiti to slough off the robotic and anaesthetising effects of industrial modernity, to immerse himself in transgressive "African" rites that would revitalise and re-sacralise him, but he was unable to recognise either the sorcerous powers of modern capitalist relations or the returning horrors of a barbarous plantation economy that had lasted for over two centuries and which continued to haunt the people of Haiti in a new guise.

THE BATAILLE – SEABROOK CONNECTION

He is in the end a westerner who "understands". Without ever yielding to the stupid prejudice of race, he puts himself on the same level as the natives: one could even say that often it is he who humiliates himself... What he understands first-hand is the intense desire that all human beings have for pushing their own limits, even taking the risk to merge with animals, plants, minerals, in order to lose their own boundaries within the great shadow of the outside, which is yet more real and alive than one's self.

- Michel Leiris, review of *The Magic Island* (1929)[60]

I'm afraid it has become only too apparent that I went for no useful, moral, scholarly, political or reasonable purpose whatsoever. I went for the joy of life, and because I believed I should love it.

- William Seabrook, *Adventures in Arabia* (1928)

In September 2010 I was invited to give a talk at *The Last Tuesday Society*, an intimate and genial mix of art gallery, cabinet of curiosities and esoteric salon in East London, hosted by the inimitable impresario of the surreal Viktor Wynd. My talk drew parallels between Bataille's theories of sacred excess and revolutionary contagion, the ritual practices of Vodou, the secret society *Acéphale* founded by Bataille in 1936, and the Bois Caïman ceremony. Towards the end of the talk I mentioned my recent reading of Seabrook's *The Magic Island* and the surprising similarity I'd found there between the author's description of his initiation into Vodou and Bataille's visions of transgressive, sacred ecstasy. When the talk was finished a man in the audience, whose name I didn't get and whom I have never seen again, made two penetrating comments that exposed me as a rather flimsy Bataille scholar. The first had to do with Bataille's familiarity with Seabrook's

---

60 *Documents 6* (1929) 334

work, which, he informed me, had been reviewed by one of his closest friends Michel Leiris in the Surrealist journal, *Documents,* that Bataille had edited between 1929 and 1930. I thanked him for pointing this out, agreeing that I certainly should have known. The second point had to do with the details of precisely who within the *Acéphale* group had offered themselves up for sacrifice. I had assumed it was the author Colette Peignot (aka "Laure"), Bataille's lover, his accomplice in deep debauchery and a central figure within this and earlier revolutionary organisations in which he had been involved.[61] The man in the audience assured me that Patrick Waldberg, another member of the *Acéphale* group and a lifelong friend of Bataille, had made it clear that Bataille intended to have himself sacrificed. I thanked him for the correction, feeling a little pierced by his comments, but happy in the knowledge that such slights were presumably inflicted by one of the "unavowable community".[62] I hoped that, before he left, we might acknowledge our *being-in-common*, but he departed promptly with neither word nor gesture of recognition.

The Seabrook connection, it turns out, is more compelling and complicated still. Not only was Leiris a close friend of Seabrook, arranging a reception for him with senior colleagues from the Trocadero on Seabrook's return from Timbuctu in 1930, but also visiting the author at his hotel sick bed in Paris before his final return to New York. The young, would-be-ethnographer even took *The Magic Island* with him on his own journey into "primal darkness", the Dakar-Djibouti mission to Africa of 1931, the experiences of which he would recount in his 1934 *sousrealist*[63]

---

61 Notably the group around the journal *La Critique Sociale*, edited by Boris Souvarine, Lauré's former partner, and *Contre-Attaque*, a political group formed by Bataille and André Breton in 1935. In Michael Surya's biography of Bataille he notes that Bataille had proposed Roger Caillois as the sacrificer (Surya 248 n20). Surya however absolutely refutes the claim that Lauré had been chosen to be sacrificed (Surya 249 n25).

62 "Unavowable community" is the name given by Maurice Blanchot to *Acéphale*, and two other communities established by Bataille in the 1930s – *Contre-Attaque* and *Collège de Sociologie* – in his 1983 book of the same name.

63 The term *sousrealist* I have taken from Petrine Archer-Straw's book *Negrophilia* (2000) where she uses it to describe the particular modality of Surrealism *lived* by Bataille and Leiris (Archer-Straw 145). It is a fitting

ethno-biography *L'Afrique Fantôme* (a book that seems to have been directly inspired by Seabrook's example). At the meeting with his "stuffed shirt" colleagues from the Trocadero, the American author arranged for a call-girl called Mimi from Montparnasse to be hooded and suspended from the balcony by her wrists, wearing only a leather skirt that he had had brought back from Africa.[64] Later Leiris would write another essay for *Documents* – 'Le "Caput Mortuum" ou la femme de l'alchimiste' – which is accompanied by a photographic portrait of a woman (presumably), in a full-head black-leather mask and collar made by Seabrook himself. Seabrook sent the photograph to Leiris from Toulon, where he was writing *Jungle Ways*. Of the image Leiris would write about the exciting metamorphosis by which man overcomes the confines of himself by "donning another skin". As Zieger points out, both Leiris and Seabrook seemed to have imagined that donning another (usually black or leather) skin would give them access to mystical realms of ecstatic experience beyond their "waning Whiteness".[65] That such techniques also involved bondage and partial tortures also suggest erotic-fantasy allusions to the sadistic practices of slave-masters, bringing the violent realities of the plantation economy into an uncomfortable proximity to the erotic practices of sado-masochism as performed in the brothels of bohemian Paris in the 1920s.

According to his second wife and biographer Marjorie Worthington, Leiris and his *sousrealist* comrades admired Seabrook because he fitted

---

epithet for a perspective on the world that was hostile to any form of idealism and pre-occupied with the experience of that which was most sinister, base and ignoble. Bataille's clearest statement against the idealism of André Breton's version of Surrealism is his essay 'The "Old Mole" and the Prefix *Sur* in the Words *Surhomme* [Superman] and *Surrealist*' in *Visions of Excess* (1985). A detailed account and analysis of the relationship between Bataille, Leiris and Seabrook is given in Susan Zieger's essay 'The Case of William Seabrook: *Documents*, Haiti and the Working Dead' (2012) *Modernism/modernity*, Volume 19, Number 4, November 2012, 737-754.

64 Worthington 108-109

65 For an account of the racial dimension of Leiris' metamorphosis fantasies see Phyllis Clarck-Taoua 'In Search of New Skin: Michel Leiris *L'Afrique Fantôme*' *Cahiers d'études africaines*, 2002/3, n167, 479-498.

so well with their "strangely distorted view of life".[66] As Archer-Straw and others have pointed out, Negrophilic primitivism was a popular trend within the Parisian avant-gardes of late 1920s and early '30s and Bataille and Leiris, like many of their Surrealist colleagues, were very much in tune with this vogue, writing numerous articles about Black Culture for *Documents*.[67] Bataille and Leiris' version of Negrophilia was informed by a politics of ecstasy that connected eroticism and death at the colonial periphery to a new fantasy of transgression as subjective obliteration.[68] And Seabrook, as Zieger and Archer-Straw argue, was *the* key figure for the construction of this excessive and ecstatic fantasy of the loss of self through immersion-communion with "der ganz Andere" (or the absolutely Other).[69] Like him they were Negrophiliacs of a particularly "wild" kind, sharing a fantasy of "Blackness" that challenged the perceived sterility, spiritual impoverishment and mindless automatism of modern western society.[70] The focus of attention in Leiris's review of *The Magic Island* reveals the general philosophical outlook shared by Seabrook and the *sousrealists*: a paradoxical idealisation of the Negro's "primitive mentality" (appropriated as a critique of the anaemic and soulless

---

66 Worthington 143

67 For an account of the reception of Black Culture in *Documents* see Simon Barker 'Variety (Civilizing Race)' in Ades and Barker (2006). The term 'Negrophilia' was used by the Parisian avant-gardes of the 1920s to describe a love of Black Culture by Whites. It has been re-deployed by Petrine Archer-Straw to analyse radicalised modes of western thinking in the 20th century.

68 Zieger 737-738

69 The term *ganz Andere*, associated primarily with the writings of the German theologian Rudolph Otto who used it to describe the numinous mental experience of the Holy, was adopted by Bataille to name "a supreme non-human being, derived from nothing, but from which the creation of the world, as much as the mimetic reproduction of the original event arises" (Gasche in Boldt-Irons 158).

70 Zieger 740. Neurasthenia was a term used during the 19th century to describe a mechanical weakness of the nerves allegedly caused by the strains and stresses of modern, urban life. It was still in use in the 1930s.

qualities of modern, western society and culture); an affirmation of *actual experience* over *aesthetic distance* (symbolically enacted through rites of initiation and debauchery); a particular focus on morally repugnant and aesthetically repellent phenomena and practices; and a pre-occupation with animal and human sacrifice as the privileged site of sacred excess, ritual transgression and ecstatic communication.

Although there is no direct evidence that Bataille had read *The Magic Island*, it is likely, given his friendship with Leiris at the time, that he did, and that his fantasies of initiation into a sacrificial sect may have been inspired by Seabrook's account. It is also a book from which Bataille *could* have learned about the Bois Caïman ceremony, something which would explain the coincidence of themes at the origin of this work in a direct way. The Bois Caïman ceremony is mentioned in a footnote to part one of *The Magic Island*, in a section concerned with the misrepresentation of Vodou as a snake-cult. Seabrook uses the story of Bois Caïman as an opportunity to discuss the alleged "hatred of whites" within the religion. Quoting directly from J. C. Dorsainvil's *Manuel d'Histoire d'Haiti* (a book that made the story part of the national curriculum for schoolchildren in Haiti in the 1920s), Seabrook, who takes an explicitly a-political view of the cult, frames the uprising more as an act of anti-White violence than an anti-slavery one. After citing Dorsainvil's description in full in the French, Seabrook goes on to mention the role of Vodou priests in the 1918-20 Cacos uprisings against the U.S. occupation, repeating the inference that Vodou is a military tool in only Haitian "race wars". In normal times, he reassures the reader, hatred of Whites "has no more place in Voodoo ceremonial than hatred and fulmination against the Germans has normally in the Christian temples of England or America".[71] From this perspective Vodou only acquires a racist aspect in times of struggles for national independence.

As Zieger has argued, the clearly counter-colonial, historical and explicitly political meanings of both the Bois Caïman ceremony and the *zombi* figure seem, at the time at least, to have eluded Seabrook, Leiris and Bataille, as did the legacy of the Black radical intellectual and militant traditions that followed directly from the Haitian Revolution.[72] What Bataille does seem to have taken from Seabrook are the erotic

---

71 Seabrook (1929) 311-313

72 Zieger 748

and racialised fantasies of ecstatic communion with an excessive Black alterity in which sacrifice, orgiastic excess and cruelty played a decisive role. Like Seabrook, Bataille was interested in making contact with the "great outside". But for him rites of sacrifice, transgression and erotic excess, were also a means of accessing the violent, disastrous and torrential forces of a Godless universe that could be put into the service of a bloody revolution. It seems unlikely then, given his philosophy at the time, that Bataille had noted the story of Bois Caïman tucked away in the appendices of *The Magic Island*, for surely, otherwise, it would have served as a significant historical precursor for the trajectory of *Acéphale* however a-political the latter was in its conception. But although Bataille does not make any explicit reference to either the *zombi* figure or the Bois Caïman ceremony in the texts of the 1930s, he does intimate familiarity with Seabrook's account of *le culte des morts* (to which a chapter is dedicated in *The Magic Island*). In 'The Use Value of D. A. F. De Sade', an open letter addressed to his Surrealist comrades in 1930, Bataille listed a range of things associated with the abject, excremental and agitational elements of the sacred: "the cult of cadavers (above all, insofar as it involves the stinking decomposition of bodies)... ritual cannibalism; the sacrifice of animal-gods; omophagia" and, in an image that could have been lifted from the pages of *The Magic Island,* "a half-decomposed cadaver fleeing through the night in a luminous shroud".[73] As with Seabrook, who took the very things that made Haiti (according to her detractors) a land of irredeemable barbarism as the "holy grail" of his quest, the agitational elements of the sacred identified by Bataille tally closely with those used to condemn Haiti as a land of atavistic savagery desperately in need of disciplinary governance. As such Bataille's fantasies of revolutionary base materialism, when considered in the context of occupied Haiti, flip over into a pretext for imperial domination. Similarly Seabrook's book appears from this perspective like a sensationalist, literary exploitation of a maligned "religion of resistance" on the colonial peripheries, that would serve as a moral justification for the violence being used against it and against poor Haitians in general.

Fantasies of sacrificial ecstasy were fundamental to Bataille's revolutionary philosophy of the sacred during the 1920s and '30s, but as his later pre-occupation with *images* of excess attests, his interest

---

73 Bataille (1985) 94

gradually became more aesthetic, psychological and philosophical than revolutionary in any strategic or political sense. In an *Autobiographical Note* written in 1958 Bataille explained that *Acéphale* was founded by former members of the militantly communist group *Counterattack* immediately after the latter dissolved, partly in response to supposed fascist tendencies within the group (himself included). The fascination with "exterior" forms of violence that bourgeois society provokes could, he believed, "lead to the worst". *Acéphale* was a "secret society" that therefore turned its back on politics, its aims being "solely religious" and its members dedicated to "a journey out of this world". The outward face of this journey was the *College of Sociology* (an informal meeting of scholars in the back room of a Paris bookstore between 1937 and 1939) and the journal *Acéphale,* dedicated to religious interpretation of the philosophy of Nietzsche. By September 1939, due to the "unendurable" nature of its mission, all members withdrew.[74]

Metaphors of darkness abound in Bataille's writing, where they are associated with the sinister, left-handed dimension of the sacred (the impure, ignoble, abject, excremental and evil) leading to a seemingly paradoxical relation to the anti-colonial politics of race he seems to have supported in the 1920s and '30s. In 'The Use Value of D. A. F. De Sade' Bataille proposed a post-revolutionary social programmeme in which the future world of human affairs would be divided into two spheres: the political-economic and the anti-religious/anti-social. It was in the service of the latter, generally Sadeian sphere, that Bataille envisioned Black communities having a central role:

> Black communities, once liberated from all superstition as from all oppression, represent in relation to heterology not only the possibility but the necessity of an adequate organisation. All organisations that have ecstasy and frenzy as their goal (the spectacular death of animals, partial tortures, orgiastic dances, etc.) will have no reason to disappear when a heterological conception of human life is substituted for the primitive conception; they can only transform themselves while they spread, under

---

74 Bataille (1986) 107-110

the violent impetus of a moral doctrine of white origin, taught to blacks by all those whites who have become aware of the abominable inhibitions paralyzing their race's communities. It is only starting from this collusion of European scientific theory with black practice that institutions can develop which will serve as the final outlets (with no other limitations than those of human strength) for the urges that today require worldwide society's fiery and bloody Revolution.[75]

Bataille envisioned a new society beyond "the stupid prejudice of race" whose coming into existence would embrace the untethered, frenzied energies of Black communities. But to suggest that these communities participate "to some extent" in revolutionary emancipation is to ignore the very "fiery and bloody" revolution that brought Haiti into existence, to say nothing of Black revolutionary and anti-slavery struggles since that time. In his enthusiasm for the role of Black communities in the coming revolution, Bataille seems to suggest a de-mythologised extraction of only the most overtly excessive and transgressive aspects of White fantasies of primitive "Blackness", exemplified in Seabrook's writing, and subordinated to the requirements of a base-materialist (or *heterological*) vision of a sacred revolution in which a presumably White cabal of neo-gnostic "spiritual directors" would collude with the "black practices" of Negros in the creation of the new society. Similarly, the defence of the pure Negro soul against the injunctions of White, western morality and technological modernity seems to have outweighed any apparent concern Seabrook had for Haiti's contemporary social and political problems or how they could be solved.[76] To the extent that Bataille envisaged a revolutionary, scientifically-orientated, White counter-intelligentsia guiding primitive and superstitious Black communities on the path towards a form of global socialism, his vision could be seen to conform to the hegemonic and stereotypical European view of international race relations at the time. In René Depestre's words:

---

75 Bataille (1985) 101-102

76 Dash (1997) 31

The creative expressions of Africans and their descendants were isolated and became a heterogeneous heap of *africanisms*, morbidly encased in the immaculate organism of the Americas. Given this racist point of view, slave revolts, political and cultural marronage and the participation of Blacks in peasant struggles were rarely considered decisive contributions to the formation of societies and national cultures in Latin America.[77]

If Bataille can be retrospectively accused of racism, it would be in the most amoral sense, recognising racism, as he did, as a "social fact", but not one founded on "epidermal metaphysics" like that espoused by Seabrook.[78] To the extent that Blackness *was* associated with "otherness" in European societies of the 1920s and '30s, and into this otherness were projected a range of barely repressed unconscious wishes and fantasies amongst self-identifying "civilised" Whites, it had become an imaginary "site" for socially abjected impulses and "terrible phantasms". In an article on 'Racism' in *Critique,* produced on the occasion of the publication of Leiris' book *Race et Civilisation* in 1951, Bataille wrote:

> Racism is a specific aspect of a deep *heterophobia* [hatred of difference], *inherent in humanity* and whose general laws we cannot avoid [...] The worst case is that of the Blacks, whose glaring difference is ineradicable. One could describe the antagonism as inevitable, to the extent that a tangible difference has a property of stability: so it is futile to argue that difference is ill-founded according to science. It is not a question of science: in racist attitudes, theory had only a secondary influence. To see racism as an evil idea is to turn away from a problem

77 Depestre 252

78 The term "somatic metaphysics" is taken from René Depestre's 1984 essay '*Bonjour et adieu à la négritude*' ('Hello and Goodbye to Negritude') in which he uses it to describe a development of the concept *Negritude* into an uncritical racial essentialism that assumes "an exclusively Black worldview within American or African societies". The essay was written explicitly as an attack on the direction *Noirisme* had taken under Duvalierism.

> whose essentials are never located in *ideas*: nor are they
> in *nature*. They are contingent and aleatory, they are
> *historic*, which is to say *human*.[79]

Bataille's indifference to the actual history, cosmology and ritual protocols of Vodou is unsurprising given the generally *atheological* and *base materialist* nature of his philosophy. Seabrook, on the other hand, accepts the gods of Vodou to the extent that they offer something more real, alive and purer than those offered by *modern* religions. But what differentiates both Bataille and Seabrook's idealisation of "black practices" from those who undertake them devoutly, is that the latter do it not for the purposes of ecstasy, frenzy and self-annihilation, but as a complex act of religious faith binding them to their gods, ancestors and communities, and as such, to their *histories*. They are aspects of a holistic religious system in which the intervention of the gods is absolutely essential, where prophesy and healing are more important to the participants than an encounter with "that which is absolutely other". Certainly it seems that the bonds of personal subject-hood are violently torn asunder during possession, but such experiences only occur when an individual has been bound to a particular *lwa* in a lifelong, mystical marriage. From this perspective Bataille writes in the spirit of those 19th century romantic abolitionists and 20th century communists who would re-write the history of the Haitian Revolution in mystical, African and occult terms, while preserving their Enlightened faith in science, natural law and dialectical materialism, however nihilistic his inversion of those ideals was at the time. He does so however, like Seabrook, in the aftermath of a world war that had seen the greatest loss of human life in modern European history, the collapse of the global economic system, the emergence of a new anti-capitalist, anti-imperialist and International Worker's Movement and the prospect of even greater human atrocities yet to come. The creation of the *Acéphale* in 1936 was in many ways a final, desperate attempt to create a new myth for a brutally dehumanised modern society in which the forces of imperative sovereignty were forming themselves into totalitarian, fascist and national socialist forms of collective organisation that were marching their militarised masses towards a new and even bloodier global cataclysm. As Michel Surya has shown, Bataille believed in

---

79 Bataille and Leiris, 71-72

neither history nor progress. The revolution he expected or "attempted to make inevitable", in the words of Simone Weil, would resemble "a catastrophe more than a peace, an irrationality rather than a rationality, a liberation of the instincts rather than their equitable ordering".[80]

Towards the end of his life Bataille would comment on four photographs, taken by the French photographer, ethnographer and *Babalawo* (Priest of Candomblé, the Yoruban-Brazilian religion) Pierre Verger, of a reputed Vodou ceremony.[81] In one often-reproduced image, the initiate seems to be drinking blood from the severed neck of a ram. A short text – entitled simply 'Voodoo Sacrifice' – accompanies photographs of a shaven-headed initiate, dressed in a white smock, their head, shoulders and arms smeared with blood and white feathers. In the article Bataille claims that the sacrificer experiences a kind of ecstasy, comparable to drunkenness, brought about by the killing of birds. To look on such images with passion, he proposed, was "to penetrate a world as far away as possible from our own... a world of blood sacrifice".[82] Bataille does not mention Haiti. Instead he identifies the ceremony as taking place in certain regions of America where the religion developed among Black slaves, originally from Africa.[83] The images, he proposes, are made all the more vivid because the photographer, in order to know the religion better, had himself become an initiate. The intimate, immediate and personal experience of sacrifice seems to have been more important for Bataille

---

80 Surya 225

81 Although Bataille identifies the images as being of a Voodoo ceremony they are in fact images of a Candomblé ceremony taken by Verger in Salvador, Brazil sometime between 1946 and 1953. In her book *Spirit Possession in French, Haitian and Vodou Thought* (2015) Alessandra Benedicty-Kokken dedicates a chapter to Bataille's misappropriation and misidentification of the actual nature of the ceremony depicted and his use of found images of possession. Benedicty-Kokken focuses specifically on the image of the sacrifice of the ram, identified in Bataille's earlier book *Erotism: Death and Sensuality*, as "Sacrifice of a Ram. Voodoo Cult". It is unclear whether the other images are from the same ceremony however. Verger, she notes, was a friend of Alfred Métraux who had visited him in Haiti while he was conducting his fieldwork there (Benedicty-Kokken 156).

82 Bataille (1989) 199

83 Bataille (1989) 201

than the places where such rites took place, their role in the protocol of Vodou rites, the religion's cosmology and metaphysics or its role in revolutionary struggles in Saint-Domingue and Haiti. As Benedicty-Kokken has pointed out, ultimately Bataille appropriates Verger's images to illustrate a thesis which ultimately identifies African-American religious practices involving sacrifice and possession-trance as essentially diabolical in nature.[84] Although Bataille's philosophy of the sacred was of a much more evolved and philosophical nature than Seabrook's, Zieger is right to point out the extent to which their world-views and libidinal orientations coincided in the 1930s. Haiti for Bataille, as it was for Seabrook, was one of those remote corners of the world that can only be penetrated by men of great "passion and imagination", men like Seabrook, who had temporarily lost himself in "the great shadow of the outside". More than a century separated the revolutionary apocalypse that Bataille envisioned erupting from the global turmoil that proceeded from the Great War and the secret sacrificial ceremony that inaugurated the Haitian Revolution, but the coincidence of Bataille's vision of a violent, contagious and unlimited expenditure of social wealth triggered by a ritual blood sacrifice with depictions of the Bois Caïman ceremony, by those who considered it a "monstrous anomaly" in the proper course of modern history, have a striking similarity that is at the very heart of *Undead Uprising*. And at the centre of the correspondences that tie these fantastical events together is Willy Seabrook, the man whose image of the Haitian walking dead would soon be re-born in celluloid as his young friend Michel Leiris wrestled his own inner demons in the middle of a "phantom" Africa.

POSTSCRIPT

In 1940 Seabrook had begun to drink heavily again after a period of relative abstinence. In the midst of his experimental research for *Witchcraft in the World Today* he received a gift from Hamilton Smith, a former colleague and editor at Harcourt Brace publishers: a Haitian

---

84 Benedicty-Kokken describes Bataille's "exoticist" appropriation of the image of the ram sacrifice as a "crime of montage" that evidences how Bataille was "completely insensitive to the concerns of anthropological integrity" (Benedicty-Kokken 157-159).

ounga charm. Despite having obviously been made for the tourist trade, the gift, made of red satin and tied with silk, seemed to have a very negative impact on Seabrook's already deteriorating mental health. Marjorie, his long-suffering second wife, hoping to relieve him of whatever emotional burdens she could, took it the rubbish heap behind the barn and burned it.[85]

85 Worthington 218

White Zombie, original promotional poster, 1932

II

SLEEP WALKING WITH ZOMBIS

MASTERS NATURAL AND SUPERNATURAL

> For this consciousness was not in peril and fear for this
> element or that, nor for this or that moment of time, it
> was afraid for its entire being; it felt the fear of death,
> the sovereign master. It has been in that experience
> melted to its inmost soul, has trembled throughout
> its every fiber, and all that was fixed and steadfast has
> quaked within it. This complete perturbation of its entire
> substance, this absolute dissolution of all its stability
> into fluent continuity, is, however, the simple, ultimate
> nature of self-consciousness, absolute negativity, pure
> self-referent existence.

> - G. W. F. Hegel 'Fear' *The Phenomenology of Spirit* (1807)

Shortly before saying goodbye to Maman Célie and his friends in the
mountains above Petit Goave, Seabrook encountered a being that
represented a supernatural counterpoint to the soul-less *zombi* that
would so disturb the author's sense of natural and supernatural orders.
Having just sat down to a dinner of chicken stew and plantains with his
gros negre friend Captain Despine, the pair were suddenly interrupted
by Rafael, the second son of his host family, telling them to get up
"immediately". Seabrook, in no mood to have his already late-arriving
dinner spoiled any further, stayed sitting, motioning Despine to do the

same. "But a mystery approaches" Rafael told him. From beyond the gate of the *peristyle* Seabrook noticed a barefoot man in ragged overalls and a torn straw hat approaching, a field labourer, "apparently of the poorest class", moving slowly "as if sleep-walking". Rafael, suddenly overtaken by rage, reached for Seabrook's throat with hands "like those of a galvanized, trembling automaton". "Up!" he tells them, "It is a god who comes...". The author, sensing the gravity of the situation, duly complied.

The sleep-walking peasant walked directly up to their table, inspected what was laid out upon it and, apparently uninterested, saluted the two men before shuffling back towards the gate where Maman Célie and the *houngan* Papa Théodore, who had arrived hurriedly in the meantime, adorned him with a bright coloured stole, surplice, ostrich feathers and necklaces like an "inanimate idol". Maman Célie quietly explained to Seabrook that this was a manifestation of one of the elder, and potentially terrible *lwa*, Ogoun Badagris.

Ogoun is the name of a Yoruban deity that is common to several New World, African-Atlantic religions including Candomblé, Macumba, Palo Mayombe, Santeria and Vodou. In West Africa he is associated with warfare, hunting and ironwork, particularly the fabrication of weapons. From the Nago family of *lwa*, Ogoun is syncretised in Haitian Vodou with the Catholic Saint Jacques Majeur, "Killer of the Moors", a tradition which began with the Portuguese Catholic influence on the Kongo aristocracy in the 15th century. In Haiti he is imagined as an equestrian warrior and a ferocious military general who controls lightning and storms and whose sacred colour is red.[1] According to Herskovits, who cites Faustin Wirkus as his source, the Cacos rebels wore this colour because of its association with this fierce, military *lwa*.[2]

---

1 Métraux 107

2 Herskovits 316-317. Deren notes that Ogoun is often an explicitly political figure and that in the region of Port-au-Prince *houngan*s who claim his patronage often belong to Masonic Orders (Deren 131 and 134). Several authors have noted that Ogoun has been fused with the spirit of Jean-Jacques Dessalines. One of the principle sources of this claim is Lorimer Denis who described seeing a *houngan* possessed by the spirit of the "terrible emperor" in 1944 (Métraux 49). Largey, in a chapter dedicated to "recombinant" myths of Ogoun in Haiti, notes how president

Soon the *hounfo* was so crowded with local people who had come to witness the presence of the god, that those closest to him, nearest the altar – upon which Maman Célie had discreetly replaced a Damballa snake staff with a thunderstone, the symbol of Ogoun – had to kneel down so that those behind could see him. When he looked upon the god-incarnate Seabrook could see only a "dazed peasant masquerading in fantastic garments". But when he looked upon the man's hands his rational faculties left him, and it seemed that he was in the presence of something "mysteriously superhuman". When at last he began to move it was as if "some monstrous, black, bedizened idol had come alive".[3] Seabrook was a little afraid of it, as they all were, and he found himself, without at first realising, chanting two endlessly repeated, monotonous minor chords along with the congregation. Something, he wrote, had got inside him:

> And because I was in that semi-hallucinatory state, I saw presently – as truly, I think, as any mortal eyes have ever

---

Florvil Hyppolite (1889-1896) is associated with the *lwa* Ogoun-Desalin in Haitian popular song (Largey 61-96). Rigaud has claimed that Toussaint Louverture worshiped Ogoun as a protector spirit (Laguerre 65). Alongside the Guede family of *lwa*, Ogoun is the only other deity to pass between the Petro and Rada rites (McArthy Brown in Barnes). Ogoun is associated by Kenaz Filan, author of *The Haitian Vodou Handbook*, with the 5th Gevurah sephirah of the kabbalistic tree of life, Officer of judgment, fire and awe whose colour is red (Filan 135).

3 The image of a person possessed by Ogoun appearing like a wooden statue is echoed in Graham Greene's *The Comedians* of 1966 where Joseph, bartender at the Hotel Trianon, is possessed by the same spirit:

> Then the *houngan* went to Joseph. He carried a red scarf, and he flung it across Joseph's shoulders. Ogoun Ferraille had been recognised. Someone came forward with a machete and clamped it in Joseph's wooden hand as though he were a statue awaiting completion. The statue began to move. It slowly raised an arm, then swung the machete in a wide arc so that everyone ducked for fear it would fly across the *tonnelle* (Greene 181).

seen it, for truth of this sort is purely subjective in the last analysis – a god descended to earth and made incarnate, accepting and devouring (for devouring is the only word when gods or beasts slake their hunger) the meats arrayed before him upon his own sacrificial altar [...] He seemed utterly self-contained, utterly unconscious of the presence of any of us. He was a god, and we were less than nothing in his presence.[4]

After speaking to the congregation in a "strange tongue of Creole and African words", making predictions and commands about the approaching spring storms and the measures to be taken against them, the god-incarnate lay down to sleep in the *hounfo*.[5] The following morning the deity had departed and only a "humble ragged Negro" lay there dozing at the foot of the altar.

Although the *zombi* and the possessed person will become peculiarly interwoven figures when the former migrates into cinema, they were for Seabrook very different kinds of being. The *zombi* represented an individual devoid of all will and subjective agency, reduced to the mere husk of a person, forced to labour *mindlessly* like a brute or *automaton*. The person possessed by a god, on the other hand, despite sharing some of the uncanny, automatic behaviour and hollowed-out subjectivity of a *zombi*, was something *superhuman*, ecstatic and miraculous. Although it seems Seabrook never experienced it personally, possession by the *lwa* represented for him the "ultimate... self-destroying illumination" which, during some ceremonies, signalled to all who were "propitiously disposed" that they could abandon themselves to "savage, joyous exhalation". Such idealisation of the "divinely unconscious automaton" before which we are "less than nothing" is further evidence of the paradoxical relationship between the *living-death* of modern, mechanical, industrialised labour and the *revitalising* "Dark Demon" of Negro mystery cults.[6] On the

---

4 Seabrook (1929) 75

5 This "strange tongue" was probably the mix of African and Kreyòl spoken in Vodou ceremonies known in Haiti as *langage* (see Dunham and Hurston).

6 The notion of a 'Dark Demon' is taken from Wyndham Lewis who, in *Paleface: The Philosophy of the Melting Pot* (1929), used it to describe the

one hand there is an abject horror of work-bound, animalistic and cadaverous mindlessness (a fate worse than death) and, on the other, a mystical idealisation of divinity-incarnate that ultimately gives way to ego-obliterating ecstasy and collective, orgiastic excess. In both cases notions of mindlessness, automatism and ego-loss play a fundamental role but their manifestations are evaluated in very different ways.

A complex semantic network of broadly philosophical terms – *master, subject, slave, thing, mind, consciousness, possession, self, ego, property, divinity, sovereignty, law* and *right* – are woven into the theoretical core of the Zombie Complex. Historical debates about Vodou, Enlightenment philosophy, revolutionary and historical consciousness, the political philosophy of the master-slave relations within the plantation and occupation economies and the relationship between divinity and individual subjectivity within the ceremonial protocols of Vodou and Christianity, all veer between the *abject* and *idealised* poles of this ego-less automatism. In so doing they follow a line of philosophical and psychological inquiry, inherited largely from Hegel and developed via Kojève, Nietzsche, Freud and Marx by Bataille and his Surrealist comrades in the 1920s and '30s, that passes directly – "like a diamond bullet" – through the forehead of that half-real being that lives on the ragged edge of things beyond either Superstition or Reason, as Seabrook put it, in the obscurest regions of *darkest* Haiti. The opposition between a super and subhuman *loss of self* echoes, in Seabrook's race-mystical terms, the dialectic of the master and slave staged in the famous section of Hegel's *The Phenomenology of Spirit* (1807). The Hegelian formulation, despite being concerned explicitly with the role of *labour, thing-hood* and *recognition* in the "trial-by-death" through which the bondsman (or slave) achieves "self-consciousness", makes no reference to the political and economic realities of New World slavery at the time of its writing, the facts of the Haitian Revolution, the conditions of plantation labour nor the institutions of trade and colonial legislation that justified and kept the mechanisms of production functioning. Hegel was however well aware of actually existing slavery in Europe's New World colonies and about the slave revolution that had taken place a few years earlier in Saint-

---

demon that had possessed Nietzsche, Lord Byron and D. H. Lawrence (Lewis (1972) 146-147).

Domingue.[7] Hegel's formulation of the master-slave dialectic grew out of his reading of Adam Smith's *The Wealth of Nations* (1776) and his understanding of the world-historical effects of the division of labour. For Hegel this division introduced a new "system of needs" (*System der Sittlichkeit*) in which the interdependence of need and labour create a "monstrous system of mutual dependency... that moves about blindly, like the elements, and like a wild beast, requires steady and harsh taming and control".[8] This vision of the integrated world economy as a vast, brute being determining *from without* the movements of remote but interwoven human aggregates is an early example of a philosopher conferring unconscious agency and imaginary sentience to an economy in much less beneficent terms than Smith's "invisible hand". The general metaphor would be taken up by Marx forty years later to account for the "alienation" effects of capitalism, this "greater thing" made up of many inter-dependent hands (i.e. an extra-human mode of production and distribution in which the autonomy of the individual worker is subsumed within a greater, systematic totality, whose impulses and reflexes – "market forces" – they are subject to). Marx's famous use of the allegory of the "dancing table" to illustrate the processes of commodity fetishism (through which labour is *abstracted* from the worker and consequently *objectified* by the general system of commodity exchange) emerges precisely within this nexus of extrinsic economic mechanisms generating *thing-like* human workers.[9] Marx would use this same formula of transposed agency

---

7 Buck-Morss proposes that Hegel's silence about Haiti had less to do with a refusal to recognise the significance of the Haitian Revolution but was more a defensive tactical move on the part of the young philosopher, living in precarious personal circumstances, who was considering his best interests in the political climate of Jena in 1806 (which was being besieged by Napoleon's forces). Toussaint Louverture, leader of the revolution in Saint-Domingue, had died in a French prison three years earlier. Any mention of the successful revolution would have been considered seditious by the invading forces who, Buck-Morss notes, ransacked Hegel's house at the time (Buck-Morss 18-20).

8 Hegel quoted in Buck-Morss 5

9 See 'The Fetishism of the Commodity and its Secret' (Marx (1976)). Engels would write openly against the "scientific" claims of Spiritualism in his *Dialectics of Nature* (1885) and E. B. Tylor, the person who popularised

from worker to object in his analysis of machines within the capitalist mode of production, conferring a kind of monstrous alien autonomy to capital itself.[10]

By using the term fetishism to describe the mysterious labour-objectifying effects of the capitalist mode of production in the "commodity form", Marx brings together two generic anthropological concepts that had historically been used to identify primitive and broadly African modes of thought during the slavery era: *fetishism* (loosely, the fallacy of misplaced concreteness) and *animism* (the fallacy of misplaced agency) which had been revived in middle of the 19th century by the Spiritualist movement whose somnambulist tables and "rappings" Marx seemed to be making reference to. As Stephan Palmié and Fred Moten have pointed out, a slave was actually a "commodity that speaks" rather than a phantasmal and imaginary one, and the *zombi* is evidently, in part, a reminder of this historical fact.[11] Neglecting the explicitly racial dimension of the new world slavery and the master-slave relations there, Hegel therefore universalised a relationship that other notable Enlightenment philosophers, like Immanuel Kant, were attempting to justify in terms of natural history and heredity.[12]

It would have been clear to Hegel that actual slaves were not simply beings of intermediate self-consciousness but explicitly *things* that were owned, used, bought, sold and done away with according to their master's desire, an idea that Bataille would return to repeatedly as the basis for the theory that *sacrifice* removed objects from the world of things (i.e. world of servitude) and returned them to the realm of sacred *immanence* from which they had been withdrawn. The master, for Hegel, was a *sovereign self-consciousness* that achieved its supreme agency

---

the term animism in his book *Primitive Culture* (1871), initially intended to use the term spiritualism in reference to the then popular new religious movement (Bird-David 69).

10 "The science which compels the inanimate limbs of the machinery, by their construction, to act purposefully, as an automaton, does not exist in the worker's consciousness, but rather acts upon him through the machine as an alien power". From Karl Marx 'Fragment on Machines' (1858) quoted in Mackay and Avanessian.

11 See Moten (2003) 'Resistance of the Object: Aunt Hester's Scream'.

12 See Bernasconi 'Who Invented the Concept of Race?: Kant's Role in the Enlightenment Construction of Race' in Bernasconi (2001).

through the control, use, exchange and negation of *things* (including "things" like *slaves*). The universe of autonomous self-consciousness was fundamentally foreclosed to the slave in this relationship. It could only be achieved either by the *negation* (destruction) of the superior being or through the recognition of self via the objects created through its labour. To quote briefly from what is a notoriously obtuse philosophical formulation, *self-consciousness* is defined by Hegel as "simple being-for-self, self-equal through exclusion from itself of everything else", its *essence* and *absolute object* being 'I' (or *Ego*). This pure abstraction of self-consciousness in *ego* reveals itself as a "pure negation of its *objective* mode". By showing that it is not a "thing" attached to any specific existence or to "life", the *ego* reveals itself as *subject-to-itself* alone (i.e. it is independent or *autonomous*).[13] Self-consciousness however only *is* by being acknowledged (or recognised) by an Other. But the recognition of a self-consciousness outside of itself means the *ego* must cancel that Other being in order to affirm its *Self*. As each independent self-consciousness seeks the death of the Other, it must risk the negation of its own ego in the process. From hence ensues the life and death struggle for the *absolute independence* of *self-consciousness* which Hegel associates with true freedom. "It is only by staking one's life that freedom is won" Hegel claims, in a proposition that chimes with the motto that heads the Haitian Declaration of Independence: *Liberté ou La Mort*.

From the Hegelian perspective the master treats the slave as his property, an *object* or a *human-thing*, lacking in subjectivity or self-hood, which he can do with as he pleases. In this sense *possession*, as a synonym for private property, refers to a *thing* that is owned (and the state of having ownership of that thing), whether that be a physical object, material good or human being, over which an individual right to use and/or destroy is exercised. Possession in a religious or mystical sense refers to the condition of having one's body, personality and will temporarily taken over and controlled by an external, supernatural entity. Thus, in simple terms, possession refers to two sides of the owned-owner relationship: the possessor and the possessed, the willing and the willed. In both cases of possession

---

13 Bataille will make much of this life-negating power of sovereign self-consciousness and the risking of life to the point of death. See Bataille (1993) 'Sovereignty'.

a thing or person is subject to the volition of an external, *superior* and *controlling* agent, the self-conscious, self-possessed and sovereign subject of Enlightenment Reason or Divine Power (which, as we know, often amount to the same).[14] In the case of *private property*, as formulated within modern political-economy, the agent of ownership is understood to be a rational, self-interested individual who is *master* of its *possessions*. There is, ostensibly, nothing mystical or metaphysical about this relationship, except to the extent that it is posited as a Legal or Natural Right. A brief survey of the development of a philosophy of property and rights in modern political economy, from Thomas Aquinas to John Locke, reveals an explicitly Christian and patrilineal genealogy of the idea, still evident in Adam Smith's notion of a benevolent "invisible hand". *The Wealth of Nations*, from which Hegel envisaged the outline of "vast animal being", represented a radical challenge to previous formulations by introducing a "sacred and inviolable" labour-based theory of property rights. The foundations of the authority by which an individual claims rightful ownership of a thing is based on a Judaic conception of the Law of God that had been economically and politically naturalised during the colonial era according to a great chain of being, in which Black slaves were likened to beasts of burden (or *chattel*), controlled as personal property by White master-owners who ultimately derived their authority and rights from God. The sundering of the legal, moral and metaphysical bases of such rights seems to have been one of the most significant changes brought about by the newly individualistic economic materialism of the Radical Enlightenment, something which Hegel seems to have ominously foreseen in the writings of Smith.[15]

In *ritual possession* a human being is transformed into a

---

14 For Depestre the basis of Eurocentrism lies in the postulation of an identity of Divine Right between the typical colonial concept of "White" and that of the "Universal Human Being" (Depestre 252).

15 Stephan Palmié takes issue with precisely this assumption, arguing that capitalism is founded on mystical principles that masquerade as objective, rational and materialist (much as Marx had proposed in his theory of commodity fetishism) (Palmié (2002)). See David S. Oderberg's 'The Metaphysical Foundations of Natural Law' for an overview of the relationship between cosmic order and natural law in H. Zaborowski ed *Natural Moral Law in Contemporary Society* (2010).

vehicle over which a *non-material* agency (i.e. a deity, divinity or demon) exercises temporary, volitional control. In Vodou this relationship is explicitly associated with a metaphysical and supernatural possession of the subject (*serviteur*) by a divinity (*lwa*). The African slaves formally treated as *capital* by their owners were spiritually "owned" by disincarnate entities that made them perform miraculous feats of endurance, self-negation and supernatural virtuosity far in excess of the utilitarian demands of their enlightened masters. In this sense the possessed slaves, locked within a brutal system of economic regulation overseen by their mortal, sovereign masters, found temporary mystical release from their physical enslavement in rites of ecstatic, trans-corporeal, de-subjectification. Several authors have noted that the Kreyòl term *lwa* seems to carry the French word for law (*loi*) within it. Kate Ramsey, for instance, while acknowledging contemporary scholarly consensus that the word is derived from the Yoruba word for Spirit or God, argues that the homology between *lwa* and *law* is more than mere linguistic coincidence and may well have been informed by "colonial ordinances, canonical statutes, and post-colonial Haitian juridical and customary laws that constrained, and thereby shaped, their practice over the course of four centuries".[16] In Vodou the possessed person is said to be ridden by the *lwa*. In this sense the relationship between *lwa* and *serviteur* is less one of ownership in strict, juridical terms. The *serviteur* owes service to, and must feed the *lwa,* in order to ensure their favour and protection, but they are not formally the *property* of the *lwa*. In Vodou a *serviteur* is said to be *married* to a particular *lwa* and their responsibilities mirror on a mystical level those expected on the profane.[17] Despite the fact that generally speaking the *lwa* do not "own" their *serviteurs,* they make very real and, at times, punishing demands upon them, their ire notoriously harsh. Erika Bourguignon, Elizabeth McAlistar, Stephan Palmié, Karen Richman have pointed out that the folklore of Vodou, and other Afro-Caribbean religions, often include stories of pacts (or contracts) made with marginal entities in which the *serviteur* of a malign spirit is ultimately *consumed* by it.[18] And as these

---

16 Ramsey (2011) 19-20

17 See Dunham.

18 See Erika Bourguignon 'The Persistence of Folk Belief: Some Notes on

authors have also noted, stories about *zombis* and cannibals on the peripheries of the Eurocentric global economy often equate the loss of control over one's life with the idea of having one's soul eaten by a demon. In this case the monstrous entity that sucks the life force from the living is imagined as the world economy itself.

The distinction, then, between a slave (human commodity) and the supernaturally possessed person has to do with the nature of the entity which exercises control over them (master, supernatural being, law, *lwa* or extra-human apparatus); the duration of this control (permanent, semi-permanent, temporary, periodic); the system of beliefs, values and cultural norms that account for and justify these relationships (slavery, capitalism, Vodou) and the institutions by which such relations are maintained and legitimated (the state, society, community, cult).[19] Being both possessed by its master, and mystically dispossessed of its soul, the Haitian *zombi* emerges at the intersection of these two versions of possession: rationalist political economy and mystical religious practice. The Haitian *zombi*, like the slave, is a being that never possesses itself, and as such never attains *subjectivity* in the Hegelian sense. And like the *possessed* slave, or Descartes' brute automaton, it is a *thing*

Cannibalism and Zombis in Haiti', *The Journal of American Folklore* Vol. 72, No. 283 (January - March, 1959) 36-46.

19 The two meanings of the word possession explicitly involve an issue of 'Will' in the dual sense of volition (Free Will) and the distribution of property after death (Last Will and Testament). In terms of the latter it was through the wills of their masters that slaves could be freed (a practice known as manumission). Wills in this latter sense evidence how the dead continue to exercise control over the living within the enlightenment continuum, much as the central role of heroic, ancestor figures and Saints within Judeo-Christian traditions reveal them to be forms of ancestor and spirit worship. As Jean-Jacques Dessalines put it in the *Declaration of Haitian Independence*:

> What are you waiting for before appeasing their spirits? Remember that you had wanted your remains to rest next to those of your fathers, after you defeated tyranny; will you descend into their tombs without having avenged them? No! Their bones would reject yours.

imagined to be driven *supernaturally* by an "outside on the inside" of which it has no conscious awareness and no recoverable memory.

REVOLUTIONARY SOMNAMBULISTS

> What is very true of Vaudoux and at the same time very remarkable is the spirit of magnetism which brings the members to dance right to the edge of consciousness.

- Moreau de Saint-Méry (1797)[20]

> For is that not what most people desire, to be dolls of that sort; to be looked after, disciplined into insensibility and blind dependence on a will superior to their own?

- Wyndham Lewis *The Art of Being Ruled* (1926)[21]

The transition from Haitian folkloric to classic cinematic zombie occurred during the 1930s when the national sovereignty of the Haitian republic was subject to a neo-imperialist occupation and the world was in the grip of the so-called Great Depression. It also coincided, in broad terms, with a modern, quasi-rationalist *episteme* that was founded upon the denigration and suppression of subaltern knowledge practices that were considered primitive, outmoded, barbaric and superstitious.[22] The folkloric Haitian *zombi* and the ritually possessed being evoked fantasies of African atavism

---

20 Saint-Méry 5. Kieren M. Murphy has argued that Moreau de Saint-Méry deliberately conflated "Vaudaux" and Mesmerism because he was deeply critical of and opposed to both practices. See Murphy 'Marooning Human Rights and Science in Colonial Haiti'. The word magnetism here was translated by Ivor D. Spencer as hypnotism in his 1985 abridged version of Saint-Méry's work.

21 Lewis (1989) 125

22 The term *episteme* is Michel Foucault's, who uses it to designate an historical knowledge paradigm upon which legitimate statements of truth are grounded. See *The Order of Things* (1966).

that had been central to the historical denial of Haiti's role in the development of global modernity at a time when the U.S. needed to win support for its imperial ambitions in the Caribbean. The right of the United States to take possession of a sovereign nation in the interests of regional stability was justified by claims that Haiti and its people must be protected from themselves, as we have seen. In this context stories about the mystical *possession* of people by ancestors, gods or demons served as an aberrant, irrational and pathological counter-narrative to the "enlightened" Christian paternalism of the White colonial authorities. The "black practices" of animal sacrifice, sorcery, cannibalism, ancestor worship, divination, zombification and possession trance, whether imagined or actual, served as a moral justification for an American civilising mission that seemed to symbolically mark the end of the Haitian revolutionary experiment. The association of Vodou with revolutionary insurrection only served to further denigrate the historical claims of the revolution and Haiti's right to self-determination in the eyes of foreigners, the revolutionary insurgents no longer seen as historical agents of Enlightened emancipation but as irrational and "possessed" savages blindly obedient to their *houngan* masters, just as the brute slaves had been to their European overlords and *zombis* continued to be to their *bokor* keepers. Mindless, ego-negating automatism, in both its idealised-ecstatic and abject-subhuman forms, served to perpetuate the myth of Haiti's need for a form of "benign" despotism that seemed to many Haitians to be taking the country back to the political conditions of its pre-revolutionary, slave-holding past.

Vaguely intuited anxieties about transforming conceptions of Natural Law and Property Rights, and the dangers of supernatural spirit possession within African slave communities, were present in Saint-Domingue before the revolution.[23] Spectacles of possession trance, the uncanny power of the *Papaloi* and *Mamaloi,* and "wild" dances like the *Vaudoux* and *Don Pedro* were regarded by colonial observers not only as throwbacks to the superstitious practices of African tribes but also as potentially subversive and oppositional practices that could "spin out of control". To be ridden by a god presented the colonial authorities with the disturbing image of people becoming vehicles for disincarnate, ancestral powers over which neither

---

23 See Saint-Méry.

the congregation nor the authorities could exercise legitimate, rational or earthly control. The colonial authorities seem to have understood that African, ancestral and potentially catastrophic "invisible powers" might be directing the slaves in their ritual dances and ceremonies. These disturbing propensities of the slaves were exacerbated by the arrival in the colony of "animal magnetism", a popular healing practice invented by the German physician Anton Mesmer, which had become something of a craze among the polite classes of French society in the late 18th century.

The popular meaning and etymological root of the word "somnambulism" is the Latin *somnus* ("sleep") and *ambulare* ("to walk"), a sleep disorder in which people perform activities as if they were awake but with no conscious awareness of doing so. The inventor of "artificial somnambulism", later to be called *hypnotism*, was one of Mesmer's most loyal followers, Armand-Marie-Jacques de Chastenet, Marquis de Puységur. Mesmer's discovery of a "universal fluid" permeating all living bodies occurred ten years earlier in 1774, when, having asked a female patient to swallow a preparation of iron filings, he attached magnets to her body, creating a feeling of "false tides". He named this phenomenon, which seemed to be present in the body of the "operator" to an exceptional degree, "animal magnetism".[24]

In 1775 Mesmer was invited by the Munich Academy of Science to pit his new therapeutic technique against a Catholic exorcist from Switzerland called Father Johann Joseph Gassner, a modest country priest who had acquired notoriety in Northern Europe for his successful treatment of patients with physical afflictions assumed to be the effects of demonological possession. Despite the theological and philosophical differences between the two healers, their therapeutic methods shared a common feature: the summoning in the patient, through the use of hands and gestures, of a crisis that necessarily preceded an "ecstatic" cure. But what for Gassner was evidence of demonic possession was, for Mesmer, an artificially induced sign of the disease that required treatment. An asthmatic would have an asthmatic crisis, an epileptic

---

24 See Walmsley Chapter 6 'Franzl and the Magnets'. Ellenberger likens Mesmer's concept of animal magnetism to the Polynesian notion of *mana*, "a universal, impersonal energy that can be stored in persons, objects, or places, and can be detected only through its objective effects" (Ellenberger 62).

an epileptic one, etc. With each repeated crisis, so Mesmer claimed, the patient's symptoms would gradually lessen. After performing a number of successful cures himself, Mesmer was able to pass judgment on Gassner: although he was an honest man, his cures were not in fact exorcisms but the effects of an exercise of animal magnetism whose blockages caused both physical and mental illnesses (though the latter category was yet to be invented as such).[25] Shortly after his success in Bavaria Mesmer moved to Paris, where he established a network of clinics called Societies of Harmony, at which he trained students in the technique. Despite animal magnetism's popularity amongst the Parisian elites, Mesmer's theories were viewed with suspicion by the nascent scientific establishment, and in 1784 a Royal Commission, consisting of some of the most important scientists of the day, was set up to investigate and assess the scientific merits of the practice and its claims.[26] The commission concluded that no evidence existed for the magnetic fluid and any therapeutic effects were solely attributable to the patient's imagination.[27] Despite the damning report, the many popular caricatures that followed in its wake and schisms within the movement, Mesmerism continued to flourish and Societies of Harmony began springing up in cities throughout France. One schism concerned the so-called Kornmann group, named after the Strasbourg financier who bankrolled it, which was led by one of Mesmer's ardent

---

25 See Ellenberger who identifies this event as pivotal for a newly materialistic conception of psycho-somatic illness and the beginnings of dynamic psychiatry.

26 The commission included several eminent figures in the history of the physical sciences including Benjamin Franklin, Antoine-Laurent Lavoisier and Joseph-Ignace Guillotin, after whose recommendation the guillotine was named.

27 In a secret report to the king, one member of the Royal Commission, A. L. Jussieu, suggested that "animal heat" was a more appropriate way to describe the mysterious power that the Mesmerist exercised over the patient (Ellenberger 65). Somewhat paradoxically, as Darnton discovered, Jussieu's attribution of magnetic effects to an "atmosphere" surrounding bodies was developed by one of Mesmer's most radical followers, Jean-Louis Carra, who integrated them into his own cosmology in which magnetic theory was applied to moral and political phenomena (Darnton 107-111).

followers Nicolas Bergasse, a lawyer from Lyons. It was the Kornmann group that set Mesmerism on the radical political path that would be epitomised by Jean-Louis Carra who promoted the idea of a worldwide "Mesmeric Revolution". An abolitionist current was also present in the group through the influence of Jacques Pierre Brissot, founder of the Society of the Friends of the Blacks.[28]

The cause of animal magnetism was taken up most successfully by the Marquis de Puységur, an Alsatian nobleman, one of three brothers, all of whom were disciples of Mesmer, who began treating peasants on their family estate in Buzancy, Northern France in 1785. Eventually, having so many patients to treat, the Marquis began magnetising an old elm tree in the centre of the local village where he could treat scores of peasants at a time.

The peasants would sit on the surrounding stone benches. Ropes were hung in the tree's main branches and around its trunk, and the patients wound ends of the rope around the ailing parts of their bodies. The operation started with the patients forming a chain, holding one another by the thumbs. They began to feel the fluid circulate among them to varying degrees. After a while, the master ordered the chain to be broken and the patients to rub their hands. He then chose a few of them and, touching them with his iron rod, put them into "perfect crisis."[29]

Later Puységur would establish the *Societé Harmonique des Amis Réunis* in Strasbourg, a quasi-Masonic organisation set up as a training centre for magnetisers, which, by 1789, on the eve of the French Revolution, had 200 members. The Strasbourg society had already begun exploring the "deep waters of spiritualism", as Darnton put it, two years before Mesmer's visit there in 1786. But it was the Lyons branch that explored the occult depths most fervently at the time, especially a group called *La Concorde* which recruited from the Swedenborgian, alchemist, cabalist and Rosicrucian members of the Masonic *Ordre des Chevaliers Bienfaisants de la Cité Sainte*, many of whom "staffed the lodge" of a secret society founded by the silk and silver manufacturing mystic Jean-Baptiste Willermoz.[30] It was

---

28 According to Walmsley, Kornmann received 24,000 livres in bills of exchange from Saint-Domingue at this time (Walmsley 152).

29 Ellenberger 71

30 Darnton 68. Willermoz was an initiate of the Order of Elus Cohens, an

Willermoz's close friend Louis-Claude de Saint-Martin who would act as a "metaphysical consultant" to the Marquis de Puységur, helping him interpret his discoveries and warning him against the dangerous influence of "astral intelligences" that his somnambulists were very probably communicating with.[31]

It was Puységur's brother Antoine-Hyacinthe, Comte de Chastenet de Puységur, a devoted follower of Mesmer himself, who, on a royal mission to map the coast of Hispaniola, first brought animal magnetism to Saint-Domingue. During the three-month journey from France to Saint-Domingue the Count set up magnetic *baquets*, tubs filled with water and iron filings from which metal rods and ropes protruded, to treat the passengers on board. Immediately on arrival in Cap-Français he installed a *baquet* in the local poorhouse and established the first *Société Magnétique* where he would evangelise Mesmer's methods and give speeches against the unnatural evil of slavery – "a state of war between master and slave" – and the perverted reason of men, who, misled by their instincts, have set up institutions based on "superstition, tyranny and errors, fertile mothers of all vices and all evil".[32] Spurred on by the Count during his stay in Saint-Domingue, animal magnetism spread through the colony overseen by a network of Mesmeric practitioners sanctioned by the doctor in Paris. A letter written by a witness of one of the Mesmeric sessions in Saint-Domingue elides with descriptions of Vaudoux ceremonies witnessed by Moreau de Saint-Méry, himself highly critical of the new trend:

---

esoteric Christian cult often referred to as Martinism that was founded in France in 1740 by Martinez de Pasqually. Martinez died in Saint-Domingue in 1774 where he had travelled to collect an inheritance. In his *Conversations: The Autobiography of Surrealism*, André Breton suggested that Mesmerism had been imported to Port-au-Prince by Martinez de Pasqually himself (Lepetit 322). Lepetit notes that in Breton's second lecture delivered in Port-au-Prince during his visit to Haiti between 1945 and 1946 he spoke at length about Mesmerism and parallels between the magnetic crises and the *crises de possession* in Vodou.

31 Darnton 69

32 Antoine-Hyacinthe, Comte de Chastenet de Puységur *Discours prononcé dans la société de l'Harmonie établie au Cap-Français* (Haïti), *pour des réceptions, en* 1784

A magnetizer has been in the colony for a while now, and, following Mesmer's enlightened ideas, he causes in us effects that one feels without understanding them. We faint, we suffocate, we enter into truly dangerous frenzies that cause onlookers to worry. At the second trial of the tub a young lady, after having torn off nearly all her clothes, amorously attacked a young man on the scene. The two were so deeply intertwined that we despaired from detaching them, and she could be torn from his arms only after another dose of magnetism. You'll admit that such are ominous effects to which women should sooner not expose themselves. [Magnetism] produces a conflagration that consumes us, an excess of life that leads us to delirium. We will soon see a maltreated lover using it to his advantage.[33]

In an image uncannily close to one invented by the Halperin brothers a century and a half later in *White Zombie* (and a stark example, should more be needed, of the ways in which slaves were treated as "living commodities" by their masters) one Artibonite plantation owner wrote a letter to his Swiss cousin which described how another plantation owner had made a large profit by magnetising a consignment of cast-off slaves bought at a low price. After restoring them to good health "by means of the tub," he was able to lease them "at prices paid for the best slaves".

The colonial authorities in Saint-Domingue generally turned a blindeye to the practice of animal magnetism, considering it a frivolous and risqué parlour game for the elite classes, rather than a significant threat to the social order. Their attitude changed however when the practice began to spread from the White land-owning circles and into those of the Mulattos, Free Blacks and slaves. Saint-Méry recounts a signal event that took place in the northern parish of Marmelade in 1786, four years before the Bois Caïman ceremony, that is the most

---

33 McClellan 177. McClellan quotes Saint-Méry on Mesmerism: "Magnetism had its disciples, its apostles, and consequently its miracles in the southern department. But it was also ridiculed, and it died. The miraculous was rejected by all faiths, except those that admit the Resurrection".

probable source for later claims that Mesmerism played a decisive role in events that ignited the insurrections of 1791.

Earlier in the year the colonial authorities began receiving reports from plantation owners of nocturnal gatherings at which slaves from many different plantations were congregating. Some plantations would become entirely deserted on these nights and one plantation owner reported seeing up to a hundred slaves at one gathering. Witnesses claimed that the slaves seemed to be involved in some form of magnetism and so the *Conseil Supérieur* of Cap-Français (of which Moreau de Saint-Méry was a member) issued a decree prohibiting the practice to all those of African descent, free or not, describing it as:

> an instrument that physics itself handles with precaution... which is easy to abuse and is apt for the tricks of jugglers who are common among the blacks and respected by them... taken over by them under the name of *Bila*... which might indicate just how far initiates or convulsionaries, the class of Macandals, might take their mad fanaticism.[34]

In June that year four slaves were brought to trial charged with being involved in the newly prohibited practice: a Mulatto called Jerome, his assistant Télémaque and two co-conspirators Jean and Julien. During their trial, whose court records Saint-Méry cites directly, eyewitnesses to these "mysterious ceremonies" claimed to have seen Jean on his knees, two crossed machetes on the ground in front of him, raising a fetish before a covered table upon which two candles were placed. The participants, holding the leaves of a raspberry bush, avocado and orange trees, and drinking spiced *tafia* (rum), would fall to the ground before being struck by Jean with a machete and miraculously "resurrected". The magnetists and their accomplices, it was claimed, also sold various sacred objects to the congregation including *maman-bila* (small limestone rocks), *poto* (red and black berries of the acacia tree) and *mayambos* (batons filled with *maman-bila*). According to Saint-Méry the magnetists also preached rebellion against their masters, claiming that the talismans they sold would protect them from harm. All four were found guilty, and though accounts vary as to their fate, it seems likely that Jerome and Télémaque were hung and

---

34 Gabriel Debien quoted in Weaver 105.

strangled in effigy, Jean was actually hung and strangled to death, and Julien was forced to assist in the execution of his co-conspirator and then returned to his master.

It is difficult now to know with any certainty if Jerome and his colleagues were actually practising Mesmerism, combining it with traditional African practices, or simply scapegoated in the interests of symbolically suppressing practices considered to be potential threats to the social order by the colonial authorities. It is also difficult to reconstruct the passage of magnetic practices and ideas from the colonial elites to the plantation slaves. The courts that prosecuted Jerome and his colleagues condescendingly described the ceremonies as "*prétendu*" (or "so-called") magnetism, suggesting that it was an attempt on the part of the slaves to emulate the European practice in their own misguided ways. Given the details of the testimony against them, it seems that Jerome and his colleagues probably were practising some nascent form of Vodou that tallied with descriptions made by Saint-Méry. Whatever the reality, parallels between what we now know about contemporary Vodou and the practice of 18th century Mesmerists suggest that they had elements in common that might have caused a local "confusion", if not in fact, then certainly in the minds of the colonial authorities. Both are based on the assumed existence of an *invisible power* that can be known only by its effects on sensitive individuals and groups; both involve the summoning of a physical and mental *crisis* that is shocking to observers and seems to be controlled by the will of the magnetist or *Papaloi*; such effects seem to be *contagious* and often have an apparently sexual nature; patients seem to fall into a *trance-like* state; at the onset of a crisis the patient is taken to a separate room where they are treated personally by the magnetist or *Papaloi*; *music* is used to stimulate the movement of the invisible forces (glass pianos the instrument of choice in the Parisian Societies of Harmony, drums and singing at the Vodou ceremony); a *metal rod* (or machete) is used to transmit the invisible force to various parts of the patient's body; and *ancient trees* were special receptacles of the invisible energy.

Good child of the Enlightenment that he was, Mesmer himself insisted that there was nothing supernatural or occult about any of the methods he developed or the forces that flowed through his patients. This was not the case for many of his followers however, whose involvement with Freemasonry and other esoteric movements seems to have opened them to the influence of planets, angels, "astral intelligences", disembodied spirits and other occult agencies. As the edifice of Enlightenment Reason and materialism gave way to the swelling torrents of Romanticism in the ensuing century, Mesmerism would become associated with a host of new superstitions from which, in the form of modern psychiatry, it would struggle for more than a century to "free itself".[35] Beyond the metaphysical and philosophical speculation that Mesmer and his followers were engaged with on the eve of the French and Haitian Revolutions, what remains in play here is the precise nature of the forces that took possession of both the Magnetist's patients and the subjects of the King and Queen of Vaudoux at one of their mysterious and shocking ceremonies. What kind of outside is it that can take away a person's self-possession and make them the plaything of forces against which they have no conscious or voluntary control? What kind of apparatus can make somnambulists, automata and "convulsionaries" of us all, regardless of race, gender or faith?

---

35 See Darnton Chapter 5 'From Mesmer to Hugo' and Ellenberger.

MASS MIND-SAVAGE CROWD

> Behind the avowed causes of our acts there undoubtedly
> lie secret causes that we do not avow, but behind these
> secret causes there are many others, more secret still
> which we ourselves ignore.
>
> - Gustave Le Bon *The Crowd: A Study of the Popular Mind*
> (1895).[36]

Despite the distinctly mystical direction that Mesmerism took after
the French and Haitian Revolutions, the materialist thread continued
in various forms, not least in the emergence of clinical psychiatry and
the theory of crowd behaviour which developed from conservative
reactions to the *contagious* "mass" insurrections witnessed during
the revolutionary period. Perhaps the most important writer in this
tradition is the French social psychologist Gustave Le Bon, who
played an important if indirect role in the development of the Haitian
Négritude movement in the 1920s.[37]

Le Bon's *The Crowd: A Study of the Popular Mind* was to have a major
influence on popular and academic theories of mass psychology at the
turn of the century.[38] Le Bon began his career in the relatively new
academic field of anthropology in the late 19th century at a time when the
discipline was significantly shaped by Darwinian evolutionary theory
and, as such, was primarily concerned with the physical differences
between human beings and other animals. Like other pioneers in the

---

36 Le Bon (2001) 5

37 Jean Price-Mars, the first Haitian author to write a modern account of
Haitian folklore, was inspired to do so after discovering, while studying
in Paris, the racist message contained in his *Les Lois psychologiques de
l'évolution des peuples* ('The Psychology of Peoples') (1898). Several years
later he would confront Le Bon privately about the issue. Le Bon, admitting
that his judgment may have been premature, urged Price-Mars to write a
book about Haiti (Magloire and Yelvington 5 and 132).

38 See Wilfred Trotter's *Instincts of the Herd in Peace and War* (1919),
Sigmund Freud's *Group Psychology and the Analysis of the Ego* (1922) and
Edward Bernays' *Propaganda* (1928).

field of physical anthropology he shared an interest in the hereditary and biological causes of criminality, deviance and madness. Paul Broca had developed a theory of cranial anthropometry according to which intelligence and personality could be measured from skull structures and in 1871 Le Bon invented a pocket cephalometer (the "Compass of Coordinates") that he used to measure the heads of local inhabitants of the Tatra mountains in Poland. Physical anthropology at that time was closely associated with the "scientific racism" of writers like Arthur de Gobineau, whose 1855 *An Essay on the Inequality of the Human Races* would also impact directly on Haitian ethnology, as we will see.[39] For Le Bon, racial inferiority and superiority were reducible to brain volumes, the latter having the more voluminous cranial cavities on average than the former. The larger the cavity the greater the capacity for intelligence, he proposed.[40]

According to Le Bon the great upheavals in civilisation were caused primarily by the modification of a people's *ideas*. The basis of all historical change therefore was a fundamental transformation of "the inherited groundwork" of a race's thought, the most important at the time being the destruction of religious, political and social beliefs ("in which all the elements of our civilisation are rooted"), and the creation of "entirely new conditions of existence" brought about by science and industry. Together these heralded a new era of crowds: "the last surviving sovereign force of modern times". Modern crowds were not so much the consequence of universal suffrage than the propagation of ideas – like "Liberty", "Equality", "Socialism", "Democracy", "Fatherland" or "Revolution" – which had slowly implanted themselves in people's minds. Drawing on the example of the recent physiological discoveries of Jean-Martin Charcot and Hippolyte Bernheim, Le Bon explained that:

> an individual may be brought into such a condition that, having entirely lost his conscious personality, he obeys all the suggestions of the operator who has deprived him

---

39 Anténor Firmin's 1885 *The Equality of the Human Races* was written as a response to Gobineau's book. In a chapter entitled 'Artificial Ranking of the Human Races', Firmin takes Gobineau to task on a number of key points, specifically the question of brain size and intelligence (Firmin 156-163).

40 See his *The Study of Races and Present-day Anthropology* (1881).

of it, and commits acts in utter contradiction with his character and habits. The most careful observations seem to prove that an individual immersed for some length of time in a crowd in action soon finds himself – either in consequence of the magnetic influence given out by the crowd, or from some other cause of which we are ignorant – in a special state, which much resembles the state of fascination in which the hypnotised individual finds himself in the hands of the hypnotiser. The activity of the brain being paralysed in the case of the hypnotised subject, the latter becomes the slave of all the unconscious activities of his spinal cord, which the hypnotiser directs at will. The conscious personality has entirely vanished; will and discernment are lost. All feelings and thoughts are bent in the direction determined by the hypnotiser.[41]

Of particular concern for Le Bon was the assumed *imitative* and *unreasoning* tendencies of individuals when they formed crowds. They did so, he claimed, not as people endowed with Reason and Free will (as Enlightenment idealists had hoped) but instead as herd animals, driven purely by desire, appetite and instinct. They were, according to Le Bon, akin to those species of being at the lower end of the evolutionary scale (i.e. women, savages and children).[42] For Le Bon the characteristics of an individual inherited from the "genius of the race" – the "innumerable common characteristics handed down from generation to generation" – were supplemented by a very different psychology once they assembled as a crowd. The individual alone was a *conscious* being, but as part of a crowd he or she became *unconscious*, their personality superseded by a crowd-mentality with an organised unity and definite direction of its own. This autonomous *mass-mind*, made of multiple, unconscious individual minds but lacking any

41 Le Bon (2001) 7

42 Le Bon (2001) 10. "It will be remarked" Le Bon writes "that among the special characteristics of crowds there are several – such as impulsiveness, irritability, incapacity to reason, the absence of judgement and of the critical spirit, the exaggeration of the sentiments, and others besides – which are almost always observed in beings belonging to inferior forms of evolution – in women, savages, and children, for instance".

specific purpose, could never accomplish tasks demanding a high degree of intelligence, any more than a "gathering of imbeciles" could. Crowd-mentalities were intent on returning civilisation to an archaic state of "primitive communism", a "barbarian" society in which the divine right of the masses would replace the divine right of kings.

For Le Bon the most powerful factor determining men's actions, whether as an individual or as part of a crowd, was race. A crowd made up entirely of Englishmen, for instance, would have a very different character than one made entirely of Spanish. In *The Psychology of Peoples* he distinguished between the "natural" races and the "historical" ones which superseded them. Races that have played a part in the history of civilisation are by definition "historical", and those that have not he called "natural". Natural Races were defined by anatomical details such as the colour of the skin and the shape and volume of the skull, the White, Yellow and Black races forming the most fundamental divisions within the species, each with its own "invariable" mental constitution based on some special, as yet unknown, structure of the brain. A race, he wrote, "is a permanent being that is independent of time". Somewhat confusingly Le Bon also associated these invariable characteristics with a race's "national character", including in the category of race Englishmen, Chinamen, Russians, Frenchmen and Spanish. Races can be divided further into the "primitive", "inferior", "average" and "superior". Within the first no trace of culture can be found and they border on a state of animality. The "inferior" races are best represented by "the negroes" who are only capable of attaining to "the rudiments of civilisation". "Average" races include Chinese, Japanese, Mongolian and Semitic peoples, while "superior" races include Indo-Europeans, Greeks and Romans. Only the latter have been capable of great inventions, sciences and industry, and they alone have shaped the highest levels of modern civilisation.

Like the person under the influence of a magnetist or *Papaloi*, the person under the influence of the crowd descends "several rungs on the ladder of civilisation", becomes an automaton, no longer guided by his will and, as such, may commit acts of "irresistible impetuosity" that his conscious personality would be morally repelled by. When men of a "higher race" form crowds they typically exhibit behaviours of a lower one. Given the theories of evolutionary racial difference expounded by Le Bon, and following a generally Cartesian model, the closer a race is assumed to be in evolutionary terms to the animal, the more it approximates the automaton or somnambulist. Thus, given the explicitly racist character of Le Bon's thought, we can also infer, following his reasoning, that the Black race is closer to the level of animal-automata than the White, and as such, its members are more prone to the unconscious and mysterious behaviour of the crowd.

> Visible social phenomena appear to be the result of an immense, unconscious working, that as a rule is beyond the reach of our analysis. Perceptible phenomena may be compared to the waves, which are the expression on the surface of the ocean of deep-lying disturbances of which we know nothing. So far as the majority of their acts are considered, crowds display a singularly inferior mentality; yet there are other acts in which they appear to be guided by *those mysterious forces which the ancients denominated destiny, nature, or providence, which we call the voices of the dead,* and whose power it is impossible to overlook, although we ignore their essence.[43]

Despite being ostensibly rational and materialist in orientation, the doctrine of racial and gender superiority which underpinned Le Bon's theory of crowd behaviour was clearly a product of his own culture, sex and nationality. That many of the claims of scientific racism have since been refuted should not distract us from the fact they were widely held amongst members of the scientific and intellectual elites of European society at the end of the 19th century, shaping the ideological contexts in which writers like Spenser St. John lived and worked. What is important for the development of the Zombie Complex is the idea that all individuals, regardless of race, allegedly become increasingly somnambulistic, "automatic" and "savage" when they are part of crowds or "masses". The more immersed in a crowd one becomes the more one's behaviour is governed by the inherited, biological automatisms of the species. For Le Bon, once the individual is subsumed within a collective social group it no longer has the autonomy of a rational, enlightened and sovereign subject such as that proposed by Kant or Hegel. Merely an atom within the aggregate, it is compelled to act

---

43 Le Bon (2001) v (emphasis added)

according to unfathomable forces rooted in the species' hereditary history, in *unison* with a mass-form of mental organisation. The correlation of a mass-form of automated crowd psychology with the new conditions of life brought about by the developments of industry and science, created the cultural conditions for the folkloric *zombi* to elide with those iconic machine-age *agents-without-autonomy*: the slave, somnambulist and robot. The elision of these four figures in early 20th century popular culture constitutes the docile and fully compliant pole of the nascent Zombie Complex.[44] But as we will see, when the fully compliant zombie figure transitions from the classic cinematic to the apocalyptic flesh-eating phase its metaphorical "mass" function changes too. No longer a being controlled from without by an external will, the zombie becomes a being driven entirely by its spinal cord, as Walter Lippmann might have put it.[45]

In his essay 'Mass Psychology and the Analysis of the Zombie: From Suggestion to Contagion' Phillip Mahoney argued that the transition from a creature produced by *suggestion* to one produced by *contagion* involves "a concomitant sublation of the figure of the tyrannical leader in favour of a horizontal, collective relation between equal members" which potentially transforms traditionally dystopian readings of the apocalyptic flesh-eating

---

44 The term "robot" was introduced to the public in 1920 through Karel Capek's play *R.U.R* (Rossum's Universal Robots). The word, derived from the Czech noun "Robota" meaning "labour" – specifically "un-free labour", "serf labour" or "*corvée*" – was in fact coined by his painter brother Joseph. The term "automaton", a synonym for "robot", has also been used in relation to somnambulists, particularly in juridical discourse. "Automatism" is a criminal defence term in English Law which denies that an accused was responsible for their actions when they committed the offense. Ironically the root Greek meaning of the term is "acting of one's own will".

45 Walter Lippmann was a journalist and political commentator who coined the term "stereotype" in its modern, psychological sense in his 1922 book *Public Opinion*. In the same work he proposed that the contemporary public acted like a "bewildered herd" driven primarily by desire, irrational impulses and animal instincts, a formula that would be fundamental to Edward Bernays' theory of public relations and the "engineering of consent" (1947).

zombie into utopian ones, an image of "the multitude" and "collective life" based not on the humanistic terms of sympathy and identification but an "inhuman... contagious formation". As it transitions from the docile to flesh-eating form the zombie figure will shake off any reference to Vodou sorcery, remote corporate control or the mysterious hypnotic power of the evil Mesmerist. But despite being thoroughly deracinated by then, it will distantly evoke memories of the slave insurrections that haunted the minds of the colonial elites in the lead-up to and aftermath of the Haitian Revolution, in which armies of revolutionary slaves laid bloody waste to the lives and livelihoods of hundreds of their former masters, seemingly without Reason or Self-consciousness (at least from the perspective of the supporters of the old order). In other words, the revolutionary slave-masses of Saint-Domingue and the post-'68 cinematic zombie hordes share characteristics of "savage" mass-beings, the product of hypnosis, suggestion or contagion, irresistibly impetuous, irrationally violent, "primitively communist" and guided by the mysterious voices of the dead inherited from their ancestral species-being. Unleashed from the cosmic order of Natural Right, and drawn "like simple organisms towards the sun", the new mass-being will return the earth to the chaotic, primordial darkness of *ignoble* human nature: the great night of "death screams and riots" in which the beautiful phrases of their masters will be drowned.[46]

---

46 From Bataille (1985) 'The Notion of Expenditure' (1933). The full quote reads as follows;

> In historical agitation, only the word Revolution dominates the customary confusion and carries with it the promise that answers the desire of the masses. As for the masters and the exploiters, whose function is to create the contemptuous forms that exclude human nature – causing this nature to exist at the limits of the earth, in other words in mud – a simple law of reciprocity requires that they be condemned to fear, to the *great night,* when their beautiful phrases will be drowned out by death screams in riots. That is the bloody hope, which, each day, is one with the existence of the people, and which sums up the insubordinate content of

THE BLACK BLOOD OF SOULLESS ROBOTS

> The Kingdom of the Dead is the only one safe from
> invasion. Those who enter are humble and obedient.
> There are no coups or Palace Revolutions in the Kingdom
> of the Dead.

> - Garnett Weston, screenwriter of *White Zombie* (1932)

> The realm of the dead is as extensive as the storage
> and transmission capabilities of a given culture...
> media are always flight apparatuses into the
> great beyond.

> - Friedrich Kittler *Gramophone, Film, Typewriter* (1999)

The first and by far the most influential of the early zombie films was
White Zombie, produced and directed by the film-making brothers
Edward and Victor Halperin in 1932. Clearly influenced by *The Magic
Island*, *White Zombie* not only borrowed some of its visual language
from Alexander King's illustrations but also referenced Article 246
of the Haitian penal code that legitimated claims about the existence
of zombification there. In the film the article is cited by the fatherly
missionary figure Doctor Bruner in order to convince Neil, the
rationally incredulous and grieving fiancé of the eponymous White
zombie, of the strange reality of the living dead. A translation of the
article was even used on publicity posters for *White Zombie*, with the
added comment "The practice of Zombiism is punishable by death in
Haiti! Yet Zombiism is being practiced in this country".[47] So although
The Magic Island did more than any other book to popularise Vodou
and zombies for American and international readers – the term first

---

the class struggle.

47 A less known precursor to *White Zombie* was a Broadway play
entitled *Zombie*. Influenced much more directly by Seabrook's
book, it ran for a brief season in February 1932, and seems to be
an indirect source of the Halperins' references to Seabrook's work
(Rhodes 85-87).

appears in Funk and Wagnall's dictionary of 1935, where Seabrook is cited as a primary source – it was the medium of cinema that brought them to a mass audience. By the time of its transition from Seabrook to cinema there had been few formal ethnographic accounts of Vodou or the cultural mythology of the *zombi*. The first ethnographic account seems to have been Elsie Clews Parsons' article 'Spirit Cult in Hayti' from 1928 in which she uses the term to describe a spirit or ghost, tracing the word's etymology to the French *les ombres* (shades). According to her informants a *ganga* (sorcerer) can turn a person into a stone or an animal, kill the animal and sell the *zombi* meat on the market, a story that accords with tales told by Spenser St. John about powerful sleeping potions used to procure "undead" human bodies for ritual consumption in Haiti, and Erika Bourguignon's research into the links between cannibalism and folkloric *zombi* mythology there.[48] For popular audiences in America however the figure of the *zombi* perpetuated a dominant colonial myth of Haiti as a land of atavistic savagery while posing a terrifying, metaphysical challenge to a "modern" western audience's assumptions about what has real, concrete existence and what is mere figment or phantasm.

White Zombie opens with a scene of villagers performing a burial in the middle of a country road to the sound of "tribal" drums and chants. The coach-driver explains to his two passengers – a soon-to-be married couple, visiting the West Indies for the first time – that the locals do this because they fear "the men who steal dead bodies". As the coach carries on its way, two disembodied eyes dissolve into the head of a cloaked figure standing beside the road. This, we discover later, is Murder Legendre, slave master, factory owner, sorcerer and hypnotist, who is accompanied by a gang of ramshackle, wide-eyed followers. "ZOMBIES!", the coach-driver shouts, before beating a hasty escape. These newly reincarnated celluloid cadavers, made to walk again and again through the "magical" medium of cinema, are people who, we learn, have been poisoned into a death-like state, taken from their graves and are now controlled using hypnosis and potions.

The figure of Murder Legendre was written with the archetypal, malign, Eastern hypnotist character Svengali in mind. Created by George Du Maurier in his 1894 novel *Trilby,* Svengali had come to represent an anti-semitic stereotype of an enchanting, exotic and

---

48 Parsons 178-179 and Bourguignon (1959)

manipulative sexual predator who promises to bring young and hopeful artists undreamed of success that he will ultimately profit from. Like the will-less somnambulist he controls and exploits, the evil hypnotist figure grew out of a century of debates within the human and social sciences about the nature of hypnosis and the closely associated theme of suggestion that began with the academic reception of "animal magnetism" in the late 18th century. The association of Mesmerism with sexually motivated charlatanry, which had been present since the Royal Commission's report of 1784, continued throughout the 19th century, during which time a veritable "theatre of hypnosis" developed in response to ongoing popular and academic debates about the reality, causes and therapeutic value of the technique. These culminated in a number of public displays of "criminal suggestibility" in (mostly) female somnambulists staged by eminent psychologists, theatrical dramatizations of the uncanny phenomena of hypnotic trance (often focusing on potential criminal relationships between hypnotist and somnambulist) and sensational stories about hypnotic crimes reported in the popular press.[49] Gilles de la Tourette, a high-profile advocate of hypnotism, student and personal secretary to the more famous Jean-Martin Charcot and a proponent of the theory that hysterics *cannot* be made to commit crimes under hypnosis, was himself the centre of a sensational hypnotic scandal in 1893 when one of his former patients – Rose Kamper – shot him in the head at his home. Despite claiming to having been "hypnotised at a distance" by Tourette (who, she believed, was in love with her), and having her will gradually "annihilated" over numerous hypnotic sessions, the court concluded that no hypnosis was involved in the crime, and that his assailant was in fact suffering from "delusional thoughts".[50] A direct reference to the earlier staging of criminal suggestibility occurs in *White Zombie* when Madeline is hypnotically compelled by Legendre to murder her fiancé Neil with a knife.

Such stories shaped the narratives of early silent films like D. W. Griffith's *The Criminal Hypnotist* (1909), Max Mack's *Der Andere* (1913), Robert Wiene's *The Cabinet of Dr. Caligari* (1920) and Fritz Lang's *Dr. Mabuse the Gambler* (1922). At the same time the cinematic

---

49 See Andriopoulos, Chapter 2, 'Staging the Hypnotic Crime' and Bogousslavsky *et al* (2009).

50 Bogousslavsky *et al* 193

apparatus was itself interpreted as a hypnotic technology by early commentators like Hippolyte Bernheim who, in 1886, proposed the existence of a "nervous light" that could explain post-hypnotic amnesia in terms of the disappearance of images no longer illuminated in the mind.[51] Thirty years later Hugo Münsterberg would write one of the earliest theories of film – *The Photoplay* – that compared the workings of the human psyche directly to that of "the cinematic apparatus".[52] Münsterberg was not alone in comparing the techniques of hypnotism to the technology of cinema. Several of the early hypnotic-themed films made explicit reference to the theoretical and clinical debates about the psychology of hypnosis and the assumed influence of hypnotic suggestion on vulnerable individuals. *Der Andere* for instance opens with a medical councillor reading from a book to a public prosecutor. We are shown a quote by the French historian, philosopher and sociologist Hippolyte Taine, which proposes that "accident, sickness or exhaustion" can produce a "double being" of which the individual has no conscious knowledge. Once such a double has been created "the sick soul in a sort of comatose state is able to commit actions which the healthy one is not aware of". The idea of an unconscious double committing terrible acts in the "guise of one's self" seems to have been a powerful fantasy in hypnosis-themed cinema and it was a pattern associated by Siegfried Kracauer with the rise of National Socialism in his influential history of German film *From Caligari to Hitler* (1947).

That it was during the 1930s, towards the end of the U.S. occupation and a time of major crisis within the global economy, that "*zombi*" entered official lexicons of the English language is important for the new meanings it would come to carry. As it transitioned into this new cultural context the associations with Haitian folklore would gradually recede into the background and the word "voodoo" would become a simple, xenophobic shorthand for assumptions about the differences between White, rational and scientific civilisation, and Black, irrational and superstitious savagery. At the same time the Anglicised zombie began to signify any kind of being whose memory, consciousness and

---

51 Andriopoulos 116

52 Münsterberg was also the author of a Taylorist tract *Psychology and Industrial Efficiency* (1913) which asked "how we can produce most completely the influences on human minds which are desired in the interest of business".

will had been artificially removed or displaced by an external agent. As such it became a figure for mass mindlessness and mass manipulation precisely at a time when cinema began to take on an increasingly instrumental role in popular politics and modern propaganda, whether in the shape of Fascism in Italy, National Socialism in Germany, Soviet Communism and other forms of collective social organisation perceived to be totalitarian from the perspective of a nascent Free World. It is not surprising then, that a number of "voodoo" and zombie films from this period made reference to armies of hypnotised zombie-slaves under the control of an evil and despotic hypnotist-sorcerer figure. *Revolt of the Zombies* (1936) for instance tells the story of an army of Cambodian zombie-soldiers telepathically controlled by a Priest-King who threatens to destroy the White race.[53] Made one year after Leni Riefenstahl's *The Triumph of the Will*, *Revolt of the Zombies* suggests some acquaintance with the mystical rebirth of Germany under the Führer. The film opens with an army General dismissing a tale being told to him by army interpreter Armand Louque:

> "No captain Louque, your splendid service as an interpreter has been appreciated, but when you try to tell me stories of Mesmerism, occultism, men-without-souls, hordes of supermen capable of annihilating armies of trained men, you make me wonder which one of us is sane."

When the *zombi* figure transitions into cinema then it takes on the characteristic of a number of other soul-less, will-less and ostensibly remotely controlled and human-like "things" (somnambulists, workers, robots and soldiers), *agents-without-autonomy* controlled by hypnotic or magical powers. In an interview for the *New York Times* in 1936 for example, Edward Halperin claimed that Henri Christophe (the ruler of the north of Haiti after the death of Dessalines in 1806) was "reputed to have built his noted Haitian fortress with *zombi* labour" (a

---

53 *Revolt of the Zombies* contains one of the first representations of the zombie's invulnerability to bullets. *King of the Zombies* (1941) contains numerous gags about zombie platoons and military camaraderie, suggesting it may well have been a product of the covert propaganda campaigns discussed in Chapter Four.

reference to the fortress Citadelle Laferrière built by the self-ordained emperor between 1805 and 1820 to protect against future attempts by French forces to re-take the country).[54] Acknowledging contemporary anxieties about emergent totalitarian politics in the early cold war era, one *New York Times* reviewer of the stage-play *Zombie* wrote:

> If zombies are those who work without knowing why and who see without understanding, one begins to look around amongst one's fellow countrymen with a new apprehension. Perhaps those native drums are sounding the national anthem.[55]

Despite being set in Haiti and made seventeen years into the U.S. occupation, *White Zombie* made no reference to the political relationship between the two nations. For this reason it is generally regarded by scholars of Haiti and Vodou as a film that explicitly harnesses fictional accounts of zombiedom for covert propagandistic purposes, denigrating Haitian culture as mired in primitive superstition while masking the realities of U.S. military intervention there.[56] As such *White Zombie* represents a fundamental transition in the nature and function of the *zombi* figure after it leaves Haiti. From thence it becomes a generic component of a popular cinematic genre terrifying the domestic audiences of an imperialist nation into *not* seeing the reality of the international power relations their government is involved in. This imaginary movement of the *zombi* figure between multiple realities will become a defining characteristic of the zombie myth as it evolves in western culture through the first half of the 20th century, advancing fundamental ontological questions

---

54 John T. McManus, 'Walking Dead in Angkor', *New York Times* May 24, 1936.

55 Quoted in Chera Kee '"They are not men... they are dead bodies!"': From Cannibal to Zombie and Back Again' in Christie and Lauro.

56 See for instance Jennifer Fay 'Dead Subjectivity: *White Zombie*, Black Baghdad' (2008), Frank Degoul's '"We are the mirror of your fears": Haitian Identity and Zombification' in Christie and Lauro and Lizabeth Paravisini-Gebert's 'Women Possessed: Eroticism and Exoticism in the Representation of Woman as Zombie' in Olmos and Paravisini-Gebert (2000).

about its existence into the spectacular field of mass culture and mass psychology, while simultaneously obscuring and distorting the regional, historical and cultural actualities from which the figure emerged. In this way the modern cinematic zombie is a spectral *fetish* in the classical psychoanalytic sense, *substituting* for an unacceptable truth a monstrous, imaginary form that is uncannily reassuring relative to the reality it *disavows*. The same pattern is present in other "voodoo" films of the period in which references to Haiti, when they are made at all, are of an entirely superficial kind, representing it simply as the "land of voodoo", an exotic, generic amalgam of stereotypical elements (tom-tom drums, the frenzied dancing of Black natives, voodoo dolls, wanga charms, human sacrifice, etc.), a land "lost in time" (but still only "six hundred miles from the Florida coast").[57] None of the films made in the 1930s and '40s make reference to the U.S. occupation of Haiti and their general tone echoes the White, paternalistic attitude toward Blacks that had been used to support arguments for colonial occupation since the 1860s.[58] Most are structured around a romance, usually between a White heroine threatened by some agent of Vodou sorcery and a White, American, hero figure who is largely sceptical about, and in-susceptible to, the primitive mumbo-jumbo. Occasionally, as in *Chloe: Love is Calling You* (1934) and *Ouanga* (1935), the love-plots were compounded by inter-racial issues that treated the presence of "Black blood" in a (seemingly) White woman as an irredeemably damning trait for her future marriage prospects, a theme found also in popular fictions set in Haiti at the time such as Beale Davis's *The Goat Without Horns* (1925). Even films made for all-Black cinemas, like *The Devil's Daughter* (1939), contained crude African American stereotypes like the ("voodoo") Mammy and wide-eyed, grinning Uncle Toms.

The bringing together of slave-master, sorcerer, hypnotist and capitalist in a figure like Murder Legendre suggests that the institution of plantation slavery might retrospectively be thought of as an effect of

---

57 There are occasional references to actual Vodou deities in some of the films from this period; *Chloe: Love is Calling You*, for example, includes a wedding-dressed, top-hatted and dress-coat-wearing female Guede figure leading the ritual sacrifice climax of the film, an image evidently modelled on photographs of Papa Nebo in *The Magic Island*. See Chapter 4 '*Live and Let Die*: Black Power and Voodoo Politics'.

58 Schmidt 232

magical and hypnotic techniques used by slave masters. Although this idea obscures the historical reality of plantation slavery as a complex system of organised economic, racial and legislative violence, the idea that a company of workers could be remotely controlled by an external, "corporate" agent was to become a characteristic feature of debates about hypnosis, crowd psychology and mass media in the early 20th century.[59] In *White Zombie*, as in all of the zombie films made before 1968, zombiedom is directly correlated with a state of somnambulism brought about by some form of hypnosis and/or poisoning, a defining feature of what I am calling here the "Classic Cinematic" phase of zombie films from 1932 to 1943. Like *zombi*-making and spirit possession in Seabrook's stories, hypnotic phenomena fundamentally challenged rationalist accounts of self-consciousness, the absolute sovereignty of the individual ego and its assumed agency. So as the Haitian *zombi* finds a new form of spectral after-life in the medium of modern cinema, it becomes an allegory for states of mass mindlessness and economic powerlessness induced by remote, hypnotising agents. In this sense the *zombi*, automaton, worker-drone and somnambulist figures all represent *agents-without-autonomy* condemned to geopolitical and historical oblivion by the combined forces of political-economy, hypnosis, narcotics and media sorcery.

In *White Zombie* Murder Legendre controls a select gang of servants, his former enemies, who now do his evil bidding, and a company of *zombi*-slaves who work in his sugar mill. When Legendre takes Mr. Beaumont (a land-owner posing as the visiting couple's generous benefactor, while secretly having amorous designs on the film's title character Madeline) to his factory, we see for the first time the *zombi*-slaves who work there. Silently and monotonously they toil at the rustic machines without speech or expression. When one of them topples into the blades of the grinding mechanism none of the others react: they are merely the soul-less, fleshy components of the automated production process. Although the shock of this scene has to do with an evocation of the brutal and dehumanising labour processes from a remote and distant past, fifteen years before *White Zombie* was playing to domestic audiences U.S. marines in Haiti had re-introduced forced labour there. An article of the Haitian Code Rural, which provided

---

59 See Andriopoulos, Chapter 2, 'Invisible Corporate Bodies'.

for the repair and upkeep of existing routes by a rotating system of local residents, was re-purposed during the occupation to justify the introduction of forced labour (the *Kové*, in Kreyòl parlance) between 1916 and 1918. As local Haitian gendarmes were expected to meet Government quotas of labourers they forcibly conscripted rural peasants from their homes at night or from their fields during the day.[60] *Kové* workers were roped together to travel between camps, worked under armed guard and would be shot if they attempted to escape. The cinematic fantasy of a supernaturally ordered manufacturing process, in which Black workers were governed by a White slave master and a cabinet of Mulatto henchmen was like a zombic-cinematic double of the actual situation in Haiti a decade earlier.[61] But if the mill scene in *White Zombie* explicitly references the horrors of actual colonial slavery in Saint-Domingue, however remotely for U.S. audiences, it would have had more immediately familiar and local connotations to the breadlines that had become emblematic of the great depression that followed the Wall Street Crash of 1929. As David Skal noted:

> the shuffling spectacle of the walking dead in films like *White Zombie*... was in many ways a nightmare vision of a breadline... Millions already knew that they were no longer completely in control of their lives; the economic strings were pulled by faceless, frightening forces'.[62]

---

60 (Ramsey (2011) 123 -127). Ramsey notes that Jean Price-Mars was himself arrested with a view to being conscripted into forced labour after making house-calls, as a local doctor, on the outskirts of Port-au-Prince.

61 Williams (1983) notes that the first group of zombies in *White Zombie* are White and Mulatto, while the latter group of factory labourers are Black, suggesting parallels with the racial and class divisions of power within occupied Haiti at the time.

62 Skal 169. The idea of having one's life controlled by "faceless, frightening forces" echoes the experiences of slaves within the plantation economy, and, as Zieger has argued, *White Zombie* did briefly, if imprecisely, connect labour practices in a fantasmatic Saint-Domingue to contemporary practices in the U.S., and therefore to a wider structure of alienation brought about by political and economic processes (Zieger 750).

Unemployed workers in the U.S. did not consider themselves slaves, which, in legal terms they were not (slavery had been abolished in the U.S. in 1865 following the 13th amendment of the constitution). They were precisely "free-labour" in a labour market governed by forces upon which their lives and welfare depended. And, like the forced labourers in occupied Haiti, they were not officially "owned". But this did not stop them feeling *possessed* in a new sense of the term, possessed by Hegel's "monstrous system of mutual dependency", the abstract mechanisms of an integrated global economy. Within this system the well-being and livelihood of masses of property-less workers was policed by a disciplinary mechanism that maintained the smooth functioning of an abstract, economic system geared towards the creation of profit for a wealthy and largely invisible social minority. From this perspective "the modern zombie" can be seen as a transitional figure by which the mysterious, occult practices of so-called primitive societies are made to coincide with the faceless, abstract forces of the modern capitalist economy. As such it becomes a metaphorical figure for beings whose capacity for resistance, agency and self-determination have been systematically suppressed or eradicated by a sovereign, external authority, be that a ruling, social elite, occupying army or an abstract economic system whose determining effects are beyond any individual's control.[63] Whether the zombie is an actual cadaver raised from the dead by "voodoo" sorcery, a simple, idiot-brute shocked into compliance by the modern factory system or an industrial labourer in a period of massive economic crisis, it walks the line between interminable drudgery and living death. In his *The Monster Show* David Skal quotes a commentator at the time of *White Zombie*'s first release who noted how the management of a cinema in San Francisco where it was playing hired people to stand in the building's lobby and bathrooms dressed in zombie costumes, "like so many potted plants". Presumably, she added, "they don't mind the overtime"[64]

---

63 As Comaroff (2002), Palmié (2002), Richman (2005), Taussig (1980) and others have noted, contemporary myths of zombiedom and sorcery amongst rural African and African-American diasporic communities are often associated more with the labour practices of contemporary capitalist economies (especially in terms of migrant labour) than with their traditional religious beliefs.

64 Skal 169

A MIND OF ONE'S OWN?

> Thus precisely in labour where there seemed to be merely
> some outsider's mind and ideas involved, the bondsman
> becomes aware, through this re-discovery of himself by
> himself, of having and being a "mind of his own".

> - G. W. F Hegel 'The Formative Process of Self-
> Enfranchisement' *The Phenomenology of Spirit* (1807)

A variation of the hypnosis-sorcery account of zombiedom recurs in
Val Lewton's 1943 *I Walked with a Zombie*, the most nuanced and
artful *zombi* film of the classic cinematic era. The plot of this West
Indian *Jane Eyre* ostensibly concerns a struggle for control of a White,
female protagonist, Jessica Holland, who is in a permanent state of
catatonic somnambulism, by two brothers, the stoic and puritanical
Paul Holland, Jessica's husband, and Wesley Rand, his charming
but wayward half-brother.[65] Set on the imaginary Caribbean island
of Saint Sebastian *I Walked with a Zombie,* like other films from the
period, makes no reference to the U.S. occupation of Haiti, which had
officially ended nine years earlier. It does however address the history of
New World slavery explicitly, its shadow contributing to the cheerless
atmosphere that pervades the film.

As the horse and trap driver who first brings Mrs. Holland's new
nurse, Betsy Connell, to the plantation explains to her, there is "an old
man who lives in the garden of Fort Holland with arrows stuck in him
and a soft and weeping look on his black face". The locals call him Ti-
Mysery and he is the figurehead of the "long-ago boat" that "brought
the long-ago mothers of us all chained to the bottom of the boat"
he tells her. A little later in the film Paul Holland explains to Betsy
the meaning of the statue of Saint Sebastian (the aforementioned Ti-
Mysery). "That's where our people came from" he tells her, "from
the misery and pain of slavery. For generations they found life a
burden, that's why they still weep when a child is born and make
merry at a burial... I've told you Miss Connell, this is a sad place".

---

65 The idea of a West Indian *Jane Eyre* would be taken up by the
Dominican-born novelist Jean Rhys in her 1966 novel *Wide Sargasso Sea*.

Paul Holland's generally pessimistic, Byronic temperament suggests a despair beyond the personal problems associated with a *zombi*-wife. His vision of the West Indies as a place of profound sadness seems to be shaped by the legacy of colonial slavery that his family was involved in. "Everything good dies here" he tells Betsy, as she watches flying-fish in the moonlight from the boat that is bringing her to the island, "even the stars". Although there are no visual references to the plantation manufacturing system, we learn early on that the master of the house is a descendant of the sugar planting family that brought the first slaves (still familiarly referred to as "ours" by their master) to the island. As they sit taking refreshments on the terrace Wesley jokes about the "mysterious" and "eerie" jungle drums, a stock-in-trade of sensationalist "voodoo films" at the time, that can be heard in the distance. He reassures the nervous new nurse that they were simply the "work drums" of the sugar mill, "Saint Sebastian's version of the factory whistle" as he puts it.

Despite perpetuating the White paternalistic and colonial pattern typical of the genre, Jacques Tourneur, the film's French-American director, and Val Lewton, its producer and script writer, seem to have understood the political-economic subtext to theories of zombiedom, the paradoxes of "possession" in former slave colonies and the challenge they posed for normative understandings of western rationalism and objectivity better than other directors of the time. A fundamental ontological problem raised by the *zombi* figure for western audiences, after the invention of cinema, was how to distinguish *objective* from *subjective* experiences and truths, *actual* and *imaginary* phenomena and *rational* from *irrational* beliefs. We have also noted how this problem has bearing on the dual meaning of possession: the rational and rightful ownership of a *thing* and the replacement of a human "soul" by an external, *supernatural* entity. In other words the *zombi*, like the somnambulist it meets in the Classic Cinematic phase, threatens the ideal of individual, self-conscious volition with that of an unconscious, remotely controlled automaton (or mere *human-thing*), troubling common-sense notions of what it means to be *self-possessed*. *I Walked with a Zombie* subtly plays on this opposition and in so doing manages to touch more directly than any of the other zombie films of the period, upon the deeper philosophical, historical and economic questions raised by the figure. Unlike other films in the genre it shows evidence of research into actual Haitian Vodou, Val Lewton having employed the Haitian folklorist Leroy Antoine, co-author of *The Voice of*

Haiti: An unusual collection of original native ceremonial songs, invocations, voodoo chants, drum beats and rhythms, stories of traditions etc. of the Haitian people (1938), as a consultant researcher for the film.[66] When Betsy takes Jessica to visit the *hounfo* in search of a supernatural cure for her condition they pass through a forest of cane following grizzly and symbolic route-markers, until they encounter the *zombi* Carre-Four, "guardian of the crossroads". The name is a reference to Kalfu or Maitres Carrefour, the Petro aspect of the Vodou *lwa* Papa Legba, master of the cross roads, messenger of the gods and "opener of paths". A deity that can be traced back to the Fon peoples of West Africa, Legba-Carrefour is honoured at the beginning of every Vodou ceremony.[67] A powerful and violent *lwa*, he controls the evil, night-time forces of the spirit world.[68] As Betsy and Mrs. Holland approach the *hounfo* we hear drums and a song to Papa Legba being sung in Kreyòl: 'O, Legba', a reputedly authentic Haitian song provided to the film-makers by Leroy Antoine.[69] At the *hounfo* Betsy consults Damballa through a hole in the temple wall. As she begins to tell the *houngan* why she has come to the *hounfo* a door opens, an arm reaches out and Betsy is pulled inside, where, to her surprise, she finds Mrs. Rand who explains to her that she has been masquerading as the voice of the great serpent deity in order to give covert western medical advice to members of the Vodou congregation. To make mothers boil the water for their babies, she explains, she had to tell them that the god Xango would kill the evil spirits in the water if they did so.[70]

---

66 Nemerov 118

67 Métraux 360

68 Although the choice of the name Carre-Four for the lead zombie is not in keeping with Vodou cosmology and belief, it has diegetic value in the film because he is portrayed as guardian of the paths that lead to the *hounfo*. However, as we will see, the association between Baron Samedi (Lord of the Cemetery), Legba Kalfu and zombies is a significant one in Vodou lore.

69 Nemerov 118. There are two other Vodou songs in the film: 'O Marie Congo' and 'Walee Nan Guinan'. The song 'Shame and Scandal' ('Fort Holland'), sung in the film by the Trinidadian Calypso singer and actor Sir Lancelot, was written about his own experience of being rejected by his family after his success in America.

70 Xango is a deity of Yoruba origin associated more with the Afro-Cuban

UNDEAD UPRISING

The tension between supernatural and rational accounts of Jessica's condition, typical of the genre, and implicated directly in the romantic plot of the film, is not reduced to a simple dichotomy of Black superstition versus White science. Instead a compromise explanation is arrived at that neither negates nor transcends the opposition. Having accidentally stumbled across Mrs. Holland walking through the grounds of the estate in the middle of the night, Betsy expresses her shock at discovering that she was a "mental case". Mr. Holland advises her to keep that idea "solidly in mind", "particularly when some of the people on the island start regaling you with local legends". "You'll find superstition *a contagious thing*" he warns, "Some people let it get the better of them". This contagiousness, a metaphor for both local superstition and local diseases, is something to which all the characters, in one way or the other, are prone. Dr. Maxwell, who had treated Mrs. Holland when she first became sick, explains to Betsy that her condition was caused by a tropical fever that burned out the base of her spinal column resulting in "a woman without any will power... a sleep-walker who can never be awakened". We eventually learn that Mrs. Rand, fearing that Jessica would destroy her family by having an affair with her second son Wesley, had caused Jessica's condition. While possessed during a Vodou ceremony she had asked the *houngan* to make Jessica into a *zombi*. After her confession Dr. Maxwell attempts to convince Mrs. Rand that she was letting her imagination "run away with her. "As I understand it" he explains, "in order to turn someone into a *zombi*, whether by poison or hocus-pocus, you must first kill that person... she was feverish, she was delirious, but I don't remember her dying or even being in a state resembling death. No coma, nothing. I'm afraid you are an imaginative woman Mrs. Rand". "Of course, of course" she replies, unconvinced and exhausted, before retiring to her room.

When Wesley Rand first meets Betsy for dinner he introduces the family *in absentia* by showing her the chairs in which they sit

---

traditions of Santeria and Palo Mayombe and Brazilian Candomblé and Umbanda than Haitian Vodou. Reputed to be a former king of Oye in Yorubaland, he is a god of fire, lightning and thunder who is syncretised in Santeria with Santa Barbara (Murphy). Like Ogoun Badagris, Shango is associated with the Nago *nanchon* in Haitian Vodou (Deren 60).

in the dining room. At the head of the table sits "the master", who faces his wife Jessica. In the corner sits "the particular property of Mrs. Rand", Wesley's mother. The visual metaphor of "the master's chair" and references to the chairs being "the particular properties of their owners", evokes the allegory of the "dancing table" which Marx used to illustrate the theory of commodity fetishism in *Das Kapital*, and which, as we have seen, was used to explain the ways in which concrete labour was magically alienated from the worker and *fetishised* into the commodity, now mysteriously animated by the abstract dynamics of a market and "governed" by the law of universal, general equivalence (the money form). And as Fred Moten has shown, slaves in the plantation economy were actually *commodities-that-spoke*, real human beings reduced to the status of mere *things*, the personal properties of their owners, whose value was measured entirely by their utility and fungibility.[71]

An important innovation of *I Walked with a Zombie* was the bringing together of the modern tradition of the hypnotised somnambulist and the folkloric Haitian *zombi* without reducing either to the logic of the other. A recurrent element in stereotypical representations of Vodou is the so-called "voodoo doll", an effigy of an individual used to exercise control over, or injure, the person represented.[72] Although such objects are largely the invention of cinema and their cultural roots European rather than African, in *I Walked with a Zombie* a blonde-haired doll, dressed by the *houngan* to look like Jessica, is used to underline the object-like nature of Mrs. Holland herself. In one of the most iconic scenes in early zombie cinema, the doll is twice placed in the hands of a blankly staring Carre-Four. Mindless *human-thing* in effigy becomes the symbolic driver of mindless *human-thing* in actuality, both wills controlled by the remote powers of sorcery, the *playthings* of forces far beyond their ken, pulling them ineluctably towards each other. The *houngan*, having eventually captured Carre-Four's negligible

---

71 Moten (2003)

72 The precursors of the stereotypical "voodoo doll" would seem to be the poppet dolls of European witchcraft traditions and the Nkondi nail-fetishes made by the Kongo people of West Africa, a tradition which has characteristics in common with that of the Haitian *ouanga* and "expeditionary" *zombi-astral* (see McAlister 1995).

attention, uses the doll to draw him forward and set his intention on the retrieval of the "real" Mrs. Holland. The encounter is of an explicit, if covert, racial and sexual order: Black, male, human, *zombi-kadav* is brought face-to-face with White, female, somnambulist in a gesture which speaks directly to a characteristic mixing of spectacular zombie-fetish tropes within the classic cinematic zombie narrative, reconnecting the cinematic *zombi* figure Carre-Four to the classic silent-era somnambulist figure Cesare from *The Cabinet of Dr. Caligari*, and Mrs. Holland to Jane, the wife of Francis in the earlier and clearly influential film. The fantasy of remotely controlling others and being remotely controlled oneself, either by the magic of cinema or "voodoo-hypnosis", is succinctly expressed in this meeting of two *human-like agents-without-autonomy,* driven by external wills or unacknowledged and unconscionable desires. (The scene is intercut with a discussion between Betsy and Paul agonising over his brother's accusation that he deliberately drove Jessica into insanity without knowing it). Meanwhile the *houngan* has attached a string to the effigy of Jessica, which, as he pulls it towards him, draws the real Jessica towards the *hounfo*. Paul and Betsy find her at the gate, where Wesley, looking somewhat en-tranced himself, explains that "they are trying to get her back" with "charms that can draw a man half-way round the world". "We believed all that when we were boys Wes", his brother responds, "but we're grown men now. We know it's all nonsense". "Do we?" Wes replies, unconvinced. That one may drive another person mad without intending to suggests that the powers of the unconscious, present at the birth of cinema, and blossoming in Hollywood in the 1940s, were of an equally mysterious nature as those of so-called "voodoo". And this is what the film seems to conclude.

Wes, evidently still in love with Jessica and desperate to end her mute suffering, opens the gate to let her pass towards the *hounfo*, following her with an arrow he has pulled from the chest of Ti Mysery/Saint Sebastian. When the *houngan* sticks a needle into Jessica's effigy we see that Wesley has used the arrow to kill his would-be lover. He then carries her body into the sea to save her from the beckoning arms of Carre-Four who has been sent to collect her. The scene of the *houngan* putting the needle into the Jessica-doll cuts directly to Wes pulling the spear out of her actual body. It is an exemplary cinematic combination of two world-views within which the Haitian *zombi* and hypnotised somnambulist meet. On one side of the cinematic cut (which is simultaneously and significantly a representational *coup de grâce*) is the hocus-pocus account of events in which the lethal act is a *magical* one. On the other side is the "actual" crime. Within the imaginary space of the cinematic narrative neither action has any more causal viability than the other. They are, diegetically speaking, mutually supportive components of the same spectral act. In this sense the scene stitches together two ostensibly distinct explanations for Wes's action (natural and supernatural), leaving the question of the causes of Jessica's zombiedom and Wes's crime (pathological or sorcerous) philosophically open, yet cinematically and narratively resolved.

The extent to which the "cinematic apparatus" and the Hollywood Studio system were part of an external, integrated, extra-human "system of needs" remotely controlling cinema-going publics at the time is a question beyond the scope of this chapter. What is clear however is that the zombie films of this period, regardless of their quality, all involved narratives in which "foreign" and "dark" powers were able to control the will of individuals and groups without them being aware or conscious of such influences. But Tourneur's film is the only one that shows awareness of the paradoxical nature of the *human thing* upon which the plantation economy was based and the economic-ontological paradoxes implied by such relations. To present the main characters of the film as the objects they own (and the empty places they are never seen to inhabit) reminds us of the spectral nature of cinematic representations in general (a theme artfully exploited by the Halperin brothers' *White Zombie*, where Neil Parker, in a drunken daze, tries to embrace the cinematic phantasm of his fianceé).

The spectral after-life granted to cinematic recordings of living beings turns them all into zombic entities in a fundamentally Vodouistic sense, their *astral* doubles caught forever in a parallel, non-physical dimension that repeats itself over and over again. The metaphorical transformation of the *zombi* from bewitched, Black, New World slave into modern, White, hypnotised somnambulist is largely a consequence of the new mass medium of cinema and its assumed suggestive powers. As such the hypnotic-zombie reiterates the epistemological problems associated with the folkloric *zombi* but re-situates them within a modern, technologically "advanced" context. The hypnotic theme in classic cinematic zombie narratives introduces a "machine age" mindlessness and new criminal and sexual anxieties to the established cluster of concerns represented by the *zombi* figure. As we have seen, what both the *zombi* and somnambulist share is a removal of their ego, consciousness and memory, and their being controlled by the will of another, usually male, and often "foreign", protagonist. In this death-like trance-state they are prone to a power of suggestion which often has a sexual or homicidal character. The *zombi*-potion hypothesis, carried over from the folkloric traditions and legal code of Haiti, also informs attempts to account for what would otherwise be considered irrational or supernatural beliefs amongst civilised and reasonable people. Alongside the sorcerous explanations of zombiedom then, the Classic Cinematic zombie introduces hypnotic and narcotic accounts which attempt to reduce the category of supernatural phenomena to the psychological and pathological in ways characteristic of a modern, scientific *episteme*. It does so, however, in order to maintain the possibility of a metaphysical and supernatural causality for involuntary and transgressive acts which has kept zombie lovers returning to the cinema in droves.

Andre Normil's dramatic evocation of the Bois Caïman ceremony showing the red-sashed Dutty Boukman, machete raised, and Cécile Fatiman, sacrificing the black Creole pig.

III
THE ROMANCE OF REVOLUTIONARY VODOU

THE ETHNOGRAPHIC RECLAMATION OF "VODOU"

A remarkable characteristic of the literature about the Haitian folk religion popularly referred to as "Voodoo" is the range of different ways authors have chosen to spell it.[1] There seems to be only one generally steadfast rule governing this orthographic diversity: "Voodoo" signifies the popular, sensationalist, Anglo-American spelling used by the uninformed to describe something they know little about, while the rest, in one way or another, indicate something more "authentically Haitian" and "academic". The most common reason for choosing any spelling other than "Voodoo" therefore is to signify a level of cultural familiarity and scholarship that distinguishes the author from the mere dilettante or ill-informed cultural exploiter of a misunderstood religion. The rule however is not set in stone. William Seabrook typically used "Voodoo" throughout *The Magic Island,* but he also included

---

1 In the literature consulted here I have encountered the following variations: "Voodoo", "Vaudaux", "Vaudou", "Vodou", "Vodoun", "Voudou", "Voudow", "Voudoo", "Voudu", "Voudoun", "Vodoun", "Vôdu", "Vodun", "Vaudoux", "Vaudoun", "Vadou", "Voudaux", "Vaudoo" and "Vaudois". See Pettinger's 'From Vaudoux to Voodoo' for a precise history of the changing uses of the term.

a discussion drawn from one of J. C. Dorsainvil's lectures about the origins of the term *vôdu* which in the Fon language of Dahomey means "spirit", a derivation most scholars now accept as the word's principle source. Why Seabrook chose to spell the word "Voodoo" rather than "Vôdu" presumably had something to do with the expectations of American audiences for whom the former was already the familiar spelling, having been introduced by William Newell in 1888 in a rejoinder to Spenser St. John. Magdeline W. Shannon however bucked the scholarly consensus in her 1983 translation of *Ainsi parla l'oncle* choosing to translate Price-Mars' "Vaudou" as "Voodoo" precisely because that was how Anglo-American audiences expected it to be spelled. Price-Mars' choice of "Vaudou", she speculates, was a nod to Moreau de Saint-Méry, a Frenchman, and one of the first to use the word in print, spelling it "Vaudoux". But Spenser St. John, an Englishman, who, as we have seen, wrote one of the most scathing accounts of the religion, spelled the word "Vaudoux" too. From Moreau de Saint-Méry to St. John this seems to have been the most common spelling, used to denote variously an Arada sect, the adherents of the cult, the serpent god they worshipped, their dance and a variety of fetish-objects.

The first use of the spelling "Voodoo" seems to have been in Newell's 1888 article in *The Journal of American Folklore* entitled 'Myths of Voodoo Worship and Child Sacrifice in Hayti' which rebuked the cannibal claims made by Spenser St. John. Newell proposed that the word was of European origin referring to followers of a 12th century French merchant-mystic called Peter Valdo, who went by the name of Valdensians or Vaudois. The slaves of Saint-Domingue, he claimed, borrowed the term from the French to refer to a witch or sorcerer. It was, unfortunately, from this point onwards that Anglo-American authors began using the spelling that carried with it the very associations of cannibalism, child sacrifice and African fetish-worship that Newell had intended to dispel. Whether or not authors have chosen to capitalise any particular spelling seems to indicate whether they consider it to be a religion in formal terms rather than an informal collection of folk customs, a form of superstitious magic or a popular term for mythical "mumbo jumbo".

In April 2003, shortly before the second coup to remove him from office, President Jean-Bertrand Aristide officially recognised Vodou as a national religion in Haiti, allowing participants to legally perform baptisms and marriages under the auspices of the Ministry of Religious Affairs. The general consensus of the board of KOSANBA (Scholarly Association for the Study of Haitian Vodou) is that the name should be spelled "Vodou", its capitalisation indicating that it is identified as a religion alongside Judaism, Hinduism, Islam, etc. Thanks to their efforts this spelling has been recognised by the U.S. Library of Congress since 2012. What is perhaps most perplexing about the debate is that the majority of the people in Haiti who actually practice the religion don't refer to it as "Vodou" at all. Instead they speak about "serving the spirits" or "serving the *lwa*". When the word *is* used it is to describe a certain kind of dance or drumming. The nearest equivalent term for an all-encompassing religious phenomena derived from Africa is "Ginen", an African, ancestral ethos and moral code regarding how one properly serves the spirits.[2] The capitalisation of Vodou then, however it is spelled, has been used largely by outsiders and non-practitioners either to praise and respect, or to denigrate and condemn, the Afro-cultural beliefs and practices of Haiti and the Haitian diaspora.

Alasdair Pettinger, who has researched this changing orthography in some depth, identifies a significant moment in the 1930s when disagreements about the spelling of the word for "Afro-cultural beliefs and practices of Haiti and the diaspora" reached a turning point. At this time writers associated with the Haitian ethnographic movement (notably Jean Price-Mars, J. C. Dorsainvil, Arthur Holly and Melville Herskovits) attempted to reclaim the term from sensationalist representations of Haitian culture before, during and after the U.S. occupation. In his *Life in a Haitian Valley* of 1937, Herskovits advocated for the spelling "Vodun", allegedly following the Kreyòl pronunciation, while also insisting on the necessity to counter the spelling "Voodoo" used by exploitative American authors like Seabrook and Craige:

> Conceived as a grim system of African practices, it ["Voodoo"] has come to be identified with fantastic and

2 In personal correspondence LeGrace Benson has noted that term *andeyo* is also used by practitioners (or *serviteurs*) of the religion. I have chosen to spell Vodou with a capital "V" in respect of the work of the KOSANBA scholars and those who have struggled to have Vodou officially recognised as a religion.

cruel rites and to serve as a symbol of daring excursions into the esoteric. Not only has emphasis been placed on frenzied rites and the cannibalism supposed on occasion to accompany them, but its dark mysteries of magic and "zombis" have been so stressed that it has become customary to think of Haitians as living in a universe of psychological terror.[3]

This, it seems, was the first moment that a lexical distinction between different spellings, one false and exploitative, the rest more or less authentic, gained some level of scholarly consensus. That it was towards the end of the U.S. occupation that alternative spellings began to gain academic currency is a sign of how much Haitian scholars of the time felt that popular Haitian culture, particularly the culture of the Black, peasant masses, so maligned and misrepresented by foreign authors and Hollywood film-makers, needed to be re-evaluated and re-represented in a more positive, accurate and favourable way. From then on the spelling "Voodoo" seemed to point away from Haiti and towards the distorted, collective fantasies of the American masses while "Vodou" (and its variants) pointed back towards the actual practices of Haitian peasants, the urban poor and their African ancestors, that had been so unfairly misrepresented by exploitative and malicious foreigners.[4]

The U.S. occupation had a profound impact on the political and intellectual life of Haiti in the 1920s and '30s. The publication of the literary journal *La Revue Indigène: Les Arts et La Vie* in 1927 signalled the beginning of a new nationalist current in Haitian letters that sought to define a distinctly Haitian school of literature in reaction to the dominant, traditional European models.[5] Inspired by the new interest in "Negro Arts" that developed with the Harlem Renaissance and in Europe (especially in Paris where, as we have seen, it was closely

---

3 Herskovits 139

4 It was, however, not a permanent state of affairs. By 1987 an exhibition at the prestigious Art Institute of Chicago would be called *Spirit and Image: The Art of Voodoo*. Then, in 1995, all the contributors to the catalogue of the exhibition *The Sacred Arts of Haitian Vodou* were encouraged to drop 'oo's and the 'n' but keep the 'ou' (Pettinger 422).

5 Ramsey (2011) 178

associated with Cubism, Dada and Surrealism), several young writers from elite families in Haiti, like Carl Brouard, Jacques Roumain and Normil Sylvain, many educated in France, sought to develop a style of literature that was highly critical of the U.S. occupation and sought to make a creative break with the literary traditions of the past.[6] The movement, which came to be called *Indigénisme*, marked the beginning of a renewed and passionate spirit of nationalism that celebrated the African roots of Haiti's peasant masses. Carl Brouard, the son of a successful Haitian businessman and German mother, even became a *serviteur* of the spirits, writing poetry in honour of the *lwa* and in praise of the "savagery" of African culture. His poem *Hymne à Erzulie* from 1928 captures something of the new spirit:

> Drum
> when you sound
> my soul screams towards Africa.
> Sometimes
> I dream of an immense jungle
> bathed in moon-light
> with hirsute, sweating figures,
> sometimes
> of a filthy hut
> Where I drink blood from human skulls.[7]

In his review of Jean Price-Mars' highly influential *Ainsi parla l'oncle* in 1928, Brouard described Vodou as "our only creation... the certain pledge of an architecture, of a literature, of a national mystique".[8] Price-Mars was the most important figure in this new spirit of Haitian letters. A medical doctor educated in Paris, his *Ainsi parla l'oncle* (So Spoke the Uncle), a collection of lectures on Haitian popular culture

---

6 Nicholls 159

7 Nicholls 161. Brouard's career traverses the first expressions of a raw Rimbaud-like Haitian *indigénisme* in the 1920s to the totalitarian tendencies of the *Noiristes* in the 1940s. By the 1930s Brouard would advocate for the restoration of a mythical Haitian past in which the *houngan* (or *Papa Loi*) was an allegorical figure for an ancient form of patriarchal sovereignty that would emerge from the Haitian *volksgeist* (See Dash (1998) 74-77).

8 Nicholls 161

and folklore, was the most influential work in the emergent discourse of Black, African and nationalist sentiment in Haiti during the ensuing decades. In it he attacked the complacency of the Haitian elites towards the unity of the nation, their cultural identification with Europe and America and their neglect of the African-derived culture of the Haitian peasant and urban masses. "Our only chance to be ourselves," he wrote, "is to not repudiate part of our ancestral heritage. And! as for this heritage, eight-tenths of it is a gift from Africa".[9] Price-Mars' re-affirmation of the African ancestral roots of Haitian national identity was intended, in part, to counter racist representations of Vodou that had been promoted before and during the U.S. occupation. In his *Une étape de l'évolution haïtienne* (A Step in Haitian Evolution) (1929) Price-Mars directly criticised misleading depictions of Vodou like Seabrook's, challenging the credibility of his accounts of so-called "Voodoo Rites", noting how Seabrook had misappropriated the work of reputable Haitian authors like Arthur C. Holly, J. C. Dorsainvil and Price-Mars himself, to give popular credence to incredible stories.[10] The distinction between religion and witchcraft, which Seabrook emphasised, was one Price-Mars considered unrecognisable by ninety percent of Haitians. Recounting in detail Seabrook's description of his own initiation into the Petro cult, Price-Mars argued that it had nothing in common with traditional initiations, which ordinarily take place over several weeks or months and require prolonged periods of abstinence. Furthermore no pigs, which are sacred to the Petro rite, were sacrificed during Seabrook's initiation. In short, Price-Mars accused Seabrook of constructing a "Voodoo" version of his own occidental, esoteric and sexual fantasies, facilitated by his new Haitian friends in the mountains above Petit-Goâve. For Price-Mars Vodou was neither a savage blight on a nation struggling to be civilised nor the stuff of White, primitivist fantasies about Blackness, but a principle source of the nation's distinct cultural identity. He was not alone in this belief. The other authors cited by Seabrook also wrote early defences of Vodou against its demonisation by the U.S. marines, the Catholic Church and their literary apologists.

---

9 Price-Mars quoted in Ramsey (2011) 179

10 There is a certain irony to this accusation given that Price-Mars himself had tried to secure the performance of Vodou ceremonies for Seabrook's observation (Ramsey (2011) 218).

THE ROMANCE OF REVOLUTIONARY VODOU

Between 1907 and 1908 Justin Chrysostome Dorsainvil, a school teacher and official in the ministry of education, wrote a number of articles for the Haitian journal *Le Matin* criticising the social hermeticism of the Haitian elites, who ignored the general population's ethnic and historical roots, proposing that the Haitian struggle against European imperialism had created a "new Creole Race" upon which the culture and politics of a new Haiti should be based.[11] Dorsainvil was also critical of the educational establishment's neglect of the racial factors underpinning the Haitian Revolution and the true ethnic character of the Haitian majority. As a corrective he penned his *Manuel d'histoire d'Haiti* in 1924, a standard high school textbook, which contains what is perhaps the first official, government-sanctioned account of the Bois Caïman ceremony. A decade earlier he had written one of the first sympathetic accounts of Vodou, an essay entitled *Vodou et Nevrose* (Vodou and Neurosis), published in book form in 1931, in which he claimed that, although Vodou was both a "religious and racial psycho-neurosis", it was also the royal road to the Haitian psyche, corresponding to the "Guinean soul" of the Haitian people.[12] Following the French theologian and philosopher Raoul Allier's *Le non-civilisé et nous* (translated as *The Mind of the Savage* in 1929), Dorsainvil argued against any *essential* difference between primitive and modern minds. Possession in Vodou, the book's central theme, was, as in other religions, "incontestably a psycho-biological pre-condition" common to all peoples and religions regardless of race. Quoting T. K. Oesterreich's *The Possessed* (1921) he proposed that only where a high degree of civilisation prevails does possession disappear or retreat into the shadows. Psychotherapy, following this argument, was a modern, scientific form of exorcism. Dorsainvil did however believe that possession trance was a particularly marked hereditary

---

11 Nicholls 152-153

12 Nicholls 153. At the opening of the book Dorsainvil strikes a positivistic scientific note explaining how, as with the earlier essay, he was not concerned with problems associated with the philosophy of religion or, more precisely, with the "metaphysics of possession". He quotes Kant's famous cautionary statement about metaphysics from 'The Only Possible Argument in Support of a Demonstration of the Existence of God': "a dark ocean without shores or lighthouses, where one must proceed like the mariner in a sea not yet navigated" (Dorsainvil 8).

trait of Africans, proposing that the propensity to possession within Vodou communities was enhanced by a sort of *accumulation héréditaire* ("hereditary accumulation").[13] Echoing Price-Mars' sublime imaginings of the African landscape in *Ainsi parla l'oncle*, Dorsainvil proposed that the psychology of Haiti's African ancestors was directly shaped by the dramatic and fearful nature of the environments in which they lived. Vodou, he claimed, was consequently a religion "born from fear" and, at its highest point, "a divination of natural forces", which it had personified into a pantheon. Under the "hereditary weight of generations" such beliefs had evolved into a "true racial neurosis" which affected families from the countryside and poor areas disproportionally due the relative absence of miscegenation with European stock amongst those populations. Despite this affirmation of the hereditary African disposition of the Haitian people, and the subsequent inappropriateness of European models of culture, politics and education there, Dorsainvil felt that the African strain was generally bad for Haitian society and politics because it drove Haitian peasants to seek ritualistic and magical solutions to real social problems, describing Vodou as Haiti's *"grand malheur"* (great misfortune).[14]

---

13 Dorsainvil 21. The discussion of the hereditary characteristics of Black Africans as a *race* has been identified as a founding one for the *concept* in modern European thought. Robert Bernasconi locates the origin of race as a formal philosophical concept in Kant's 'On the Use of Teleological Principles in Philosophy' from 1788. In the essay Kant defines race as "a conjunction of causes placed originally in the line of descent of the genus itself in order to account for a self-transmitted peculiarity that appears in different interbreeding animals but does not lie in the concept of their genus" (Bernasconi 40). For Kant *race* differs from human *variety* in that it is an inevitable and *radical* peculiarity that announces a common descent. A "deviate form" rather than a *degeneration of* the common line, race predisposes its members to specific teleological purposes (Bernasconi 41). According to Kant, racial variation, which occurs because of the species' natural adaptation to climate, is irreversible. The root stem of which all races are deviate forms was assumed by Kant to have been White (Bernasconi 23-24).

14 Dorsainvil 33. Since Dorsainvil several authors have attempted to account for the psychology of spirit possession in terms of specifically racial genetic traits, universal psychological propensities or a combination

Price-Mars disagreed with Dorsainvil's thesis, proposing instead that the term "psychoneurosis" was only appropriate for the small group of *serviteurs* who participated directly in the Mysteries of the Divinities and who were ridden by the *lwa*, but not for the majority of the adherents to the cult. Following Pierre Janet and Joseph Babinski (Charcot's assistant and proponent of the theory that hysteria is an effect of suggestion, or *pithiatism*), Price-Mars proposed that hysterical symptoms were the effects of "pathological suggestibility" which tended towards the "dissociation of the personality". Correcting Dorsainvil's diagnosis of possession as a form of hysteria, Price-Mars argued that Vodou possession was more likely to be an effect of suggestion and that the inner sect of *serviteurs* were subject to a pathological "mythomaniac constitution" characterised by an "involuntary propensity to fabrication" and the tendency to "realise nervous crises". This psychopathological tendency was "essentially hereditary" and transmitted from parents to children. Such a genetic inheritance was not simply attributable to race however, as the example of similar pathological constitutions in other races (and Moreau Saint-Méry's claims about the "magnetic" influence of the Vaudoux dance on certain Whites) attests.[15] The extent to which possession trance, one of the defining characteristics of Haitian Vodou, was the consequence of an essential racial heredity or a universal propensity of any human population under specific environmental conditions, was to remain a question for ethnographers for several decades to come. As Magdeline

---

of both. Bourguignon, who has probably investigated the phenomena more widely than others, convincingly demonstrates that possession-trance is a universal human potential with culturally relative forms of manifestation, sometimes involving music and drumming, sometimes not (Bourguignon (1973)). In Haiti those forms contain embedded histories of the nation – its heroes, battles, the African ancestors, tribal deities, etc. – in coded patterns of performed custom and ritual. That these patterns have historically been performed by the blacker populations is a consequence of a cultural and racial hierarchy that has been present since the colonial era. In other words, the history of slavery, its revolutionary overcoming and the explicitly *epidermal* distributions of violence that characterised it are "built-in" at the level of culture, but there is no necessary reason to assume a specific race-determined gene-expression in these cultural patterns.

15 Price-Mars (1983) 133-134

Shannon notes in a footnote to *So Spoke the Uncle*, in 1954 the Haitian psychologist Louis Mars wrote an article – 'The Phenomena of Possession' – which argued that possession must be viewed in the light of the economic distress of "anxiety-ridden" Haitians, "a people waging a heroic struggle against the pitfalls of ignorance and misery", for whom its cathartic role was an affective necessity. Louis Mars' socio-economic interpretation of possession trance was furthered by Rémy Bastien and others who generally rejected the "mental illness" hypothesis.[16]

Kate Ramsey has shown how the established laws against Vodou in Haiti were exploited by the U.S. army to justify their "civilizing mission" there and to conscript forced labour into road building projects. She also notes how sensationalist accounts of Vodou by ex-marines like Craige and Wirkus were considered by members of the Haitian elite, who wanted to clear Haiti's name of the taint of primitivism, to be deliberate acts of national-cultural sabotage.[17] Arthur C. Holly's *Les daïmons du culte voudu* (1918) was written with the explicit intention of countering the negative stereotypes of Vodou being exploited by U.S. marines in the first few years of the occupation. Holly was a son of the first African-American Bishop of the Protestant Episcopal Church in Haiti, James Théodore Holly, abolitionist, Freemason and ardent advocate of the capacity for Black self-governance in the Caribbean.[18] His tone in *Les daïmons* typifies the emerging *Indigéniste* sensibility of the time in its criticism of those elite Haitians who feigned the manners of Europeans and Americans joining them in denigrating and denying the importance of Haiti's African past: that "luminous landmark and the most living and fecund centre of religious humanity".[19] "Now more than ever" Holly wrote, "is the moment to try to cleanse our ancestral cult of the stain which has been put upon it. In this, much of the honour of the African race in general is involved, and much of the dignity of our posterity, of us Haitians".

---

16 Price-Mars (1983) 134 n15

17 Ramsey (2011) 159

18 See James Theodore Holly, *A vindication of the capacity of the Negro race for self-government, and civilized progress, as demonstrated by historical events of the Haytian revolution: and the subsequent acts of that people since their national independence* (1857).

19 Holly quoted in Seabrook (1929) 314

Defending Vodou against uninformed and widespread accusations that it was a form of Satan worship, Holly invoked the "luminous spirits" that would protect the nation when the tainted image of Vodou had been cleansed:

> And then, from the depths of our valleys, from the gorges of our mountains, from the forests whose century-old trees have shielded the sacred meetings of our ancestors in epic times, will rise in the air, mingled with mysterious effluvia, the songs of joy of the legions of Invisibles who watch over us – as in the past they inspired and protected the invincible founders of our independence – happy to see us reestablish the chain of union and fraternity between blacks and Mulattoes in an unalterable sentiment of piety, of love toward the Old Divinities, the Ancestors, the immortal and revivified Mother-country.[20]

In *Dra-Po* (1928), written under the pseudonym Her-Ra Ma-El, Holly would make explicit his belief that Vodou represented an essentially pan-African-American religious form. The book is dedicated to his "Congénères Africain" and claims to have been made with the cooperation of the Invisibles (the "natural guardians of the African Race"). Following the tenets of Theosophy, Holly proposed a "universal spirit" in which all lives and divinities partake, including those that will direct the African race into the future, assisting them in the creation of a *"Collective Theocratique"* of "inviolable solidarity".[21]

The *Indigénistes'* intellectual counter-attack against stereotypical misrepresentations of Vodou in the 1920s and '30s coincided with the first wave of academic ethnographers to visit Haiti.[22] Perhaps

---

20 Seabrook (1929) 316

21 Holly (1928) III

22 As noted earlier, there had in fact been a handful of ethnographers in Haiti before and during the occupation. These included Elsie Clews Parsons, the American anthropologist, folklorist and pioneer feminist, who was the first ethnographer to discuss the folkloric Haitian *zombi* in 1928, and Robert Burnett Hall, an American anthropologist who studied the

the most influential of these was Melville Herskovits, pioneer of African-American Studies, who first passed through Haiti with his wife Frances in 1928 after making contact by letter with Price-Mars.[23] Herskovits had already made a name for himself in New York as a champion of the Harlem Renaissance and an advocate of Negro assimilation in the U.S., and he was a central figure connecting the ethnographic study of contemporary African cultures to those of Haiti. After a brief meeting with Price-Mars on the docks of Port-au-Prince the two men began a long correspondence that eventually led to Herskovits's three-month stay in the Mirebalais valley in 1934 where he undertook his first fieldwork in Haiti. A significant early topic of discussion between the two men was Seabrook's *The Magic Island,* which Herskovits described in a review for *The Nation* in 1929 as a "work of injustice" and a "sensational exploitation of the lives and customs of the Caribbean Negro peoples".[24] In *Life in a Haitian Valley* Herskovits attempted to distance himself from sensationalist accounts of Vodou like Wirkus's and Seabrook's, describing possession as a perfectly normal phenomenon within the pattern of Haitian culture, dismissing Dorsainvil's thesis as "somewhat simplistic".[25]

Société Congo in La Gonâve in 1929 while it was under the "governance" of Lieutenant Faustin Wirkus, the "White King of la Gonâve". Wirkus had himself carried out archaeological fieldwork on the island and amassed a collection of Native American artefacts (Hall 687).

23 Magloire and Yelvington 152

24 Quoted in Magloire and Yelvington 158

25 Herskovits 143 n11 and 147-148. Ironically, Herskovits's host on his first trip to Haiti was John Houston Craige, the U.S. Marine Captain and chief of police in Port-au-Prince at the time, who would go on to write two of the most sensationalist accounts of Haiti during the occupation: *Black Bagdad* (1933) and *Cannibal Cousins* (1934). Ramsey's work reveals how the anthropologist and police chief also shared a six-year correspondence after their meeting. Craige, a self-acknowledged White Supremacist, modelled himself as an amateur anthropologist and a "long distance research assistant" to Herskovits (Ramsey (2011) 66). More ironic still is the fact that their correspondence also disparaged Seabrook's book despite Craige's more extreme raiding of colonial tropes. On the publication of *Cannibal Cousins*, while disagreeing with Craige's race theories, Herskovits praised it as "one of the most exciting books I have read in many a long

Of Seabrook's account of his Petro initiation Herskovits wrote that "on the basis of its inner inconsistencies" it should be considered a "masterpiece of misstatement and misinterpretation".

In 1932 a group of Price-Mars' former students, who, during the 1920s had begun calling themselves the three D's after the surnames of their founders (Lorimer Denis, Louis Diaquoi and François Duvalier) formed a group called the Griots after the tradition of African storytellers and magicians who preserve the customs of the tribe. Carl Brouard and the poet Clément Magloire (aka Saint Aude) joined the group shortly afterwards. In 1938, with financial aid from Brouard's father, then mayor of Port-au-Prince, they founded the journal *Les Griots*.[26] The ideology of the Griots, for which David Nicholls coined the term *Noirisme*, emphasised the African roots of Haiti's past and appealed to their fellow Haitians to reject the culture of Europeans and their American cousins.[27] They celebrated the great civilisations of Africa, taking the Harlem Renaissance as a clarion call for a global, pan-African awakening. Unlike their mentor Price-Mars however, who saw himself as an heir to Joseph Anténor Firmin, the Haitian lawyer, diplomat and anthropologist whose 1885 *De l'égalité des races humaines* rebuked the scientific racism of authors like Arthur de Gobineau, the Griots believed that fundamental differences between races were rooted in biological factors that dictated the appropriate forms of government for people of different heredity, aligning themselves with anti-colonial struggles for Black Nationalism in Africa. Like the *Indigénistes* who preceded them, the Griots looked to Vodou as a unifying force in the national psyche, a force that was essentially African in nature, a "crystallisation of the origins and psychology of the Haitian people" and "the supreme factor in Haitian unity".[28] Black leaders from Haiti's revolutionary past, like Macandal, Dutty Boukman, Toussaint Louverture, Jean-Jacques Dessalines and Henri Christophe (Holly's "invincible founders of our independence") were lauded as national heroes and defenders of the masses, personifying

---

day" (Ramsey (2011) 330 n228).

26 Nicholls 168-169

27 Nicholls 167

28 Denis and Duvalier quoted in Ramsey (2011) 250

the genius of the Haitian race.[29] And like Dorsainvil, Holly and Price-Mars, the Griots identified the Mulatto elites as the major obstacle to the progressive transformation of Haitian society.

WAR ON VODOU

The rise of a Black nationalist movement in Haiti was in large part a reaction to the overtly racist nature of the occupation there, a racism that, from the perspectives of the *Indigénistes* and Griots, was shared by the Mulatto elites who collaborated with an occupying force made up largely of marines from the still segregated southern states of America. Divisions between the nascent Black nationalist movement and the elites were exacerbated by the latter's support for the suppression of native practices legally identified as *les sortilèges* (spells), a term which, according to the Haitian penal code which had been in place since 1835, included the making of *ouangas, caprelatas, vaudoux, donpèdre* and *macandals*.[30] Under the client government of Philipe Sudre Dartigeunave "Vaudou" was officially considered to be, alongside "ignorance", one of the two ills that had hindered the economic and cultural development of the Haitian people. In 1916, one year into the occupation, Haiti's minister of justice and religions issued a circular announcing the government's plans to overthrow all "altars of fetishism" and to "destroy superstition as quickly as possible".[31] U.S. marines, who had only three articles of the Penal Code translated into English (the two others, as noted earlier, being against "vagrancy" and "poisoning people into a death-like state"), set upon a systematic campaign against the traditional peasant customs and practices known to the marines as "Voodoo".[32] Rural police officers were enlisted to

---

29 Nicholls 171

30 Ramsey 58

31 Ramsey (2011) 148

32 As Ramsey shows, Vodou was explicitly associated with forms of "savage warfare" waged by the Cacos rebels and also deemed a threat to American business in Haiti. Officials in Haiti's courts, according to a confidential report written to the chief of Naval Operations in March 1920, were also tainted by the corruption of "Vaudoism" (Ramsey (2011) 144-147).

enforce the law and those accused of said practices were fined and sentenced to six months of *kové*.[33]

Although the persecution of Vodou would continue throughout the occupation with varying degrees of intensity, there developed alongside it stories of its miraculous resilience to suppression. Price-Mars and Herskovits recounted popular narratives told to them about appearances of the Virgin Mary at the sacred waterfalls of Saut D'Eau that inspired Vodouists that their faith would not be destroyed. Herskovits and Price-Mars told how, responding to a vision of the Virgin in a palm tree at Ville Bonheur, a Catholic priest, with the help of an American officer, attempted to shoot the vision out of the tree. Having failed to do so they cut the tree down and the vision slowly ascended into the sky. When the priest returned to his house he found it had burned down along with everything in it. He died shortly afterwards from a paralytic stroke. The marine who shot at the virgin allegedly went mad and was found wandering aimlessly in the woods.[34] The miraculous resilience of the Vodou faithful in the face of their religion's persecution seems to have fuelled fantasies amongst U.S. marines about the threat it posed to their authority, and it became widely believed by them that the Cacos rebels were actively using the powers of Vodou against the U.S. forces. One of the most sensational stories was that of Lawrence Muth who, as we have seen, was captured, murdered and his organs allegedly eaten by rebels after a skirmish in the mountains beyond Mirebalais. The discovery of a grimoire in the possession of Benoît Batraville, the rebel leader who allegedly ordered Muth's execution and dismemberment, furthered rumours that the Cacos were using magic. The story of Muth's death and the legends surrounding it would become part of marine lore during the occupation.[35]

---

33 *Kové* is the Kreyòl term for *corvée*, a forced labour system used by a state for public works. It was introduced to Haiti by Henri Christophe after the revolution, who used it to build fortifications against a potential French invasion. See Chapter Three of Ramsey's *The Spirits and the Law*, 'Penalizing Vodou and Promoting "Voodoo" in U.S.-Occupied Haiti, 1915-1934). Testifying to the U.S. Senate committee hearing on the occupation of Haiti in 1921, General Eli Cole, when asked about the main conditions compelling the invasion in 1915, told them that "Voudauxism was rampant" (Ramsey (2011) 130).

34 Herskovits 383-284

35 Renda 66

In the process of persecuting Vodou many U.S. marines used the opportunity to amass collections of the artefacts that, under Article 407 of the Penal Code, they were required to confiscate for "burning or destruction".[36] The most prized of these were drums, believed by the marines to be the main source of communication between guerrilla units. In *Black Bagdad* (1933) John Houston Craige lists the collection of artefacts he had amassed in his Philadelphia home, the centrepiece being a six foot Arada drum.[37] So while films like *White Zombie* and *Drums O' Voodoo* were playing to both Black and White audiences in the United States, promoting stereotypical images of "voodoo" practitioners and the primitive superstitions of "jungle" savages, U.S. marines in Haiti were destroying *hounfor* and the artefacts they found there, while hoarding the best pieces as trophies of their civilising mission. Later soldiers like Craige and Wirkus would capitalise on their experiences by writing books that exceeded Seabrook in terms of their "calculated sensationalism".[38] Wirkus would even return to La Gonâve after his tour of duty in 1932 to film the early "docudrama" *Voodoo*, a film which included footage of "authentic" native dances and ceremonies alongside staged scenes of the ex-officer himself rescuing an actress who was about to be fed to a jungle deity.[39]

One might have assumed that after the withdrawal of American troops in 1934 the persecution of Vodou would have abated somewhat. This was not the case however. President Sténio Vincent, who had been elected to office during the occupation in 1930, immediately adopted a more authoritarian attitude than his predecessor Louis Borno, and in 1935 he issued a decree that tightened the prohibition against *les sortilèges*, now identified as *pratiques superstitieuses* (superstitious practices), which, for the first time, included animal sacrifices.[40]

---

36 Ramsey (2011) 162

37 Ramsey (2011) 163

38 Ramsey (2011) 166

39 Senn 238. The film seems to have been lost.

40 Ramsey (2011) 177. Informants of George Eaton Simpson who conducted fieldwork in Haiti in 1937 told him that so-called "dances without sacrifices" had been invented towards the end of the occupation to "circumvent the law" (Ramsey (2011) 188). The presence of animal sacrifice at Vodou ceremonies seems to have become a distinguishing

THE ROMANCE OF REVOLUTIONARY VODOU

Vincent was a staunch supporter of Haiti's French cultural heritage, the Roman Catholic Church and Haiti's economic relations with the United States. Five years after the law was changed it became the basis for a renewed campaign against Vodou, this time waged by the Catholic clergy, with the blessing of then president Élie Lescot. For *Noiristes* like Brouard, Denis and Duvalier, the continued offensive against Vodou signalled a distancing of the Mulatto elites from the popular values of the Haitian masses, and the anti-superstition campaign strengthened their belief that the fundamental fault-line in the cultural politics of Haitian nationalism was a racial one.

Between 1941 and 1942 the Catholic Church, the clergy of which was predominantly French, set about the most systematic campaign against Vodou in the nation's history. Alfred Métraux, who arrived in Haiti with his wife and fellow ethnographer Rhoda Métraux in 1941, witnessed the campaign first-hand and would describe it in detail in his 1958 *Le vaudou haïtien*. He recounts seeing vast pyramids of drums, painted bowls, necklaces and talismans in the backyards of presbyteries "all awaiting the joyous blaze which was to symbolise the victory of the Church over Satan". He also recounts stories, told to him during his field work in the Marbial valley eight years later, of the "expeditions" led by Father Lavalas (meaning "torrent" or "cleansing flood"), so named because of the force by which he executed his mission. The *curé* and his followers uprooted all the large crosses in family cemeteries believing them to be symbols of Baron Samedi, "King of the Dead", and women accused of being *Loup-Garou* (werewolves) were dragged before the priest to be exorcised. *Bois servis* (sacred trees) were exorcised by the *curé* too, as the *rejetés* (renouncers of Vodou) hurled rocks at them. Anti-superstition handbooks written to guide the campaign specified that it was necessary to "truly destroy everything: to smash bottles, jugs, to tear up pictures, to pull up and burn poles and crosses, to take away stones, remove necklaces, crush the *cayes-lwas* (homes of the spirits), to cut down the *bois servis*, to profane all that which is

---

feature in post-occupation Haiti between so-called "folkloric dances" and their authentic counterparts. It seems that through the entire occupation period informal "licenses" for Vodou ceremonies were granted by the local officers of rural constabularies, the *chef de section*. Seabrook describes at length the circumstances around his attempt to secure such a license for his Petro initiation in *The Magic Island* (Seabrook (1929) 21-27).

served superstitiously".[41] Ramsey recounts how one *curé* took on his mission with such "frenzy" that he had a physical breakdown and began spitting up blood.[42]

Inspired by the so-called *Kanpay rejete* of the late 1930s (a wave of popular renunciation of Vodou by former practitioners), the Bishop of Gonaïves, Monsignor Paul Robert, wrote a pastoral letter pointing out the absolute incompatibility of religion and superstition (by which he meant "the collection of religious beliefs and practices that came from Africa").[43] The church subsequently drafted an anti-superstition oath which all Catholics were expected to swear, promising they would never give food offerings to the *lwa*, would destroy (or have destroyed) all "fetishes and objects of superstition" and would bring their children up exclusively in the Roman Catholic faith.[44] A special catechism was published declaring the *houngan* to be the "principle slave of Satan" and the *lwa* to be his manifestations. Reflecting awareness of current affairs in Europe, the church newspaper *La Phallange*, described the campaign as a "spiritual *blitzkrieg*".[45] Resistance to the anti-superstition campaign amongst the Mulatto elites seems have intensified when it spread from the countryside to the capital, and therefore from the peasants to the middle and upper classes of Haitian society, who reacted strongly to the indignity of having their faith questioned so publicly. After shots were fired outside a church in the Delmas suburb of Port-au-Prince where oaths were being administered, the Lescot government withdrew its support for the campaign.

---

41 Métraux 323-358

42 Ramsey (2011) 201

43 Ramsey (2011) 194-195, Nicholls 182, Métraux 339-340

44 Métraux 341. Métraux suggests that the anti-superstition campaign was in part an anti-Protestant one too (Métraux 351). Ramsey corroborates his claim, pointing to a version of the anti-superstition oath that included the promise never to become Protestant (Ramsey (2011) 197).

45 Nicholls 182

FOUNDING OF THE BUREAU OF ETHNOLOGY

> If the dead impose on us not only their physical constitution but also the pattern of our thought... by what absurd wager would one try to disengage our Haitian society from its racial origins four or five centuries ago.

> - Jean Price-Mars *So Spoke the Uncle* (1928)[46]

> Vodou is at once a religious and politico-social fact... To the degree that it's not too strong to say that the more one penetrates the mysteries, the more the history of Haiti will reveal her secrets.

> - Lorimer Denis and François Duvalier 'The Gradual Evolution of Vodou' (1944) [47]

Political life in post-occupation Haiti was characterised by an over-arching spirit of nationalism divided between two broad factions: those in favour of retaining the *status quo* of bourgeois, Mulatto hegemony and those seeking a greater shift in the distribution of wealth and power. In terms of the latter there were those who saw the problem primarily in terms of colour and race (the *Noiristes*) and those who saw it in terms of economics and class (the Socialists).[48] In 1925 a group of young *Noiristes* and Socialists formed *La Nouvelle Ronde* hoping to resuscitate the turn-of-the-century nationalist movement by drawing attention to the literary innovations of Black American and French writers and applying them to the Haitian situation. In 1927 they founded *La Revue Indigène*. A key figure on the Left was Jacques Roumain, imprisoned for subversive activities by President Sténio Vincent in 1933 before escaping to Europe, America and

---

46 Price-Mars (1983) 104

47 *L'evolution stadiale du Vodou: de la culture populaire et des origines ethniques du peuple haïtien* (The Gradual Evolution of Vodou: On the Popular Culture and Ethnic Origins of the Haitian People) (1944) quoted in Johnson 12.

48 Nicholls 165. See also Mathew J. Smith's *Red and Black in Haiti: Radicalism, Conflict and Political Change, 1934-1957* (2009) which traces the internal cultural politics of Haiti during this period.

Cuba (via Martinique).[49] While in exile Roumain consolidated his friendships with Langston Hughes, Richard Wright (the blacklisted actor and author of *Native Son* (1940) and the first author to use the expression "Black Power" in his 1954 book of the same name) and other pan-African writers and intellectuals associated with the Harlem Renaissance and the American Communist Party.[50] During the 1920s many Black intellectuals, especially those who had been educated in Europe and inspired by the "Black Surrealism" of writers like Aimé Césair, Jules Monnerot and Léopold Senghor, began to consider Vodou, much as Seabrook had done, as an authentic expression of the popular Black soul of the Haitian masses.[51]

The debate about Nationalism and Vodou was profoundly shaped by the central but complex role of race in the country's colonial and revolutionary history, and by the philosophical and political issues raised by 19th century race theory. In 1885 the Haitian anthropologist, journalist and politician Joseph Anténor Firmin published *De l'égalité des races humaines* (On the Equality of Human Races), a response to Arthur de Gobineau's *Essai sur l'inégalité des races humaines* (Essay on the inequality of the human races) from 1855, a formative work in the development of scientific racism.[52] A monarchist, dismayed by the political and social consequences of the French Revolution,

---

49 Smith 14-22, Fowler 204-211

50 Smith 21, 57, Fowler 142, 206

51 Métraux 343. See Richardson for a survey of the reciprocal relationship between Surrealism, the *Négritude* movement and Caribbean politics between 1932 and 1946. Jules Monnerot was a close colleague of Leiris' and Bataille's in the 1930s, and one of the founders of the College of Sociology (1937-39). He fell foul of his Surrealist comrades later in his life when his politics veered away from communism and towards the extreme right of the French National Front.

52 Gobineau, who explicitly used the example of Haiti as evidence of what happens when a Black nation introduces white forms of governance, was writing at the time of the government of Faustin Soulouque, the first post-revolutionary Haitian leader to be publicly associated with *le Vaudoux* (Ramsey (2011) 79). As Ramsey shows, it was during and after Soulouque's regime that disparaging accounts of Vodou by foreigners began to proliferate, such as the notorious *affaire de Bizoton,* exploited by Spenser St. John in his *Hayti, or the Black Republic* (Ramsey (2011) 80).

Gobineau, like Le Bon, argued that the human race can be divided into three major groups – Yellow, Black and White – and that history was solely the creation of the latter.[53] Blacks, he believed, were at the foot of a ladder of civilisation they could never climb.[54] The highest pinnacle of racial civilisation was Aryan aristocracy whose genealogy could be traced back to the biblical Adam. Inevitably, according to Gobineau, miscegenation would lead to the demise of White civilisation, citing Haiti as an example of what happens when European forms of government are imposed on people of an inferior race. Firmin, in response, proposed that all races were capable of great human achievement, advocating a fundamental universalism of human qualities and potentials and rejecting what he called the "biological fatalism" of race theorists like Gobineau.[55] Followers of Firmin, like Price-Mars, accepted a hereditary lineage connecting Haitians to peoples of Africa but rejected the assumption that such links had a determining effect in the fields of society, culture or politics.[56] The Griots on the other hand embraced Gobineau's theories arguing that psychological and socio-cultural characteristics differed considerably between European and African peoples and that the Haitian mentality was "unconsciously governed by African heredity".[57] Contrary to Gobineau however, they pointed to the splendours of previous African civilisations as evidence of the Black race's capacity for cultural achievement of the highest order. And echoing Le Bon, whose race theories had prompted Price-Mars to write *Ainsi parla l'oncle*, they proposed that the biology of a racial group determines the "collective personality" of its societies. The *Noiristes* rejected Marxism and the

---

53 According to René Depestre one of Duvalier's political influences was Joseph De Maistre, a key figure in the French counter-enlightenment, harsh critic of the French Revolution and staunch supporter of hereditary monarchism. In a meeting with Depestre in 1958 Duvalier described De Maistre as his "alter-ego" (Munro (2007) 82).

54 Nicholls 127. Nicholls notes that Gustave Le Bon proposed fundamental changes to the French colonial policy of assimilation based on the premise of fundamental racial differences.

55 Firmin 139, 145, Nicholls 129

56 Nicholls 130

57 Smith 24

egalitarian universalism of Firmin as race-specific forms of Creole, European and Francophone political thought.[58] Racial authenticity therefore lay at the heart of Griot ideology and, as Matthew Smith points out, Gobineau's idea that Africans were naturally inclined to paternalistic and despotic forms of governance would prove instructive for the later career of François "Papa Doc" Duvalier, as we will see.[59]

Despite the specific requirement that all objects of superstition be destroyed during the anti-superstition campaigns, many were secretly salvaged, Métraux himself managing to save a cache of artefacts which he had shipped to the United States to be deposited in the Smithsonian Institute. Shocked by the scale of the offensive, Métraux was convinced that Vodou would eventually be eradicated completely from the country. He was not alone in his fear. Jacques Roumain arrived back in Haiti in 1941 after several years of exile. He and Métraux met in July that year and subsequently travelled together on a one-month trip to Ile de la Tortue, off Haiti's northern coast, where together they witnessed the severity of the campaign.[60] In a number of articles for *Le Nouvelliste* Roumain vehemently criticised the anti-superstition campaigns and later that year he founded the Bureau D'Ethnologie de la République d'Haiti. As its first director he set about protecting and preserving Haiti's threatened cultural heritage. Élie Lescot, the president who had initially endorsed the anti-superstition campaign, publicly supported the new project, perhaps as a way to deflect accusations that he was the "co-author of [the campaign's] most deplorable excesses".[61] One of the first tasks of the bureau was to develop an ethnographic teaching programme based on a collection of artefacts salvaged from the anti-superstition campaign. One week later Price-Mars created a private, educational Institute of Ethnology that would also make use

58 Smith 27. Jean Price-Mars supported *Négritude*, the literary and ideological movement created by Aimé Césaire, which promoted international Black solidarity, but not the *Noirisme* of the Griots, which be believed would inevitably lead to despotism. For an overview of the *Négritude* movement, its historical relevance for Haitian politics and culture and its transformation into a "somatic metaphysics", see René Depestre's 'Hello and Goodbye to Negritude'.

59 Smith 25

60 Ramsey (2011) 212

61 André-Marcel D'Ans quoted in Ramsey (2011) 212

of the bureau's collection.[62] In the ensuing decades the bureau and institute became centres of a new *Mouvement Folklorique* in Haiti within which the *Indigénistes*, Griots and foreign ethnographers found a common ground for their mutual defence of Vodou as the essential and exceptional cultural characteristic of Haitian national and historical identity.

THE MYTHOPOESIS OF BOIS CAÏMAN

There is a scene in the film adaptation of Graham Greene's 1966 novel *The Comedians* where the artist nephew of the Minister for Social Welfare, whose body was found at the beginning of the story in the empty swimming pool of the Hotel Trianon, explains to the morose and faithless hotel-owner Brown that he is going to a Vodou ceremony that night to summon the African gods who will help him fight the Tonton Macoute and overthrow the Duvalier dictatorship.[63] The particular *lwa* to be summoned will be Ogoun Ferraille, the Dahomean warrior and metalworker spirit who, as we have seen, is syncretised in Vodou with Saint Jacques Majeur. "My grandmother came from Africa" young Philipot tells Brown proudly, "and her gods are the only ones that can help me now. I've pretended to be Western for too long". During the ceremony, in which a black cock is sacrificed by an unlikely-looking though reputedly authentic *houngan*, Joseph, the bartender from the Trianon, is possessed by the spirit of Ogoun. He sprays the terrified Philipot with rum and taps his palms and soles with the flat of a machete before the young painter is initiated into the cult.[64]

---

62 Ramsey (2011) 214

63 In the novel Brown, the narrator, notes an image of Duvalier on the *poteau mitan*: "Between us stood the pole of the temple, stuck up, like an aerial, to catch the passage of the gods. A whip hung there in memory of yesterday's slavery, and, a new legal requirement, a cabinet-photograph of Papa Doc, a reminder of today's." (Greene 178)

64 In a short promotional film made by MGM for *The Comedians – The Comedians in Africa* – the director Peter Glenville explains how the person who plays the part of the *houngan* was an actual Vodou priest, proudly proposing that there are authentic aspects of the secret rites in the film

Ogoun Ferraille, along with Erzulie Dantor, Mambo Marinette and Ti Jean Petro, are the four *lwa* most commonly associated with the Bois Caïman ceremony. Young Philipot's recourse to his mystical powers was represented by Greene as the desperate act of an innocent and misguided idealist who had succumbed to the romantic fantasy of "Revolutionary Vodou".[65] By the time of Papa Doc's reign of terror (between 1957 and 1971) the idea of Vodou's insurrectionary credentials had become an essential component of the foundation myth of African-Haitian nationalism. But for Greene, already deeply sceptical about the emancipatory value attributed to the religion after a visit there in 1963, Duvalier had cut short any potential paths for "Vodou liberation", containing them, and the nation, within his own mystical personality cult.

In the scholarly field of Haitian Studies scepticism about the role of Vodou in the Haitian war of independence is seen by some as a revisionary strategy in an ongoing racist and imperialist campaign to deny the historical truth about the religion and its world-changing powers.[66] For others, as we will see, the role of Vodou in Haiti's

---

that will never have been seen before. One such scene includes a shot of the *houngan* biting the head off a black rooster before sprinkling its blood on a vévé of a Vodou drum. The actor who played the *houngan* was in fact a Haitian painter from Paris called Max Pinchinat (Diederich 119). In 1977 Pinchinat had a gallery dedicated to his works in Port-au-Prince (*Black Enterprise* magazine Vol 7, no.9 1977, 34).

65 It is well known that at the time of writing *The Comedians* Greene was undergoing a profound crisis of faith which is expressed throughout the novel. His literary biographer Michael Brennan has noted that Duvalier's assumed adoption of the Baron Samedi persona, which seems to have been largely Greene's invention, represented for the author a "black comedy", in which Papa Doc personified an inverted Christianity from which there was neither escape nor redemption.

66 See for instance the artist, performer, playwright and human rights attorney formerly known as Marguerite Laurent, who, under the guidance and inspiration of her eponymous *lwa* Ezili Dantó, advocates for the Haitian Right to Self Defence decreed by the Goddess at Bois Caïman and for a Black-ruled, Boukman Prayer, and Eh Bomba! Chant inspired independent nation. See http://margueritelaurent.com (accessed 10/09/14).

revolutionary history is a romantic myth that is at best contradicted by historical fact, and at worst one of the reasons for Haiti's social and political under-development.[67] The myth of Haiti's African past, and the central role of Vodou in the construction of an authentic and unique cultural identity, came to the fore during the U.S. occupation and the rise of the *Indigéniste*, *Noiriste* and folkloric currents in Haitian cultural life in the decades that followed. By 1953 the Haitian historian and elder statesman Dantès Bellegarde would describe the Bois Caïman ceremony in ways that had by then become familiar to all elite-educated school children there:

> During the night of 14 August 1791 in the midst of a forest called Bois Caïman, on the Morne Rouge in the northern plain, the slaves held a large meeting to draw up a final plan for a general revolt. They consisted of about two hundred slave drivers, sent from various plantations in the region. Presiding over the assembly was a black man named Boukman, whose fiery words exalted the conspirators. Before they separated, they held amidst a violent rainstorm an impressive ceremony, so as to solemnize the undertakings they made. While the storm raged and lightning shot across the sky, a tall black woman appeared suddenly in the center of the gathering. Armed with a long, pointed knife that she waved above her head, she performed a sinister dance singing an African song, which the others, face down against the ground, repeated as a chorus. A black pig was then dragged in front of her and she split it open with her knife. The animal's blood was collected in a wooden bowl and served still foaming to each delegate. At a signal from the priestess, they all threw themselves on their knees and swore blindly to obey the orders of Boukman, who had been proclaimed the supreme chief of the rebellion. He announced as his

---

67 See for example Lawrence Harrison 'Haiti and the Voodoo Curse: The Cultural Roots of the Country's Endless Misery', *The Wall Street Journal*, February 5th, 2010. Harrison was the director of USAID in Haiti between 1977 and 1979 and author of *Underdevelopment is a State of Mind: The Latin-American Case* (2000).

choice of principal lieutenants Jean Francois Papillon, Georges Biassou, and Jeannot.[68]

Despite the general acceptance of the myth of Bois Caïman in most popular histories of the revolution, some historians have disputed whether the ceremony actually took place, and one in particular, Léon-François Hoffmann, proposed in 1991 that the story was fabricated by a malevolent French colonist and plantation physician, Antoine Dalmas, whose intention was to denigrate the slaves and distance the colonial elites from the African-born insurgents. Hoffmann's claims caused something of a scandal within the Haitian studies community at the time and the debate was rekindled by the publication of David Geggus' *Haitian Revolutionary Studies* in 2002.[69] After taking a thorough look at Hoffmann's claims, sources and alternative accounts, Geggus concluded that a ritual ceremony probably did take place sometime around August 21st, but that the facts pertaining to it,

---

68 From Bellegarde's *Histoire du Peuple Haïtien* (1953) quoted in Geggus. Bellegarde was an influential member of the *La Ronde* generation of writers and poets at the end of the 19th century. A politically liberal Mulatto, defender of French cultural values in Haiti, a nationalist critic of the U.S. occupation but also of the *Noiristes*, whose racial theories he felt undermined the unity of the country, Bellegarde also rejected the idea that Vodou could serve as a unifying spiritual force for an independent Haiti (Nicholls 176-177). Then Minister of Education, Bellegarde wrote the preface to Dorsainvil's 1925 *Manuel d'Histoire d'Haïti*, which contains the model for Bellegarde's account. (Magloire (1998) 15).

69 Daniel Simidor and Rachel Beauvoir-Dominique accuse Geggus and his colleagues of ignoring oral accounts of the event, versions symbolically encoded into Vodou ritual, pilgrimage traditions and local folklore, and of having a French bias (http://www2.webster.edu/~corbetre/haiti/history/revolution/caiman.htm (accessed 10/09/14)). Beauvoir-Dominique makes three significant claims towards the end of her criticism: i) that Morne Rouge, where the event purportedly took place, is the contemporary site of an important Islamic cult (Boukman, according to some, was a Muslim), ii) that contemporary informants claim that "Semi-Islamic" secret societies were responsible for "closing the circle" of the ceremony, and iii) that the *regleman* (ceremonial protocols) of Bois Caïman were based on those of Haitian secret societies (or "Makaya").

which are thin on the ground, have been significantly embellished by subsequent historians seeking to emphasise the African and slave-led currents within the revolution (and therefore at the foundation of the Haitian nation).

Antoine Dalmas' account of the events in *Histoire de la révolution de Saint-Domingue*, purportedly written two or three years after them but not published until 1814, is based on the testimony of three slaves captured after an initial, well-documented public gathering of coach-drivers and slave-drivers (the "slave elites") from one hundred different plantations at the Lenormand De Mézy estate on Sunday August 14th 1791. A smaller gathering allegedly took place a few days later in a wooded area called *La Caïman* (the Alligator) at which a pig was sacrificed, its blood drunk and its hairs taken to make protective amulets for the upcoming insurrection. According to Dalmas the captives said that the pig was "surrounded by fetishes" and sacrificed "to the all-powerful spirit [*genié*] of the black race". That such "an ignorant and besotted caste would make superstitious rituals of an absurd and sanguinary religion serve as a prelude to the most frightful crimes", Dalmas concluded, was only to be expected of them. And that was it. So how did the story of Bois Caïman develop from such a basic schematic account to the established myth we know today? And more specifically how did the characters Dutty Boukman (reputed *houngan*, rebel leader and author of the famous Boukman Prayer), the *mambo* Cécile Fatiman, the old sabre-wielding priestess and the *lwa* Erzulie Dantor, Ogoun Ferraille, Mambo Marinette, Ti Jean Petro, all find themselves cast into this *"operetta sanguinaire"* of Haitian independence?[70]

Geggus argues convincingly that two meetings, one large, open and public, the other smaller and clandestine, seem to have been conflated over time. Dalmas clearly distinguished between the two: a first at which plans for the rebellion were drawn up and a second, smaller gathering, shortly afterwards, at which a pig was sacrificed and its blood drunk. The second historical version of events, also allegedly based on eye-witness accounts, is Hérard Dumesle's *Voyage dans le nord d'Haïti* of 1824 which also distinguishes between the two meetings, the pig sacrifice occurring at the second. Dumesle was a

---

70 The term used by Haitian novelist Fernand Hibbert and quoted by Hoffmann (Hoffmann in Geggus and Fiering 341).

senator from the southern city of Les Cayes and his version, according to Geggus, seems to have drawn on local oral history, taking the form of a poetic invocation rather than an historical description, and embellished with Hellenic rather than African mythical references. Poetic license seems to have allowed him to introduce a "young virgin" who used the pig's entrails for divination. Dumesle was also the first to include a prayer to *Bondye* (God), presumably crafted by the author and only attributed to Boukman thirty years later:

> "...This God who made the sun,
> who brings us light from above,
> who raises the sea, and who makes the storm rumble,
> That God is there, do you understand?
> Hiding in a cloud, He watches us,
> he sees all that the whites do!
> The God of the whites pushes them to crime,
> but he wants us to do good deeds.
> But the God who is so good orders us to vengeance;
> He will direct our hands, and give us help,
> Throw away the image of the God of the whites who
> thirsts for our tears,
> Listen to the liberty that speaks in all our hearts."[71]

Hoffmann alleges that Dumesle's account owes much to a fanciful version of events described by a radical French abolitionist called Civique de Gastine, who published an account in Paris in 1819. It was this text that introduced the anti-Christian tone to the proceedings, dramatising them with a storm, the divination of entrails and the sworn oath. It may also have been influenced by another Frenchman, Antoine Métral, whose 1818 *Histoire de l'insurrection des esclaves dans le Nord de Saint-Domingue* introduced an oration and a young priestess. Not until French abolitionist Victor Schœlcher's *Les colonies étrangéres dans l'Amérique et Haiti* (1840) does Boukman appear in Dumesle's scenario, but at the first meeting at Lenormand rather

---

71 Geggus 78-79. Thylefors notes how a local *Vodouisant* in Port-au-Prince in 2004 recited a version of the oath in which God or *Bondye* is associated with the "God of the whites" and *Granmèt* with the "God of the Blacks" (Thylefors 80).

than the second at Caïman.[72] The Bois Caïman oath is not directly attributed to Boukman until the third plausible eye-witness account of the ceremony, Céligny Ardouin's *Essais sur l'histoire d'Haïti* (1853), which includes oral testimony gathered from 1837 onwards, notably from the ex-soldier Paul Ali who he interviewed in 1841.[73] In Ardouin's account however there is no evidence of Boukman being a Vodou priest, a widely held and popular belief both within and outside of Haiti, the ceremony reputedly presided over instead by an unidentified priestess.[74] A fourth, and much later account, Étienne Charlier's *Aperçu sur le formation historique de la nation haïtienne* (1954), was passed on to the author by the grandson of Cécile Fatiman, wife of the Haitian general and president Louis Pierrot, which casts his grandmother, a woman of mixed Corsican and African descent, as the unidentified priestess in the proceedings. No more details were given. This seems to be the single, formal historical source regarding Cécile Fatiman's reputed presence at the ceremony.

So up until 1853 the basic historical details of the Bois Caïman ceremony were: i) a small, secret meeting of rebel slaves at a place called Caïman somewhere on the Choiseul estate on the Plain du Nord, ii) the reputed presence of the rebel leader Dutty Boukman, iii) a pig "surrounded by fetishes" sacrificed to the "God of the Blacks" and its blood drunk, iv) its hairs taken as protective amulets for the forthcoming insurrection and v) the reputed presence of a young priestess (later identified as Cécile Fatiman). The Boukman prayer, its author's status as a *houngan*, the anti-Christian tone of the proceedings, the lightning storm and the reading of the pig's entrails, all appear to be embellishments sprung from the romantic fancies of abolitionist Frenchmen, post-occupation Haitian nationalists and indigenous Vodou lore (mostly gathered long after the event). The

---

72 Schœlcher was in fact highly critical of what was known in Haitian law at the time as *les sortilèges*, blaming it, in part, for the deplorable state of the nation under President Boyer (Ramsey (2011) 65).

73 Geggus 88-89

74 Geggus points out that there is no formally documented evidence of Boukman being either a *houngan* or a Maroon leader, two common claims which seem to be the product of French Romanticism and indigenous lore. The claim is made by many authors including Deren, Dorsainvil, Fouchard, Heinl and Heinl, and Nicholls.

claim that Boukman announced the names of his lieutenants at the meeting seems to be largely Bellegarde's invention.

So how did this story come to be consolidated as the Vodou foundation myth of Haitian nationalism in the 20th century despite the lack of substantial, historical evidence for it? To answer this question we need to fast forward to the *Indigéniste* reaction to the U.S. occupation of Haiti between 1915 and 1935. It was then, as we have seen, that the first serious ethnographic and speculative historical accounts of Vodou began to be written. Throughout most of the 19th century descriptions of "Vaudoux" tended to be of an extremely negative and sensationalist kind, its presence considered a blight of African atavism that condemned Haiti to irredeemable barbarism. There does not seem to have been a remotely sober account of the religion published between Moreau de Saint-Méry's description of a "Vaudoux" ceremony in his encyclopaedic survey of Saint-Domingue from 1797 and Duverneau Trouillot's 1885 *Esquisse ethnographique: Le Vaudoun apercu historique et evolutions*, the first formal ethnographic account of the religion.[75] And it was this conspicuous lacuna regarding the actual practices and beliefs of Vodou that the authors associated with the *Indigéniste* movement set about rectifying during the occupation.

Written when he was an official in the ministry of education, Dorsainvil's *Manuel d'histoire d'Haiti*, which contains the first official, government-sanctioned account of the Bois Caïman ceremony, refers to the revolutionary *"intelligence délié"* (non-linear intelligence) of Louverture, Boukman and Biassou which was transmitted to the slaves during the rite.[76] In it Boukman is identified as a Jamaican-

---

75 Price-Mars (1983) 140 n.131 Eugene Aubin's description of "Voodoo" temples and spirits in *En Haïti: Planteurs d'autrefois, nègres d'aujourd'hui* of 1910 is also an important early corrective to the misrepresentations.

76 Dorsainvil quoted in La Martine 79. The notion of non-linear intelligence is an interesting one for debates about how the plantation slaves, most of whom spoke no French, could become conscious of their "revolutionary destiny" in the *universal enlightenment* sense transmitted from France. Dorsainvil's concept of an *intelligence délié* seems to be a way of reconciling the apparent contradiction. For an analysis of the historical and philosophical problem of the Haitian slave's understanding of "universal human rights" see Nesbitt's *Universal Emancipation: The Haitian Revolution and the Radical Enlightenment* (2008). Nesbitt makes

born *"N'gan"* of Vodou, "the principle religion of Dahomeans", who gathered a large number of slaves in a clearing in the Alligator Woods, close to Mourne-Rouge (Red Mountain) to recite his prayer.[77] During a raging storm, an old Negress appeared, dancing and waving a great cutlass around her head, plunging it into the pig and distributing its blood to the attendants. The story was re-told in Price-Mars' *Ainsi parla l'oncle*, which included the embellishments of a *mapou* tree (a tree sacred to Vodou rites), "cabalistic signs" drawn on the ground by a priestess, the sacrifice of a wild boar, the reading of its entrails and a rendition of the Boukman prayer.[78] Haitian novelist and biographer of Toussaint Louverture Stephen Alexis composed a lurid version of the events in which Boukman wore a red robe, carried a glittering sword, and sacrificed a gazelle, a pig and goat, all of which were disembowelled and their entrails poured out so that Boukman's followers could plunge their hands into them.[79]

---

only one reference to Vodou in this context, which he claims, citing Michel Laguerre, "contributed to both a nascent Haitian conception of a universal right to freedom and a corollary awareness of a specificity of the experience of exploitation and suffering under slavery" (Nesbitt 43). But he does not identify any aspects of Vodou practice or cosmology that would support the proposal. Laguerre's claim, which Nesbitt footnotes, is that Vodou was a language for expressing and resisting cultural assimilation and "the focus for the development of political consciousness so far as it allowed the slaves to be aware that their values were different from those of the whites" (Laguerre 70). But like Nesbitt, Laguerre does not identify any specific aspects of Vodou ritual to support his claim except that it was an expression of the "collective memory of slaves" in which African cultural traditions were "preserved and perpetuated" (Laguerre 70). Beyond this expression of an awareness of cultural and epidermal differences between the slaves and their masters, which was presumably readily apparent, no claims are made by either author for any nascent, revolutionary function of Vodou other than the often repeated claim, derived from Drouin De Bercy via Moreau de Saint-Méry, that the slaves "usually sang" an anti-White song – the famous "Eh! Bomba!" chant during Vodou initiation ceremonies (Laguerre 69).

77 Dorsainvil quoted in La Martine 79

78 Price-Mars 47

79 McAlister in Polyné 204

The first Anglophone author to transmit Dorsainvil's version of events to an English-speaking public was, once again, William Seabrook, who cites the section of the *Manual* verbatim in the footnotes of *The Magic Island*. He also quotes at length from a lecture he attended in 1924 at which Dorsainvil discussed the African roots of Haitian Vodou, correlating its philology and pantheon with contemporary and historical Dahomean culture and emphasising the revolutionary role of the Vodou cult:

> The colonists tolerated all the noisy dances of the slaves, but feared the Voodoo ceremonies. They instinctively feared this cult with its mysterious air and felt confusedly that it might be a powerful element of cohesion for the slaves. They were not mistaken, for it was from the bosom of a Voodoo ceremony that the great revolt of the Santo Domingo slaves began.[80]

In keeping with his theory of possession as a racial psychoneurosis (and echoing Saint-Méry's descriptions of the "Vaudoux" rites), Dorsainvil proposed that the attendants at the Bois Caïman ceremony were inspired to believe in their invulnerability through a form of (hypnotic) auto-suggestion. In *So Spoke the Uncle* Price-Mars describes Bois Caïman as a "wholly voodooistic ceremony" from which, "during thirteen years of violence, of privations, or torture", the Negroes drew their faith, enabling them to "confront death and achieve the miracle of 1804".[81] Dorsainvil and Price-Mars seem to be the principle source of the accepted myth about the revolutionary role of Vodou at Bois Caïman for Anglo-American authors after Seabrook, not least C. L. R. James, whose 1938 version of events in *The Black Jacobins* includes an amended Boukman prayer imploring the slaves to throw away the symbol (rather than the image) of the god of the Whites. In his essay 'The Belief System of Haitian Vodoun' (1945) George Eaton Simpson cites Dorsainvil as his principle source, and Maya Deren, in *Divine Horsemen: The Living Gods of Haiti* (1953), cites Simpson in turn, repeating the inclusion of the old Black woman who performs the sacrifice. Alfred Métraux quotes the Bois Caïman section from

---

80 Dorsainvil quoted in Seabrook (1929) 291 and 312-313

81 Price-Mars (1983) 155

Dorsainvil in its entirety in *Voodoo in Haiti*.[82] Métraux includes an important opening sentence from Dorsainvil's account: "To put an end to all holding back and to obtain absolute devotion, he [Boukman] brought together a great number of slaves". The notion of "absolute devotion" is a recurrent one in such accounts echoing the concern expressed by Moreau de Saint-Méry about the relation between the "Vaudoux" kings and queens and their followers:

> Once this system of domination on the one side and of
> blind submission on the other is established, the leaders
> set times and dates for future assemblies.[83]

Like C. L. R. James and Michel Laguerre, Aimé Césaire will also claim that the African slaves chanted a favourite song during the uprising:

> Eh! Eh! Bomba! Heu! Heu!
> Canga, bafio té!
> Canga, mouné de lé!
> Canga, do ki la!
> Canga, do ki la!
> Canga, li![84]

Following Price-Mars' example both authors translated the chant as "We swear to destroy the whites and all that they possess; let us die rather than fail to keep this vow".[85] The chant, originally cited but un-translated by Moreau de Saint-Méry in his 1797 description of a

---

82 Métraux 42

83 Moreau de Saint-Méry (1985) 2

84 "One does not need education or encouragement to cherish the dream of freedom. At their midnight celebrations of Voodoo, their African cult, they danced and sang, usually this favourite song" (James 18).

85 Price-Mars (1983) 111. Césaire suggested the chant was sung at the Bois Caïman ceremony itself (Césaire 178). However, as Geggus points out, not only is this an entirely speculative claim, but the best literal translation of the chant, which seems to be a magical binding chant dedicated to a Kongo deity called Mbumba, is:

"Vaudoux" ceremony, seems to have first been translated into French by Drouin de Bercy in his *De Saint-Domingue* of 1814 as: "We swear to destroy the whites and everything they own, will die rather than renounce our oath".[86] It is to this explicitly anti-Vodou source that Price-Mars owes the translation that would be taken up by James and Césaire. According to James, who seems have derived the idea from Dorsainvil and Price-Mars, via De Bercy, the colonists knew this song and tried to stamp it out along with the Vodou cult with which it was linked. "In vain" he writes "For over two hundred years the slaves sang it at their meetings, as the Jews in Babylon sang of Zion, and the Bantu today sing in secret the national anthem of Africa".[87] By the 1960s then, as a consequence of the ideological re-imagining of events that attempted to put an essentially Black, African and emancipatory "Vodoun intelligence" back at the centre of the nation's revolutionary origins, the Boukman Prayer and Eh! Bomba! Chant had become established components of the popular myth of the Bois Caïman ceremony and the revolution it inaugurated.

Eh, serpent Mbumba
Stop the blacks
Stop the whites
Stop the ndoki
Stop them. (Geggus 79)

86 De Bercy's book was written to support France's plans to re-invade Haiti and re-introduce slavery there. In a footnote Price-Mars questions de Bercy's translation claiming that the words "Aia bombé" are of Taino origin and noting that King Henri Christophe had made the song a national anthem (Price-Mars (1983) 111).

87 James 18. James' use of the myths of both the Boukman Oath, and the Eh! Bomba! Chant were part of a more general political imperative to construct the Haitian Revolution as a template for Black Socialist emancipation on an international scale.

SUMMONING THE LWA OF INSURRECTION

But how did particular *lwa* come to be associated with the ceremony? The answer seems to lie in the blossoming of ethnographic interest in Haitian Vodou inspired by Dorsainvil, Holly, Price-Mars and others that culminated in the founding of the Bureau of Ethnology in 1941. As more knowledge of the rites, traditions and belief systems of actual Haitian Vodou was acquired, so authors and intellectuals interested in its African roots began to speculate on what kind of rite might have been enacted at Bois Caïman. Meanwhile increased international ethnographic interest in Vodou that flourished from the 1930s to 1950s led to a rare period in pre-Duvalier Haiti when the strict legal prohibitions on the cult were temporarily relaxed and the traditional religion became one of the nation's state-sanctioned tourist attractions. This in turn seems to have coincided with a growing pan-African and nascent, international Black Power movement for which the Haitian Revolution was a source of historical inspiration and racial pride. From these perspectives the specific ritual and historical details of the rite enacted at Bois Caïman became an object of explicitly political and ideological significance in pre-Duvalier Haiti.

The only recurring details in the eye-witness accounts of the Bois Caïman ceremony were, as we have seen, the name of the location, a gathering of revolutionary slaves and the sacrifice of a black pig "surrounded by fetishes" and dedicated to "the god of the blacks" whose blood was drunk. These latter elements are the basis for most speculation about the religious nature of the gathering. There are two dominant and contradictory ethnological interpretations: one that sees it as a Dahomean blood rite, binding the participants to secrecy and "absolute obedience" to their leaders, and another that sees it as a sacrificial Petro rite invoking various violent, warrior *lwa*.[88] Dorsainvil

---

88 A third, less widely accepted version of events proposes that a conglomeration of "dark matter entities" associated with the Makaya-Simbi cult was created in a special Petro-Zandor rite. In this version of events, Marinette-Pié-Chèche, along with other lesser known deities (Ti-Jean Petro, Krabinay, Simbi-Yan-Kita, Mondongue Moussai, and Prince Zandor), became part of a revolutionary "egregor" (or mystical grouping) that has yet to be appeased. During the ceremony Boukman reputedly

seems to be the source of the first interpretation, a view shared by Price-Mars, Métraux and others, and one consolidated by Herskovits's comparative ethnography of African and Haitian traditions in the 1930s and '40s. According to Robin Law, a contemporary authority on the issue, in Dahomey such rites were binding pacts that ensured solidarity, unlimited confidence and secrecy amongst those involved.[89] At times these included the sacrifice of a pig. Given that such oaths had been associated with earlier slave uprisings in the Caribbean and that the Fon (from the Dahomey/Benin region) were more established in northern Saint-Domingue than the Congolese, this seems like a plausible interpretation.

It has not been universally accepted however because pig sacrifice is not practiced in contemporary Rada ceremonies, the rites associated with Dahomean traditions in Haiti. This has led several authors to speculate that the ceremony was a Petro (i.e. Congo) rite, whose *lwa* are considered more malevolent, angry and war-like than those of the Rada rite. Such interpretations seem to be based primarily on the findings of modern Vodou ethnography. Maya Deren, for example, confidently claimed the ceremony as a Petro rite because of the pig sacrifice. The *lwa* of the Petro pantheon, to whom pigs are often dedicated, she described as embodiments of a "cosmic rage" against the fate Africans suffered because of slavery.[90] The association of the violent Petro *lwa* with the spirit of insurrection, combined with the sacrifice of a black pig, suggests that the rite may have been dedicated to Erzulie Dantor, the fiery and violently protective mother deity, syncretised after the revolution with the Black Madonna of Częstochowa, whose favourite offering is a black pig.[91] Deren repeats the

---

entered into a Zandoric "composite state" with the human sacrifice Jean-Baptiste Vixamar Legrand "whose blood was drunk like that of the sacrificed hog" (Crosley 234). Vixamar Legrand subsequently became a powerful *lwa* in the Petro Zandor rite in which he is known as 'Guard of the Bizango'. (Crosley 178). The source of the Petro Zandor and Vixamar Legrand legends appears to be Mercedes Foucard Guignard's *Le Légende des Loas: Vodou Haitien* (1993).

89 See Robin Law 'La cérémonie du Bois Caïman et 'le pacte de sang' dahoméen' (2010).

90 Deren 62-63

91 Erzulie Dantor's association with the Black Madonna presumably began after the cult of the Black Madonna of Częstochowa was brought

claim, originally made by Odette Mennesson-Rigaud and Lorimer Denis in an essay written for the *Journal of the Bureau of Ethnology* in 1947, that "even today the song of revolt 'Vive la Liberté' occurs in Petro ritual as a dominant theme".[92]

The figure of Marinette, another violent, female deity from the Petro pantheon, mystical wife of Ti Jean Petro and close in spirit to Erzulie Ge-Rouge, also seems to have entered the myth through an association of allegorical elements combined with the story over time. Marinette is identified in Haitian Vodou with the Catholic figure of *Anima Sola* whose broken chains are a clear symbolic reference to the breaking free from slavery. Deren associates Marinette with the old cutlass-waving woman who appears in Dorsainvil's 1925 account, suggesting that this was perhaps the first Mambo Marinette (or the first person to have been possessed by her). But only after Étienne Charlier's *Aperçu sur le formation historique de la nation haïtienne* in 1954 did the old Black woman potentially possessed by the *lwa* Marinette become retrospectively associated with the reputed *mambo* Cécile Fatiman. The presence of a young virgin priestess has been part of the legend since 1818, and the old Black woman seems to have been formally introduced by Dorsainvil in 1924. Cécile Fatiman however is usually described as a light-skinned *mulâtresse*.[93]

More recent ethnographic research by Rachel Beauvoir-Dominique and Eddy Lubin, critical of the "Cartesian logic" of Dalmas' report, points out that August 14th, the date of the first meeting – and for some of the Bois Caïman ceremony itself – is the annual feast day of Erzulie Kawoulo, a spirit associated with secret societies and popularly believed amongst *Vodouisants*, they claim, to be the *lwa* that possessed the priestess at the ceremony.[94] It is a feast day shared with Notre-Dame

---

to Saint-Domingue by Polish soldiers who were part of Napoleon's legions in Haiti before defecting to the side of the rebels. The few remaining members of the Polish battalion were some of the only Whites spared after their purging in the massacres which followed the Declaration of Haitian Independence in 1804 (Heinl and Heinl 117-119).

92 Deren 62

93 Dayan 47 *Mulâtresse* is the French colonial expression for a woman of African and European descent.

94 Ramsey (2011) 43

de l'Assomption, patron saint of the colony after whom the cathedral in Cap-Français was named, and a festival celebrated by slaves before the revolution, notably Christianised slaves from Congo. August 15th is the contemporary date for honouring Kongo *lwa*, including Papa Ogou at Nan Soukri in Gonaïves.[95] Such calendrical correlations seem to suggest that Catholic saints had as significant a role in the ceremony as "the gods of the blacks", an interpretation complimented by revolutionary leaders like Macaya and Romaine Rivière ('Romaine la Prophétesse'), who reputedly received military instruction directly from the Virgin Mary.[96] But there is no concrete historical evidence to substantiate any of the ethnographic claims that particular *lwa* were summoned at Bois Caïman, or that the rite was primarily Congo, Fon, Nago, Rada, Petro or another, more secret, rite. Furthermore, the correlation of specific Vodou *lwa* with established Catholic saints also points to a distinctly Christian, rather than purely African influence, on the revolutionary spirit of the slave masses, and, as the example of Saint Jacques Majeur clearly demonstrates, history supplies us with many examples of Catholic saints that have been summoned to inspire the downtrodden masses to rise up in mystery-driven warfare against their oppressors.

Whatever interpretation we give to the Bois Caïman ceremony, it will necessarily be speculative given the lack of historical evidence, the scant knowledge of the actual religious and cultural practices of African and Creole slave communities prior to the revolution, and their cultural suppression throughout most of the 19th century. What is more certain is that the creation of the myth of Bois Caïman during this period, and its popular consolidation by the middle of the 20th century, served explicitly ideological and hegemonic purposes: to rescue from potential historical oblivion the central role of African slaves in the most successful slave revolt of modern history, to put Vodou at the heart of Haitian national unity and identity, to associate it with revolutionary prowess and to culturally re-enfranchise the peasant and poor urban majority who were predominantly imagined

---

95 See Rey for a survey of the Kongolese Catholic influences on Haitian Vodou, not least the cult of Saint James which had already become associated with the African spirit of Ogun before Congolese slaves arrived in Saint-Domingue (Rey 272-273).

96 Ramsey (2011) 45

to be "in the service of the spirits". In the process of attempting to reconcile African mysticism with pan-African Black Nationalism and International Socialism, the role of Christian eschatological currents seems to have been largely written out of the story, despite the reputed involvement of African spirits of revolution working through and with them. More recently however the myth of Bois Caïman has been used to endorse Black Christian Liberation Theology as a discourse of "black freedom from below".[97]

SACRIFICE, FETISHISM AND THE BLACK GOD OF LIBERTY

The animal dies. But the death of the animal is the becoming of consciousness.

- Georges Bataille 'Hegel, Death and Sacrifice' (1955)[98]

Something which we must never tire of saying to the people is that liberty, reason, truth are only abstract beings. They are not gods, for properly speaking, they are part of ourselves.

- Antoine-François Momoro, "First Printer of Liberty" (1793)

Stories about the presence of *fetishes*, and by inference of *fetishism*, amongst the pre-revolutionary slaves of Saint-Domingue have unavoidable racist and Eurocentric meanings in the context of what Michel-Rolph Trouillot has described as the "unthinkability" of the Haitian Revolution amongst the majority of scholars at the time. One philosopher who chose to *not* think through the consequences of the Haitian Revolution was Hegel, an eminent modern thinker who played a significant role the development of the concept of fetishism and its elevation into a universal category of human cognitive evolution. Hegel inherited the concept from the Dutch merchant Willem Bosman who,

---

97 See Aristide and Joseph.

98 Bataille and Strauss 9

while working for the Dutch East India Company, used it to describe serpent worship at the slave port of Ouidah in Benin, West Africa in 1703. The presence of fetishism in stories about the Haitian Revolution was often used to propose an irrational account of the psychology of the slaves, one driven by a "primitive mentality" that destined the slaves to superstition and its political expression, "Primitive Despotism", rather than "Enlightened Republicanism".[99] It is a formula that continues to haunt foreign perceptions of Haiti, having found a recent contemporary expression in evangelical Christian stories that the earthquake of 2010 was punishment inflicted by God for a pact with Satan made at Bois Caïman.[100]

Scholarly debate about the historical construction of the dichotomous pair "primitive" and "civilized" has a long and august history, and the concept of fetishism has had a central role to play, closely associated with the often mutually re-inforcing concept of *animism* (i.e. the assumption that a vital, incorporeal soul can be attributed to inanimate things). Both words came to define the psychology of peoples assumed to be less cognitively developed than modern Europeans. As the case of Bosman shows, the term fetishism in its modern sense develops out of trading relations between Africans and Europeans from the 16th to 18th centuries, a period in which the transatlantic slave trade brought millions of Africans to the Americas. Over two centuries of global trade the word's meaning shifted from one used to identify European witchcraft artefacts (and objects of "false-faith") to one describing material goods that were subject to irrational and ritualistic processes

---

99 The concept of a "primitive mentality" is associated with the writings of the French philosopher and ethnologist Lucien Lévy-Bruhl whose *Les fonctions mentale dans les sociétiés inférieures* (1910), translated in 1926 as *How Natives Think*, was to have a significant impact on theories of primitivism within 20th century Modernist art practices and debates about "Negro Arts". According to Lévy-Bruhl the thinking of "primitive peoples" is *pre-logical*, in the sense that it does not conform to the rules of modern, European thought, and *mystical*, because it involves belief in, and participation with, "supra-sensible" forces. See Lucien Lévy-Bruhl *The 'Soul' of the Primitive* (1965).

100 McAlister, Elizabeth 'From Slave Revolt to a Blood Pact with Satan: The Evangelical Rewriting of Haitian History' (2013)

of evaluation by Africans.[101] The shift can be generally understood as a consequence of an increasingly rationalist, scientific and Enlightened world-view that sought to relegate superstition, "blind faith" and the chimeras of "magical thinking" to earlier, "savage" stages of universal, civilized progress. It was on the basis of early accounts of African culture, written by those involved in the trade, that Charles de Brosses developed a general theory of fetishism to describe an ethnological category of magical belief shared by West Africans and Egyptians. His *Du culte des dieux fétiches* of 1760 was the beginning of a universal theory which, under the influence of Darwinism a century later, would identify fetishism as a characteristic of a primitive, developmental phase in the evolution of all religious thinking proper, and a practice associated explicitly with Africans who, by implication, were assumed to be less developed in evolutionary, cultural and cognitive terms. For Hegel, the philosopher of the universal unfolding of the Spirit of History, fetishism was associated with a stage of human consciousness immediately prior to its properly *historical* form. It was "precisely that object of the spirit that failed to participate in the idea, which never experienced a dialectical negation and *aufhebung* to a truth beyond its natural materiality".[102] Hegel repeated Bosman's claim that Africans would make a fetish of "the first thing that comes their way", be that "an animal, tree, stone or wooden figure". He used the concept specifically to argue that Africa was "unhistorical", that the African mind lacked the category of "the Universal", was "pre-dialectical" and, consequently, that Africans were led to "absolute dependence" on Kings and Priests. In other words, fetishism was a mode of thinking that characterised those unable to achieve the level of abstract and conceptual thought necessary to realise and comprehend the higher purposes of the One God and the "Empire of Right".[103] It was a belief that was to prove particularly enduring and influential in the 19th century, when attacks on Haitian democracy questioned the fitness of the liberated African slaves for enlightened self-governance. By the middle of the 19th century then, just as Marx was about to use it to account for the alienation of human labour in the age of machines and

---

101 See William Pietz 'The Problem of the Fetish, I' (1985), 'II' (1987), 'IIIa' (1988).

102 Pietz (1985) 8

103 Hegel (1956) 94

the "magical" conversion of qualitative labour into abstract (exchange) value, the concept of fetishism had developed into a complex and multi-purposed notion with a number of generic and broadly irrational characteristics of thinking: the fallacy of misplaced concreteness; the misattribution of spiritual and causal powers to inanimate things and immaterial beings; idolatrous delusion; and an ambiguous relation of control between persons and objects.

From the first accounts of the Bois Caïman ceremony to those taught to school children in Haiti today, the sacrifice of a black pig to the "God of the Blacks" and the collective drinking of its blood to bind the oath of revolutionary insurrection are essential elements of the story. The central role of the pig sacrifice in every representation points to a problem at the philosophical core of *Undead Uprising*: that is the revolutionary value, meaning and efficacy of ritual blood sacrifice and its place within a modern political theory of progressive social change.

As Price-Mars and others have shown, the religious practice of sacrifice has been used to serve a number of different purposes in different cultures and circumstances. Most generally they are the propitiation of, communion with, homage to and participation in the life of a deity, and the intercommunication between the profane and sacred worlds.[104] All of these were understood and recognised by Georges Bataille as means of accessing a sacred dimension of communion-communication (or what he called *animal intimacy*) that had been almost entirely lost in modern secular societies. But, according to Price-Mars and others, sacrifice was also the means by which a community or individual demonstrated devotion to divine and super-natural beings *beyond and superior to themselves*. As such they conform to a theistic conception of universal creativity, force and order, something which Bataille's philosophy was profoundly opposed to. His was a radically *atheistic* conception of the sacred in which animal sacrifice puts participants in contact with the violent, disastrous and torrential indifference of a limitless (Godless) universe.[105] But the coincidence

---

104 Price-Mars (1983) 136

105 Bataille (1986) 62. Perhaps the most significant expression of Bataille's thinking on this issue is a section of a study on the thought of Alexander Kojève, the Russian émigré philosopher who introduced Bataille to the

of a revolutionary theory of sacrifice, such as Bataille pursued in *Acéphale* and the College of Sociology, and the mythopoetic re-writing of the Bois Caïman ceremony by Haitian scholars in the ensuing decades, points to a trans-historical knot that connects these seemingly very distant revolutionary myths of "sacrifice" and "racial holocaust".

In the hands of *Noiriste* writers like Carl Brouard, Lorimer Denis and François Duvalier in the 1930s and '40s, the centrality of the pig sacrifice was a way of putting Vodou – the "hereditary" religion of (Black) Africans – at the centre of a National creation myth intended to counter Eurocentric versions of the Haitian Revolution that saw it primarily as the post-colonial legacy of French Republicanism disseminated to the Black slaves by White revolutionaries. In so doing they needed to emphasise the sacrificial nature of the ceremony, a gesture which emphasises the *pagan* nature of the founding rite, the "participation mystique" of the conspirators, and their "blind" religious and military devotion to their deities, ancestors and leaders.[106] As Price-Mars put it, "it was through an actual bloody sacrifice that the strife was inaugurated in their camp and assumed the mystical character which the chiefs steadfastly retained until victory was won".[107] A certain "Vodou mystique" then, very close in nature to the notion of fetishism as it was constructed by European thinkers in the 19th century, was used to account for the hypnosis-like relationship between the slave revolutionaries, their leaders and the animating spirits of their African gods.

Such theories developed alongside the emergent discourses of ethnology, ethnography, anthropology and group psychology within which debates about racial difference had a central role. Nineteenth century Haitian intellectuals like Anténor Firmin were actively engaged in these debates. Following the lessons of social philosophers from Aristotle, through Bentham and Kant, to Comte, Tylor and Spencer,

---

work of Hegel, first published in 1955 under the title 'Hegel, Death and Sacrifice'.

106 The term is Lévy-Bruhl's, used to describe a mystical tie between persons and objects in which the distinction between them becomes impossible to distinguish. As we have seen, this is a defining characteristic of a general theory of fetishism too.

107 Price-Mars (1983) 137

Firmin challenged the claim that Blacks were unable to rise above the condition of fetishism and totemism, taking to task contemporary French social scientists like Georges Pouchet, author of *De la pluralité des Races Humaines* (1858), who had argued that monotheism was a racially determined belief system that Central Africans, Australians and people from "the northern lands" were unable to achieve, and that the subsequent "moral inequality" of the human races was an established scientific fact.[108] Although Firmin considered the White race the most culturally evolved at the time, pioneering a progressive and positive scientific path that all races would follow, this was not due to any innate inequality between the races but a consequence of historical contingency.[109] Moreover Black cultural development had been significantly limited by the transatlantic slave trade, the ideological interests of which were served directly by spurious scientific theories of hereditary and racial inferiority. Consequently Firmin strongly criticised those Europeans who accused Black slaves of intellectual inferiority while forgetting the methods used to keep them from developing their fully human potentials.[110] Like the British anthropologist E. B. Tylor, who argued that survivals of outmoded social practices continue as superstitions in modern societies, Firmin challenged the idea that fetishism was a "special product of the African mind". He dismissed such claims as false on both empirical and logical grounds, arguing that fetishistic cults had existed amongst all human races, not least the Greeks and Romans, "two of the most intelligent peoples in ancient history". Firmin also challenged the portrayal of Blacks as a more temperamentally cruel and bloody race, particularly

---

108 Firmin 43. Anténor Firmin, one of three Haitian members of the Paris Anthropology Society, published *The Equality of the Human Races (Positivist Anthropology)* in Paris in 1885. It remained uncommented on by the society and generally ignored by 20th century historians until it was re-published in 2000. See Carolyn Fluehr-Lobban, 'Anténor Firmin and Haiti's Contribution to Anthropology'.

109 Firmin 355. "This unique level of development is due not to any particular virtue of the race, but to its constant effort to develop its natural abilities. The White race has journeyed along a progressive path which all other human groups must follow." In this sense Firmin seems to be in accord with Hegel.

110 Firmin 333

accusations made about their inherent propensity to cannibalism and human sacrifice, pointing out examples of similar atrocities committed by the White race like the Inquisition, the Albigensian crusade and slave trade, and noting records of cannibalistic practices in the pre-history of different races, including the European. Similarly, he argued, there was ample evidence in the historical records that human sacrifice had been practiced by many races, including the Hebrews, Greeks, Romans and Scandinavians.[111] Opposing the racial theories of Gobineau, Pouchet and Paul Broca (founder and secretary of the Society of Anthropology in Paris, of which Firmin was a member) he showed that people of African descent had proven themselves proficient in a range of artistic and academic disciplines, thus refuting hereditary race theory by example.[112] And in response to the perceived errors in the pseudo-scientific theory of essential racial inferiority and superiority, Firmin proposed a broad integrative science of anthropology that would include the disciplines of "ethnography" (the description of peoples) and "ethnology" (the systematic study of the same people from the perspective of race) and "anthropology" proper, which concerns itself with the true nature of man in his difference from other animals. Following Comte, who had argued that, cognitively speaking, fetishism is more conducive to the development of positive philosophy than the religious or metaphysical stages, Firmin proposed that African peoples, in their "indifference to the more external aspects of religious worship", were ideally suited to "the emancipation of reason":

> Never having experienced the sort of religious
> fanaticism and dogmatism now choking the Caucasian
> race, Blacks are ready to evolve toward rational and
> positivist conceptions which are consistent with
> the working of the universe and its attendant moral
> order. There is no need to destroy in their minds any

---

111 Firmin 353

112 Carolyn Fluehr-Lobban notes how once, when Firmin defended his thesis to the Paris Anthropology society, Clemence Royer, a translator of Darwin's *On the Origin of Species*, asked if his intellectual abilities and presence at the society might not be the result of some White ancestry (Fluehr-Lobban 1).

hereditary influences which might be refractory to philosophical thinking; they are naturally receptive to the right ideas.[113]

And nowhere was this more the case than in Haiti where the descendants of African slaves had inherited the responsibility from the Haitian Revolution to set an exemplary rationalist example to all African peoples.[114]

Unsurprisingly Firmin was to have a significant influence on the *Indigéniste* movement in Haiti, not least on Jean Price-Mars, who would write a biography of Firmin towards the end of his life.[115] But unlike Firmin, other writers associated with the movement sought to identify essentially African hereditary traits in the psyche and culture of the Haitian masses, an essentialism, it was argued, expressed most clearly in the culture of Vodou. It was from the work of Gobineau, complemented by hereditarian currents within *Indigéniste* writers like Dorsainvil and Holly, that Francois Duvalier and the *Noiristes* developed a racial theory of Black Nationalism which built on his ideas of an essential African mentality, while inverting his assumptions about the cultural inferiority of the Black race. They argued for a Black and hereditarily African revolution of cultural values that would be politically appropriate for the Haitian nation, a vision which would come to fruition under the presidency of Duvalier between 1957 and 1981.

In the period between Arthur Holly's *Les daïmons du culte voodu*, the first literary attempt to reclaim the religion as a source of national pride, and the election of François Duvalier in 1957,

---

113 Firmin 342

114 Ramsey 94. Gobineau, on the contrary, had identified Haiti as evidence of this theory of the inferiority of the Black race and its unsuitability to European forms of governance. Black Africans, he argued, have an innate tendency to prefer despotic forms of government maintained by violent force and discipline. Hegel made a similar argument, as we have seen, but unlike Gobineau, he did not consider these tendencies to be innate to the race. They were instead a consequence of environmental and geographical factors.

115 *Joseph Anténor Firmin* (1978).

the legend of Bois Caïman had become a national foundation myth in which Vodou was widely believed to have been a revolutionary force unifying the slaves, their leaders and their ancestral African gods through rites of blood sacrifice and binding oaths. Stories about the summoning of specific Vodou *lwa* at Bois Caïman, popular since the 1920s, seem to have been invented long after the supposed event. This does not prevent them from having a real, socially cohesive and spiritual value in Haiti. Far from it. Since Vodou ostensibly operates outside the confines of rationalist and scientific *epistemes*, established notions of material and historical causality are elided by various forms of revolutionary mysticism, be they Christian, Marxist, Fascist, African or Racial. What counts for the spheres of political and cultural formations is not the factual or evidential historical "truths" about Bois Caïman, but the mythopoetic value of the stories that have accrued to it. The *Indigénistes* sought a Vodouistic significance in the signal event of the Haitian Revolution and the nation's subsequent independence, but to do so, paradoxically, required them to perpetuate mythical ideas about Vodou inherited from colonial authors like Moreau de Saint-Méry, Antoine Dalmas and Drouin de Bercy, who associated the cult with fetishism and the unfitness of Black African slaves for Enlightened self-governance, and more sympathetic foreign "Friends of the Blacks", who held romantic and violently atheistic views about the slaves' "natural religions". It does not seem to matter whether the source of the claims about Bois Caïman were made by sympathetic or hostile authors, whether they were seeking to idealise or denigrate the role of Vodou in the revolution. The African slaves who ignited the first fires of revolution in 1791 were represented as people who could act without moral constraint ("without holding back") and with "blind devotion" to their leaders, two qualities condensed into the mythical idea of a Dahomean Blood pact combined with a Revolutionary Oath. It is perhaps not surprising then that François Duvalier would describe the Bois Caïman ceremony in his 1968 *Eléments d'une doctrine* in terms of the summoning of an insurrectionary racial holocaust:

> ... [T]hey celebrated the ceremony of Bois-Caïman
> during which they all swore to take vengeance against

the White colonizers by iron and fire. A grand
Vodou priest called Boukman became the terrible
organiser of the slave revolt. Hallaou, Hyacinthe,
the Lafortunes, all Vodou priests made fanatic by
their African beliefs, pulverized the Northern plains
of Haiti so that the burning flames of a thousand
glowing houses could be seen as far as the Bermuda
Islands. The African beliefs thus served to gather the
slaves in the face of the conquest of the Independence
of Haiti.[116]

The recurrent motifs of "blind allegiance", "supernatural
inspiration" and "suicidal fervour" on the part of the rebellious
slaves follows the same pattern of contemporary racist denigrations
of the uprising and subsequent revolution. This paradoxical
inversion of White racist representations of Black insurrection
into an image of radical, emancipatory and essentially religious
mysticism, points obliquely to what I have been calling elsewhere
the Zombie Complex: i.e. the situation in which a mythical figure
of an "unthinking" being, *living-in-death,* takes on two generally
polarised modes of behaviour: one totally subject to the will of an
external agency (Fetish, God, King, Priest, Divinity, Master), and
an other beyond any form of reasonable human control (savage and
barbaric insurrectionary). I am not attempting to suggest that there
was anything "zombic" about the slaves who organised themselves
to overthrow colonial rule in Saint-Domingue and fought a thirteen-
year war to achieve national independence, only that a certain
historical framing of the events has meant that the sacrificial Vodou
ceremony at Bois Caïman has, in popular history, superseded what
was probably the key event at which the revolution was actually
planned (i.e. the Lenormand De Mézy meeting which took place a
week earlier and at which hundreds of slaves were in attendance). In
the process the "non-linear intelligence" of the revolutionary slaves
has been configured in terms of "blind obedience" to their *houngan*
leaders and an expression of a "cosmic rage" unleashed by the
summoning of ancient African gods and dead ancestors by blood
sacrifice, a picture that finds its chimerical expression in popular

---

116 Duvalier quoted by Thylefors, 75 (Translation by Markel Thylefors)

xenophobic narratives about Voodoo-horror and spectacular visions of a "revolutionary" zombie-apocalypse.

Original cover painting by James Meese for Ian Fleming's
Live And Let Die, published by Perma Books, 1956

IV

LIVE AND LET DIE:
BLACK PROPAGANDA AND VODOU POLITICS

RISE OF THE BARON

> Without the discipline of service and obedience, fear
> remains formal and does not spread over the whole
> known reality of existence.
>
> - G. W. F. Hegel 'The Formative Process of Self-
> Enfranchisement' *The Phenomenology of Spirit* (1807)

> It is not enough to hold this monster, the most recent
> form of the sacred teratology, up to horror or ridicule,
> one must also understand how he dies and sustains
> himself. The plundering he does is in proportion to the
> degeneracy and insanity of the bourgeois world.
>
> - Michel Surya[1]

At the climactic sacrifice party of *Chloe: Love is Calling You* (1934),
Mandy, the "voodoo" Mammy of this largely forgotten and forgettable
film, dances around a bayou bonfire wearing a white tutu, tail coat
and top hat, the iconic garb of the Vodou *lwa* Baron Samedi, perhaps
the most popularly recognised Vodou figure in Anglo-American pop

---

1 Surya 182

culture after the folkloric Haitian *zombi*. Baron Samedi is a major deity within the contemporary Vodou pantheon, sometimes syncretised with Saint Martin de Porres, the Mulatto Dominican lay-brother from Peru, beatified in 1837, and considered to be the first Black Catholic saint. Lord of Death, the cemetery and the crossroads, and brother of Mait Carrefour, Baron Samedi is also master of the *zombi*.[2] Chief of the unruly and lascivious Guede family of spirits, the Baron shares many of the identifying features of that line (top hat, dark glasses, frock coat, skulls and crossbones). Strangely, as Katherine Smith has noted, the earliest accounts of Vodou make little mention of him.[3] Yet by the late 20th century Baron Samedi had become what Leah Gordon has called the poster boy for the religion.[4] So how did this figure become so iconically associated with popular images of Vodou while having largely slipped the attention of early ethnographers?

Smith, who has studied the historical texts and traced the figure's rise to popular prominence, suggests that the lack of references to "the Baron", his cult's somewhat marginal status in relation to other rites within the religion and its evident roots in the Port-au-Prince area, all indicate that the Guede cult is of a relatively recent origin.[5] The title of Baron, she claims, is derived from a rank within Freemasonry, noting that Masonic lodges have existed in Haiti since long before the revolution, especially in the port towns, and that several prominent Mulatto leaders of the Haitian Revolution were members of French lodges on both sides of the Atlantic.[6] The historical and contemporary

---

2 Cosentino (2012) 26 and Deren 69. Deren proposes that the terms Samedi and *zombi* share a common root in the Taino word *zemi* (spirit of the dead, the soulless living or fetish stone) (Deren 70). He is closely related to Baron Cimetière and Baron la Croix (Hurston 223).

3 Katherine Smith 'Genealogies of Guede' in Cosentino (2012). Arthur C. Holly's 1918 *Les Daïmons Du Culte Voudo* contains an early account of the Guedes, interpreting the name as a derivation of the word "guide" as in "spirit guide" (32).

4 Leah Gordon 'Guede: The Poster Boy for Vodou' in Cosentino (2012)

5 Hurston suggests that the cult emerged in Miragoane, a port town in Western Haiti (Hurston 223).

6 These included Vincent Ogé and Julien Raimond, French lawyers who spoke for Mulatto rights in the first year of the French revolution, Toussaint

symbolism of the Baron bears this out. Coffins, spades, hammers, rulers and saws, morning coat and top hat are also, significantly, symbols of the undertaker.[7]

Smith traces this cluster of symbols back to a novel by Jean Baptiste Picquenard *Zoflora; ou, La bonne negresse* (1800) in which a libertine planter makes an association between Freemasonic symbols, sorcery and "the great Zombi, or in other words, the devil".[8] This early use of the term *zombi* may have been derived from the Bantu word for the creator God, *Nzambi*. But, according to Ackerman and Gauthier, this derivation wasn't noted in a scholarly context until 1962.[9] The authors propose instead that the term is probably of mixed-African origin, derived from a range of words referring to a number of related entities including: spirit, corpse, devil, the invisible part of a man, the spirit of a dead person, a body without a soul, night bogey and revenant. Significantly, as the Haitian concept of the *zombi* attests, it can refer to either a body without a soul (*zombi kadav*), or a soul without a body (*zombi astral*).

Louverture, leader of the Haitian Revolution, André Rigaud who fought against the British in Saint-Domingue in the 1790s and Alexandre Pétion, president of the southern republic of Haiti from 1807-1818 (Buck-Morss 64). Buck-Morss notes that G. W. F. Hegel may also have been a Mason, as was the author of the first positive account of Haitian independence – *An Historical Account of the Black Empire of Hayti* (1805) – Marcus Rainsford.

7 The similarity between Vodou ceremonies and Masonic rituals has been noted since the late 18th century. One priest described the nocturnal gatherings of slaves before the Revolution as "a sort of religious and dancing masonry" (Dayan 151). Métraux notes the existence of *lwa* Masons: Agassu, Agau and Lingkessu (Métraux 157). Though I have found nothing to corroborate the suspicion, certain aspects of the *zombi*-making myth correspond to initiation rites within Freemasonry, notably the rite of the third degree, which includes the mock murder, burial and resurrection of Hiram Abiff, chief architect of the Temple of Solomon, using a substitute secret word replacing the one lost with the death of the architect.

8 Smith in Cosentino (2012) 86. The novel includes a character called Boukmant, a ferocious Negro and Maroon chief who torments the White planters by "incursions into their possessions" (Piguenard [sic] 145).

9 Ackermann and Gauthier 469

The first literary use of the term *zombi*, referring to an ostensibly re-animated corpse, seems to have been *Le zombi Du grand-Pérou ou La comtesse Du Cocaigne* ('The Zombi of Grand Peru or the Countess of Cocaine') by the enigmatic, libertine poet-convict Pierre-Corneille Blessebois, published in 1697. Blessebois worked on slave ships between Africa and the Antilles and was sold into indentured labour himself in Gaudaloupe in 1681. The story tells of a Black aristocratic woman who wants to gain control over a husband that is not respecting her. To do so she makes use of a magical technique – the so-called "zombi" – that makes her invisible. A few lines later the term, which seems to be local to the Antilles, is used for the first time, without explanation, later to be replaced by "ghost". That the term was used so early in the French Antilles does not seem to have been addressed by most orthographic and scholarly histories of the term. *Zombis* don't seem to have been mentioned again in French literature until Moreau de Saint-Méry's 1797 history of Haiti, where, along with *revenants* (ghosts) and *loupgaroux* (werewolves) they are given as an example of primitive superstitions that existed there. It was also used by Saint-Méry to identify a snake-deity of African origin, also known as "Le Vaudoux".[10] In the labyrinthine orthographies of early commentators on Haitian belief and custom then, the concepts of "Vaudoux", "Zombi", "Devil", "Ghost" and "Serpent Deity" were often conflated.

The first explicit mention of Guede, a century after Picquenard's *Zoflora*, occurs in a novel by the Haitian writer Antoine Innocent – *Mimola; ou, l'histoire d'une cassette* (Mimola; or, the Story of a Money Box) – which recounts in some detail a Vodou rite of the feeding of the dead in which a goat is sacrificed to Guede in order to appease an ancestral spirit.[11] Four years later, in 1910, the travel writer Eugène Aubin would explain that Guede is one of the Ginen family of Vodou spirits, describing a "dressed cross" inhabited by Guédé Baron Samedi, "master of the cemetery".[12] The first formal ethnographic mention of the cadaverous *lwa* (after Holly's more esoteric account in his 1918 *Les daïmons du culte voudo*) seems to be in Elsie Clews Parson's 'Spirit Cult in Hayti' (1928) in which she describes the *lwa* Gédé Nibo, who, like

---

10 Saint-Méry 1

11 Smith in Cosentino (2012) 88

12 Smith in Cosentino (2012) 88. Commentators seem unsure about which family of spirits the Baron belongs to. Deren points out that he is sometimes associated with Petro and other times with Rada (Deren 69).

those he takes possession of, talks through his nose, his jaw tied and nostrils stuffed with cotton in the manner of the recently deceased.[13] She also describes a *Ba-Un-Samedi* (a name she interprets as 'Gives, or for Saturday') who is a *grande diable*, like Ogoun, but worse. He is a clown at whom you must not laugh or you may laugh forever. He wears a coat and hat and carries a cane.[14] In *Ainsi parla l'oncle* (1928) Price-Mars makes a brief mention of the Baron, a "minor god", associated with the popular masses (or the *pep la* in Kreyòl), an association that Smith emphasises throughout her essay.[15] Price-Mars describes the "grotesque... caricatures of prayer" dedicated to these common gods and proposes that "the accumulation of nonsensical phrases, the triviality of the languages, the clumsy inaccuracies of the wording" typifies the milieu "in which and for which it was written".[16] In *Life in a Haitian Valley* Herskovits echoes earlier accounts of Guede as a gravedigger, master of the cemetery and a spirit unpopular with the other *lwa*, "tolerated rather than favoured... 'He is a zombi and is fed apart'; as the Haitians say: 'The *lwa* are like other human beings. They will not mingle with the dead, and Guede is of the dead'".[17] Zora Neale Hurston echoes the somewhat derogatory tone struck by Price-Mars, claiming that Guede belongs to "the blacks... and the uneducated blacks at that". "Nothing in Haiti is quite so obvious" she writes, "that this *lwa* is the deification of the common people". A spirit of class antagonism and social criticism, the Mulattos will have nothing to do with him she writes. She also proposes that the cult originated amongst outcaste *bossales* in Miragoane, a port town in Western Haiti, its most celebrated meeting place being a bridge over a lake there.[18] In *Haiti Sings* Harold Courlander, the American ethnomusicologist who did fieldwork in Haiti in the 1930s, tells a story about how, during Louis Borno's

---

13 Parsons 158

14 Parsons 162

15 Price-Mars (1983) 169-170

16 Price-Mars (1983) 170

17 Herskovits 318

18 Hurston 223. This is the same bridge upon which Hurston stages a fanciful literary description of a meeting of the *Secta Rouge* secret society(Hurston 211-217). The *Secta Rouge* and the Guede worshippers had at times, she claims, fought upon this bridge.

presidency in the middle of the U.S. occupation, a group of *houngans* were spontaneously possessed by Guede and marched on the National Palace wearing tall black hats, long black tail coats, smoked glasses and black skirts over their black trousers.[19] As they passed through the streets a crowd of revellers joined the Guedes and the riotous throng passed through the gates of the National Palace unmolested by the guards, where the possessed *houngans* demanded money from the president. Caught in a compromising position between the anti-Vodou sentiments of the Mulatto elites, the occupying U.S. forces and the pro-Vodou will of the popular crowd, Borno gave the *houngans* the money they requested and the Guedes promptly dispersed. A popular Haitian song, recorded by Courlander, commemorates the symbolic victory of Papa Guede over the president.[20]

In *Voodoo in Haiti* Alfred Métraux recounts how, during the anti-superstition campaign of 1948, Father Lavalas uprooted a large cross from a family burial place. At the site of such impiety a crowd of women became possessed by Baron Samedi, Baron Lacroix and other members of the Guede family and began shouting "Do you think you can get rid of us like this? All you are burning is wood. Us, you will never burn. Today you throw these crosses into the fire but soon you will see another kind of fire burning in this valley."[21] Métraux associated the rites of Guede with the *pères-savane*, itinerant funerary priests "standing outside the competence of hungan and mambo" who perform sacraments and funeral rites and have become "the official representatives of the Catholic Church in the bosom of paganism."[22]

---

19 Smith in Cosentino (2012) 91

20

> Papa Guede is a handsome fellow!
> Papa Guede is a handsome fellow!
> He is dressed all in black
> To go up to the palace!
> When he's dressed all in white
> He looks like a deputy!
> When he's dressed all in black
> He resembles a senator! (Courlander (1960) 58-59)

21 Métraux 347

22 Métraux 333

They are counterfeit *curés* who are treated with irreverence and indifference, "catechists or sacristans on the loose... good for nothings who took their function very lightly".[23] He tells the story of a parodic Guede ceremony he witnessed on his feast day of November 1st when a group of *hunsi* (Vodou initiates), all possessed by the spirit, received a special catechism from a *houngan*, himself possessed by the *lwa*, to which they responded with blasphemous obscenities.[24] They were duly given high ranks in the Military and Church of the Dead.[25]

But once again, it seems to have been Seabrook, *bête noire* of respectable Vodou scholars, who popularised the early image of the Baron and his cross-dressing "cult of the dead" for American and European readers. Seabrook's descriptions and accompanying photographs of the *culte des morts*, particularly the sunglasses-wearing, cigar-smoking, top-hatted, tail-coat and wedding-dress-wearing figure of Papa Nebo, were the most likely inspiration for "Mammy" Mandy's wardrobe. It was Arthur Holly, author of *Les daïmons du culte voudu* (and whose image of an altar of crosses illustrated Price-Mars' *Ainsi parla l'oncle*) who first introduced Seabrook to the *culte des morts*.[26] Seabrook was a regular visitor to Holly's pharmacy in downtown Port-au-Prince and considered the doctor a friend. One day he consulted Holly about rumours he had heard about a reputed cult of the dead, which, the doctor confirmed, did exist. Most

---

23 Métraux 334

24 Although Métraux does not make the connection, presumably such performances are intended to parody the anti-superstition oaths imposed on Vodouists during the 1941 campaign.

25 Métraux 349

26 In an interesting aside Smith notes that in his book *Dra-po*, Holly traces the liturgical language of Vodou back to an ancient African Hebrew, analysing "Guede Nibo," "Bawon Samdi," "*zonbi*," and other well-known spirit names and liturgical vocabulary. While the Bawon and *zonbi* carry meanings that would be familiar to contemporary Vodouists, the analysis of "Guede Nibo" is surprising to Smith. Holly traces the name Guede to "Gehede" from the same origin as the English word "behead" (and by extension to "armies who behead"). He then compares the Rubenites, an ancient tribe of Israel, to the Cacos and those who "decapitated" President Guillaume Sam (Holly (1928) 240-41 and Smith 90). And, one might add, those who decapitated Sergeant Muth a decade later.

members of the Petro and Rada cults however would have nothing to do with them: "These people," he said, "are necromancers... though the word necromancy does not exist in our creole vocabulary".[27]

After a series of disappointments and false leads, Seabrook was eventually introduced by Holly to Classinia, a country girl and "Nebo" of the *culte des morts,* who would take the author to a nocturnal ceremony described in some detail in a chapter entitled 'The Altar of Skulls'. Before said altar, made of a simple table covered with a red and white checkered table-cloth, and upon which skulls, bones, a shovel, a pick-axe and candles were lain, Papa Nebo stood, dressed in a white muslin skirt, long-tailed black frock coat, high-silk hat and smoked goggles. When consulted by the people in attendance there came from the throat of this "sexless oracle of death" a series of "deep, rasped gutturals, strung together on meaningless vowel monotones: 'Hg-r-r-r-u-u-u-hgrr-r-r-o-o-o Hgr-r-r-a-a-a-a-a Oh-h-h-h-uu-uu-uu-uu- Bl-bl-bl-ghra-a-a-a- Ghu-u-u-u-u-u–'".[28]

> It was like the prolonged death-rattle from a windpipe choked with phlegm or blood; it was those horrid sounds in skillful savage simulacre... The oracle was talking with the dead, in the subhuman vernacular of death itself - or so it must have seemed to the ears of the waiting listeners.[29]

Seabrook then recounts a story told to him about the nocturnal rites of the *culte des mortes.* Going to a graveyard in the middle of the night

---

27 Seabrook (1929) 82

28 Seabrook (1929) 85. As Smith notes the notion that Guede might be "sexless" is highly unusual. Ordinarily Guedes are very lascivious and often sexually obscene. Interesting to note, however, an early articulation of the flesh-eating zombie groan.

29 Seabrook (1929) 86-87. Seabrook is less overtly dismissive than some of his literary predecessors about the reality of this type of necromancy, conceding that, even though there was "ample scope for the charlatanry and profitable fraud" that "superstitious peasants universally suffered at the hands of rapacious sorcerers", all those involved in the ceremony believed in what they were doing.

the necromancers knock two gravestones together to awaken Baron Samedi – "a big black man with a long white beard" – who grants them the rite to open the grave and exhume the body.[30] They then use parts of the body to make tools more effective, to give cowardly people courage and to concoct *ouanga* charms.[31] Seabrook then makes the distinction, picked up by Leiris and challenged by Price-Mars, between the malefic rites of the *culte des mortes* and Vodou rites proper.[32]

But by far the most widely known image of the Baron comes not from ethnographic literature, sensationalist or sober, but from the 1973 film version of Ian Fleming's 1954 novel *Live and Let Die,* in which the deity played a starring role that would consolidate his association with "Hollywood Voodoo" in the ensuing decades.[33] In the film version James

---

30 Seabrook (1929) 88

31 In a footnote Seabrook corrects a misleading tale, circulating at the time amongst White Americans in Haiti, that Sergeant Muth, whose murder was discussed in the previous chapter, was the victim of the *culte des morts* (Seabrook (1929) 322).

32 He does however note that all over Haiti peasants are on "curiously intimate terms with their dead and seem almost totally devoid of that special, unreasoning terror of graveyards, ghosts, 'haunts' and dead bodies". To illustrate the point he tells the story of a celebration he came across while traveling through the mountains between Morne Rouis and Les Verettes. In a compound there he found people celebrating the death of an elderly man of the community. The said gentleman was sitting on a chair in a place of honour in the main room, nearest the food and the rum, fully dressed, propped up in a position that made him look as life-like as possible, while his family fed him rum and cigarettes (Seabrook (1929) 89).

33 The actor who plays Baron Samedi, Geoffrey Holder, was a renowned Trinidadian dancer, choreographer and painter who famously modelled for the Harlem Renaissance photographer, and author of the notorious novel *Nigger Heaven,* Carl Van Vechten, in the 1950s. Holder was invited to New York by Agnes De Mille in 1954 where he taught at the Katherine Dunham dance school. The same year he appeared as Baron Samedi in the Broadway musical *House of Flowers* based on a short story by Truman Capote. Holder, who choreographed some of the dance sequences, first wore the distinctive black and white face paint worn by the burlesque Baron in *Live and Let Die* for the play (Polk in Cosentino (2013) 135).

Bond takes on Harlem drug lord Mr. Big who runs a network of nightclubs and restaurants, from New Orleans to New York, through which he operates a heroin distribution business. Mr. Big lives a double life as Dr. Kananga, the evil dictator of an imaginary Caribbean island called San Monique who employs a mysterious henchman called Baron Samedi.[34] During the opening sequence of the film an FBI agent, who is watching a funeral procession in New Orleans while staking-out one of Mr. Big's restaurants, asks a short, grey-haired, suited and bespectacled man who has quietly appeared behind him, "Whose funeral is it?" "Yours", the man replies, before stabbing him in the side and having him lifted into the passing coffin. The quiet, little assassin has a marked likeness to François Duvalier, the unlikely-looking "Voodoo Tyrant" who notoriously stole the bodies of his enemies from their funerals in order to use their body parts for necromantic purposes.[35] In the next scene we see another FBI agent bound to a pole in San Monique in the midst of a Voodoo ceremony where he is ritually killed by a goat-masked priest wielding a green mamba.

By the time *Live and Let Die* made it to cinema François Duvalier had been dead for two years, his presidency-for-life passed on to his son Jean-Claude in 1971. But the idea of a Black demagogue-cum-drug-baron would have been popularly associated in the English speaking world with Papa Doc, the eponymous "Voodoo Dictator" of Haiti.[36]

Baron Samedi appeared in a number of films before and after *Live and Let Die*, including Juan Ibáñez's *Isle of the Snake People* (1971) and Paul Maslansky's *Sugar Hill* (1974).

34 In the original novel Mr. Big is himself identified as emulating the character of Baron Samedi and there is no Dr. Kananga alter-ego.

35 The scene seems to reference a story associated with Duvalier's reign of terror when he had the body of Clément Jumelle, his former finance minister, taken from his funeral cortege in front of hundreds of mourners (Diederich and Burt 137-139). The claim that Duvalier would use bodies for necromantic purposes has been made by Diederich and Burt, Abbott and others. The scene was also replicated in Graham Greene's novel *The Comedians* (1966) and the film adaptation of it the following year.

36 The term "Voodoo Dictator" is taken from 'Papa Doc: The Black Sheep', which may have been the most widely seen popular representation of Haiti under Duvalier for western audiences at this time. A similar term – "Tyrant Vodouist" – was used in 1963 in leaflets dropped over Haiti

By the late 1960s it had become widely accepted in the international press and popular media that François Duvalier had deliberately cultivated an image of Baron Samedi in order to consolidate his deathly credentials in Haiti. The claim was made most emphatically in the 1969 documentary 'Papa Doc: The Black Sheep', an episode of the *Whicker's World* travel programme made for British television.[37] In the key sequence of this dictator-damning documentary, the globe-trotting super-journalist Alan Whicker strolls through a Haitian cemetery explaining how, in Haiti, when a person dies, "decomposition is sometimes allowed to set in to make sure that enemies or sorcerers don't dig up the dead man and make a zombie, a work slave out of him". "These heavy stone slabs" he continues, touching one of the sepulchers, "are an added insurance that the dead won't rise, to exist forever more, as zombies". The scene then cuts to footage of a dimly-lit Vodou ceremony, presumably staged for the film, intercutting images of possession, ritual drumming, dancing, much shouting, wailing and chickens being twirled around by mambos. Whicker then continues his narration:

> One reason why, after two centuries, the Catholic Church still finds it so difficult to cope with Vodou, is that this free-wheeling cult, without written codes or hierarchy,... has managed to integrate into itself almost all the symbols and ceremonies of the Roman church. For example the cross of Christ doubles for the sign of

---

by opposition groups based in the Dominican Republic (Diederich and Burt 202).

37 Although the claim is made in several places – notably Cosentino (2012), Diederich and Burt (1969), Dunham (1969), Nicholls (1979) 234, Heinl and Heinl (2005) 540, Johnson (2006) and Smith (2011) – Duvalier himself does not seem to have made it personally. Diederich and Burt's *Papa Doc: The Truth About Haiti*, written the same year as Whicker's documentary was broadcast, contains a final chapter, written in distinctly Whickeresque tones, that contains an account of Duvalier's relationship to Guede-Baron Samedi. The book was, however, published three months after Whicker's documentary was broadcast. Dunham's *Island Possessed*, in which she suggests an intentional association with the Baron on the part of Duvalier, was also published in 1969.

> Baron Samedi. Baron Samedi personifies death itself, he
> is the most powerful, the most dreaded of the Gods in the
> Vodou pantheon. He's always dressed in black, always
> wears dark glasses, and of course, for the great mass of
> Haitians today, we know who personifies Baron Samedi.

The film then cuts to Papa Doc being interviewed by Whicker. "Haiti is not the country of Vodou", the President explains. "They said I was a *houngan*. A priest of Vodou. They say that in the international press. Why? We were facing an international and political conspiracy set up by certain great nations". "Which nations do you believe is leading this conspiracy then?" Whicker asks. "Several White nations. And they spend many millions since 1963, not only to overthrow the President Duvalier but to destroy the Fatherland, our Fatherland. To destroy I say, to destroy our Fatherland." The choice of date is significant. It was the year that the myth of Papa Doc as Baron Samedi came to international attention after Graham Greene published an article for the *Sunday Telegraph* - 'The Nightmare Republic' - which first made the claim that Duvalier impersonated the Haitian Lord of the Dead.[38]

Surprisingly Ian Fleming made the association between his imaginary Vodou super-villain and Baron Samedi three years before Duvalier's rise to power. So although by 1973 publics in the English-speaking and Latin American world may have had some familiarity with the deathly despot, this was not the case in 1954, when, like Baron Samedi, he was largely unknown outside of Haiti.[39] Significantly the fifteen years that divided the novel and the film saw the rise of international, Pan-African and Black Nationalist movements, with roots in the Harlem Renaissance and the *Indigéniste*, *Noiriste* and folkloric movements in Haiti, that would form the backdrop to Duvalier's rise to power in the 1950s. These movements would also influence the U.S. Black Power movement of the late 1960s that was

---

38 Diederich (2012) 28

39 As we will see, between 1954 and 1956 Duvalier had been forced into hiding due to suspicions that he was plotting against President Paul Magloire. Before then, though known in Haiti, Duvalier was little known in the outside world, except, that is, to ethnographers who visited the Bureau of Ethnography in Port-au-Prince.

parodied in the 1973 film.[40] It seems highly probable therefore that the portrayal of Mr.Big/Dr.Kananga in the film version of *Live and Let Die* was written with Duvalier in mind. But how did Fleming come to make the connection with Baron Samedi as early as 1954?

---

40 In his interview with Duvalier in 1969, Alan Whicker asks him directly about his relation to the Black Power movement in the United States, and his reputed claim that he was its founder. "No, no, no. What Black Power movement? Black Power is in the states. It's for the states, for the Negroes living in the states. I said that I want to get for Haiti the leadership of the legal or the Black world because we have been the first to become independent with our guns against White people, against French people. And we got it in 1804".

> But with the progress that science has made... we cannot afford Machiavelli to return. One or two more such returns on a large scale will, under existing conditions, mean the end of white civilisation, and possibly the white race itself.

- Irving Babbitt[41]

> Anonymity was the chief tool in his trade. Every thread of his real identity that went on record in any file diminished his value and, ultimately, was a threat to his life. Here in America, where they knew all about him, he felt like a negro whose shadow had been stolen by the witch-doctor. A vital part of himself was in pawn, in the hands of others.

- Ian Fleming *Live and Let Die* (1954)[42]

Fleming was still closely connected with fellow agents from the international secret services when he wrote *Live and Let Die,* and many of the ostensibly comic-book elements of the plot are very close to the kinds of operations he had been involved in during WWII. Between 1939 and 1945 Fleming worked for British Naval Intelligence liaising on behalf of Admiral John Henry Godfrey (the model for Bond's boss "M") with the Secret Intelligence Service, Political Warfare Executive, Special Operations Executive and Joint Intelligence Committee.[43] One of his principle roles was to invent propaganda fictions that could be used as disinformation to confuse the enemy. Working with the Political Warfare Executive, charged with spreading rumour and propaganda in enemy countries during WWII, Fleming became an expert in so-called "Black Propaganda", false information purporting to be from one side of a conflict but actually coming from the opposite.

---

41 Quoted in Lewis (1989) 102

42 Fleming 2

43 Chancellor 28

He personally set up, along with Donald McLachlan, future editor of *The Daily Telegraph*, unit NID 17 Z, a special operation that used the cover of a false German radio station called Atlantiksender to broadcast misleading messages to U-Boat crews in the mid-Atlantic. In 1941 Fleming met 'Wild Bill' Donovan, head of the OSS (Office of Strategic Services, later to become the CIA) who was canvassing ideas for a U.S. intelligence agency. In the next few years Fleming, working for a division of MI6 called the British Security Coordination, founded by the industrialist William Stephenson, the "Quiet Canadian", made several trips to New York where he operated ostensibly as a security advisor for U.S. ports.[44] Part of the BSC's mission in the U.S. was to mobilise pro-British opinion in the Americas and to convince Americans that going to war in Europe was a good thing.[45] To do so the BSC developed a number of covert strategies for promoting anti-Nazi sentiment in the U.S., including the hiring of sham astrologers predicting disaster for the German dictator. One of its most successful operations was to suggest that Hitler's ambitions extended across the Atlantic to South America, a theme already present in sensationalist, Vodou-themed novels like Beale Davis's *The Goat Without Horns* (1925). One particularly successful operation involved the dissemination of an allegedly German-produced map, stolen from a courier's bag in Buenos Aires, showing Hitler's ambitions in the region. President Roosevelt publicly endorsed the map as authentic.[46]

In 1941 Monogram Pictures, a Hollywood company specialising in low-budget action and adventure films, released *King of the Zombies*, the first zombie film to include a secret German military plot against the United States. The film opens with a plane lost at night "somewhere between Cuba and Puerto Rico", its pilot trying to make

---

44 Lycett 127. It was Fleming's earlier career as a journalist for Reuters, taking him to Soviet Moscow in 1933, that laid the foundations for his intelligence career during the war.

45 See William Boyd 'The Secret Persuaders' *The Guardian*, Saturday 19th August 2006.

46 Boyd. Elizabeth Abbot recounts that the president of Haiti at this time, Élie Lescott, declared war on the Axis powers five hours before the U.S. did. On hearing this Hitler allegedly asked "Where is it, this Haiti?" After having it pointed out to him on a map he said "When the war is over, I swear I will turn it into my stables" (Abbot 53).

contact with the ground. We discover from Mr. Bill's valet Jeff that this is the same location that one Admiral Wainwright's plane disappeared a week earlier.[47] The pilot picks up "some new lingo" (German) on his radio from directly below them and so decides to land on the island. After crash-landing in a graveyard the trio hear the sound of tom-tom drums which lead them to a "creepy looking" jungle mansion, the residence of the Austrian Dr. Sangre, his *zombi* butler Momba and somnambulist wife Madame Sangre. Dr. Sangre quickly denies that any radio broadcasts are being sent from the island. Jeff, because he is Black, is forced to stay in the servant's quarters in order not to set a bad example to the others. As he is led down to the basement by Momba he asks "you ain't by any chance a member of the Mystic Knights of the Bengatas is you?... No?... Harlem never was like this". In the basement he meets a crone-cook, an attractive young maid and the *zombis* that Dr. Sangre has created to run his espionage mission. It turns out that Sangre is using an ancient Druidic rite of transmigration mixed with "voodoo magic" to transfer the souls of the dead into the bodies of the living in order to extract their secrets. Admiral Wainwright, who was on his way to Panama on "some sort of mission for the government", has been captured and put into a trance. In the by-then standard climactic Voodoo rite, a masked Dr. Sangre, who has hypnotised his servants into thinking they are dead, transfers Wainwright's soul into the body of his hypnotised niece. His plan is foiled at the last minute when "Mr. Bill" manages to turn the hypnotised *zombi*-slaves against him.

Two years later Monogram would release *Revenge of the Zombies*, another schlock-horror comedy in which a Dr. Max Heinrich Von Altermann, who is communicating directly with Hitler via a radio transmitter, attempts to create an army of the living dead for the Third Reich. Once again Mantan Morlant added racist comic relief as Jeff the cowardly valet. Although there is no evidence to suggest that these films were directly shaped by the black ops of the BSC their content fits quite precisely with what is known about their propaganda mission at the time. More importantly perhaps, they perpetuate the typical

---

47 Jeff the valet, played by Mantan Morlant, is the heavy-handed, racial comic relief for this otherwise po-faced comedy horror. Typically he is cast as the superstitious and cowardly Negro against the rational and sensible White hero figure.

paternalistic image of heroic, White males cutting through the sinister, anti-American and hybrid forms of European-African mumbo-jumbo in foreign lands that Fleming's Bond character would emulate in the decades to come.

Early in *Live and Let Die* Fleming has Bond visit Harlem, or 'Nigger Heaven' as the chapter is called.[48] The account was based on an actual visit the author made to Harlem in 1950 with his guide and character-model for Felix Leiter in the novel and film, Ernie Cuneo, a liaison officer between the OSS, the FBI and the BSC during the war.[49] Cuneo, a lawyer and former advisor to President Roosevelt, was one of the first operatives to be contacted by British intelligence in 1940. He was described by William Stephenson as the head of Franklin's "brain trust", a reference to the group of advisors close to the president in the 1930s. Cuneo was tasked with feeding intelligence items about Nazi sympathisers to friendly journalists (like Walter Lippmann) who were "stealth operatives in their campaign against Britain's enemies in America".[50] During a night spent with two local detectives patrolling the dance clubs of Harlem, Fleming met a local crime boss who was reputedly the inspiration for Mr. Big.[51] Fleming's choice to cast his villain as a Black man, in keeping with the over-arching Vodou theme of the novel, may also have been informed by rumours within the U.S. intelligence sector at the time that the NAACP (National Association for the Advancement of Colored People) was in fact a front for the Communist Party of America.[52] Fleming has his hero comment on the novelty of his invention of a Black super-villain:

---

48 A name taken from the title of Carl Van Vechten's 1926 novel set during the Harlem Renaissance. The expression "nigger heaven" originally referred to the balconies of 19th century American churches that were reserved for Black people (Worth 464).

49 Cuneo would become a good friend and inspiration to Fleming, the author dedicating his last novel, *Thunderball,* to him.

50 After the war Cuneo created a group of investors, including Fleming and his childhood friend Ivar Bryce, another BSC operative and conceiver of the fake Hitler map of America, to gain control of the North American Newspaper Alliance.

51 Chancellor 42

52 Lycett 237

"I don't think I've ever heard of a great negro criminal before," said Bond... "They don't seem to take to big business. Pretty law-abiding chaps I should have thought, except when they've drunk too much." "Our man's a bit of an exception," said M. "He's not pure negro. Born in Haiti. Good dose of French blood. Trained in Moscow, too, as you'll see from the file. And the negro races are just beginning to throw up geniuses in all the professions – scientists, doctors, writers. It's about time they turned out a great criminal. After all, there are about 250,000,000 of them in the world. Nearly a third of the white population. They've got plenty of brains and ability and guts. And now Moscow's taught one of them the technique."[53]

The theme of a secret communication network between Vodouists, often operating to foil the amorous intentions of a sceptical White hero figure, has been a characteristic trait of pulp adventure stories set in Haiti since the 1920s.[54] Sometimes the system uses smokes signals, often secret signs, and, almost inevitably, "talking drums". Like the characters in *King of the Zombies* and *Revenge of the Zombies*, Fleming associated the secret codes of German U-boat commanders (which he had helped decode during the war) with the secret language used by Mr. Big on his ship *Secatur*:

The FBI, with the help of Naval Intelligence, had tried listening to the Secatur's wireless. But she kept off the air except for short messages before she sailed from Cuba or Jamaica and then transmitted *en clair* in a language which was unknown and completely indecipherable. The last notation of the file was to the effect that the operator was talking in a "Language", the secret Voodoo speech only used by initiates, and that every effort would be made to hire an expert from Haiti before the next sailing.[55]

---

53 Fleming 18

54 See for instance Beale Davis's *The Goat Without Horns* (1925) and George Terwilliger's *The Devil's Daughter* (1939).

55 Fleming 35-36. The French expression *langage*, as Katherine Dunham

In keeping with a general paranoia about the subversive potential of Black radical and Pan-African Nationalist movements in America during the cold war, the main political threat to White, Anglo-American "Free-World" imperialism was imagined as a Soviet-funded, Mulatto-led, Black criminal underground network using Vodou "mumbo-jumbo" and terror tactics to control its operatives.[56] In the 'Big Switchboard' section of the novel, a reference to the underground communication network set up by Mr. Big, Captain Dexter of the CIA warns one of the police officers in the station not to trouble the "Big Man" prematurely:

> "D'you want a race riot?" objected Dexter sourly. "There's nothing against him and you know it, and we know it. If he wasn't sprung in half an hour by that black mouthpiece of his, those Voodoo drums would start beating from here to the Deep South. When they're full of that stuff we all know what happens. Remember '35 and '43? You'd have to call out the militia."[57]

When Bond tells Dexter that he'd like to take a visit to Harlem with Felix Leiter he is also warned not to stir up any trouble: "The case isn't ripe yet. Until it is, our policy with Mr. Big is "live and let live".' Bond looked quizzically at Captain Dexter. 'In my job,' he said, 'when I come up against a man like this one I have another motto. It's "live and let die".'"[58]

---

notes, is used by Haitians to describe the "secret" language (a mixture of different African tribal dialects) of ceremonial songs within Vodou and spoken by those ridden by the *lwa* (Dunham 107-108).

56 Richard Lawless has identified this as the "Voodoo Extortionist" angle of Haiti's historically bad press (Lawless 20).

57 Fleming 36. The reference here is to the 1935 Harlem Riot that was sparked by rumours of the beating of a teenage Puerto Rican shoplifter. It has been described as the "first modern race riot", one that symbolically marked the end of the optimism of the Harlem Renaissance (Jeffrey Stewart). The 1943 riot took place after an African-American serviceman was shot and wounded by a police officer. An account of the riot is contained in James Baldwin's *Notes of a Native Son* (1955).

58 Fleming 37-38

Released at the height of the Blaxploitation era, the *Live and Let Die* film was full of stereotypical representations of Harlem Blacks as hustlers, pimps, numbskulls, players, prostitutes and pushers. It was also, coincidentally, shortly after the FBI's COINTELPRO (Counter Intelligence Programme) of 1956-71 that had targeted organisations like the Civil Rights Movement, the Congress for Racial Equality, the NAACP and the Black Panther Party in the manner of the "black ops" developed by the OSS. One of their most controversial tactics was the promotion of a notorious *Black Panther Coloring Book*, allegedly produced by the Panthers as educational material, and distributed to households in potentially sympathetic White neighbourhoods, which showed images of White police officers, depicted as pigs, being murdered by Black men, women and children.[59]

The principle source of Fleming's knowledge about Vodou was Patrick Leigh Fermor's travelogue of the Caribbean *The Traveller's Tree* which he has Bond read in his New York hotel room, while the secret agent is researching his future adversary.[60] Fermor, a personal friend of Fleming, and similarly a former secret service operative for the British during WWII, visited Haiti in 1947 during a period of rare affluence and openness, sometimes referred to as the Haitian Renaissance. It was an era that saw a flourishing of Haitian art and culture, the founding of the Centre D'Art and the emergence of a thriving tourist industry for which folkloric Vodou ceremonies became a mainstay.[61] There was a gradual loosening of restrictions of Vodou under Dumarsais Estimé, the first *Noiriste* president of Haiti since the occupation, who had come to power in the so-called Bloodless Revolution of 1946. During this time the Haitian elites, recognising the economic potential of Haiti's "native" culture, relaxed their anti-Vodou sensibilities and, in the words of Sidney Mintz and Michel-Rolph Trouillot, under Estimé's leadership, "Vodou became folklore; and folklore could be sold".[62]

---

59 Jorgenson 314

60 Fleming makes the point of plugging his friend's book, noting "This is one of the great travel books... published by John Murray at 25s." (Fleming 25 n1)

61 Cosentino (2013) 27. The Centre D'Art, established by the American painter Dewitt Peters, and opened in 1944 was to become the centre of the Haitian Renaissance of the late '40s and early '50s.

62 Quoted in Smith in Cosentino (2013) 94. Matthew J. Smith notes

Fermor describes in great detail a number of Vodou ceremonies he and his companions attended while in Haiti, none of them legally sanctioned.[63] Whatever the official view of the ceremonies, they seem to have been frequent, the author visiting three in one heady night.[64] Twenty pages of Fermor's travelogue contain surprisingly detailed accounts of the history and mythology of Vodou that seem to have escaped the attention of most historians of the religion's representation in popular culture.[65] They include a meeting with one Father Cosme, a Catholic priest who had been personally involved in the anti-superstition campaigns; a long section reflecting on the nature of possession-trance which references the writings of Dorsainvil and Louis Mars, author of *La crise de possession dans le vaudou* (1946); an account of the various African peoples constituting the pre-revolutionary Haitian masses; their contributions to the religion; descriptions of the major deities (including Baron Samedi and his consort Madame Brigit); the nefarious branches of the faith and associated superstitions; Vodou cosmology and metaphysics; first-hand accounts of possessions by Guede, Baron Cimetiére, Général Criminel and Capitaine Zombie and even detailed accounts of Vodou initiations. Fermor confesses that he had become somewhat obsessed by the religion: "As night fell, we would listen for the first faint roll of drums with the anxiety of dipsomaniacs waiting for opening time".[66]

After leaving Haiti Fermor travelled to Jamaica where he visited "Commander" Fleming at Goldeneye, the house he had built on

---

that once it became obvious to the Haitian elites that Haitian folklore and Vodou could be exploited for the benefits of tourism, they began to actively support it. This changing attitude was significant enough for the U.S. minister in Haiti to write a report in 1942 discussing the topic (Smith 213-214).

63 Ramsey has noted that from the occupation onwards informal "licenses" had to be acquired by the appropriate authorities for anyone wishing to conduct a ceremony. Whether such restrictions had been lifted is not possible to ascertain from Fermor's account, but as Ramsey points out, few of the formal ethnographers of Vodou between the '30s and '50s discussed the delicate issue of "staged" rituals.

64 Fermor 258

65 An exception being Alfred Métraux who includes Fermor in the bibliography of his *Voodoo in Haiti* of 1957.

66 Fermor 273

the northern coast named after the WWII sabotage operation he had helped mastermind.[67] Fermor, who was generally open-minded, scholarly and sympathetic to both Vodou, Haiti and Haitians, would have presumably spoken to Fleming about his recent experiences there. In *Live and Let Die* Fleming quotes at length from one of Fermor's descriptions of a Vodou ceremony, selecting the most appropriately macabre and fantastical details:

> Bond turned over the pages, occasionally passages combining to form an extraordinary picture in his mind of a dark religion and its terrible rites... At the edge of the crowd we came across a little hut, scarcely larger than a dog kennel: "*le cage Zombi*". The beam of a torch revealed a black cross inside and some rags and chains and shackles and whips: adjuncts used at the Ghédé ceremonies, which Haitian ethnologists connect with the rejuvenation rites of Osiris recorded in the Book of the Dead. A fire was burning in which two sabres and a large pair of pincers were standing, their lower parts red with the heat: "*Le Feu Marinette*", dedicated to the goddess who is the evil obverse of the bland and amorous Maîtress Erzulie Fréda Dahomin, the Goddess of Love. Beyond, with its base held fast in a socket of stone, stood a large black wooden cross. A white death's head was painted near the base, and over the crossbar were pulled the sleeves of a very old morning coat. Here also rested the brim of a battered bowler hat, through the torn crown of which the top of the cross projected. This totem, with which every peristyle must be equipped, is not a lampoon of the central event of the Christian faith, but represents the God of the Cemeteries and the Chief of the Legion of the Dead, Baron Samedi.[68]

These passages are the only reference to the actual culture of Haiti in Fleming's novel. Throughout the book there are however scattered references to the theme of corpses and graveyards. The Harlem

---

67 Fermor 327

68 Fleming 26-28 and Fermor 253.

nightclub he is taken to by Leiter, for instance, is called The Boneyard. There he and Leiter witness a stage show worthy of Seabrook: "The whole scene was macabre and livid, as if El Greco had done a painting by moonlight of an exhumed graveyard in a burning town."[69] When he meets Mr. Big for the first time the villain is described as having the complexion of a "week old corpse in the river" with "bulging eyes" that seem to devour anything they rest on (the greying corpse-like complexion of Mr. Big is played upon in the film version too).[70]

Although Fleming makes sensational and superficial use of Fermor's considered experiences of Vodou and Haiti, *The Traveller's Tree* brings us closer to the political life of the country in which François Duvalier would soon make a profound impression. One of Fermor's main informants about Vodou, the French priest Father Cosme, had been active in the anti-superstition campaign that had influenced the *Noiriste* backlash that would ultimately help bring Duvalier to power fifteen years later. Father Cosme spoke to Fermor about Vodou marriages to Erzulie Fréda Dahomin, the construction of *wanga* charms by *bokors*, the evil demons of Vodou and of the secret societies of "wizards" who sacrifice the *cabrit sans cornes* (the goat without horns). The *curé* lamented that, under president Estimé, Vodou had been de-criminalised, expressing fear that it might evolve into a "new sort of state religion" under the influence of the "Seraphic Doctors of Voodoism": Jean Price-Mars, Melville Herskovits and J. C. Dorsainvil.

In the account of his stay in Haiti Fermor keeps noticing a mysterious and striking figure, whose "air of deep-eyed and spectral aloofness, his pallor and fragility and the gypsy-like neglect of his appearance" left a distinct impression on the author. The man seemed to have been remotely observing his group, first after a performance of a play about Macandal, disrupted by a *Noiriste*, anti-bourgeois mob, and again when they leave the last of three Vodou ceremonies in the early hours of a Sunday morning. Before leaving Port-au-Prince Fermor makes

---

69 Fleming 55.

70 Fleming 64. The chapter describing Bond's arrival in Jamaica on the trail of Mr. Big's smuggling operation is called 'The Undertaker's Wind', the name given by sailors in the Cayman Islands to an on-and-off shore breeze that blows the bad air out of the island at night. 'The Undertaker's Wind' was the original working title for *Live and Let Die*.

the man's acquaintance outside a patisserie on the Champs de Mars. He introduces himself as Clément Magloire-Saint-Aude, poet. "Lyric? Epic? Romantic? Symbolist?" Fermor asks. None of these, he replied. He was a Surrealist.[71]

---

71 In *Refusal of the Shadow: Surrealism and the Caribbean*, Michael Richardson describes Magloire-Saint-Aude as "one of the greatest poets of both Surrealism and the Caribbean" (Richardson 28). André Breton, who visited Haiti between 1945 and 1946 with Pierre Mabille and Wilfredo Lam, and gave several influential lectures there, was to have a significant impact on young poets and artists at the time, particularly those associated with the literary journal *La Ruche*. See René Depestre 'André Breton and the Emancipation of Poetry' (1974).

PAPA DOC'S VODOU NATION

> The few people to come from the degraded part of society, from its servile sections, could be integrated by the armed fascist state not as people but as the flesh of a "sickening slaughter", entirely metamorphosed into its opposite: patriotic glory... The fascist revolution turns the masses it seduces against themselves. Nothing remains of them except militias subject to the god-master.

> - Michel Surya on Georges Bataille's 'The Psychological Structure of Fascism' (1933)[72]

> Foreign journalists and scholars in search of exotic buffoons have enjoyed painting François Duvalier as an incoherent madman, a black Ubu, a tropical Caligula who would spout any amount of nonsense at any time. This mocking attitude comes partly from the national shame that Duvalierist practices have inflicted on Haitian pride. But that condescension also concealed a strategic counter-attack by the Haitian bourgeoisie, a counter-attack that survived the departure of the Duvaliers.

> - Michel-Rolph Trouillot *Haiti: State Against Nation*[73]

Magloire-Saint-Aude was one of the founding members of the Griots, a group whose cultural goal, as expressed in the journal of the same name, was to reverse the historical repression of Haiti's African heritage, to affirm it as the racial background of the nation and its people, and to give "dark skinned Haitians more control over Haitian affairs".[74] As we have seen, the Griots had grown out of an earlier group, *Les Trois D*, named after its members Louis Diaquoi, Lorimer Denis and François

---

72 Surya 178-179

73 Trouillot (1990) 192

74 Nicholls 168, Largey 192, Laguerre 103

Duvalier.[75] Diaquoi, a radical nationalist, journalist and the driving force of the group, died early at the age of twenty-five. Denis, the son of a Black senator and trained in law, would become the director of the Bureau of Ethnology between 1946 and his death in 1957, during which time he penned a number of influential articles celebrating the African ancestry of the Haitian people and promoting Vodou as "the transcendent expression of racial consciousness before the enigmas of the world", along with his colleague François Duvalier.[76] Duvalier, at the time of Fermor's meeting with Saint-Aude, was the Director of Public Health for the Estimé government.[77]

It was during Denis' directorship of the Bureau of Ethnology that Duvalier began to study Vodou in depth, developing friendships with the many *houngans* and *mambos* who would help form the base of his popular support amongst the peasants and urban poor during his 1957 election campaign. In 1944 Duvalier and Denis had co-authored *The Gradual Evolution of Vodou: On the Popular Culture and Ethnic Origins of the Haitian People,* an essay that outlined Duvalier's later political ideology.[78] Duvalier and Denis portrayed Black leaders of the past as the heroic defenders of the Haitian masses and as "the true guardians of national independence", while Mulatto leaders like Pétion and Boyer, they claimed, had betrayed the people and turned the national interests into their own.[79] From this perspective Jean-Jacques Dessalines became the iconic hero figure of a *Noiriste* ideology of racial-class conflict, with Vodou configured as the driving force for a Black, Nationalist independence movement. The same year their essay was published Duvalier accepted an offer by the Inter-American Affairs Commission to be one of twenty Haitian doctors to join the graduate school of public health at the University of Michigan. There he studied for two semesters as part of an international programme to control the spread of the degenerative disease yaws, second only to malaria as Haiti's main health problem.[80] On his return Denis

---

75 Nicholls 168

76 Denis and Duvalier quoted in Nicholls 170

77 Diederich and Burt 55

78 Laguerre 102-103

79 Nicholls 171

80 Diederich and Burt 50

introduced Duvalier to his professor Daniel Fignolé, whose political party *Mouvement Ouvrier Paysan* (Movement of Workers and Peasants or MOP) had been founded to mobilise Haitian Blacks against the Mulatto elites. Duvalier duly became the party's general-secretary.[81] In the elections of 1946 Fignolé was unexpectedly beaten by the relatively unknown Dumarsais Estimé, Duvalier's former high-school teacher and an outspoken critic of the U.S. occupation, who had been expelled for sedition under the presidency of the pro-American Mulatto Louis Borno. His election as the first Black president since the occupation was greeted positively by *Noiristes* and shortly afterwards Duvalier was appointed as Director of Public Health on the basis of his position in the MOP and his work in eradicating yaws from the country.[82] It was during his time working as a doctor to the rural poor in a clinic in the Gressier region that Duvalier had acquired the epithet "Papa Doc", a term of endearment following a pattern of familiarising popular names for statesmen in Haiti.[83]

Despite his early popularity Estimé found it difficult to control the conflicting interests within Haitian politics and to maintain the much-needed economic confidence of the U.S., a pattern that would plague all post-occupation presidents. In an attempt to placate the country's former occupiers, Estimé began to openly oppose the radical student and workers movements that had previously supported him, leaving his followers from the lower classes in disarray. Their disunity played into the hands of the Mulatto elites and, when Estimé tried to push through legislation that would allow him to run for a second term in office, he was popularly opposed and eventually overthrown in a Mulatto-backed *coup d'état* led by the former chief of police of Port-au-Prince Paul Magloire.[84] An ardent anti-communist, friend of the United States and the Catholic Church, Magloire presided over a period of

81 Diederich and Burt 53

82 Diederich and Burt 53

83 Diederich and Burt 49. Elizabeth Abbott has claimed that Duvalier was profoundly affected as a teenager by the image of a mother treating her son for yaws (Abbot 8). According to Michel-Rolph Trouillot Duvalier gave himself the name Papa Doc following the examples of previous Haitian leaders like Toussaint Louverture (Trouillot (1990) 194 n4).

84 Diederich and Burt 58

relative peace and prosperity between 1950 and 1956.[85] It was during this period that, with the help of U.S. investment, the nascent tourist economy that emerged under Estimé was consolidated and Magloire's international acceptance endorsed by a portrait on the cover of *Time* magazine in February 1954. Duvalier, who was bitterly opposed to Magloire, refused the offer of an office in his government and instead continued to work for the Inter-American Cooperative Health Service. Aware of Duvalier's political loyalties, Magloire became suspicious about the doctor's activities and later that year Duvalier went into hiding.[86] In his self-imposed internal exile Duvalier immersed himself in literature, notably Machiavelli's *The Prince* (reputedly read to tatters) and the study of Vodou, while quietly plotting the overthrow of the president.[87] In 1956, in the midst of the turmoil caused by anti-Magloire student protests, Duvalier formally announced his candidacy for the upcoming presidential election.

From the outset Duvalier's mission took on the character of a religious crusade, the "humble country doctor" portraying himself as a divinely chosen personage who embodied the Nation in person.[88] He maintained the image of a good Catholic while reputedly promoting his reputation as a Vodouist.[89] In its simplest form Duvalier's doctrine was that Haiti was Black, should be ruled by Blacks, that ethnic cohesion is founded

---

85 Diederich and Burt 60

86 Diederich and Burt 66

87 Diederich and Burt 66 and Abbot 61. The source of the claim seems to have been Duvalier's one-time second-in-command and commander of the Tonton Macoute, Clément Barbot. (Heinl and Heinl 540).

88 For detailed accounts of Duvalier's rise to power see Abbott, Diederich and Burt, Dupuy, Heinl and Heinl, Nicholls and Trouillot (1990).

89 Several authors, including Abbott, Heinl and Heinl and Diederich and Burt, have made this claim. But, as we have seen, Duvalier himself publicly denied practicing Vodou. Dunham, who is cited by Johnson, does recount that Duvalier had had the bones of Dessalines disinterred to use for magical purposes but she does not claim that these rumours were generated by Duvalier himself, as Johnson suggests (Dunham 172, Johnson 8), only that he made the date of Dessalines' death a national holiday and that candles were kept burning at his tomb day and night.

on Vodou, and that the national faith must have a national leader.[90] If Vodou was the authentic essence of the nation, race and religion, then the state should be the political realisation of that essence. Exploiting the disjuncture between "State" (wealthy urban, Catholic, White and Mulatto elite) and "Nation" (poor, rural, Black and Vodouist masses), Duvalier enlisted the support of previously disenfranchised segments of the population such as peasants, poor urban Blacks, women and the expatriate Middle-Eastern business groups.[91] His ultimate intention however was not the political and economic improvement of the lives of impoverished Haitian masses but to capture political power for the Black bourgeoisie.[92]

Duvalier's campaign seems not to have been taken seriously by his opponents at first.[93] Playing down his *Noiriste* sympathies for the U.S. – where they were associated with communism – Duvalier cast himself as the mystical and moderate successor to Estimé, whose "Bloodless Revolution" of 1946 he said "broke the circle of iron... and infused the entire country with new blood".[94] At the same time masked supporters of Duvalier, known as *Cagoulards,* invaded the slum districts of Port-au-Prince to terrorise non-Duvalier supporters, while pro-Duvalier sheriffs in the south arrested his opponents' supporters and kept them in jail until the election was over.[95] At the end of a wave of armed

---

90 Bastien and Courlander 61

91 Abbott 64, Dupuy (2007) 32. Duvalier created the *Faisceau Féminin* (Women's Torch) group who campaigned for the women's vote. One of the most dedicated activists of the movement was Rosalie Bosquet, who would later become Madame Max Adolphe, ruthless Commandant of the Tonton Macoute.

92 Dupuy (2007) 32

93 Diederich and Burt 76-95

94 Smith 184

95 Smith 185. Trouillot notes that the origin of the term *cagoulards* comes from European Fascist organisations who hid their faces behind ski-masks (Trouillot (1990) 189). Dupuy however sees their origins in the *zinglins* created by Emperor Faustin between 1847 and 1859 (Dupuy (2007) 35). Bob Corbett noted that the term was revived during the pre-Aristide era as the *zinglendo,* a term used to describe criminal paramilitary organisations (see 'The rule of Faustin Soulouque (Emperor Faustin I) March 1, 1847 –

clashes between the supporters of the main presidential candidates – Louis Déjoie, Daniel Fignolé, Clement Jumelle and Duvalier – a number of pro-Fignolé rioters were gunned down by Haitian soldiers on the orders of General Antonio Kébreau, leader of the military junta who were overseeing the elections. By the end of the campaign, with Fignolé, the only other viable candidate still running, forced into exile in New York, Duvalier was elected president on September 22nd 1957.[96]

Once in power Duvalier ordered the *Cagoulards*, who were under the control of Clément Barbot (the "Robespierre of the Duvalier Revolution" as the Heinls have called him, and future head of the *Milice de Volontaires de la Sécurité Nationale* (VSN), later popularly known as the Tonton Macoute) to round up and harass supporters of any opposition groups.[97] The new president quickly set about bringing the army under civilian control, convincing Kébreau, then commander of the Haitian army, that several of his inferiors were plotting against him. Having retired or exiled these officers, Kébreau was deprived of any potential support he had against Duvalier and was subsequently replaced in 1958 by Maurice Flambert, who was himself replaced

---

January 1859', Bob Corbett, 1995).

96 Smith 178-185

97 Nicholls 215-216 and Heinl and Heinl 452. Fort Dimanche is the notoriously brutal prison built during the Duvalier era. Constructed originally by the French, it was used as a military facility by American Marines during the 1914 – 1934 occupation. Trouillot notes that the name Tonton Macoute for Duvalier's secret police predates the formal creation of the VSN in 1962. Its commanders were predominantly middle-class urban dwellers and landowners, many of whom did not formally join the VSN. Although the Haitian language distinguishes between Tonton Macoute and *Milisyen* (civil militia) Duvalier was keen to keep the association between the two strong in the public imagination. The choice of uniform for the VSN – blue denim shirt, pants and hat and red kerchief – is that of the Vodou *lwa* Papa Zaka, spirit of agriculture, whose colours are also those of the Haitian flag (before Duvalier changed it in 1964) and of the Cacos rebels. While the lower class Macoutes were drawn from the popular classes and paraded on the street, the middle class Macoutes tended to wear civilian garb (Trouillot (1990) 190).

the same year.[98] The army were eventually superseded by the Tonton Macoute – effectively the president's personal militia – who were drawn primarily from the lumpenproletariat, Vodou hierarchy and the rural *chefs de section* (controllers of rural regions traditionally drawn from the local community).[99] In 1960, anxious about the growing power of Barbot, who effectively ran the country when the president was ill, and was reputedly planning a coup, Duvalier arrested and imprisoned him in the notorious Fort Dimanche.[100] By 1960 all unions, except that of the taxi drivers who brought tourists from the ports, were dissolved and their leaders arrested or forced into exile.[101] Initially on good terms with the Roman Catholic Church – even including, for the first time, a Catholic priest in his cabinet – Duvalier had not forgotten the anti-superstition campaigns of the 1930s and '40s and, in 1959, under the pretext that the National Union of Secondary School teachers (many of whom were Catholic priests) had been infiltrated by communists, twenty student leaders were arrested and the high-profile priest Père Etienne Greinenberger, superior of the Holy Ghost Fathers, was expelled from the country.[102] In 1962, the Bishop of Gonaïves, Mgr. Robert, who had also been active in the anti-superstition campaign, was expelled on the grounds of having "organised and tolerated the pillaging of archaeological and folklore riches of the diocese".[103] The final break with the Catholic Church came in 1964, when a presidential decree was issued accusing the Canadian Jesuits of plotting to overthrow the government. The same year Duvalier expelled the Bishop of the Episcopal Church, also accused of conspiring against him. With the

---

98 Nicolls 216

99 Dupuy (2007) 35. By 1962 there were twice as many VSN as regular army and police (10,000). On the changing role of the *chefs de section* before and after the U.S. occupation see Jean L. Comhaire 'The Haitian *Chef de Section*', *American Anthropologist*, Vol. 57, 1955, 620-624

100 Nicholls 217. Released in 1962 Barbot went underground and allegedly plotted to kidnap Duvalier's children. It was during this time that Barbot told a journalist from the *Washington Post* that the president wanted to kill 300 people a year (Diederich and Burt 237).

101 Nicholls 218

102 Nicholls 222, Heinl and Heinl 559-560

103 Nicholls 224

Catholic and Episcopal Churches effectively, if temporarily, spiritually disarmed, Zacharie Delva, chief of the Macoutes and a reputed *houngan*, performed a public *Cérémonie Bois Cayman* on the steps of the cathedral, at which a pig was sacrificed and its blood drunk from a chalice.[104]

On April 1st that year Duvalier made himself president for life, pronouncing to the Haitian people that he had a Holy Mission to fulfil. The decision was ratified in June by a plebiscite in which more people voted than lived in the country, and the horizontal red and blue bands of the national flag were replaced by the vertical black and red bands of the flag used by Dessalines.[105] *The Catechism of the Revolution*, a collection of Duvalier's writings compiled that year by Jean Fourcand, claimed that Duvalier was the living embodiment of the five founders of the nation: Dessalines, Toussaint, Pétion, Christophe and Estimé.[106] The collection also contained Duvalier's self-styled Lord's Prayer read by all school children before lessons. By 1965 the consolidation of Duvalier's power had been achieved, as the most pressing political opposition in the country were either exiled, assassinated or imprisoned.

A year later the acclaimed Catholic novelist Graham Greene published perhaps the most scathing and famous account of life in Haiti under Duvalier – *The Comedians* – which brought a nightmare vision of the country to a highbrow, international literary public. He depicted in harsh and harrowing detail the methods used by Duvalier and the Tonton Macoute to maintain their hold on power, with several events in the novel based on actual stories reported to Greene by his good friend and *Time* journalist Bernard Diederich.[107] Several times in the novel Greene repeated a claim he had first made in an article for the *Sunday Telegraph* in 1963, that Papa Doc Duvalier considered

---

104 Heinl and Heinl 561

105 Heinl and Heinl 582-583

106 Nicholls 233

107 One such scene was the abduction of the corpse of Clément Jumelle. Stories about Duvalier's alleged use of Vodou and necromancy, such as the one that he planned to use Jumelle's body for nefarious purposes, were generated by the Catholic newspaper *Le Phallange*, after it was reported that police refused to let the body be blessed (Diederich and Burt 139).

himself the living embodiment of Baron Samedi, Lord of the Dead. This, it seems, was the first time anyone outside of Haiti had made a journalistic association between the Black despot and the Vodou Lord of the Dead, first expressed in fiction by Greene's compatriot and former British intelligence service colleague Ian Fleming nine years earlier.

THE END POINT OF COMEDY

> So haunted and given over to the superstition of the tragic, Greene creates and re-creates through photographed characters those phantasmagoric scenes dominated by fatality, a Greenian fatality ending up in an absurd human condition.

> - 'Graham Greene or the Scaring Machine' from *Graham Greene Démasqué* (1968)[108]

In Fleming's 1954 *Live and Let Die* Mr. Big does not have the Kananga alter-ego that appears in the 1973 film version of the book. He is instead a Haitian-born Mulatto called Buonaparte Ignacio Gallia, "head of the Black Widow Voodoo Cult and believed by that cult to be Baron Samedi".[109]

> The rumour had started that he was the Zombie or living corpse of Baron Samedi himself, the dreaded Prince of Darkness, and he fostered the story so that now it was accepted through all the lower strata of the negro world. As a result he commanded real fear, strongly substantiated by the immediate and often mysterious deaths of anyone who crossed him or disobeyed his orders.[110]

---

108 Max *et al* 53

109 Fleming 17

110 Fleming 20. Somewhat uncannily, given the later facts of Papa Doc's life, Mr. Big had only one Achilles heel: "chronic heart disease which had, in recent years, imparted a greyish tinge to his skin." Fleming 21. Fleming

This description is uncannily close to claims made about Duvalier by foreign journalists during his "reign of terror" in the mid 1960s. The popular source of this association, as we have seen, was Greene's article of 1963. But Duvalier himself seems not to have made the claim, his silence on this issue treated by subsequent commentators as evidence of its veracity. But as we have seen Fleming's uncannily prescient association of a ruthless Black "strong-man" emulating Baron Samedi, master of the *zombis* and a *zombi* himself, prefigures Graham Greene's use of the analogy by nine years. Could it be that Greene deliberately created the rumour as a kind of journalistic "black op" in order to attack Duvalier by subtly exploiting the recognisable combination of the Baron Samedi-Mr. Big figure, sinister Black adversary of the heroic White super-secret agent Bond, already disseminated to English-speaking publics?

Greene was familiar with the Bond novels, joking about *Dr. No* with Diederich as they travelled along the Haitian-Dominican border in 1965.[111] Greene had also stayed with Fleming at his Goldeneye residence in Jamaica where the author had offered to loan him the villa if he would write a foreword to his omnibus of Bond novels (to which Greene reputedly replied that he'd rather pay rent than write a foreword).[112] It seems probable, given Greene's familiarity with Fleming and his novels, that the association of Duvalier with the Baron was shaped by his reading of *Live and Let Die*. As we will see, Diederich, who claims to have personally witnessed Duvalier speaking as the Baron from the presidential balcony in 1963, himself attributed the association to Greene.[113] Like Fermor, and a host of other celebrated European and American writers, Greene had first visited Haiti during the presidency of Estimé when, as we have seen, the country became something of an "exotic" mecca for thrill-seeking and globe-trotting journalists and authors. Having first met in Haiti in 1954, the year *Live and Let Die* was published, Diederich and Greene met again in the Dominican Republic in 1965 when Diederich was in forced exile from Haiti and Greene was suffering from depression and doubts about his religious faith. The two men (along with the exiled Haitian priest Jean-Claude Bajeux, whose family had recently been disappeared

---

himself died seven years before Duvalier in 1964.

111 Diederich (2012) 81

112 Diederich (2012) 82

113 Diederich (2012) 28

by the Macoutes) took a tour of the Dominican-Haitian border, a journey that would supply the much-needed inspiration for Greene's 1966 novel.

The New Zealand-born Diederich perhaps did more than any other foreign journalist living in Haiti at the time to alert the outside world to the atrocities taking place under the reign of Duvalier. But it was Greene who wrote the article that would bring wider international attention to Diederich's claims.[114] In the *Sunday Telegraph* article Greene compared the "unconscious nightmare world of the Haitians" – in which "the Ego and the Id seem joined in unholy matrimony" – to that of Hieronymus Bosch.[115] In it he first put forward the rumour, purportedly at large in Haiti at the time, that Baron Samedi was living in the presidential palace "and his other name is Duvalier".[116] By 1969 the association would be an established truth in the minds of the foreign journalists, not least because of Diederich and Burt's *Papa Doc: The Truth About Haiti Today* in which the first public appearance of Papa Doc *as* Baron Samedi was "officially" reported.[117] The manifestation reputedly occurred when a delegation from the OAS (Organisation of American States) arrived in Haiti in 1963 to investigate reports of civil rights abuses there (six months before Greene's *Sunday Telegraph* article). On the morning of their arrival Duvalier reputedly filled the city with "*kleren*-soaked peasant mobs" who amassed before the National Palace.[118] Placing himself in front of a row of ambassadors from the OAS, each flanked by an armed Macoute, Duvalier sat

---

114 *The Sunday Telegraph* in 1963 was edited by Donald MacLachlan, Fleming's boyhood friend, colleague in British Naval Intelligence (notably the Atlantiksender radio project) and conceiver of the Hitler map hoax for the OSS. McLaghlan had first employed Greene to write an article on Cuba under Castro in 1963 (Sherry 145). It was on this trip that Greene visited Haiti and witnessed first-hand life under Duvalier.

115 Brennan 119-120

116 Brennan 120

117 As a "welcome" to the delegation of the OAS Duvalier organised an impromptu carnival on the streets of Port-au-Prince, hauling thousands of peasants into town and plying them with free rum (Diederich and Burt 215).

118 Heinl and Heinl 574

silently and unblinking for fifteen minutes, before cursing them "in the foulest Creole possible".[119] Then, parading the delegates on the palace balcony, Duvalier addressed the cheering crowds in their native language:

> Bullets and machine guns capable of daunting Duvalier don't exist. They cannot touch me... Haitian people, lift up your hearts to the spirits of the ancestors, prove that you are men, put marrow in your bones, let the blood of Dessalines flow in your veins... I take no orders or dictates from anyone, no matter where they come from. No foreigner shall tell me what to do. As President of Haiti, I am here only to continue the traditions of Toussaint Louverture and of Dessalines. I am even now an immaterial being.[120]

Echoing this scene from six years earlier, the final image of Duvalier in Diederich and Burt's *Papa Doc* describes him on the palace balcony addressing "the throng" below in "the high-pitched nasal gibberish that is the hallmark of those possessed by the Guédé *lwa*".[121] According to them, the "mystic... broken-field rambling" that Duvalier had developed as way of speaking to foreign journalists during his election campaign – seemingly designed to avoid answering their questions – had evolved into the subhuman gobbledegook of Guede-Baron Samedi himself, at the height of his charismatic and deathly powers.[122]

---

119 Diederich and Burt 215. The claim that Duvalier was deliberately impersonating Baron Samedi was repeated in Heinl and Heinl (574).

120 Heinl and Heinl 575. The speech itself does not seem to suggest a possession by the Baron, which, presumably, would have been far more offensive, vulgar and gibberish-filled.

121 Diederich and Burt 393

122 Diederich and Burt 86

SECRETISM, JU JU JOURNALISM OR ZIN?

Konplo pi to pase wanga (Conspiracy is stronger than a wanga charm).

- Haitian proverb

I see no difference when the changeover of chemistry and personality are made whether they are due to real or symbolic acts, the effect on man and society seems to be about the same.

- Katherine Dunham[123]

A film-adaptation of *The Comedians*, starring the superstar couple Richard Burton and Elizabeth Taylor, followed quickly on the heels of Greene's novel in 1967. Unable to film in Haiti, Duvalier having banned both the author and the book from the country, it was shot in Dahomey, described in an MGM promotional film as "geographically, culturally and ethnically... the place in the world most like Haiti". It was also, significantly, the ancestral home of Vodou according to most authorities on the subject. Duvalier's initial reaction to Greene's novel was dismissive, telling a European television crew that it had "no literary merit whatsoever".[124] The year before, perhaps in response to the popular reception of *The Comedians* novel, Papa Doc had decided to patch up his relations with the Vatican and create a wholesome image of Haiti that would attract more tourism. Gradually he began to suspect that Greene's novel was part of a larger international conspiracy to sabotage these plans. When news reached him of plans to make a film of the novel he was convinced.[125] On hearing that it would be shot in Dahomey he was reputedly "apoplectic", declaring it an act of treason by a nation that was the ancestral of home Vodou.[126]

---

123 Dunham 165

124 Diederich (2012) 114

125 Diederich (2012) 116

126 Diederich (2012) 115-117. Duvalier reputedly believed that Greene

In response Duvalier had the Haitian Foreign Ministry produce a special bulletin denouncing Greene and the conspiracy he was part of – *Graham Greene Démasqué* – written by staff members of the ministry and distributed to all foreign diplomatic missions in Haiti. In it Greene was described as a liar, a cretin, a stool pigeon, an unbalanced sadistic pervert, a former torturer and a drug addict.[127] It included an essay by Yves Massilon, a "protocol officer" at the Ministry, which claimed that Greene and Fleming had worked with the communist double-agent Kim Philby, and that both the novel and film were deliberate acts of espionage against Haiti.[128]

In his authoritative work *From Dessalines to Duvalier* David Nicholls suggested that claims to supernatural authority made by Duvalier himself "fade into insignificance when compared to those made by his supporters", people like Jacques Fourcand, compiler of Duvalier's *Catechism of the Revolution*.[129] And, one might add, by his detractors too. The seed of the myth of Papa Doc as Baron Samedi seems to have been sown to English speaking audiences by Greene, first in 1963, then again in 1966. The association was consolidated in 1969 by Diederich and Burt, Dunham and Whicker, from whence it has become an established fact of Duvalier-lore repeated consistently since then. But the extent to which Duvalier was himself a faithful practitioner of Vodou is still a disputed issue, and something that he publicly denied, accusing foreign journalists of concocting the legend.[130] Stories about him reading the entrails of goats, sitting in a bath wearing a top-hat and seeking council from the gods, sleeping one

---

was working for the CIA.

127 Diederich (2012) 125

128 Diederich (2012) 122-123

129 Nicholls 232

130 See 'Papa Doc: The Black Sheep' where he accuses foreign journalists of inventing the story that he was a *houngan*. Diederich and Burt suggest that while working at the Bureau of Ethnology both Duvalier and Denis were initiated as *houngans* (Diederich and Burt 47). One of the first accusations by a foreign author that Duvalier was a practicing *houngan* seems to be Alfred Métraux in *Voodoo in Haiti* (1959/1972) but he is sceptical about the claim, arguing that it seems to be based largely on the fact of his scholarly interest in the religion (Métraux 55).

night a year on the tomb of Dessalines, and consulting with mediums and the severed heads of dead enemies, seem to have come from disenchanted former colleagues and survivors of his terror tactics, who recounted their stories to journalists like Diederich, Burt and Elizabeth Abbott.[131] Nicholls, on the other hand, suggests that such stories were probably fabricated by Duvalier's enemies in a social milieu within which unfounded rumours were a cultural norm.[132] Rémy Bastien, in his essay 'Vodoun and Politics in Haiti' (1966), argued that only if Duvalier did *not* believe in Vodou could he have expected to impose his will on his *houngan* collaborators. Duvalier's will, Bastien wrote, "is supported by his pretense of conformity and by the repeated "proofs" that he possesses magical powers to a superlative degree. In the event that this magical prestige does not suffice, he holds a trump card: armed force."[133]

What seems certain, regardless of whether Duvalier deliberately impersonated Baron Samedi, is that the fictional figure of a "Voodoo Dictator" using his mystical powers to manipulate both his own people and foreign agents was created four years before Duvalier came to power by a former British intelligence officer who was by then a world-famous popular novelist. The image of Haiti under Duvalier created by

---

131 Diederich and Burt 355

132 Nicholls 234. Nicholls does however suggest that Duvalier himself cultivated a reputation for having occult powers and that claims to the same made by foreign journalists only strengthened his authority among the Haitian masses. The same point is made in the overtly propagandistic and denigratory television documentary *Haiti: Papa Doc and his People*, made for channel WTVJ-Miami in 1966, in which the narrator suggests "The practice of Vodouism in Haiti is not frowned upon by the country's president François Duvalier. On the contrary a superstitious people are more easily controlled than an enlightened people. It is not known whether Duvalier actually embraces Vodou himself, but he seems content in letting the populace believe he does".

133 Bastien 60. Bastien notes the cruel irony that this "regression" of Haitian political life was brought about by a learned minority, likening it to what Julien Benda has called *la trahison des clercs* (the treason of the learned). "The Haitian clercs", he wrote "mistook their passionate interest in folklore for the active care they should have taken of their illiterate brothers" (Bastien 62).

Graham Greene exploited Voodoo-horror tropes already established in the imaginations of western audiences, albeit in a much more high brow way than his friend and fellow intelligence operative. And it was presumably under the influence of such journalistic "facts" that the makers of *Dr. Terror's House of Horrors* would recast the "Great God Damballa" in place of the ubiquitous Duvalier-Baron Samedi figure on the island of "Paiti" in 1965, exploiting tropes that had been common to sensationalist representations of Haitian Vodou since Moreau de Saint-Méry.

Although facts about the stories associated with Duvalier cannot be corroborated, they are very much part of the myth that Duvalier reputedly perpetuated about himself.[134] In an article from the *Journal of the American Academy of Religion,* one that takes journalistic accounts like Abbot's and Diederich and Burt's on face value – 'Secretism and the Apotheosis of Duvalier' – Paul Johnson has argued that the authority of Vodou's initiatic knowledge was theatrically staged by Duvalier in order to create the appearance that he had special access to mystical powers.[135] Johnson uses the term *secretism*, adopted from Georges Simmel, upon which the essay rests, to name the active use of secrecy as the source of group identity, involving the promotion of the reputation of special access to restricted knowledge, and the successful performing or staging of such access.[136] He proposes the Kreyòl word *zin* (gossip that has no original source) to describe how Duvalier cunningly utilised the effects of Vodou rumour to maintain the popular idea of his access to secret and forbidden knowledge.[137] He would allegedly spread stories that he was seriously ill in order to flush out potential conspiracies against him, have the bodies of murdered enemies stolen from funeral processions in order to perpetuate the

---

134 What seems certain is that any *hounfort* that did not comply with his wishes was eradicated and that in 1960 Duvalier increased the taxes on Vodou rites "to the point that at Easter many *hounforts* in Port-au-Prince could not afford to hold their traditional Guédé ceremonies". At the same time he insisted that his image be pinned on every *poteau-mitan*. (Diederich and Burt 358-361).

135 Johnson 3

136 Johnson 19

137 Johnson 14

idea that he was making *zombis* of them, and design the uniform of the Tonton Macoute – a soft hat, denim pants, red bandana, and sunglasses – to match the sartorial code of the *lwa* Azaka.[138] But the victims of these groundless rumours seem to have been as much the foreign journalists who wrote about Haiti at the time as Haitians themselves. It was in their writings and television programmes that the myths about Duvalier tended to become established truths. Johnson for example, like several other authors, retells the story told to Elizabeth Abbott by the ethno-musicologist Harold Courlander, about a meeting he had with Duvalier in a darkened room lit only by twelve candles. Although no reference is made to the Baron in the original text, and Duvalier is wearing none of his typical attire (except a black suit), several subsequent authors have cited this as an example of Duvalier's deliberate use of the image. But Abbott's book was not published until 1988, thirty years after said meeting, long after the myth had become an established truth amongst foreign journalists.

It seems clear that François Duvalier was an extremely cunning and ruthless dictator who knew enough about Vodou to use its symbolism and mythology to consolidate his power amongst the disenfranchised majority of poor Haitians. But this is not the same as being a practitioner of Vodou, a claim he denied, as we have seen. What is much less open to speculation is Duvalier's mystical identification with previous Haitian presidents, whom he believed himself to be the reincarnation of, and his admiration for French reactionary, anti-democratic philosophers and political leaders like Arthur de Gobineau and Joseph de Maistre. In 1959 he had posters put up across Port-au-Prince declaring "Dieu, the great worker of the Universe; Dessalines, the supreme artisan of liberty; Duvalier, architect of the new Haiti".[139] Rumours that he slept one night of the year on the tomb of Dessalines may well be pure *zin*, but he certainly made the date of Dessalines' death a national holiday.[140] Duvalier used his knowledge of Haitian

---

138 Johnson 11. Azaka (also Azacca, Zaka or Couzin Zaka) is a peasant *lwa* of agriculture and harvest. Azaka and Guede are considered to be brothers by *Vodouisants* (Deren 109).

139 Diederich and Burt 140

140 Dunham 162. Duvalier's identification with Dessalines is significant in several ways. Firstly Dessalines was himself reputedly both a practitioner

history to construct a myth of himself as the living incarnation of a series of revolutionary Black leaders (Dessalines, Louverture and Estimé), an ideological and populist strategy against the Mulatto elites and White foreign powers and a practical means for communicating with rural peasant and urban working class communities. Certainly many of the leaders of the Tonton Macoute were *houngans* and *mambos* drawn from the complex network of Vodou communities and temples throughout the country, and it was they who maintained the state of violence that their leader depended upon to secure his hold on power. As *chefs de section* they were able to control large portions of the country whose populations were predominantly practicing *Vodouisants* and their intimate knowledge of the religion served the purposes of consolidating power for Duvalier far more effectively than his own ever could have. In creating a state of permanent terror, maintained by a voluntary, national security force drawn from the ranks of those who had been traditionally denied power, he accomplished a new stage in the "gradual evolution" of the cult that he had outlined in 1944. Duvalier treated Vodou as the unofficial national religion, while maintaining the state religion as ostensibly Catholic. As Johnson has put it, echoing the scepticism of Greene about the possibility of "Vodou Liberation" in Haiti, Duvalier managed to build a nation-state of "the people" that would be turned against them in their own religious tongue.[141] But Vodou alone could not keep Duvalier in power, and it was, relatively speaking, a minor factor determining his control of the state. The real factors that ensured his hold on power were the purging of the armed forces of any potential rivals; a strategy of constantly rotating senior officers; strictly controlling access to weapons that could be used against him; concentrating them in the hands of the palace guard and secret police; expelling all church leaders who had any involvement in anti-superstition campaigns or left-wing organisations; banning trade

---

of Vodou and also a violent suppressor of the cult. Secondly Dessalines was one of the first Haitian leaders to be transubstantiated into an immortal within the Vodou pantheon, becoming Papa Ogou Dessalin, an avatar of Ogun, the fiery African warrior spirit. And finally Dessalines was the first Black Emperor of Haiti, the official founder of the black independent nation and a violent purger of Whites from the nascent republic (Laguerre 66 and Johnson 4).

141 Johnson 5-6

unions; imprisoning, expelling or killing any potential enemy, real or imagined; and cultivating positive "donor" relations with the U.S. based on the idea that Haiti under Duvalier was a disciplinary bulwark against communism in the Caribbean.[142]

The myth of Papa Doc as Baron Samedi, *houngan*, master of Black arts and "King of the Zombies" was a convenient one for foreign journalists and film-makers who had a ready supply of macabre stereotypes of Voodoo-horror to draw on. In his book *Haiti's Bad Press* (1992) Robert Lawless examined popular media representations of Haiti under Duvalier in the 1960s. Two magazines that could be found on the coffee tables of middle-class American homes at the time, he noted, *Reader's Digest* and *Life*, carried articles with subtitles like "A Voodoo-Touched Tyrant Exhausts Patience of U.S. and His People" and "Murder, Torture, the Black-Magic Rituals of Voodoo – These are Among the Administrative Techniques of François Duvalier".[143] Such titles clearly exploited earlier colonialist and xenophobic representations of Haiti as a land of black magic rites, human sacrifice and unspeakable horrors that many of the intellectuals and writers discussed in the last chapter had worked hard to counter and correct. As Nicholls has pointed out, simplistic and sensationalistic accounts of Haiti under Duvalier portraying it as a country in which a majority of desperately poor, discontented and rebellious peasants and urban workers were forcibly held down by a mystical Vodou dictator and his private army of cut-throat henchmen, passes too easily over the complex history of political, cultural and social relations that made Duvalier's dictatorship possible, and the tradition of terroristic means by which previous Haitian presidents held on to power.[144] But they also chimed with the opinion of the international White and Mulatto business class and Catholic clergy of Haiti, whose economic and spiritual power

---

142 Duvalier's anti-communist stance was not merely expedient, as Nicholls has shown. Duvalier constantly reiterated his criticism of Marxism, expressing his allegiance to the western side of the cold war. In a message to the legislative assembly in 1966 he declared that his government stood for the "defence of Christian civilisation against atheist materialism and the intolerance of a leveling and inhuman communism" (Nicholls 232).

143 Lawless 82

144 Nicholls 15

Duvalier had dispossessed them of, and for whom Graham Greene was an international and respected literary spokesperson.

What seems clear is that François Duvalier *was*, as he himself publicly claimed, subject to an international campaign of what Rosalind Shaw has called "Ju Ju Journalism", a genre in which the reputed magical practices of vilified figures or groups are used to undermine their credibility and justify international military, political or economic action against them.[145] In this sense the literary and journalistic case made against Duvalier by the likes of Greene, Diederich and Burt, Whicker, Abbott and Heinl and Heinl, particularly those containing unsubstantiated claims about his involvement in the nefarious aspects of Vodou and his alleged emulation of Baron Samedi, conform to a pattern we have already seen in the writings of Spenser St. John, Stephen Bonsal, John Houston Craige and Faustin Wirkus. For a brief decade, between 1946 and 1956, Haiti seemed to have turned the negative stereotypes of its history and culture into something to be celebrated and taken seriously by academics, intellectuals and politicians both within and outside Haiti, a source of unifying national pride and tourist revenue. But as Rémy Bastien lamented, after the excesses of Duvalier "the horrible crept back into the press and we read of gory offerings, of human sacrifices performed in the very basement of the national palace in Port-au-Prince. Seabrook is back".[146] What has so far remained obscured however is the extent to which "the return of Seabrook" was also a product of "ju ju journalism" connected to the political fictions of Ian Fleming and Graham Greene, as it was the occult work of Duvalier himself.

The association between Baron Samedi and *zombis* has been present since the figure first appeared in literature in 1804, and the Baron's trajectory into sensationalist representations of Vodou in western popular culture clearly exploits this association above all others. If *zombis* were the undead lumbering slaves of Vodou sorcery, the Baron appears twenty years later as their sinister funereal master, migrating from the sensationalist travelogue of Seabrook and the

---

145 See Rosalind Shaw 'Robert Kaplan and "Ju Ju Journalism" in Sierra Leone's Rebel War: The Primitivising of an African Conflict' in Meyer and Pels *Magic and Modernity: Interfaces of Revelation and Concealment* (2003).

146 Bastien 40

counter ethnology of the *Indigénistes,* back into the travel writings of Fermor and eventually into the pulp and cinematic spectacle of Fleming's Bond. What we start to see happening by the 1950s is a kind of circuitous symbolic relay occurring between the "genuine" ethnography of Haitian Vodou, its sensational misrepresentations in the West, and an overtly propagandistic use of the myth of "Voodoo Power" by Duvalier's enemies and detractors. Fleming's invention of a Black super-villain, deliberately identifying himself with Baron Samedi in order to keep his subjects in a state of permanent terror, prefigured Duvalier by three years. Is it possible that Duvalier could have known this and designed his act to exploit fears and anxieties about Haiti and Vodou already seeded by Seabrook and Fleming in the western popular imagination? This would be very good *"zin"*, but in whose service would it be operating? Or pushing the logic of "black propaganda" even further, what if the myth of Papa Doc Duvalier, the "Voodoo Dictator", living embodiment of Baron Samedi, reducing Haiti to a nation of entranced *zombis*, was a covert strategy to discredit Black Nationalist politics in America, Europe and Africa in the late 1960s, as Duvalier himself claimed?

Donald Cosentino has proposed that Duvalier ushered in the "Age of Bawon Samdi". But as we have seen *Live and Let Die* was written before Duvalier's rise to power when few people outside of Haiti would have recognised either the bespectacled country doctor or the top-hat wearing Master of *Zombis*. Wasn't it Seabrook, Fermor and Fleming who actually sowed the archetype of the Baron into the popular imagination of Haiti in the English speaking world, and Greene who returned him to Haiti in the form of a propagandistic defamation of Duvalierism? In other words, isn't it more appropriate to suggest that it was Fleming, Greene and Diederich who actually ushered in the Age of Baron Samedi, effectively casting Duvalier into a role forged from sensationalist Vodou myth, international moral outrage at his brutality towards the people of Haiti, his duplicitous manipulation of U.S. interests and their anti-communist agenda and the rise of a powerful international Black Power movement that sought inspiration from the Haitian Revolution and romance of revolutionary Vodou. By the time of Whicker's 'Black Sheep' documentary in 1969, the association between François Duvalier and Baron Samedi had become consolidated in the western media: Papa Doc *was* the incarnation of the Haitian Lord of the Dead, and the Haitian people a nation of terrorised *zombis* controlled by an army of Vodou-using thugs. As Whicker put it towards the end of 'Papa Doc: The Black Sheep':

> Believing himself secure from enemies, protected by gunmen and the Vodou power lying within the number 2 – his presidential inauguration was on October 22nd – Papa Doc, hushed and curious with that sinister smile, seems unconcerned and unaware, as his stricken nation sinks deeper into its zombie trance, watched by a critical but helpless world.

By the time of Whicker's journey to Haiti, the Haitian *zombi* had largely been forgotten by western audiences. Since its comedic apotheosis in the 1950s it had become a nostalgic, and somewhat conscience-ridden figure of exotic, spooky fun for children's "horror" matinees. But in the hands of Greene and Whicker it would once again become a metaphor for an entranced nation of terrorised subjects and their brutal subjugators, the Haitian people cast as barely-living monsters of misfortune shackled to a delusional dictator who believed himself Lord of the Dead.

In their extensive and well researched history of Haiti – *Written in Blood: The Story the Haitian People 1492-1995* – Robert and Nancy Heinl include many of the accusations about Duvalier's involvement with Vodou reported and repeated by their journalistic colleagues. Towards the end of the chapter on Duvalier – 'I am the State' – they recount a story about Papa Doc's burial. When he died in April 1971 his body was placed in a refrigerated glass box, watched over by 22 soldiers and 22 Tonton Macoute for two days. On the day he was buried something unfathomably preternatural took place:

> At the gate of the Cimetiere, sentry post of Bawon Samedi, a mysterious event transpired: suddenly from nowhere, with a fierce howl and dark coil of dust, a mighty wind swirled up from underfoot and obscured the sun. There was a shriek of horror. Musicians dropped instruments, mourners trampled each other to escape they knew not what; *miliciens* fired rusty Mausers in the air.

Duvalier has burst the grave, men cried, and is loosed upon earth. There is no hiding place.[147]

POSTSCRIPT

At a Vodou ceremony in Upper Belair in Port-au-Prince in 1976, Michel Laguerre, author of *Voodoo and Politics in Haiti*, was surprised to see a *houngan* wearing a dark suit and black hat, heavy reading glasses and holding a pistol in his right hand. When Laguerre asked another priest to identify who this was the spirit of, he was told that it was *lwa* 22 Os (22 Bones), so named after the magic number on which Duvalier was elected president and the date that his soul passed over quietly in the presidential palace.[148]

---

147 Heinl and Heinl 598-600, Abbott 163. Robert D. Heinl was the former Chief of the U.S. Naval Mission to Haiti from 1949-1953.

148 Laguerre 118

PART TWO

fig. ii AXIS OF LIVING DEATH

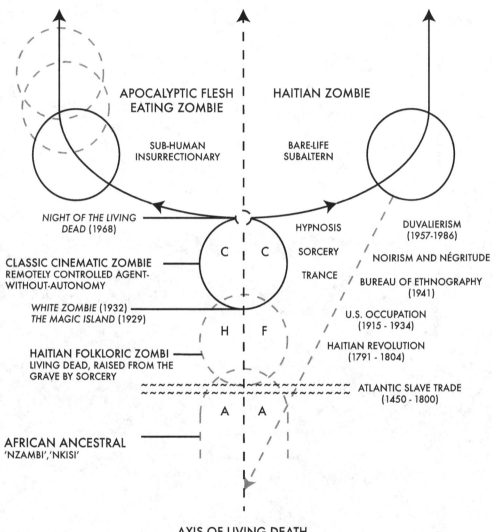

ZOMBIE APOCALYPSE

ZOMBIE NATION

APOCALYPTIC FLESH
EATING ZOMBIE

HAITIAN ZOMBIE

SUB-HUMAN
INSURRECTIONARY

BARE-LIFE
SUBALTERN

*NIGHT OF THE LIVING
DEAD* (1968)

HYPNOSIS

DUVALIERISM
(1957-1986)

SORCERY

NOIRISM AND NÉGRITUDE

CLASSIC CINEMATIC ZOMBIE
REMOTELY CONTROLLED AGENT-
WITHOUT-AUTONOMY

TRANCE

BUREAU OF ETHNOGRAPHY
(1941)

C   C

U.S. OCCUPATION
(1915 - 1934)

WHITE ZOMBIE (1932)
THE MAGIC ISLAND (1929)

HAITIAN REVOLUTION
(1791 - 1804)

H   F

HAITIAN FOLKLORIC ZOMBI
LIVING DEAD, RAISED FROM THE
GRAVE BY SORCERY

ATLANTIC SLAVE TRADE
(1450 - 1800)

A   A

AFRICAN ANCESTRAL
'NZAMBI','NKISI'

AXIS OF LIVING DEATH

Night of the Living Dead, original promotional poster, 1968

V

NO MORE ROOM IN HELL

UNDEAD UPRISING

And as soon as he stepped out of the boat a man from the tombs came to meet him, a man with an unclean spirit who dwelt among the burial caves; by this time no one could bind him, not even with a chain, for he had often been bound with fetters and chains and had snapped the chains and broken the fetters. Nobody could tame him. All night and day among the tombs and the hills he shrieked and gashed himself with stones. On catching sight of Jesus from afar he ran and knelt before him, shrieking aloud, "Jesus, son of God most High, what business have you with me? By God, I adjure you, do not torture me." (For he had said, "Come out of the man, you unclean spirit.") Jesus asked him, "What is your name?" "My name is Legion," he said, "because there are many of us inside." And they begged him earnestly not to send them to some distant place.

- Mark 5: 2-10

It was the hour I had heretofore most dreaded, just after
the night rain with soil and humus stirring and everything
alive gloating over the death of something while in the
process of feeding on it.

- Katherine Dunham *Island Possessed* (1969)[1]

Before our eyes, death embodied by a dead person
partakes of a whole sticky horror; it is of the same nature
as toads, as filth, as the most dreadful spiders. It is
nature, not only the nature that we have not been able to
conquer, but also the one that we have not even managed
to face, and against which we don't have the chance to
struggle. Something awful and bloodless attaches itself
to the body that decomposes, in the absence of the one
who spoke to us and whose silence revolts us.

- Georges Bataille *The Accursed Share Vol. 3*[2]

1968 heralded a fundamental shift in the popular image of the *zombi*
signalled by the release of George A. Romero's *Night of the Living Dead*,
the first in a new genre of zombie films that would relegate the Haitian
folkloric *zombi* and classic cinematic zombie-sleepwalkers to relics
of a bygone era.[3] From *Night* onwards there are no more Svengali-
like controllers of remote minds, no more witch-doctors with *ouanga*
charms or "voodoo dolls" capturing the souls of feckless visitors to
primitive and exotic lands, no *zombi* work slaves labouring mindlessly
in the mill and no top-hatted Baron Samedi laughing manically in the
cemetery. From here on the *zombi* no longer looks back to Haiti, or the
politics of race, colonialism and the international power relations that
pertain to it.[4] There is no more before. The new flesh-eating zombies,

---

1 Dunham 255

2 Bataille (1993) 216-217

3 *Dawn of the Dead* (1978), *Day of the Dead* (1985), *Land of the Dead* (2005)
and *Diary of the Dead* (2007).

4 There have been some exceptions to this general rule, such as *Isle of
the Snake People* (1971), *I Eat Your Skin* (1971), *Sugar Hill* (1974) and *The*

an abominable reincarnation of (in)humanity at the end of history, are returning from death for no known reason, forming marauding hordes of cannibal ghouls, hell-bent on turning each of *us* into one of *them*. After *Night of the Living Dead* (excepting one famous reference to Vodou in *Dawn of the Dead*[5]) the Haitian *zombi* becomes merely a mythical ancestor in the new zombie lore whose causes are ultimately academic. When asked what caused the new zombie plague, Romero has simply said "God changed the rules".

The genealogy of the flesh-eating zombie figure can however be traced back to a transitional, post-war period when the Haitian folkloric and classical cinematic zombies migrated into pulp science-fiction, horror literature and cinema in the late 1940s and early '50s, eventually becoming a figure of spooky fun rather than existential terror. Overtly racist comedy-horror films like *King of the Zombies* (1941) and *Zombies on Broadway* (1945), where the *zombi* figure was still associated with "voodoo mumbo-jumbo", paved the way for the comedic apotheosis of the figure which, after Romero's intervention, passed into films like *The Return of the Living Dead* (1985) and *Shaun of the Dead* (2004).[6] One of the widely acknowledged innovations of

---

Serpent and the Rainbow (1988) (discussed in Chapter Six). For a summary of *zombi* and Vodou-themed films see Bryan Senn's *Drums of Terror: Voodoo in the Cinema* (1998).

5 In a much referenced scene the four surviving protagonists survey the prison-sanctuary of the shopping mall that they have made their home from its balcony, as the zombies outside paw relentlessly at its closed doors. They reflect on what makes them keep coming back to the mall:

Francine – "They're still here."
Stephen – "They're after us. They know we're still in here."
Peter – "They're after the place. They don't know why. They just remember. Remember that they want to be in here."
Francine – "What the hell are they?"
Peter – "They're us that's all. There's no more room in hell."
Stephen – "What?"
Peter – "Something my granddaddy used to tell us. You know Macumba? Vodou. Grandad was a priest in Trinidad. He used to tell us 'When there's no more room in hell, the dead will walk the earth'."

6 *The Return of the Living Dead* is an excellent example of what the

Night was to invert the popular image of the zombie as a kitsch figure of spooky fun, injecting it with a deadly new cannibalistic vitality.[7] In this sense the zombies of *Night* are doubly zombic, having been given a second lease of horrific, cinematic un-life after their apparent comedic decline in the 1950s.

The re-birth of the *zombi* (from now on "zombie") in apocalyptic, flesh-eating mode also marked the beginning-of-the-end for the zombie colour bar, which, as we have seen, was pretty much obliterated by the final decades of the last century. There are no reasons for them and no reasoning against them, their destiny and ours total, imminent and meaningless, and there is nothing any race, creed or colour can do about it. It is perhaps this absolute negation of human difference that allowed the apocalyptic cannibal zombie to become an allegorical cipher for any array of subjugated, marginalised, vilified or persecuted social or cultural groups, from American blue-collar workers to Palestinians in the occupied territories, a tendency that Romero and his commentators have been highly conscious of. At the time of *Night*'s production however, the cultural politics shaping the consciousness of both the film-makers and their audiences were of a very particular kind.

Romero began making television commercials and short children's films for the *Mister Rodgers* television show in Pittsburgh in 1963 with his film company *The Latent Image*. This was the year that saw George Wallace become Governor of Alabama, famously announcing "segregation now, segregation tomorrow, segregation forever"; the

Australian film-maker and writer Philip Brophy identified in 1983, shortly before the Video Nasty controversy, as "Horrality", a portmanteau term combining "horror", "textuality", "morality" and "hilarity", that persuasively captured a certain excessive and comical turn in horror films of the 1980s (See 'Horrality – The Textuality of Contemporary Horror Films', *Screen*, Vol. 27, January-February 1986). It could also be read as a slapstick version of Bataille's theories of abject and erotic excess, including a graveyard striptease by a death's head-crotched punk dreaming of being eaten by old men and a headless torso running wild in a medical supply warehouse.

7 Romero continues to play on the residual comedic character of the shuffling zombie figure, perhaps most effectively in the shopping mall zombies of *Dawn of the Dead* (1978) and the "Bub" character in *Day of the Dead* (1985).

subsequent desegregation campaign in Birmingham led by the Southern Christian Leadership Conference; the violent suppression and mass arrest of Civil Rights protesters by the Birmingham police department, under the direction of Eugene "Bull" Connor; the bombing of buildings accommodating SCLC leaders (reputedly by the Ku Klux Klan) and the bombing of the 16th Street Baptist Church (in which four African American girls were killed); the 'March on Washington for Jobs and Freedom', at which Martin Luther King Jr. delivered his 'I Have a Dream' speech; and the assassination of the African American Civil Rights activist Medgar Evers by the White Supremacist Byron de la Beckwith. It was also the year that President John F. Kennedy, five months after giving his famous Civil Rights Address, in which he said "Race has no place in American life or law", was assassinated; President Lyndon B. Johnson escalated the U.S. war in Vietnam on the grounds of defending America against communism; and Malcolm X gave his 'Message to the Grass Roots' speech in which he outlined the difference between the Black and Negro revolutions, giving the example of the communist revolution in China as a model for Blacks in America.[8] The Black Power movement that emerged from the *Négritude*, *Noiriste* and Black radical traditions of the 1930s, '40s and '50s had been consolidated into an international revolutionary movement, that, as we have seen, was the target of FBI counter-intelligence operations in 1960s America. In Haiti, the traditional home of the *zombi*, François Duvalier was using the mythology of Black nationalism and Vodou against his own people, turning the country into what foreign journalists called a "Zombie Nation" ruled by a "Voodoo Dictator".

---

8 In the speech Malcolm X describes an image that could have been taken from the script of *Night of the Living Dead*: a little Chinese girl during the Communist Revolution holds a gun to the head of her "Uncle Tom" father before pulling the trigger, "setting a good example to us all". Luckner Cambronne, a loyal deputy in the Duvalier government, once said "a good Duvalierist is ready to kill his children, or children to kill their parents" (Heinl and Heinl 555). It was also in 1963 that the abuses of the Duvalier regime first came to international, public attention. That year Dr. Jacques Fourcand, president of the Haitian Red Cross, gave a speech in response to anti-Duvalier movements in Haiti, that threatened a "Himalaya of corpses": 'the dead will be buried under a mountain of ashes because of serving the foreigner" (Diederich and Burt 203).

By 1968 the war in Vietnam was fully escalated, Malcolm X had been assassinated by members of the Nation of Islam, large-scale race riots had broken out in New York, Philadelphia, Watts, Chicago and Detroit and Haiti's reputation as a "bulwark against communism in the Caribbean" was firmly maintained by Papa Doc.[9] The same year Romero and his team in Pittsburgh, having acquired a 35mm movie camera in order to make an advert for a soap-detergent called Calgon, formed a new company called *Image Ten* with the idea of making a "Bergmanesque *Virgin Spring*-type movie" called 'Whine of the Fawn', a love story about two teenagers in the middle ages.[10] When the script failed to find funding, Romero and his team decided to make a "commercial" horror film based on Richard Matheson's 1954 novel *I Am Legend,* that would capture the sense of a world "going to hell in a handcart".[11]

The plot of *I Am Legend* centres on Robert Neville, a solitary "last man" figure who fights for survival against the rest of what was "humanity", now transformed into a marauding horde of photosensitive, vampire-mutants by a cataclysmic, global pandemic triggered by an atomic war. The excessively claustrophobic story is told entirely from Neville's perspective, the seemingly sole survivor, trapped in his fortified home, protected by garlic chains and crucifixes, ceaselessly besieged by vampires during the night, and foraying into the outside

---

9 I have not been able to trace the origin of the much used epithet "bulwark against communism" but it is interesting to note that shortly after Dessalines' Declaration of Haitian Independence in 1804, *The Spectator* in New York published a letter by 'An Injured Man of Color' that praised the General for creating a "united and valiant people" who were "an unconquerable bulwark against an empire of treachery, violence and unrelenting ambition" (White 179). White Americans, White notes, needed to create a bulwark to prevent another Haiti "in their own back yard".

10 *Birth of the Living Dead*

11 The book had already been adapted for cinema by Ubaldo Ragona and Sidney Salkow as *The Last Man on Earth* (1964) on whose script Matheson had worked. The lurching vampires in *The Last Man on Earth* were an inspiration for Romero's "ghouls" four years later. Other precursors for the new zombie appear in *Zombies of Mora Tau* (1957) which introduced the idea of a zombie epidemic.

world only during the day to salvage what resources he can, killing every sleeping vampire he finds. Gradually slipping into alcoholism and depression as he reflects on the futility of his fate, Neville decides to find an antidote to the virus by experimenting on living vampires brought back to his newly created home-cum-laboratory. After years of solitary experimentation Neville meets an apparently uninfected woman, Ruth, who explains how she and her husband survived the epidemic. Suspicious of her reaction to his stories about killing vampires, Neville decides to test if she has the virus. On discovering that she does, Ruth knocks Neville unconscious. He wakes up to find a note explaining that she had been sent to spy on him by a newly formed society of vampires that is waging a war of extermination against the first generation of mutants. After being captured by the shock troops of the New Vampire Society, Neville finally realises that he was himself the last remnant of a dying species, a monster incarnate, "a new superstition entering the unassailable fortress of forever", before he is publicly executed in front of a crowd of "white faces".[12]

---

12 Kathy Davis Patterson, drawing on a long history of literary interpretations of Bram Stoker's *Dracula* as an allegory for racial "otherness", situates Matheson's novel in the context of Civil Rights struggles in the mid '50s, arguing that, by pitting a solitary White, male hero figure against the "black plague" of vampirism, Matheson was expressing widely held fears about Black-White integration and "the monstrosity of blackness" amongst middle-class Whites of the 1950s. Although the arguments are not entirely convincing, there are clear references in *I Am Legend* to the discourse of minority Civil Rights claims at the time. In one section Matheson has Neville make a sarcastic and drunken speech in support of vampire rights:

> Ah, see, you have turned the poor guileless innocent into a haunted animal. He has no means of support, no measures for proper education, he has not the voting franchise. No wonder he is compelled to seek out a predatory nocturnal existence. Robert Neville grunted a surly grunt. Sure, sure, he thought, but would you let your sister marry one? (Matheson 32)

See Kathy Davis Patterson 'Echoes of Dracula: Racial Politics and the

Like Matheson, Romero did not conceive of the monsters of *Night of the Living Dead* as *zombis* in a traditional sense, but as "ghouls", the word used by characters throughout the film. The term derives from the Arabic *ghul* (meaning "one who seizes"), a legendary demon associated with wastelands, deserts, derelict buildings and graveyards, with a reputation for feasting on human flesh, living or dead. Popularised amongst English readers by *The Arabian Nights*, the ghoul made its first cinematic appearance in the 1933 British horror film *The Ghoul*, a year after the first zombie film. In the film Professor Morlant, dabbler in the black arts, seemingly comes back from the dead to protect the secret of eternal life. By the time Romero came to make *Dawn of the Dead* ten years later however, he was using the term zombie instead, as did most of the apocalyptic zombie films that followed in *Night*'s wake.[13] The popular acceptance of the zombie moniker to describe the undead, apocalyptic cannibal seems to have been consolidated during this time. The markedly new behaviour of the flesh-eating zombie, the absence of any external or intended cause for the condition and the terminal absolutism of the *Living Dead* narratives, all suggest that it represents an entirely new kind of entity, whatever its ancestral or semantic roots may be.

In Rob Kuhns' documentary about the film, *Birth of the Living Dead*, Romero said that for him and his team in 1968 *I Am Legend*

Failure of Segregated Spaces in Richard Matheson's *I Am Legend*'.

13 A significant exception to this rule is the series of Italian-made zombie films produced after *Dawn of the Dead*. A re-edited and re-scored version of Romero's *Dawn of the Dead* was released in Europe as *Zombi* in 1978. A year later Lucio Fulci made *Zombi 2* (otherwise known as *Zombie Flesh Eaters* and *Woodoo*) which opens to the sound of a tribal bongo and a shrouded body rising from a hospital bed in a jungle hut before being unceremoniously shot in the head. It transpires that on the island of Matool, near St. Thomas in the Caribbean, a British doctor has been struggling to fight a disease that turns the dead into walking corpses. *Zombi 2* makes use of ultra-generic tropes from earlier zombie films: superstitious natives believing in legends about zombies and "voodooism", ubiquitous voodoo drumming and wailing and generally Black zombies. The film culminates not in a traditional voodoo sacrifice party but the now generic zombie siege. *Zombi 2* also seems to owe a significant debt to *Zombies of Mora Tau* (1957) which introduced the first under-water zombies.

was an expression of the popular anger they felt all around them at the time, and the creation of a race of ghouls was at once a way of depicting "revolution" and expressing the hopeless rage that was felt in the face of the perceived failures of the Civil Rights and peace movements of the 1950s and '60s.[14] "I think mostly that the sixties didn't work," Romero explained, "we thought we had changed the world or were part of some sort of a reform that would make things better. And all of a sudden it wasn't any better, it wasn't any different". Romero seems to be proposing that the spectacular rise of the flesh-eating zombie represents a species-being sublimation of this impotent, mass rage into the insatiable predation of the living dead. "The dead are coming back to life. That's the revolution. That's what's missing".[15]

Despite the recurrent millennial, and generally Christian eschatological explanations for the flesh-eating zombie plague, there is something starkly secular and virulently materialist about their incarnation which lays waste to idealist, transcendental or theological resolutions of the narratives[16] Questions about whether the new zombies are actual or imaginary beings, or the consequence of empirical or supernatural causes (à la Seabrook, Hurston, Davis and the early *zombi* films) are ultimately rendered meaningless by the ever-escalating threat they pose for humanity as a whole. There is, after all, no antidote for death, and death is everywhere on the loose. This stark truth presents the living protagonists with rather bleak prospects: not a future of meaningless, drudging slavery but a brutal and often painful death, followed by a violent mutation into a living-dead feeding-machine that will gnaw the world we once knew into oblivion. Importantly, flesh-eating zombies return to "post-life" in whatever corporeal state they died, however injured, dismembered or putrescent. As such they often take on a much more carcass-like form than their *zombi kadav* precursors. In Romero's 1985 *Day of the Dead* for instance, a scientist

---

14 In the 2002 apocalyptic zombie film *28 Days Later*, the virus that leads to the zombie outbreak, unleashed when animal rights activists raid an animal-testing laboratory, is called "Rage".

15 Romero in *Birth of the Living Dead*

16 Kim Paffenroth's *Gospel of the Living Dead: George Romero's Visions of Hell on Earth* (2006) explicitly frames the *Living Dead* sequence as a Christian morality cycle meditating on the contemporary human vices of racism, sexism, self-destructive materialism and individualism.

nicknamed Frankenstein tries, as Neville had done, to discover how the zombie plague works. In his laboratory he has a number of zombies in various stages of dismemberment, including one for whom only the spinal cord and vertical column remain, and another whose innards spill onto the floor through its ribcage. This cadaverous tendency has intensified since the inception of the flesh-eating zombie, with film-makers exploring the extreme limits of corporeal re-animation and living-dead functionality.

Like Le Bon's hypnotised mass-being, flesh-eating zombies are driven primarily by their brainstems and the compulsions of untold biological automatisms. They are, as many commentators have noted, *all drive*. The horror of the new zombie, then, is one of pure organic animism, abject *life*, an appalling, predatory vitalism, pared down to a network of reflexes that cannot be stilled. Importantly the new zombies, unlike their somnambulist and folkloric *zombi* ancestors, have no referent, actual or assumed, in the real world (except that is, for the predatory zombie-automaton that lives in us all). In this sense they are entirely spectacular entities and as such don't raise the same kind of ethical and philosophical questions as their predecessors. This is not to say the apocalyptic cannibal zombie is not an entity that raises philosophical questions. On the contrary, it has generated volumes of speculative thought and even entered the lexicon of consciousness studies in the form of the so-called "p-zombie".

The Philosophical Zombie migrated into the philosophy of consciousness in the 1970s through the writings of Robert Kirk, who proffered it as an imaginary foil for a series of thought experiments, claims and counter-claims generally referred to as the "zombie problem". It was a hypothetical being, physically indistinguishable from a normal human being except that it lacked "sentience". Since then the "p-zombie" has been used to stage debates about the relationship between consciousness and the physical world, between "imaginability", "conceivability" and "possibility", and as a way of addressing the "other minds" problem (i.e. how can one know if others have minds?). These are all problems that have been associated, if somewhat tangentially, with the zombie's previous incarnations, but rarely, until recently, were they pursued with the same level of intellectual and philosophical enthusiasm. Since the zombie-problem gained currency in the field of consciousness studies, the figure has come to be addressed from a variety of philosophical perspectives.[17] But the kind of questions it raises do not concern the *actuality* of the entity as it is popularly recognised and understood. The folkloric *zombi*, like the hypnotised somnambulist and the slave to which they both refer, is, on the contrary, a being whose *possibility* and *actuality* are very much at stake in the narratives constructed around them and around their audiences.

MEDIA ZOMBIES AND THE TELEVISION REVOLUTION

Wars, revolutions, civil uprisings are interfaces within the new environments created by the electronic media.

- Marshall McLuhan *The Medium is the Massage* (1976)[18]

If we understand the revolutionary transformations caused by new media, we can anticipate and control them; but if we continue in our self-induced   subliminal trance, we will be their slaves.

- Marshall McLuhan, *Playboy* interview, 1969

In light of the horrors and atrocities of 20th century wars both Matheson's vampires and Romero's zombies raise questions about what it is to be human and the meaning of genocidal violence. As such the tradition of apocalyptic cannibal zombies has been read as the popular cultural accompaniment to anti and post-humanist debates within philosophy during the latter half of the 20th century. The apocalyptic zombie, particularly when addressed in bio-political frameworks, has been used to reflect upon contemporary configurations of the "human"; it has been historically constructed in legal, political and philosophical terms. As many commentators have also noted the zombies of *Night of the Living Dead* reference an apocalyptic sensibility

---

17 See, for example, the collection *The Undead and Philosophy: Chicken Soup for the Soulless* (Greene and Mohammad) in which zombies are addressed from the perspectives of Aristotle, Descartes, Hobbes, Locke and Spinoza and 'The Zombie Invasion of Philosophy' issue of *Philosophy Now*, Issue 96, May-June 2013.

18 McLuhan and Fiore 9

that was widely felt during a decade that had seen the suppression of the Civil Rights and free-speech movements in the U.S., widespread rioting in urban centres throughout the United States, the first televised war in Vietnam, and the assassinations of John F. Kennedy, Robert Kennedy, Medgar Evers, Malcolm X and Martin Luther King Jr. (the latter, coincidentally, on the day that *Night* was being driven to New York to find a distributor). There is little doubt the apocalypse represented in *Night* references a perceived sense of a descent into madness and barbarism felt by many at the time.[19] And as with the events abroad, horrific images of atrocities and violence at home made their way into the living rooms of every middle class and blue collar American home, a social fact referenced by the newscasts watched by the besieged characters in *Night of the Living Dead* and many of the films that followed in its wake.

The sixties heralded a new era in the distribution of spectacular images of social conflict, human disasters and political violence through the medium of television. Since *Night of the Living Dead*, broadcasts about the coming disaster have been a generic trait of zombie films, the besieged survivors desperately seeking news about the extent of the plague through the remaining radio and television channels.[20] By the end of the century the sound and image of a television broadcast being interrupted or a video recording being scrambled and terminated had become the pathognomonic signs of the genre.[21] Between 1950 and 1970, the period in which the zombie transitioned from parodic

---

19 1968 was of course a year of tumultuous events on a global scale: Prague Spring (January), the Tet offensive (January), the iconic execution of Viet Cong commander Nguyen Van Lem (February), the My Lai massacre in Vietnam (March), Grosvenor Square anti-war protests in London (March), student uprisings in Paris (May) and the Tlatelolco massacre of hundreds of students by police and military in Mexico City (November).

20 *Night of the Living Dead* included appearances by actual television personalities from the Pittsburgh area like the horror show presenter "Chilly Billy" Cardille, and Chuck Craig, a television newscaster, lending the film an air of "televisual" authenticity. *Dawn of the Dead* (1978) begins in a television studio on the eve of the apocalypse.

21 Yann Demange's *Dead Set* (2008), written by Charlie Brooker, is an excellent example of a television-age zombie apocalypse narrative, made for television and made on the set of the reality TV show *Big Brother*.

figure of spooky fun to a terrible new flesh-eating horror, television had become the dominant medium of broadcasting and spectacular entertainment in western societies.[22] Unlike cinema, which in the 1950s and '60s was still subject to *de facto* segregation, television transcended the geographical and ethnic divisions of American society, the news broadcasts from around the nation and the world made available to all regardless of colour, creed or nationality.[23] By the 1960s the term "zombie" had also come to describe any person who displayed behaviour that was deemed unconscious, involuntary and automated, particularly when it was associated with blindly repetitive habit, political conservatism, deference to authority and work-place compliance, and the new habitual mode of television viewing quickly became associated with "zombie behaviour". In a 1969 interview for *Playboy* magazine the Canadian media theorist Marshall McLuhan picked up on the zombie metaphor to describe those afflicted with what he called the "Narcissus trance" effect of the "technological extensions of the human nervous system" and, in particular, the electronic technology of television:

> Because of today's terrific speed-up of information moving, we have a chance to apprehend, predict and influence the environmental forces shaping us – and thus win back control of our own destinies. The new extensions of man and the environment they generate are the central manifestations of the evolutionary process, and yet we still cannot free ourselves of the delusion that it is how a medium is used that counts, rather than what it does to us and with us. This is the zombie stance of the

---

22 In 1950 only 9% of American homes had a television. By 1960 it was 90% (U.S. Library of Congress).

23 The Negro Circuit of cinemas that existed during the Jim Crow era continued unofficially after they were deemed unconstitutional in 1965, partly as a consequence of the residual ghettoization of African-American communities in major urban centres. Even though the grindhouse cinemas at which *Night of the Living Dead* was first shown were often an exception to the segregated pattern, audiences at some cinemas were still largely African-American. This may explain the decision by the Walter Reade Organisation to put *Night of the Living Dead* and *Slaves* on a double-bill.

technological idiot. It's to escape this Narcissus trance that I've tried to trace and reveal the impact of media on man, from the beginning of recorded time to the present [...] It is not an easy period in which to live, especially for the television-conditioned young who unlike their literate elders, cannot take refuge in the zombie trance of Narcissus narcosis that numbs the state of psychic shock induced by the impact of the new media.[24]

McLuhan's zombic reference point here is the classic cinematic figure which, as we have seen, elides with the hypnotised somnambulist, worker-slave and, later, the "mindless consumer".[25] More specifically, in McLuhan's terms, a media zombie is a person who does not understand that "the media is the message", not its hypnotic and zombifying content.[26] His use of the trope demonstrates how far the zombie had come from its roots in western accounts of Haitian folklore in the previous century, as the medium of television began to replace cinema as the popularly perceived apparatus of mass persuasion. For McLuhan the zombie figure represented the behavioural effects of new media on certain segments of the population, effects that distracted their attention from the holistic, evolutionary transformation that both humans and their technological extensions were immanently caught up in. He was obviously not proposing that television viewers become walking cadavers or flesh-eating ghouls, but simply that, entranced as they were by the content of the new technology, they were unable to perceive the broader changes being brought about in

24 McLuhan 1969

25 This is most famously represented by Romero's *Dawn of the Dead* (1978) which is set in a shopping mall. It is perhaps the most commented on of Romero's *Living Dead* films and one particularly popular for Frankfurt School-inspired readings of the zombie as an allegory for "mindless consumerism" and ideological "mass deception".

26 McLuhan's insight was that understanding media depended on perceiving the changes in "scale, pace and pattern" of human behaviour brought about by the development of new media. In other words it was not the messages delivered by the medium that were important, but the way the media themselves changed the behavioural patterns of its users (see *Understanding Media* (1964)).

society as a whole.[27] They were the new zombies of techno-historical consciousness-less.

The deracination of the zombie figure after Romero was in many ways the product of a society dominated by the new, integrationist medium of television, through which everyone was potentially controlled by the centralised command-structure of national television networks, and equally free to witness the same barrage of "real" horror from around the globe. The flesh-eating zombies created by Romero took the Haitian myth of the zombie as a resurrected corpse and re-vitalised it in a cultural context in which television was seen by some to be *the* contemporary medium of social control. And they did so in ways that removed any residual ethnological and psychological causality or interpretation for this horrific, but entirely fictional, state of being. Despite this ostensible assimilating reach however, national network television could not over-code and erase the residual racial tensions and the history of racist violence that continued to underpin American politics in the cold war era, and within McLuhan's media zombies and Romero's flesh-eaters there continued to dwell the spectre of their "black slave" ancestors, those monsters of misfortune, whose rage had not been mollified.

---

27 McLuhan was one of the sources cited by Deleuze and Guattari in *Anti-Oedipus* (1972), where they make reference to the collapse of the "Gutenberg Galaxy" and the reduction of communication to flows brought about by what McLuhan called "the electronic revolution" (Deleuze and Guattari 240-241).

BLACK SOULS ON COLD WAR ICE

By capturing black men in Africa and bringing them to slavery in America, the white devils *killed* the black man – killed him mentally, culturally, spiritually, economically, politically and morally – transforming him into a "Negro," the symbolic Lazarus, left in the "graveyard" of segregation and second class citizenship. And just as Jesus was summoned to the cave to raise Lazarus from the dead, Elijah Muhammad has been summoned by god to lift up the modern Lazarus, the Negro, from his grave.

- Eldridge Cleaver *Soul on Ice* (1967)[28]

Often the concept of alienation is used to qualify the fantastic loss of identity inherent in slavery. This concept only inadequately covers the sterilization that threatens the cultural personality of the colonized Black man. In this case the concept of "zombification" is a more appropriate one. It is no coincidence that the myth of the zombi, which originated in Haiti, is equally well known in other American countries.

- René Depestre 'Hello and Goodbye to Negritude' (1984)[29]

The television networks thought that riots in the north might replace the now absent police dogs, fire hoses, cattle prods and mounted state troopers of the south in entertainment value. They each dispatched top-flight task forces to cover the rioting in full colour. Antonioni announced plans in Rome to do a technicolor movie concerning the riots. It would involve one man's agony in trying to decide whether to throw a brick at the police

---

28 Cleaver 95

29 Depestre 256

and the entire movie would take place in a kitchenette apartment. Marcello Mastroianni would play the lead in blackface.

- Sam Greenlee *The Spook Who Sat by the Door* (1969)[30]

Despite the marked differences between apocalyptic flesh-eating zombies and their Vodou precursors, there are reasons not to completely reject racial readings of the figure, especially during the transition phase of the late 1960s and '70s, and in light of the persistent racial themes played out in Romero's films. In his *Gospel of the Living Dead* Kim Paffenroth identifies racism (alongside the vices of sexism, materialism and individualism) as the most consistently decried social ill in the series.[31] From the central Black protagonist Ben in *Night of the Living Dead*, who eventually dies at the hands of an all-White zombie-shooting party, through the racist, rogue cop at the beginning of *Dawn of the Dead,* who uses the alibi of zombie-extermination to kill Black and Hispanic "scum", to "Big Daddy", the central Black zombie of *Land of the Dead,* who eventually leads an army of zombie comrades against the last fortress of the Living, there are implicit and recurrent racial themes contained in all of Romero's zombie films.

Many critics have commented on the significance of Duane Jones in *Night*, a classically trained Black actor, who plays the lead role of Ben, the resilient hero figure and only survivor of the zombie siege, who is killed the next morning by a vigilante group.[32] African American actors in mid 1960s films were generally depicted as passive and benevolent, rarely forthright, affirmative and strong. And when they were, like Sidney Poitier in *In the Heat of the Night* (1967), where the Black detective he played returned a slap in the face to a White plantation owner, it was widely perceived as scandalous. Generally African American actors were expected to "play Black", either stereotypically or as a commentary on contemporary racial issues. After casting Jones as Ben, the producers of *Night of the Living Dead* decided not to change the script in light of his colour (a decision which

---

30 Greenlee 128

31 Paffenroth 18

32 See for instance Higashi in Dittmar and Michaud (2000), Waller (2010) and Kee in Christie and Lauro (2011).

Romero later suggested might have been a mistake, explaining that they were simply trying to be "hip").[33] Jones' heroic role as the sole-survivor of an otherwise all-White cast broke with earlier cinematic stereotypes and expectations in ways rarely seen in horror or any other genre of cinema at the time. His death at the hands of a "lynch-mob" has similarly not gone unnoticed by commentators. White police officers with barking attack dogs, accompanied by young White men with shot-guns, shooting everything not like them in sight, was a clear reference to southern Sheriffs like Bull Connor who had ordered the use of fire hoses and police dogs against civil rights protesters in Alabama in 1963.[34] As many African Americans knew only too well, in many parts of the United States in the 1960s Blacks, like flesh-eating zombies, could be killed with impunity, a message underlined at the end of the film, when Ben is killed just like one of the ghouls. No one in the film ever comments on Ben's race, or anyone else's for that matter, and Romero has denied intending to make an overt statement about race-relations in the film.[35] But whether by accident or design, the producers of *Night* managed to make a highly race-conscious film precisely by ignoring the race of its characters and actors. Pointing towards an extrinsic racist subtext without definitively proposing it as *the* subtext, Romero opened an enduring interpretative door by which the apocalyptic zombie figure implicitly references the contemporary politics of racial violence (Foucault's historical "race war") while pointing to something more inhuman and absolute (i.e. a total (r)evolutionary species-war).

---

33 *Birth of the Living Dead*

34 Connor's decision to suppress the anti-segregation movement by "all means necessary" eventually backfired, in part because of the level of media attention his actions received. Hundreds of journalists from national and international media outlets captured photographs and footage of the police tactics leading to a national public outcry against the situation. The events seem to have prompted John F. Kennedy to give his Civil Rights Address in June 1963, ultimately hastening the enactment of the 1964 Civil Rights Act.

35 When asked whether he was trying to make a social comment on race Romero told an interviewer for *Time* magazine in 2010 that it was an accident based on the choice of Duane Jones as the lead ('Ten Questions for George A. Romero' *Time*, Monday, June 07, 2010).

Kuhns' documentary explicitly identifies the rise of a revolutionary Black Power movement and the race-riots in Watts in 1965 and Newark and Detroit in 1967, as the social context that *Night* was intended to comment upon.[36] In the film, historian Mark Harris proposes that at this time the idea of the American ghetto began to take hold of popular public consciousness, as the image of Black politics in America shifted from the non-violent protests of the Civil Rights Movement to one of anger, organised insurrection and urban conflagration. Despite the explicit symbolic correlation between the image of Black insurrection and the zombie apocalypse in the living dead sequence, critics have generally read Romero's zombie films as anti-racist allegories emphasising the absurdity of human difference in the face of such a ubiquitous and universal threat.

Initially distributed in late 1968 on the Grindhouse circuit of cinemas in New York, *Night of the Living Dead* was also booked for afternoon matinees where low budget horror films were aimed primarily at children.[37] Despite some early hostile press that accused the film-makers of cashing in on traumatised kids, the film did so well on the children's matinee circuit that the National Association of Theater Owners selected it as their "exploitation picture of the month" in June 1969. Later that year it was re-released on a new double-bill with the steamy, antebellum Civil Rights-inspired drama *Slaves* (1969). Although Romero found the association of *Night* with *Slaves* ridiculous, it is perfectly understandable from the perspective of a radical Black consciousness familiar with the enslaved African roots of the zombie figure.[38] At the same time, one can understand why Romero would not see the connection, so far were his "ghouls" removed from their

---

36 Romero in *Birth of the Living Dead*.

37 Uncertain about how best to market *Night of the Living Dead* its promoters initially had it screened as part of "monster double-bills" on the children's matinee circuit. One scathing review of the film by Roger Ebert accused the film-makers of deliberately trying to "make a fast buck" by traumatising children before new censorship laws were introduced. Throughout the review Ebert refers to the central character Ben simply as "the Negro". See Roger Ebert 'Just another Horror Movie – Or is it?' *Chicago Sun Times*, January 5th 1969.

38 In the documentary *Birth of the Living Dead* Romero asks "How does THAT connect?"

Haitian ancestors. And perhaps this is one key to the bifurcation of the Zombie Complex at this point: the new zombies carrying with them an echo of their ancestors and the revolutionary history of Haiti, while at the same time denying any credence to earlier myths and the ideologies of essential racial difference they were used to maintain.

Herbert Biberman, the director of the largely forgotten film *Slaves*, was famous for being one of the Hollywood Ten, a group of film-makers who were cited for contempt of Congress after having refused to answer the questions of the House of Un-American Activities Committee that was tasked with uncovering communist activity in America in the 1940s and '50s.[39] In 1954, after having spent six months in prison, he went on to direct *Salt of the Earth,* a fictional account of a miners' strike in New Mexico in 1951 that used the actual miners and their families as the cast. After a visit to New York in 1952 Biberman became convinced that a Black Liberation movement was taking off in the United States and decided to make a film about it. The first proposal was a film about the life of Frederick Douglass staring Paul Robeson, but the project never materialised.[40] His next idea was to make a film version of *Uncle Tom's Cabin.* The screenplay was titled *Slaves* but the final film, not finished until 1969, bears little relation to the earlier script. One critic described *Slaves* as an exploitation film in which Black actors are forced to play White stereotypes in blackface, and a *New York Times* review of the film in July of the same year described it as "a kind of cinematic carpet bagging project in which some contemporary movie-makers have raided the antebellum South and attempted to impose on it their own attitudes that will explain 1969 black militancy"[41] An indication of the political innocence of Biberman was an article he wrote for *The New York Times* during the making of *Slaves* called 'We Never Say Nigger in

---

39 The HUAC was originally set up in 1938 to uncover U.S. citizens with Nazi ties.

40 Dick 80

41 Vincent Canby, "'Slaves' Opens at the DeMille: Militancy Depicts Life in Antebellum South Dionne Warwick Plays Mistress in Debut', *The New York Times,* July 3rd, 1969. Another of the Hollywood Ten, Dalton Trumbo, went on to write the screenplay for Stanley Kubrick's *Spartacus* in 1960, another slave rebellion-themed film, and one that helped to end the blacklist after President Kennedy crossed the picket line to watch it. Dick 80-81.

Front of them'.[42] In it Biberman explains how the production company negotiated in Louisiana with businessmen who used the "n-word" but never in front of Negroes. The article explains how the company found extras for the film from the local unemployment bureau and Baptist church, describing their performances as "marvels of non-acting" and presents the production of *Slaves* as a triumph of progressive, liberal multiculturalism:

> On our sets, Black and White plantation owners and fieldworkers, Northern film craftsmen and Southern film craftsmen, actors who earn a million dollars a year and old illiterate people who earn $1.60 an hour, Northern liberals and Southern Conservatives, Wallace supporters (and undoubtedly, among the 100 to 200 persons working on our sets, several members of the KKK) met and worked together. All were cooperating in the heat of the South in making a film attacking the institution of slavery and projecting the dignity, the talent and the intellectual and moral stature of all the blacks, even in slavery.

One can only speculate how *Slaves* would have been received by audiences who saw it on a double-bill with *Night of the Living Dead*. Given the strange mix of steamy inter-racial "man woman truth" between Dionne Warwick and Stephen Boyd, the moribund Christian piety of Luke (played by Civil Rights activist Ossie Davis[43]) the lead-slave character, and the constant refrain of low-key, "African" drumming that repeats seemingly at random throughout, one can imagine that *Night* would have come as a refreshing, if chilling blast of fresh Pennsylvanian air after this sordidly maudlin melodrama.

---

42 Biberman, Herbert 'We Never Say Nigger in Front of Them', *The New York Times*, January 19th, 1969

43 A personal friend to Malcolm X, Jesse Jackson and Martin Luther King, Jr., Davis was instrumental in organising the 1963 March on Washington for Jobs and Freedom. Davis was also the director of a number of race-themed films in the 1970s including *Gordon's War* (1973), the story of a Black Vietnam vet who returns home to find his neighbourhood overrun by drug-dealers and addicts.

Slaves is not without interest however in terms of the overlap of Black radical politics and the deracination of the zombie figure after 1968, not least because of the light it casts on divisions between the reformist Christian ethos of the Civil Rights movement and revolutionary Marxism of groups like the Black Panthers and the All-African People's Revolutionary Party.[44] Set in Kentucky in 1850 the plot revolves around the central character Luke, a slave who is sold with his pregnant wife to the seemingly benevolent plantation owner Mr. Stillwell for whom he becomes a horse-trainer. Stillwell is in debt to the slave-trader Mr. Holland who proposes entering into a partnership breeding Blacks instead of horses. Stillwell's Christian conscience prevents him from even discussing the issue. Meanwhile Luke tells his wife that he is saving up to buy the freedom for her that he himself has been promised by his master. Stillwell refuses the partnership, but, with insufficient cash to pay him, Holland suggests to Stillwell that he takes Luke as payment. When Stillwell says that this too is out of the question Holland reminds him "He's not yours to free, I got a chattel on all your chattel". In the evening Luke leads the other slaves in prayer that Stillwell be made an example by God to all other slave-masters so that they will "let his people go". During hymns the master interrupts to tell Luke that he will be sold that night. Two slaves must be sold so the rest can be saved, he explains to them. Luke and his fellow slave Jericho are sold in New Orleans to Nathan MacKay, a cruel slave-master from Boston, son of an abolitionist preacher who is "long on scruples but pretty short on money". "I play a game with the species", he explains to two women who question his morals at the market, "with the times, and with myself. I mean to win. The only way for me to keep this rotted existence of ours from turning me like a screw into its rotted wood is to turn the screw myself". When asked if he likes "darkies" he replies "most of them better than I do whites. Some of them very much indeed".

---

44 The A-APRP was founded by Kwame Nkrumah, the communist president of Ghana in 1968. Stokely Carmichael, first Black leader of the Student Nonviolent Coordinating committee (SNCC) and later Honourary Prime Minister of the Black Panther Party, joined the A-APRP in the 1970s.

MacKay has a house filled with African sculptures and a bitter, drunken wife Cassy (played by Dionne Warwick) with whom he has a sadomasochistic sexual relationship. While shaving he explains to Cassy that the money he has used to buy her earrings and a necklace came from his father's church's bank, and that his father's money is now being used to underwrite his own slave-holding plantation, "whose darkies turn it into more money to give to the church to invest in missionaries for Africa". "Corruption is the salt and pepper of existence", he tells her.

MacKay gets the best lines in the film. In one important scene he delivers an impressive rhetorical defence of the pragmatics of the economic institutions of slavery against Christian double standards and the Romantic liberal sentiments of his northern slave-owning colleagues.

> "We'd better all understand this 'Darkie' we own gentlemen. He's the only self-reproducing machine in the world. You gotta know how to run him. I first met him in Africa as a young man when I ran a ship in the illegal slave-running trade. Before I settled down here in the very legal slave-driving cotton trade... I packed Blacks into my ships until you couldn't walk the decks. Every morning we threw the dead and the rebellious overboard. They were not easy those voyages. But we could turn a profit if we got 40% of them here alive".

He goes on to propose that all one needs to know about human beings can be explained by a story told to him by an old African chief whom he bought slaves from. "In the soul of a free man" he had told him, "a little slavery and a lot weigh the same. So they do in the soul of a slave. So when you chain him, just as well chain him firm. Brilliant man. He was as black as coal. He would find your views... romantic, dangerous". Having commanded Luke to refill the tray of his guests, MacKay explains that, judging by Luke's facial characteristics, his people probably came from the Songhai tribe who, three hundred years ago, had a university in Timbuktu where they could perform cataract surgery. The film cuts to Luke, regarding himself in a mirror. MacKay continues: "I believe origins can crop up even after ten generations, unless they're kept weeded out. What do *we* create? Surgeons, sculptors or *niggers*?"

UNDEAD UPRISING

The film culminates with MacKay lashing Luke for the impertinence of a failed escape attempt as Luke defiantly tells his fellow slaves watching on "We gonna bust this bondage even if it takes a hundred years. We gonna protect one another. We gonna love one another. We gonna take care of one another [falling to the ground] because our God is a Freedom God!" The scene dissolves into a flashback of Luke's wife, the last time he saw her, telling him that they would never see each other again. More sounds of the lash as they fall, his wife sobbing, into an echoing darkness and Luke dies.[45] The last lines of the film go to the master, as his stables burn behind him: "Everything is in hand Gentlemen. Nothing has changed. Nothing *really* has happened. There are always plenty of niggers in the world".

At the same time Biberman was working his miracles of co-operative multi-culturalism in Shreveport, Louisiana, Eldridge Cleaver, then Minister of Information for the Black Panther Party, was making explicit use of the zombie metaphor to describe the "living-dead" character of middle-aged White America in the '60s and the reaction of White youth towards it. It was another indication of the growing ubiquity of the term at the time to describe those bound in their behaviour to conservative and outmoded values and beliefs:

> The white youth of today have begun to react to the fact that the "American Way of Life" is a fossil of history. What do they care if their old baldheaded and crew-cut elders don't dig their caveman mops? They couldn't care less about the old, stiffassed honkies who don't like their new dances: Frug, Monkey, Jerk, Swim, Watusi. All they know is that it feels good to swing to way-out body rhythms instead of dragassing across the dance floor like zombies to the dead beat of mind-smothered Mickey Mouse music.[46]

Cleaver would also describe the condition of "the black man" within the U.S. carceral, military and industrial complex, suffering the long wait for spiritual and political redemption, in zombic terms.

---

45 Luke's death does however lead to the conflagration of the plantation they had been planning.

46 Eldridge 81

246

In the 'Lazarus, Come Forth' section of *Soul on Ice* Cleaver conflates two distinct biblical personages of the same name, likening Elijah Muhammad's notion of Black destiny to Jesus raising Lazarus from the grave. Cleaver claims that this is the interpretation held by Black Muslims about the history of Negroes in America.[47]

Although the evocation of colonial slavery associated with the Haitian folkloric *zombi*, and carried over to the classic cinematic zombie, is largely absent in the apocalyptic phase, there is a residual trace of a zombie revolt against their living masters, as is assumed to happen when *zombis* get a taste of salt. The theme of an undead uprising of the historically aggrieved and vengeful Black, slave dead is however rarely stated explicitly. Although the theme of the vengeful dead is often alluded to, particularly when the apocalyptic narrative is aligned with eschatological religious prophesies about the resurrection of the dead at the end of days, or when, as has recently become the case, the zombies start to become conscious of the way they are being treated by the living, these are exceptions.[48] As a general rule when the undead rise up they are no longer individuals with memories, souls or conscience. Instead they are resurrected in body alone, their personalities substituted by simple, irrepressible and predatory compulsion. And although it would be a stretch to align Cleaver's thinking with Romero's in any direct way, there is a Christian eschatological current in both that seems to acknowledge a reincarnated rage against an irrational, unjust and hypocritical world-order "going to hell in a hand-cart".[49] Within

---

47 Elijah Muhammad did equate Black people with the Lazarus of the testament of Luke, and the Parable of the Rich Man and the Beggar, whom he associated with slavery. He also understood this Lazarus to be destined to be risen from the dead. In the parable after the death of the rich man he begs Abraham to send Lazarus to give him a drop of water, to quench his infernal thirst. Abraham refuses. He then asks if Abraham will send Lazarus to warn his family about hell. Abraham once again refuses saying "If they do not listen to Moses and the Prophets, they will not be convinced even if someone rises from the dead".

48 See for instance Romero's *Land of the Dead* (2005) in which the zombies, led by Big Daddy, begin to express anger at the extermination of his kind and, more recently, in Dominic Mitchell's television drama *In the Flesh* (2013).

49 One exception is the 1974 blaxploitation film *Sugar Hill* – a reference

the contemporary critical discourse on the popularity and enduring appeal of the zombie apocalypse narrative there is the recurrent theme of a traumatic, historical substrate of collective experience, according to which the zombie uprising is an allegory for various forms of disenfranchised and subordinated groups and populations whose collective loss and suffering, like that of the Haitian slaves who rose up against their slave masters. In this way, a century after Gustave Le Bon identified the "voices of the dead" that animated the heterogeneous, insurrectionary and hypnotised crowd, the righteous vengeance of the aggrieved, Black, slave-dead finds its de-sublimated collective expression in the spectacle of a universal cannibal apocalypse.

BIFURCATION OF THE ZOMBIE COMPLEX

When the bi-polar myth of the zombie splits into two main branches after *Night of the Living Dead* the maniacal, insurrectionary branch is represented most emphatically in the continuum of Romero's *Living Dead* sequence. The cultural context in which the flesh-eating zombie was born was primed far more by a general sense of globalised, cold war catastrophe than widespread consciousness of new world racism and the colonial history of the Caribbean. Romero's creation of the apocalyptic flesh-eating zombie therefore effectively de-cultured the figure, making it a generally sub-human, flesh-eating, zero-degree race-figure in a total and final species war. It is, following Anténor Firmin, a speculative *anthropological* being (i.e. it raises philosophical questions about what it is to be human, the difference between the human and non-human etc.) rather than an ethnological (i.e. culture or race specific) one. The moribund, disciplinary branch is represented by the continuity of the Haitian folkloric *zombi*, re-purposed as an image of life-under-Black-despotism during the Duvalier dictatorship. This branch, which continues to be informed by folkloric myths of the *zombi* as either a person risen from the dead by sorcery or subject to the

---

to the wealthy part of Harlem made famous by residence of Black millionaires there during the Harlem Renaissance – in which a "Voodoo Queen" calls on Baron Samedi and his chrome-eyed army of the dead to take vengeance on a group of honky hoodlums who have killed the lead character's boyfriend.

hypnotic and will-depleting effects of some external power, as we will see in the next chapter, represents the continuation of a traditional *zombi* lineage of maximum passivity and compliance starkly contrasting with the irrepressible new zombies of insurrectionary apocalypse. In this sense, like the Haitian *serviteur*, subject to possession trance and the *lwa* that possesses them within the structure of traditional and highly localised religious practices, it is still a distinctly *ethnological* being. At the same time the notion of the zombie as a person subject to the unconscious, disciplinary will of an external agent, be that the blind forces of political economy, sinister media corporation, secret forms of governance or the technological extensions of the human nervous system, continues to inform contemporary notions of the media or "techno-zombie": a being controlled by its own expressive-cybernetic dependency on a techno-commercial milieu of ubiquitous tele-mediated programmeming to which it is euphemistically "enslaved".

Romero has repeatedly said that what interested him about *I Am Legend* was the idea of one civilisation replacing another by pure predation and that he imagined a new society devouring the old as a kind of "zombie revolution"[50] It is this insistence on the inevitable, (r)evolutionary overcoming of one species of human by another that underpins what several writers have identified as the fundamentally post-human dimension of the *Living Dead* sequence.[51] Commentators on the transformation of the zombie figure as it passes from the classic cinematic to the apocalyptic flesh-eating phase have noted the marked historical consequences of WWII on certain anti-humanist and nihilistic tendencies within the popular culture of the time that seemed to culminate in social reactions to the Vietnam War.[52] Within these fictions the alleged source of the flesh-eating zombie plague is often assumed to be a genetic mutation caused by nuclear radiation or scientific experiment gone awry, and the excesses that cannibal apocalypses often evoke resemble, in parodic form, the atrocities of the death camps, the decimation of Hiroshima or Dresden, or events like the My Lai massacre, which was famously reported by the press in gory detail in 1969. Unlike the traditional return-to-order

50 Rick Curnutte 'There's No Magic: A Conversation With George A. Romero' *The Film Journal*, October 2004

51 See Christie and Lauro and Boluk and Lenz.

52 See Lowenstein's *Shocking Representation: Historical Trauma, National Cinema, and the Modern Horror Film* (2005).

narratives of horror films in the '40s and '50s, at the end of apocalyptic cannibal films the protagonists are typically left in a world of abysmal and hopeless despair. Writers like Gerry Canavan have even proposed that the *actual* exercise of racist biopower upon living populations (such as those that occurred in New Orleans after Hurricane Katrina or the 2010 earthquake in Haiti) and the *fictional* representation of zombies in popular culture, are components of a uniform modality of power. Citing the African cultural theorist Achille Mbembe, and echoing the earlier formulations of Hegel and Bataille, he writes that "Sovereignty in this (post)colonial valence operates in accordance with a zombic logic of quarantine and extermination: 'sovereignty means the capacity to define who matters and who does not, who is disposable and who is not'."[53] Some psychoanalytically informed commentators on the zombie genre have also suggested that the employment of "graphic visceral shock" is a means "to access the historical substrate of traumatic experience".[54]

---

53 Canavan 176. Developing Mbembe's concept of "necropolitics" (a post-colonial re-configuration of Foucault's theory of biopower) Canavan proposes that:

> the zombie's strange persistence at the site of imperialism's limit fuels necrosis in biopower while in the same moment bolstering the capacity of resistance in those people whom biopolitical institutions have declared socially dead.

As with many contemporary critical commentators on the zombie figure, Canavan seems to collapse the fictional flesh-eating zombies of Romero with the mythical *zombis* of Haitian folklore and actual chattel slaves during the plantation era. "Social Death" is a term used by Orlando Patterson and others to describe the general condition of slavery. See Patterson *Slavery and Social Death – A Comparative Study* (1982).

54 Adam Lowenstein quoted by Christie in *Better off Dead* 76. Several authors have made psychoanalytic readings of the zombie figure, most significantly perhaps Gilles Deleuze and Felix Guattari in their 1972 *Anti-Oedipus: Capitalism and Schizophrenia,* where they famously describe the zombie as "the only modern myth... mortified schizos, good for work, brought back to reason" (Deleuze and Guattari 261). In brief, Deleuze and Guattari's schizo-analytic understanding of zombiedom refers to a modality of modern capitalism in which death is encoded as a form of

A marked difference between folkloric Haitian *zombis*, classic cinematic zombies and their apocalyptic flesh-eating progeny has to do with numbers. While the former tended to be exceptional, singular beings, apocalyptic cannibal zombies are an escalatory mass phenomenon, a voracious collective of heterogeneous subhumanity. In this sense their uprisings have more overtly political and revolutionary meanings than previous incarnations. Apocalyptic zombies are more like an insurrectionary mass of berserkers than a gang of de-humanised plantation slaves or a labour-force of industrialised drones; the animalistic contagiousness and absolute moral indifference of their violence is a spectacular parody of the kind of revolutionary "night of blood and death screams" imagined by Bataille in the 1930s. Their feasting on our flesh, like that of any animal eating another, is, in Bataillean terms, the limit case of base animal intimacy and the unconscionable, unavoidable condition of a-theological immanence.[55]

Phillip Mahoney has noted how the apocalyptic tone of the early theory of crowds anticipates later representations of large-scale zombie invasions, possessed by what the American psychologist Boris Sidis called "the demon of the demos", a demon capable of "throwing the body politic into convulsions of demoniac fury".[56] Such "fleeting moments of rhetorical excess" in the late 19th century discourse of crowd psychology become, Mahoney claims, "the very substance and focal point of later zombie films".[57] As such, allegorical readings of the apocalyptic zombie

---

social control tied to the guilt associated with the transgression, real or imagined, of the taboo on incest (Deleuze and Guattari 75). In capitalism they write: "Everything labours in death, everything wishes for death" (Deleuze and Guattari 337-338). Stephen Shaviro, one of the first cultural theorists to apply Deleuze and Guattari's ideas to the apocalyptic flesh-eating zombie in his influential *The Cinematic Body* (1983), proposed that Romero's zombies represent "a rebellion of death against its capitalist appropriation" (Shaviro 101). His work has been influential on a number of zombie-themed critical commentaries such as Patricia MacCormack's *Cinesexuality* (2008) and Jason Wallin's 'Living...Again: The Revolutionary Cine-Sign of Zombie-Life' in Jagodzinski (ed) *Psychoanalysing Cinema: A Productive Encounter with Lacan, Deleuze and Zizek* (2012).

55 Bataille (1992)

56 Sidis 311-313

57 Boluk and Lenz 115

horde have a far more political and insurrectionary meaning than their precursors. Their newly anthropophagous drive to convert *us* into *them* has been read as an allegory for the nihilistic, mindless insurgency of the structurally disenfranchised, unemployed, redundant and socially worthless human refuse of the late capitalist system. Steve Beard for instance has argued that apocalyptic cannibal zombies represent the condition of structural unemployment as a social plague, "those workers and consumers who, since the flash-point of 1968 – when the crisis in the old Fordist system blew up – have been thrown on the scrap-heap":

> Economically extinct, socially displaced, they return to devour those who have survived them. Less the lower class citizens of the monster world and more disenfranchised underclass of the material world, they are a projection of postmodern capitalism's worst anxieties about itself [...] No longer representative of the faceless masses of Fordism, they instead refer to the hollowing out of this constituency by a post-Fordist organisation of labour. Once released from the vampiric embrace of capital, the Organisation Man becomes little more than a vagrant in a suit.[58]

Mahoney quotes Boris Sidis who took up Le Bon's analogy of the hypnotised crowd member in ways that echo claims made by Hegel and others about African fetishism a century earlier, and prefigure those that will re-emerge in analyses of spectacular consumer fetishism and media censorship debates later in the century:

> The crowd contains within itself all the elements and conditions favourable to a disaggregation of consciousness. What is required is only that an interesting object, or that some sudden violent impressions should strongly fix the attention of the crowd, and plunge it into that state in which the waking personality is shorn of its dignity and power, and the naked subwaking self alone remains face to face with the external environment.[59]

---

58 Beard 76-78

59 Sidis 300

Mahoney proposes that the "metaphorical overdetermination", "figurative excesses" and "absence of a single determining feature" may be what most positively define both crowds and zombies. Such overdetermination, he argues, is built upon a "constitutive emptiness" (or "uncanny featurelessness") that we are compelled to "fill-in". As such, zombies and crowds represent what Giorgio Agamben, in *The Coming Community* (1993), has called a "whatever singularity": "limbo life-forms connected not 'by any common property, [or] identity,' but through their very lack of positive features".[60] From such perspectives the zombie-plague becomes metaphorical of a "faceless mass" of heterogeneous post-humanity, the subhuman "living refuse" of a world which can no longer put them to work and upon which they are "driven to feed".

---

60 Boluk and Lenz 116

the Serpent and the Rainbow

Bill Pullman stars in Wes Craven's cinematic adaptation of Wade Davis's *The Serpent and the Rainbow*, 1988

VI

RETURN OF THE HAITIAN ZOMBI

AGENTS OF THE CURSE

In her book *Infectious Rhythm: Metaphors of Contagion and the Spread of African Culture* Barbara Browning cites a letter written to the editor of the *Journal of the American Medical Association* in 1986 by a Dr. William Greenfield, a family medical practitioner from Illinois, entitled 'Night of the Living Dead II: Slow Encephalopathies and AIDS: Do Necromantic Zombiists Transmit HTLV III/AIDS During Vodouistic Rituals?'[1]. What is so surprising and yet symptomatic about the title is the casual and apparently jocular connection being made between the apocalyptic zombie films, pure cinematic fictions with next-to-no narrative relation to the Haitian folkloric *zombi*, and speculation about the spread of an *actual* disease reputedly amplified by regional *zombi*-making practices in Haiti. In short, the traditional Haitian folkloric *zombi* of legend is woven seamlessly into its apocalyptic, flesh-eating counterpart in an apt illustration of how different versions of the zombie figure have been made to elide in ways that perpetuate sensationalist and xenophobic fantasies about Haitian culture within discourses ostensibly far removed from ethnography, cultural studies or "ju ju journalism". This seemingly incidental elision of two very distinct modes of mythical zombie demonstrates the elasticity of the

---

1 Browning 27. The title is presumably the journal editor's rather than Dr. Greenfield's.

figure and how, despite profound discontinuities between differing versions of it, the most developed contemporary form can still be reconnected to its folkloric origins.

Haiti has an important place in the history of HIV/AIDS, being the second country to be associated with the disease. First identified in the United States in 1981 and given the acronym GRID (Gay Related Immune Deficiency), by 1982 doctors working in clinics in Florida began to notice the same set of symptoms amongst Haitians fleeing life under Duvalierism, and the name was changed to the acronym we use today. By the early 1980s in Haiti and the U.S. people were describing the disease as "4H", a reference to the four known vectors of contagion: homosexuals, heroin-users, haemophiliacs and Haitians.[2] The Miami-based doctor Arthur M. Fournier, one of the first to recognise the pattern of symptoms amongst the refugees, called the book about his twenty-five years treating the disease *The Zombie Curse*.[3] Similarly David Black, author of *The Plague Years: A Chronicle of AIDS, the Epidemic of our Times*, writing of the first evidence of toxoplasmosis discovered in the brain of a dead Haitian

---

2 Although the epidemiological metaphor that Greenfield's title plays on, and Browning's book brilliantly unpacks, often expresses implicitly racist and xenophobic configurations of the African and Haitian diasporas, there are significant anti-reactionary versions of it, most famously Ishmael Reed's 1972 novel *Mumbo Jumbo* which traces the history of the fictional Jes Grew virus from Africa to the United States. Browning reclaims the image-idea of an epidemiological African diaspora to critique the socio-economic inequalities which underlie its migrations.

3 Arthur M. Fournier *The Zombie Curse - A Doctor's 25 Year Journey in to the Heart of the AIDS Epidemic in Haiti* (2006). The title is a reference to what Fournier describes as a "metaphysical malady" that makes doctors ask why certain people get certain diseases and what their "risk factors" are, while ignoring the glaring socio-economic fact that the poor always suffer most from any epidemic (Fournier xx). Paradoxically, because *zombis* do *in fact* seem to be a local, ethnological being, his use of the term in this context undermines the ideal of universal socio-economic justice and human equality, re-affirming the very Haitian "exceptionalism" (Trouillot) it is intended to dispel. The meaning suggested by Fournier is further undermined by his choice to name the first part of the book, which opens with a chapter on the Haitian Boat People: 'The Curse Descends'.

in a Florida Hospital, described it as "a clue from the grave, as though a zombie, leaving a trail of unwinding gauze bandages and rotting flesh, had come to the hospital's Grand Rounds to pronounce a curse".[4]

Greenfield's letter appeared when the origin of HIV/AIDS was still a matter of wide-ranging speculation. His theory was based principally on two known factors in the contemporary knowledge of the disease: a recent report on the electron microscopy of the brains of AIDS fatalities that showed similarities to those of the bovine degenerative disease scrapie, and the high incidence of the disease in Haitian and Sub-Saharan African populations. Greenfield proposed that there was sociological evidence to suggest that AIDS may be more closely related to diseases like Kuru (a degenerative neurological disorder endemic to the Fore tribe of Papua New Guinea and transmitted by funerary cannibalism practices) and Creutzfeldt-Jakob disease (an incurable degenerative neurological disorder caused by the ingestion of infectious proteins or "prions", commonly known as Mad Cow Disease). His sociological evidence was a recently published account of *zombi*-making practices in Haiti that reported the use of the brains of "relatively fresh cadavers" in the making of a sorcerer's poisons. "The manner of handling human brain and other tissues", Greenfield proposed, "could easily result in autoinoculation with infectious viral particles". Given that many Haitians were Vodou *serviteurs,* and some members of secret societies (or "Bizangos") who were suspected of using human blood in their rituals, lay Haitian Vodouists, Greenfield concluded, may be unsuspectingly infected with AIDS by ingestion, inhalation or dermal contact with contaminated ritual substances. The principle source of Greenfield's ethnographic information was a book published a year earlier that would breathe new cinematic life into the largely forgotten Haitian *zombi,* eventually bringing it back into the Hollywood limelight, Wade Davis's ethnobotanical study of the Haitian *zombi* and the secret societies who make them, *The Serpent and the Rainbow.*[5]

At the time of the identification of HIV/AIDS in the Haitian refugee community in Florida, Haiti was ten years into the presidency

---

4 Black 41

5 Greenfield's other sources of information include Milaud Rigaud's *Secrets of Voodoo* and Alfred Métraux's *Voodoo in Haiti.*

of Jean-Claude Duvalier, Papa Doc's reluctant heir. When Baby Doc, as he quickly became known, inherited the presidency at the age of nineteen, few in Haiti expected him to hold on to power for very long. Notoriously lethargic and often incapacitated by barbiturates when not fishing, hunting and racing cars and motorbikes, during the early years of his presidency Jean-Claude deferred his presidential responsibilities to his mother Simone, his sister Marie-Denise and Luckner Cambronne, the high-ranking Duvalierist, his father's second in command and head of the Tonton Macoute. Despite his well-known indolence and evident lack of enthusiasm for the job, Baby Doc, the "mild-mannered Playboy", remained popular with the Haitian people for the first few years of his dictatorship. Less-flatteringly, those more critical of the new president labelled him "basket-head", a Creole term for someone of limited intelligence. By the end of the decade he was, surprisingly, still the president. Moreover, he seemed, at least to some outside observers (most importantly the U.S. government), to be in the process of rectifying the wrongs of his father and "liberalising" Haitian society. In his first scripted speech to the Haitian National Assembly he vowed that: "The United States will always find Haiti on its side against Communism", sweet words to a White House in which the recently elected Richard Nixon was installed. Soon the new airport in the capital was bringing tourists in numbers not seen since the Magloire era, many for "quickie divorces" offered by the Catholic Church. Thousands of exiled Haitians, thinking it now safe to return, did so, along with several high-profile African-American celebrity visitors like Muhammad Ali and Dick Gregory. This new international acceptability also drew in American aid money in amounts only dreamed of by his father, and by the end of the 1970s it had become Haiti's main source of income. Meanwhile the system of repressive and ruthless social controls instituted by Papa Doc (one in twenty Haitians at the time was a member of the VSN/Macoutes) was effectively running on auto-pilot, buoyed up by the kick-backs flowing in from the tourist trade and aid economy. Attempts to cover up the true extent of poverty, hardship and the continued civil rights abuses in the country were undermined by the business practices of high-ranking figures like Cambronne, whose blood-plasma business, Hemo Caribbean, earned him the nickname "Vampire of the Caribbean". His company extracted plasma from the blood of desperately impoverished Haitians, sending five tonnes a month to American labs directed by

Cutter Laboratories, Dow Chemicals and others. Rich in anti-bodies as a consequence of the country's many diseases and exceptionally high infant mortality rate, the blood was bought at a cost of $5 per pint and resold to the States for $35. Cambronne also had a lucrative line in cadavers, much prized in American medical schools because their lack of fat made them easier to dissect. One apocryphal story tells of how, when criticised for the mouldy condition of the corpses on their arrival in the U.S., Cambronne reputedly retorted "Tell them I'll start shipping the bodies up alive. Then when they need them they can just kill them".[6] Despite such macabre business ventures, Haiti under Baby Doc still managed to successfully project to the outside world a reformed image, and in 1977, conscious of the likely implications of a new U.S. president committed to international social justice (Jimmy Carter), Jean-Claude Duvalier publicly ratified the Inter-American Convention on Human Rights and released 104 political prisoners. Meanwhile hundreds more still rotted in the same cells where his father had incarcerated them. Baby Doc christened the new national ideology Jeanclaudism, and in 1979 he even orchestrated "democratic" local elections with carefully handpicked candidates.

In 1980 Jean-Claude married Michèle Bennett, the daughter of a wealthy Mulatto merchant, in a spectacular public ceremony costing $5 million. Michèle Bennett's extravagancies seemed to know no bounds. Regularly exceeding the $100,000 monthly allowance she received as "First Lady of Haiti", her marriage to Jean-Claude drove deep divisions between him and his mother and the so-called "dinosaurs" of Duvalierism that would eventually lead to the collapse of the dynasty. Such extravagant displays of opulence only served to highlight the abject poverty in which the majority of Haitians continued to live, and by 1980 tens of thousands of Haitian refugees had risked the perilous journey from Haiti to Miami seeking asylum in the United States.

In September 1980 116 Haitians, unable to endure the misery of life in Haiti any longer, climbed into a derelict boat and set sail for Miami. Forty kilometres from the coast of Cuba the boat began to list and its captain managed to deposit its passengers on a tiny, remote and uninhabited island called Cayo Lobos in the Bahamas, before sailing away surreptitiously during the night. With hardly any food to forage and little shelter or fresh drinking water, the castaways eventually

---

6 Abbott 172

began, one by one, to die. Unable to bare his plight any longer, one young man decided to try and swim towards whatever fate awaited him. Miraculously he was found by a Bahamian fishing boat and the story of the plight of his fellow castaways became international news. When the Bahamian government contacted the Haitian government asking what to do with the refugees the response was brutally frank: "We have no boats to rescue these people. Do with them what you will". When the Bahamian coastguard arrived to remove what a national newspaper described as "pariahs of the Caribbean" the Haitians linked arms in a human chain and refused to be taken. Tear gassed and beaten into submission by the coast guards, the Haitians were eventually forced onto the ship and returned to Haiti, the whole gruesome episode caught on film by a CBS news crew. The plight of the so-called Haitian boat people, and by inference, the poor and wretched masses of Haitians under Jeanclaudism, could no longer be hidden from the world. But unlike the Cuban refugees escaping communism in Cuba, the U.S. government identified the Haitian boat people as economic, rather than political migrants. With thousands of illegal Haitian immigrants in U.S. detention centres, and growing awareness of the presence of HIV/AIDS within Haitian refugee communities, xenophobia against the so-called Haitian boat people grew in the United States and the newly elected president Ronald Reagan created a *cordon sanitaire* around Haiti policed by the U.S. coastguard. It was over this *cordon* that an adventurous Canadian ethno-botanist flew with letters of introduction and a "medical research" allowance in the spring of 1982 in search of "real-life" *zombis*.

THE SERPENT AND THE RAINBOW

Wade Davis's *The Serpent and the Rainbow: An Astonishing Journey into the Secret Society of Haitian Voodoo, Zombis and Magic* is an adventure story-cum-ethnographic autobiography that tells the tale of the author's daring journey to the very "frontier of death" and his discovery of the secrets of zombification. Two years later the book would be made into what Barbara Browning has described as "one of the most astonishingly racist and xenophobic films ever to depict Haiti and Vodou", a gory Hollywood horror film directed by Wes Craven, the then-famous director of the popular *Nightmare on Elm Street* series of films.[7]

Wade Davis, a former logger and park ranger from British Columbia, was an ethnobotanist and anthropologist based in Harvard who had spent several years researching and photographing various tribal groups in Latin America and sampling their botanical remedies. Modelling himself on his mentor Professor Richard Schultes, the reputed discoverer of psychedelic mushrooms, Davis adopted the image of an intrepid *Boy's Own* explorer, venturing heroically into remote and dangerous lands, a fearless voyager into the psychotropic realms of indigenous botanicals and native mysticism. The book, which became a bestseller translated into ten languages, tells the story of his journey to Haiti in 1982 to seek the secrets of the reputed *zombi*-making formula alluded to in Article 246 of the Haitian Penal code, first mentioned by Seabrook, later by Zora Neale Hurston, and used in *White Zombie*.[8] Hurston, who had dedicated a chapter of her book to *zombis* (by then popularly known outside of Haiti due to the success of the Halperin brothers' film and those that followed in its wake) was something of a role model for Davis. Like him she set herself the task of "discovering the secrets of the zombi" and was the first respectable ethnographer to describe an encounter with a reputedly "real" *zombi*, Felicia Felix-Mentor, who she met and photographed in a hospital in

---

7 Craven's reputation for extreme horror films dates back to his 1972 *Last House on the Left*, a re-make of Bergman's *Virgin Spring* set in a Vietnam-era United States, that was listed as a Video Nasty in the U.K. due to the extreme scenes of sexual violence it depicted.

8 Hurston 195-196, 203-205

Gonaïves in 1936. Davis notes that Hurston was in fact very close to arriving at the same conclusions as him, but that her accounts of the role of secret societies in the creation of *zombis* was largely ignored by Haitian scholars who, smarting from the sensational publications that had emanated from the United States, did not consider Hurston's claims as worthy of further speculation.[9]

Davis's journey to Haiti began when, on the recommendation of Schultes, he was invited to a reception at the exotically decorated East Side Manhattan apartment of Dr. Nathan Kline, a famous psychiatrist and pioneer in the field of psychopharmacology.[10] There he was introduced to Heinz Lehman, another famous psychopharmacologist who, like Kline, had developed successful chemical treatments for psychiatric disorders in the 1950s.[11] Kline and Lehman begin to tell Davis a series of anecdotes about people who had crossed the threshold of death, like an assumed corpse in the New City morgue who had leaped up during their post-mortem and strangled a mortician who promptly died of shock, and a young woman in a Sheffield mortuary who, despite being certified dead from a drugs overdose, still showed signs of life on a cardiogram. Davis was then shown documentation from the case of a Clairvius Narcisse, a Haitian man who, having been pronounced dead in 1962, was now alive and resettled in his village in the Artibonite Valley. Narcisse's family, Kline explained, believed that

---

9 Hurston herself notes how when she was first told about the *Cochon Gris* secret society by a yard-hand, an upper-class Haitian guest who was visiting her at the time privately scolded him for telling such things to a foreigner who might "go off and say bad things about Haiti" (Hurston 203).

10 Kline was the developer of the anti-psychotic drug Reserpine in the 1950s synthesised from the psychedelic Indian Snake Root. It was used specifically for the treatment of schizophrenia. Kline also developed early drug treatments for clinical depression. Along with Manfred Clynes, Kline coined the term "cyborg" in 1960 to describe self-regulating human-machine systems designed for space travel.

11 Lehman was a famous advocate for the de-criminalisation of marijuana and the clinical value of psilocybin. John Lennon, to whom *The Serpent and the Rainbow* is co-dedicated, spoke at the Le Dain Commission hearings into the non-criminal use of drugs in 1969 at which Lehman was an expert witness.

he was the victim of a Vodou cult who had turned him into a *zombi*.

Narcisse had come to Kline's attention through a former student, Lamarque Douyon, the director of the *Centre de Psychiatrie et Neurologie* in Port-au-Prince where Narcisse had been treated since 1980. The Mars and Kline Centre, as it was also known, was opened in 1958 after Nathan Kline visited Haiti and witnessed first-hand the terrible conditions of the asylums there. He was approached for help by Louis Mars, son of Jean Price-Mars, and author of 'The Story of the Zombie in Haiti' (1945) and *La crise de possession dans le vodou* (1946), who was the only fully trained psychiatrist in the country at the time. Three nurses, two doctors and two attendants from Haiti were invited for an eight-month stay at the Rockland State Hospital in New York to train with doctors there in preparation for returning to Haiti to work as clinical psychiatrists. The building of the clinic was funded by three American drug companies who would supply the necessary medications.[12] From its opening in 1958 the clinic had been directed by Douyon, the first person to write about Narcisse in an article entitled 'Les zombis dans le contexte vodou et Haitien' in the Haitian medical journal *Haiti Santé* in 1980. Douyon himself had trained as a psychiatrist in Montreal with Ewen Cameron, president of the Canadian, American and World Psychiatric Associations and infamous for having been a chief investigator for the CIA-funded MK-ULTRA experiments in the 1960s in which non-consenting patients were experimented on in "psychic driving" experiments using massive doses of electroshock therapy and LSD.[13] Douyon, with whom Kline had been collaborating since 1961, had examined fifteen other cases of reputed zombiedom but only Narcisse's seemed to be genuine. Lehman and Kline believed there must be a material explanation for the condition, presumably some sort of drug. "Finally", Davis writes, "I knew what they wanted from me". His assignment was to travel to Haiti, find the Vodou sorcerers responsible for the preparation, obtain samples of poison and antidote while observing their preparation and documenting their use. And this is precisely what he did.

In ways reminiscent of Seabrook's *Magic Island* sixty years earlier, Davis's book, despite having an ostensibly scholarly intention, is

12 Platt 122

13 Davis (1985) 59

written in an explicitly novelistic, first person-narrative style, fusing elements of travel adventure, detective fiction, zombie films and his now characteristic New Age polemic. The book opens with an account of his first trip to Latin America during which, on a journey through the jungles between Columbia and Panama, he and his traveling companions were saved from almost certain disaster by the sudden appearance of a black jaguar. The "shamanic apparition", which gave Davis the spirit to continue onwards by pointing them in the direction of safety, would become something of a leitmotif in the film version of his book (which Davis helped script), in which an Amazonian shaman transforms into a Haitian *bokor* during a psychedelic hallucination. Davis's account of his visit to Nathan Kline's apartment in New York has all the qualities of a 1940s film noir, with Davis in the role of a private detective being offered a contract by a wealthy and mysterious client. Kline's daughter Marna Anderson, who he describes as looking like a Renoir model, plays the potential love-interest for the hard-boiled ethnobotanist. The dialogue between Davis, Lehman and Kline is straight '40s zombie movie, the aged and respected scientists discussing things "beyond western reason" with a younger and sceptical neophyte who is about to be sent on a journey to "the Frontier of Death" (the title of Chapter Two). As he stares at his own reflection in the window of the train from New York back to Boston, the passing frames race by "like so many childhood fantasies alive in colour and light", kaleidoscopic visions from previous shamanic encounters blur into his sleep like cinematic dissolves, splicing real-time seamlessly into memories of earlier adventures.[14]

Davis arrived in Haiti in April that year with introductions to Lamarque Douyon, Max Beauvoir (the *houngan* of *houngans* and self-styled spokesperson of Vodou) and Marcel Pierre, a Vodou priest who a

---

14 More a Left Coast David Attenborough than James Bond, several commentators have noted the similarities between Davis's literary persona and the fictional Indiana Jones, created four years earlier by George Lucas and Steven Spielberg. See for instance Cosentino (2012) and Kevin Thomas's *Los Angeles Times* review of Craven's film 'Good, Evil Clash in 'Serpent and Rainbow'' (Feb 5th 1988). Like Davis, Indiana Jones also had an ethnographic mentor in the figure of Abner Ravenwood, whose daughter Marion acts as the love-interest in the several of the Indiana Jones films.

year earlier had been interviewed by the BBC in a documentary about the case of Clairvius Narcisse and had given the film-makers a sample of reputed *zombi* powder. As soon as he had dropped his bags off at the hotel, Davis visited Beauvoir at his *peristyle* in Mariani, a *hounfor-cum-nightclub* in the south of Port-au-Prince.[15] Beauvoir explained to him that the secrets of the *zombi* lie not in the poison, but the person who makes it: "the *bokor*, a priest who serves with the left hand". Later, after attending his first Vodou ceremony, one of the regular services staged for tourists by Beauvoir at his compound, he meets Rachel Beauvoir, Max's daughter, who will be his main companion and guide through his many adventures there. It is Rachel who introduces him to Marcel Pierre, the *houngan/bokor* from whom Davis purchases his first sample of *zombi* powder and the promise of a demonstration of its preparation.[16] When they returned to *peristyle* de Marianna after meeting Marcel Pierre four men were waiting for them. They wanted to know what Davis was doing in Haiti. The one Davis assumed to be in charge took the powder Marcel Pierre had given him and poured it into his palm, stirring it with a finger. "This is too light to be anything", he says. The other men laugh. When they are gone Davis asks Beauvoir who they were. Important *houngans*, he is told.

After having spent some time searching for Datura, the plant that he suspected to be the main ingredient in the *zombi* powder, Davis visited Lamarque Douyon at the *Centre de Psychiatrie*. Douyon gave Davis a dossier which contains paperwork about the Narcisse case and

---

15 Max Beauvoir ran *peristyle* de Mariana from 1974 to 1994, after which he fled from Haiti to Washington D.C. fearing for his life because of his opposition to President Aristide and his closeness to the Duvalier regime (Tapper). Browning notes a personal communication with Laurent Dubois who described Beauvoir as "one of the central organisers of the political mobilization in defence of Vodou that responded to the *dechoukaj* attacks on temples, *houngans* and *mambos*; and in a way his work with Davis was perhaps as a previous (ultimately failed...) attempt to challenge representations of Vodou... He is a complex figure who is part of a larger move amongst *houngans* and *mambos*... who have chosen to try and develop a counter-representation of Vodou in order to defend the religion." (Browning 100 n20)

16 It was during the preparation of the *zombi* powder sample that Davis describes the processes noted by William Greenfield.

the much cited Article 246 of the Haitian Penal code (which, following Seabrook and the Halperins, Davis mistakenly identifies as Article 249). In conversation Douyon likens the condition of zombiedom to the clinical diagnosis of catatonic schizophrenia, dispelling any mystical explanation for the condition and instead blaming it on the actions of criminals. For Davis the *zombi* represented a much more complicated set of symptoms that, he believed, must be rooted in the structures and beliefs of the Haitian peasant society. Narcisse, who contrary to the popular myth of Haitian *zombis* was able to speak, had explained to doctors that he had been conscious during the entire process of his burial. Some time later he had heard his name being called from inside the grave, was taken from the cemetery by a *bokor* and his assistants, beaten with a whip and wrapped in a black shroud, before being passed between different groups at night. Eventually he was forced to work at a sugar plantation for the next two years, escaping by chance after one of the captives, beaten for not eating for several days, killed the *bokor* with a hoe in a fit of rage. "With the death of the master" he explained, "the zombies dispersed" Narcisse told Davis that after his exhumation from the grave he was subject to eight days of judgment. When asked by whom he replied, "They are the masters of the country and they do as they please".

Although Davis comments little on the recent history of Haiti at the time of his visit, in a section entitled 'Lessons of History' he recounts the knowledge imparted to him by Max Beauvoir during their many herb gathering forays into the Haitian countryside. He refutes popular historical stories about Touissant Louverture, Jean-Jacques Dessalines and Henri Christophe being guided by "lofty libertarian visions" and instead suggests that all of them, during the revolution and its aftermath, wanted to install themselves "at the top of a new social order". Louverture had been a willing collaborator with the French in their attempt to restore French authority to the island, and Dessalines had maintained the dream of an export economy of chain-gang labour until his assassination in 1806. Both sought to make Roman Catholicism the formal religion of the new republic and to suppress the Vodou cult.

As Davis learns more about the cosmology and mysteries of Vodou imparted to him by Max and Rachel Beauvoir, he slowly comes to realise that zombification is a very special form of ritual punishment meted out by the secret societies that govern rural Haitian communities, according to rules and rituals inherited from the Maroon bands that fought in the revolution, continuing their martial traditions with the harshest of esoteric discipline. In contrast to the revolutionary historical leaders of Haiti, all of whom wanted Haiti to be a Catholic country, Davis represents Vodou, *houngans* and the Bizango as models of an indigenous form of mystical democracy. "Vodou is a quintessentially democratic faith", he writes. "Each believer not only has direct contact with the spirits, he actually receives them into his body". Despite paying little attention to the recent political history of Haiti, Davis does note several instances in which images of Papa Doc, Baby Doc and Michèle Bennett appear in the *mise-en-scène* of his adventure, such as the prominent portrait of François Duvalier in Douyon's office at the *Centre de Psychiatrie*, the dozens of pictures of Jean-Claude Duvalier and his wife that surround Narcisse's sister Angelina (along with the many small red and black flags that match her dress), and the hundreds of images of Baby Doc at the Bizango *peristyle* they visit in Gonaïves. The significance of the red and the black will slowly dawn on Davis as he comes to realise that they are the specific colours of the secret society, echoing the flag created by Dessalines after the founding of the republic, and re-introduced by Papa Doc after he made himself president for life in 1964.

After returning to Harvard with the zombie powder he made with Marcel Pierre and a sample of all the significant ingredients, Davis deposited the specimens at the Museum of Comparative Zoology in Cambridge. There they are discovered to contain neurotoxins that could conceivably induce a state resembling death, including one, as the "fish expert" tells him, known to anyone familiar with the last chapter of Ian Fleming's *From Russia with Love* in which James Bond is poisoned into a near death state by the venom of a puffer fish. Davis eventually concludes that the key ingredient to the zombie powder is the powerful and generally lethal poison known as tetrodotoxin. As soon as he had the results he needed he was advised by Nathan Kline to send a sample to Professor Leon Roizin at the New York State Psychiatric Hospital who would test a solution of the powder topically on laboratory animals. Having tested the emulsion on rats and rhesus monkeys, both of which were sedated into a catatonic state, Roizin concludes that the powder contained active ingredients that could work as a powerful narcotic.[17] "Whatever this powder contains", Roizin told

---

17 In the section where Davis describes visiting Roizin he expresses,

him, "it acts very quickly and completely modifies behaviour". When Davis asks Roizin, rather disingenuously, what the powder might be used for, he replies by asking if Kline had ever spoken to Davis about "experimental hibernation".[18] Nathan Kline's interest in the zombie potion, we learn, had to do with the development of potential drugs for the artificial hibernation of "cyborgs" during long-term space missions.

Having isolated the compounds that could feasibly be used to put a person into a death-like state, Davis was still fascinated by the ritual process by which a person was chosen to be made into a zombie, and the crimes for which it was a punishment. "It was a potent idea," he wrote, "one that, if I were to accept the council of my advisors, was

---

in exemplary *National Geographic* style, his sadness at seeing "an entire wall of metal cages rattled with the frantic movements of animals [rhesus monkeys] that had never called out for a mate". Roizin tapped on one of the cages and "the captive lunged violently, knocking its teeth against the thin bars". "Passive they are not" Roizin comments. Although the scene does not make it into Craven's film it is echoed in two future apocalyptic zombie-themed films, that, in different ways, exploit the broadly bio-political theory of zombies proposed by Davis: Danny Boyle's *28 Days Later* (2002) which begins in an animal research laboratory in Cambridge (U.K.) where scientists are infecting chimpanzees with a virus called "Rage"; and the zombie doctor that snarls against the wall of its glass cage in Marc Foster's *World War Z* (2013). One of the consequences of the convergence of *fictional* infectious, cannibal zombies, claims about *actual* Haitian *zombis*, the discovery of HIV/AIDS amongst Haitians in the early '80s, and the hypothesis that HIV/AIDS seems to have passed from primates to humans in sub-Saharan Africa, is the rarely acknowledged, yet barely suppressed, mythical revival of evolutionary, racial archaism, common in 19th century race theory, that considered Black people as genotypically closer to our primate ancestors. See Hahn and Sharp 'Origin of HIV and the AIDS Pandemic'.

18 In an article published shortly after Wes Craven's film was released, Professor Roizin expresses embarrassment at his depiction in Davis's "novel", maintaining that he had been promised by Kline that the powders would be thoroughly analysed, and that the results of these first experiments would stay "just among friends". According to Roizin the experiments were never repeated or scientifically verified (Booth 275).

fraught with danger. After all, I was in effect asking who actually ruled rural Haiti".[19] The third and final section of the book – 'The Secret Societies' – documents his return to Haiti in 1984, this time without the support of his financial backers, to discover the secrets of the Bizango societies who controlled the zombification process.[20]

SECRET GOVERNANCE

In the years between Davis's first and second visits to Haiti, Jean-Claude Duvalier's hold on the reins of power had started to slip, not least because his wife Michèle kept forcing them from him with increasing severity and regularity.[21] Her father Ernest Bennett, known locally as "The Godfather" due to his involvement in the Columbia-Haiti-U.S. drug trade, had been granted a virtual monopoly on coffee exports, while the Duvaliers set up numerous "dummy agencies", drew millions of dollars from the national bank that, when not used for Michèle's notorious shopping binges in Paris (for which she hired a private Concorde), were spirited away to private, offshore accounts. A New York law firm, charged with reclaiming the monies that the Duvaliers had stolen, wrote that: "The Duvaliers treated Haiti as if it was their private property. Their dictatorship did not permit them to make a distinction between the goods of the State and those of the Duvalier family. They behaved as if Haiti was their feudal kingdom and the coffers and revenues of the State their private property."[22]

---

19 Davis (1986) 216

20 The Bizango is one of several names for one of many secret societies in Haiti. Other names include the Caporaleta, Cochon Gris, Les Cochons-sans-Poils, Galipotes, Makandal, Mandingue, Mazanxa, Regiment, San Manman, San Poèl, Secta Rouge, Shanpwell, Vlanbindingues, Voltiguers and Zobop. Hurston was the first writer to make public the connection between secret societies and zombification.

21 Davis's return journey to Haiti was delayed for a year because Nathan Kline died unexpectedly while undergoing routine surgery in a New York hospital in 1983 and within 48 hours David Merrick, the project's principle financial backer, suffered a debilitating stroke that left him incapacitated.

22 Abbott 251

External factors had also added to the already unbearable burden of the Haitian masses. In 1978 African Swine Fever was discovered in pigs in the Dominican Republic and, in an attempt to save the Haitian pig population upon which the rural economy was dependent, the Haitian authorities eradicated all pigs in a swathe along the border region. By 1979 it seemed likely that the attempt to halt the spread of the disease had failed and so in July 1981 an agreement was signed with the Inter-American Institute of Cooperative Agriculture for the slaughter of all Haitian pigs within two years. In the eradication programme, which began in May 1982 and ended in December 1983, an estimated 1.2 million pigs were killed and the Haitian peasant economy, already devastated by the effects of hurricanes, deforestation and soil erosion, was left in ruins, forcing millions to seek work in the capital.[23] Perhaps the greatest direct blow to the Duvalier dynasty was struck that same year when Pope John Paul II made a flying visit to Haiti during his tour of Latin America. Thinking it an opportune moment to show the world the magnanimous face of Jeanclaudism the regime spent $4 million on a lavish, red carpet reception. But in his speech to the thousands of poor Haitians who thronged to see him the Pope famously said in Kreyòl, "things must change". "There must be a better distribution of goods, a fairer organisation of society, with more popular participation, a more disinterested conception of service on the part of those who direct society" he told them. In a final snub to the Duvaliers, Pope Jean Paul refused their invitation to an extravagant feast laid on in his honour, dining instead with Catholic priests. A year later the first intimations of the simmering revolt that would force the Duvaliers into exile began in Gonaïves where, after a pregnant woman was beaten to death by Macoutes, an international food distribution warehouse was attacked and two days of rioting ensued.

There is little mention of such events in *The Serpent and the Rainbow*, although, as we will see, the popular uprisings that began in 1984 form a backdrop to the 1988 film version of the book. It was in Gonaïves

---

23 As many commentators have noted, the Creole pig was a fundamental part of the Haitian peasant economy. Easy to keep and raise, in times of hardship or when revenue was needed for special occasions, the pigs could be sold. See Leah Gordon and Anne Parisio's film *A Pig's Tail* (1997) which tells the story of a *houngan*'s attempt to find a surviving Creole pig for a Vodou ceremony.

however that Davis would discover the secrets of the organisations that controlled the rural departments of Haiti. Herard Simon was the chief *houngan* who had first questioned Davis about his activities in Haiti at *peristyle* Mariana, and it was at his compound in Gonaïves that Davis was introduced to a group of *houngans* who offered to show him the complete secrets of the *zombi*-making process (i.e. not only how to prepare the poison but how to administer it, wake the *zombi* and control it). Simon was formerly the head of the Macoutes for all of the Atibonite valley (in which Gonaîve is located). He may also have been the *houngan* who would reputedly sacrifice two newly born infants for Jean-Claude and Michèlé Duvalier on the eve of their final departure from Haiti.[24] Though now retired Simon still "ran things" there as Rachel explained. In a description reminiscent of Seabrook's image of the "dark mother of mysteries", Davis describes Simon as having a special kind of presence "a charisma hot to the touch":

> There was something frightening about him, a latent violence that was both ancient and tribal. It seemed as if he bore within him the exploding energy of an entire race; as if his skin, stretched so thin over his massive body, lay ready to split, to release some great catastrophe of the human spirit.

It was during one of their visits to speak with Simon that Davis makes the association, noted earlier, between himself and Indiana Jones. Having arrived at his compound and discovered that Simon was not there, Davis and Rachel Beauvoir decide to wait in a small cinema in Gonaïves where he could usually be found. There they watched a very poor quality print of *Raiders of the Lost Ark*. According to Davis, during the climax of the film, when the spirits rush out of the Ark of the Covenant to kill anyone watching, "pandemonium gripped the theater". "Amid shouts of 'Loup Garou' – the werewolf – someone screamed a warning to pregnant women, and another cautioned all

---

24 Diebert 350, Abbott 324. Diebert refers to the person who performed the ceremony as the Gonaïves *houngan* Hérard Simon, presumably the same person. Abbott, however claims that he was called Ernst Simon and personally described the ritual he performed in which he paid $400 for the babies which normally cost only $40. She does not however cite the source of this information.

of us to tie ribbons around our left arms". At the end of the film they discover that Simon was there watching it too. Afterwards, while discussing the scene where Indiana Jones is trapped in a crypt full of snakes, Simon told them that "Someone born with a serpent's blood could do it [...] otherwise it had to be a mystical thing... Only a fool would attempt to dance alone in the jaw of a lion". That the chapter in which the scene occurs is called 'Dancing in the Lion's Jaw' suggests that Davis self-consciously identified with the Indiana Jones character. It is perhaps not surprising then that Wes Craven will choose to emulate the climax of *Raiders of the Lost Ark* in the film version of Davis's book.

It is from Simon that Davis learns about the difference between a *zombi-astral* (a "spirit *zombi*" kept in a ceramic *govi* jar or *canari*) and a *zombi corps kadav* (a poisoned and resurrected person); that there are four different preparations for *zombis* (*Tombé Levé*, *Retiré Bon Ange*, *Tué* and *Levé*); that the best potions were made during the summer months; and that *Datura*, a powerful and highly toxic hallucinogen, did indeed have a role to play in the process, not in the making of the *zombi* however but in the *maintaining* of a person in a zombic state. Simon introduces Davis to the presidents of a number of secret societies from whom he learns the seven laws whose infractions may cause a person to be punished by them.[25] Like Michel Laguerre, whose 1980 essay 'Bizango: A Voodoo Secret Society' he makes reference to, Davis proposes that the sect's origins lie in Maroon bands that had been active since before the revolution and who acquired a reputation as poisoners and *malfacteurs* during the colonial era.[26] After

---

25 They are:

i) Excessive ambition at the expense of family and loved ones

ii) Displaying a lack of respect for one's fellows

iii) Denigrating a Bizango society

iv) Stealing another man's woman

v) Spreading slanderous rumours that affect the well-being of others

vi) Harming members of one's family

vii) Action which prevents another from working the land.

26 Laguerre himself, following Saint-Méry, proposes that the name Bizango is derived from the name of a cluster of islands off the coast of Kakonda, between Sierra Leone and Cape Verde, called the Bissagot

the revolution Maroon organisations continued to exist in the form of secret societies with their own specific variety of Vodou traditions (such as the Bizango passport which gives holders special passage between regions and villages at night and the monthly evening rallies during which members of the sect march through the local areas arresting anyone not permitted to be out). Davis claims that the Maroon sects attracted a "new class of slave" drawn from the higher, educated and militaristic castes of African society. The legislative powers of the sects, he proposes, derive from similar African secret societies like the Poro and Leopard societies of West Africa.[27] In Davis's account of the Haitian revolution the Maroons are cast as betrayed and forgotten war heroes who, after the presidency of Henri Christophe, found "a new and remarkable means of protecting their freedom". Davis also suggests that the ceremony of Bois Caïman was organised by secret Maroon societies who would play a central role in the early stages of the war of independence. (Davis' version of the event includes jagged lightning, the old woman "quivering in the spasms of possession", the "voices of Ogoun" who called for the cutlass, the "foamy blood" of the black pig, the naming of the revolutionary leaders and the Boukman oath).

With the help of a young man called Isnard, who explains to them that, contrary to popular Haitian lore, the cult was not evil but a place of security and support for those initiated into it, Davis and Rachel Beauvoir eventually managed to attend a Bizango ceremony. Once reluctantly accepted into the confidence of members, Davis learned that many of the *chefs de section* in rural Haiti, those with responsibility to liaise with the government authorities for their regional communities, were often *houngans* and presidents of secret societies. They were the leaders, in effect, of the secret government of all of rural Haiti, each

---

islands. Slaves from these islands formed Maroon communities during the colonial era (Laguerre 71-72).

27 During the reign of Jean-Claude Duvalier a special presidential branch of the VSN/Macoutes was created called the *Léopards* who were trained by former U.S. marines and funded by the CIA under the auspices of a Haitian-U.S. company called Aerotrade Inc. (Heinl and Heinl 614, Sprague 36-37). According to Sprague members of the *Léopards* would later serve in various paramilitary organisations and Baby Doc himself trained with them.

society having a ruling body, called the *chef d'etat-majeur* (made up of Emperors, Presidents, Queens and Vice-Presidents), and complex layers of minor offices modelled upon French military and civil organisations. At the ceremony in Archaie, north of Port-au-Prince, a president of one of the societies gives a speech about the origins and meaning of the Bizango:

> Another meaning of the Bizango is the meaning of the great ceremony at Bwa Caïman. They fall within the same empire of thoughts. Our history, such moments, the history of Macandal, of Romaine La Prophétesse, of Boukman, of Pedro. Those people bore many sacrifices on their breasts. They were alive and they believed! We may also speak of a certain Hyacinthe who as the cannon fired upon him showed no fear, proving to his people that the canon were water. And that of Macandal! The one who was tied to the execution pole with bullets ready to smash him but found a way to escape because of the sacrifice he did.[28]

Later the emperor of another Bizango society, Jean-Jacques Leophin, explains to Davis that the word Bizango comes from the word Cannibal. "You find this word in the Red Dragon or the books of the Wizard Emmanuel", he tells the author:

> Bizango is to prove that change is possible. That is why we say "learn to change". We are in the world, and we can change in the world. Everyone says that the Shanpwel change people into pigs, but we say this only because it

---

28 Davis (1986) 247. In his *Vodou Quantum Leap* (2000) Reginald Crosley develops a thesis proposed by Henry Claude Innocent in a 1995 article for the Haitian newspaper *La Nouvelliste* that the Vodou leaders of the Haitian Revolution practiced a rite called Petro-Zandor first created by the legendary Don Pedro (after whom the Petro cult is said to be named) which was developed by Makandal and later called the Simbi-Makaya cult. At Bois Caïman the Simbi-Makaya cult reputedly created a powerful *egregor* (or conglomerate) of "dark matter entities" to help them fight the revolutionary war (Crosley 108).

teaches that everything is relative. You may think that you and I are equals, are humans with the same skin, that we're two "pigs," or "donkeys," or even "invisible." This is what is called Bizango changing. That is what it means.[29]

Finally Leophin tells Davis that the people in government in Port-au-Prince must cooperate with the Bizangos. "We were here before them" he says "and if we didn't want them, they wouldn't be where they are. There are not many guns in the country, but those that there are, we have them".[30] Then in one of the rare references to the recent political life of Haiti and one which suggests a direct link between the Bizangos and Duvalierism, Davis explains how the Duvalier revolution, "often misrepresented in the Western press and remembered only for its later brutal excesses",

began as a reaction on the part of the black majority to the excessive prominence of a small ruling elite that dominated the nation politically and economically for most of history.[31]

The speed with which François Duvalier was able to organise the Macoutes, Davis proposes, was because of the use he made of the Bizango secret societies that reached into "every corner of the land". Repeating the claim that Papa Doc emulated the spirit of Baron Samedi, whom he says is popularly associated with secret societies in Haiti (and noting "well-documented" overlaps between membership of the Bizango and the Tonton Macoute), Davis finally suggests that Duvalier himself might have been the symbolic or effective head of the network of secret societies. The book ends with Davis and Rachel Beauvoir drinking drafts of two green potions administered to them by the president of a Bizango society, after which the two initiates entered a "long silent passage, and for the next month, were strangers to sunlight".

---

29 Davis (1986) 251

30 Sprague notes that under the auspices of Aerotrade Inc. the CIA were able to import weapons into Haiti for use by the *Léopards* (Sprague 36-37).

31 Davis (1986) 255

ALTERED STATES

> If the last two and a half years of Haitian politics look like a badly dubbed movie where the words and gestures do not always match, it is because something is wrong with the script that most observers chose to read.

> - Michel-Rolph Trouillot *Haiti: State Against Nation* (1990)[32]

> I promised the people of Haiti that this film was going to be a fair representation of their country, and that the film would look at voodoo as a well-rounded thing with both a light and dark side. I truly believe that I have accomplished that.

> - Wes Craven, director of *The Serpent and the Rainbow* (1988)[33]

Published the same year as Wes Craven's film adaptation of his earlier book, *Passage of Darkness*, Davis's scholarly follow-up to the novelistic *The Serpent and the Rainbow*, contains much the same information but composed, this time, in a dry academic manner.[34] That he should

---

32 Trouillot (1990) 224

33 Muir 27

34 Critical reactions within the scientific community to the publication of Davis's two books were summarised (after the release of Craven's film) in a 1988 article for *Science* by William Booth called 'Voodoo Science'. One of the most vociferous critics was C. Y. Kao from the State University of New York Downstate Medical Centre in Brooklyn, who accused Davis's book of being a fraud. In 1984, after his first trip to Haiti, Davis sent samples of the powder to Kao, then in Japan, for analysis. When Kao publicly criticised Davis's findings in a 1986 article in the academic journal *Toxicon*, Davis reputedly accused him of "old fashioned jealousy". The three different laboratories that tested the powders found remarkably different levels of tetrodotoxin in the same samples, and the conclusions of the doctors assigned to analysing them varied widely. There were no pharmacologists or toxicologists on Davis's doctoral dissertation committee at which he presented the first version of his 'Ethnobiology of the Haitian Zombie'

have chosen to publish another version of the story so soon after *The Serpent and the Rainbow* is odd. Could it be that he wanted to redeem his academic reputation after the release of Wes Craven's film? Given the royalties that he must have received for its sale, and the popular interest the film must have generated, it was presumably not a financially motivated decision. Dedicated to his father, prefaced with a prestigious foreword by the notable historian of African culture in the Americas Robert Farris Thompson, and with an introduction by his mentor Richard Evans Schultes, no reference is made in it to the film version of the earlier book or the circumstances of the sale of the film rights to a cultural institution generally seen as contributing more than any other to the popular denigration and misrepresentation of Haiti and its indigenous culture. The book however does conclude, as did the earlier one, with some reflection on the likely role of the Bizango secret societies in post-Duvalier Haiti. Davis proposes, finally, that it was the Bizango who were "in no small part" *responsible* for the collapse of Jean-Claude Duvalier's government, which had distanced itself from the secret societies.[35] Davis cites in support of the claim Michel Laguerre, who noted a coffin carried on the heads of two protesters in 1986 with the words "Jean-Claude Duvalier, You belong in here" on it, indicating to him that a council of elders from a secret society had ruled against Baby Doc. Un-cited press reports even proposed that a group of Bizango leaders had ultimately persuaded Duvalier to step down from power.[36] Ending with a quote from Michel Laguerre,

---

and Davis reputedly paid $300 for each sample of voodoo-powder "an enormous sum of money" Booth notes, in a country which is "one of the poorest [...] in the Western Hemisphere". But it was not the payment but the non-consensual exhumation of the body of a baby girl in order to make the powder that seems to have caused the most ethical concern amongst fellow anthropologists and medical scientists. Davis reputedly defended himself from these accusations by assuming the stance of a "participant observer".

35 This suggestion contradicts several made by Elizabeth Abbott who claims that the Duvaliers performed regular services to the *lwa*, not least on their last night in Haiti when they had two unbaptized babies sacrificed to curse the presidential bed (Abbott 324).

36 Once again this is contradicted by Abbott and Heinl and Heinl who claim it was leaders of the Haitian military and presidential guard

Passage of Darkness concludes on a note that echoes the warnings made by Spenser St. John a century earlier:

> From now on every constitutional president will need to have a functional knowledge of voodoo [*sic*] if he or she wishes to become a popular and successful leader among the Haitian masses. [...] That, perhaps, will be the most significant legacy of the Duvalier regime.[37]

Davis has said little about the circumstances by which his book became a Hollywood movie. In an interview with CBC's Peter Gzowski in January 1986 he defended the explicitly novelistic and cinematic style of the book (which one could be forgiven for thinking was written as a potential film script) by saying that, "as a scientist", he had wanted to reach a popular audience. Because Canadian tax payers had paid for his education, he argued, his research should be written up in a style that was accessible to them. Later, in an interview with Andrew Lawless, he explained that he was happy to be offered $20,000 a year for the options on the book, and that as part of the deal it had been agreed that Peter Weir – director of *Picnic at Hanging Rock* (1975) and *The Last Wave* (1977), who had recently had success with *The Year of Living Dangerously* (1982) – would direct the film, and Mel Gibson, star of the latter, would play the lead. In the end both turned the offer down and the film "fell into the hands" of Wes Craven. Ironically the film version of his book, which Davis claims to have hated, perpetuated (despite Craven's best intentions) the very pulp-fiction stereotypes of Haiti and Vodou that both author and director had reputedly aimed to dispel.[38]

After the fall of the Duvaliers Haiti was ruled by The National Council

---

who forced Jean-Claude Duvalier to resign, primarily Henri Namphy, Prosper Avril (presidential guard) and Williams Régala (head of the Haitian secret service) (Abbott 326). They may of course have been members of secret societies too, as the Leopard Society/Leopard Corps connection suggests.

37 Davis (1988) 290

38 Andrew Lawless 'The Shaman from Harvard - Wade Davis in Interview'. Elsewhere Davis has described Wes Craven's film as "one of the worst Hollywood movies of history" (Broderick 176).

of Government (or CNG), the provisional military government of the former army general Henri Namphy, who had conspired against the Duvaliers and negotiated their departure with the U.S. government. Namphy inherited a country in turmoil. The collective euphoria of the masses who had suffered such extremes under Duvalierism turned on their oppressors the Tonton Macoute in a violent purge that came to be known as *dechoukaj* (or "uprooting") overseen by the army, who refused to intervene. After decades of civil humiliation the army were once again seen as heroes. Properties belonging to the Bennett family and others associated with the regime were ransacked and destroyed and the new government freed all political prisoners (along with several hundred convicted rapists, murderers and drug dealers) and disbanded the Macoutes. With the Duvaliers having left only $2 million in the National treasury, the U.S. government hastily released $25 million of blocked aid money, a national literacy programme was announced by the new government and former exiles returned to the country in their thousands. The euphoria was short-lived however. The country was still starving and where once there had been Macoutes, bandits now murdered with impunity as the anti-Macoute *dechoukaj* spilled over into renewed and open aggression against Vodou practioners in what seemed to be a revival of the anti-superstition campaigns of the 1940s.[39] In the countryside the *chefs de section* still maintained control of the rural police but were now ruling alongside the army rather than *Macoutes*. Within six weeks, after an audacious tap-tap driver who overtook an army captain's staff car was arrested, five civilians were murdered by the *Léopards* in the protests that ensued. In April 1987 when a crowd of several hundred protestors marched to Fort Dimanche to pay respect to all those who had died in the "dungeon of death", the commandant of the prison ordered his men to open fire with machine guns that had been mounted on the roof, killing six and injuring many more. It seemed to many that, no sooner had it gone, than the old order was being violently restored.

Wes Craven and his team landed in Port-au-Prince in March 1987, arriving in what must have been a particularly trying situation to shoot a Hollywood feature film. It was something of an understatement then to have the lead character of the film say on his arrival in Haiti, that

---

39 *Dechoukaj*, a Kreyòl agricultural term meaning "uprooting", was the name given to the popular purging of Tonton Macoute and the destruction of symbols of the Duvalier regime.

it had "revolution in the air". With the screenplay cleared personally by Namphy, the crew and cast worked under the auspices of the Department of Culture, the army providing security in what was a highly volatile situation.[40] After meeting the president personally the crew went scouting for locations. In a cemetery in the capital graves had been torn open and skeletons lay everywhere. When Craven asked his guides what had happened he was told that during the "revolution" six months ago, the people had gone to the tombs of the families of the Tonton Macoute, tore the bodies out and "flung them around the cemetery". The filming was beset with problems from the start. In an interview in 2010 Craven said that at first they were treated like heroes because they were coming to give Haitians work, but any time they threatened not to satisfy their needs, the workers would pick up stones and threaten to kill them.[41] In the northern town of Milot, where the crew had camped to film a pilgrimage at the ruins of Sans Souci palace, the film's producer Robert Cohen was convinced to hire 9,500 extra Haitian nationals on top of the planned 500. But when no satisfactory payment could be agreed with the negotiators more money was extorted from them by machete.[42] According to John Muir, the author of *Wes Craven: The Art of Horror,* at a ceremony designed to "appease his unhappy extras" the director was nearly forced to drink pig's blood.

With Davis acting as remote advisor, the script was developed on location by the writers Richard Maxwell and A. R. Simoun. According to Craven, Maxwell was very interested in alternate systems of reality and had been given an introduction by Davis to one of the people who had prepared the *zombi* powder (presumably Marcel Pierre). Maxwell had asked the *houngan* for an initiation into Vodou. When Maxwell came back to the compound after the reputed initiation he could no longer "focus his thoughts" and refused to leave his room for the next few days. Eventually, after going "totally insane", Maxwell had to be put on a plane and sent back to Miami. This was on the first day of shooting. As a consequence Craven and his team had to adapt the script to "what the place was".

---

40 Muir notes that during shoot the crew were forced to purchase "insurrection insurance".

41 Interview at the Aero Theatre, Santa Monica, February 21st, 2010

42 Rob Cohen from an interview with Candice Russell in 'Bone Chilling look at Good, Bad of Voodoo' *Sun Sentinel,* February 9th, 1988.

What effect the psychological breakdown of the main scriptwriter had on the final film we can only surmise. What is clear is that the "alternate reality" angle, which had been one of the most powerful and innovative aspects of Craven's earlier and highly successful *A Nightmare on Elm Street*, is brought into the foreground in the film.[43] "For a person from another culture," Craven explains, "I mean a totally different mind-set culture, you just couldn't quite shoot the same script you went out there with."

> It's the first time I think I realised how much of a construct our "reality" is and how some cultures can have a completely different idea of what reality is, what consciousness is, and switch in and out of characters in ways that they can eat a glass and not get hurt somehow, I don't know how, but suddenly you realise that you're not in Kansas any more.

The film opens with a red-lidded black coffin being polished at a waterside workshop in Port-au-Prince in 1978. Four armed thugs arrive, the leader with powder on his arms, and take the coffin away. In the next scene we see a torch-carrying Baron Samedi figure but now in top hat, dinner suit and skull face leading the coffin down a crowded Port-au-Prince street. The camera pans across a large painting of Jean-Claude and François Duvalier looking in opposite directions as the coffin is deposited in front of a hospital building. The Baron character laughs manically as he waves his gun around the local people who make for the safety of their homes. The opening credits end with a shot of a man's head in silhouette lighting a cigarette, his gaze looking up towards the hospital window, where a distressed woman, dressed in red and black, looks out. The man with the cigarette, we will learn, is Captain Dargent Peytraud, sinister commander of the Tonton Macoute

---

43 Part of the enduring horror-value of the *Nightmare on Elm Street* series is the way in which waking reality and sleep are interwoven. The plots revolve around a killer, Freddy Krueger, who murders teenagers in their sleep. The plot was inspired by stories Craven had read about in the *LA Times* in the 1970s which told of three Khmer migrants from Cambodia to California who had tried to stop themselves going to sleep, so great was their fear of nightmares. All eventually died when they could no longer stay awake.

and, of all the characters in the film, the closest to Herard Simon. Unlike Simon however, who ultimately befriends Davis, Peytraud is no friend of his character in the film (played by Bill Pullman) or the Max Beauvoir character (played by Paul Winfield, the veteran African-American actor). In relation to previous films discussed here, Peytraud is a Dr. Kananga cum Murder Legendre character who embodies the "dark presence" that is felt by Dennis Alan throughout the film. Zakes Mokae, who plays Peytraud, also appeared in the film version of *The Comedians* as the suave, sunglasses wearing Macoute Michel who "interrogates" Major Jones at the beginning of the film. (The two roles are surprisingly continuous, Peytraud being the older Michel, now higher up in the Macoute hierarchy).

In the next scene we see a man called Christophe Durand being pronounced dead in the hospital room in front of a nurse and relatives, before being buried in a cemetery. From inside the coffin we see a tear roll down his temple as his sister calls out his name. The film then cuts to the "Amazon Basin" six years later. As a helicopter lands in a jungle clearing we hear the voice of Dennis Alan reading from his "field-notes". He tells the story of his meeting with a native Shaman who, sensing the same strange feeling as he, makes him drink a psychedelic concoction. The anthropologist then has an hallucination where he is attacked by a jaguar which chases him through the jungle, until, when the jaguar finally catches him, he discovers that it only wants to play. The shaman watches Alan rolling on the floor, laughing as he wrestles with his invisible "animal spirit". A wind suddenly comes up and the other natives run for cover. Alan unveils the shaman, who, after shielding himself in a blanket, has transformed into the *bokor* Peytraud. The terror-stricken anthropologist is then dragged through a hole into the earth, helped on his screaming way by black arms reaching out through the walls of the pit. Falling into a black abyss he awakes on the jungle floor. Everyone has gone and his pilot is dead. "Something much more evil or powerful than the shaman and his men has killed my pilot" the narrator says, as his avatar flees past smoking skulls impaled on sticks in the river bed, "I know this as clearly as I feel the darkness and cold closing in on me". Eventually, as in Davis's original book, the jaguar leads him back to civilisation.

In Craven's film Nathan Kline's East Side apartment is transformed into the glass fronted offices of Boston Biocorp where Alan meets Professor Earl Schoonbacher (the Schultes character) and Dr.

Cassedy (the Kline-Lehman character), the company's CEO. When Schoonbacher explains that Alan was guided out of the jungle by his animal spirit Cassedy responds "Well here at Boston Biocorp, we deal in science and medicine, not magic. So whether you came here by jaguar or Mercedes Benz, I really don't care. What I care about is that you came back with a sample bag full of plants and native medicines that no one has been able to collect". Then, as in the book, he is asked what he knows about zombification before being shown the case notes of Christophe Durand (i.e. Clairvius Narcisse). Cut to the streets of Port-au-Prince, Alan's voice-over repeating the oft-cited fact that Haiti "is one of the poorest countries in the world".[44] "I had expected a certain sense of oppression" he says "but what I hadn't expected was that the dark presence from the Amazon would instantly come over me here [the camera cuts to a large pile of garbage in the street] as sure as a cold hand falling on my shoulder". He also didn't expect Dr. Duchamp (the Lamarque Douyon/Rachel Beauvoir character) to be a woman.

Marielle Duchamp, played by Cathy Tyson, fresh from her debut in Neil Jordan's *Mona Lisa* (1986), now speaking with an awkward, pseudo-Kreyòl accent (much of which seems to have been dubbed in post-production) plays the director of the local hospital, where Alan is introduced to his first *zombi*, Margrite. When Margrite raises her head to answer his questions we hear the signature sound of pan-pipes accompanied by the frenetic and maniacal screaming of Diamanda Galas. Cut to a close-up of Margrite's wide eyes intercut with Alan's. Having lost his first staring game with the living dead, Alan says: "Well, she sure can't tell us anything".[45]

---

44 I have not been able to trace the precise historical source of this hackneyed epithet, one that the Haitian scholar and poet Jean-Claude Martineau has described as so ubiquitous as to have become Haiti's "second name" in popular journalism (Martineau, Jean-Claude 'The Other Occupation: The Haitian Version of Apartheid' *Covert Action Quarterly*, Spring 2005). The earliest use I have found is in the Inter-American Cooperative Report on Agriculture Haiti Agriculture Sector Assessment (1988) which notes that according to 1984 statistics Haiti was "one of the poorest countries in the western hemisphere". The epithet seems to have gained prominence during Jean-Claude Duvalier's presidency, since when Haiti's global poverty ranking has remained high.

45 The scene recalls Zora Neale Hurston's description of Felicia Felix-

Margrite's silent scream was a warning, he reflects, as the scene cuts to a folkloric Vodou ceremony, at a touristic *peristyle* reminiscent of the one in which Baron Samedi first appears in the film version of *Live and Let Die*. There he meets the benevolent but mysterious Lucien Celine, the Max Beauvoir character. In one of several sentences in the film that seems to have been dubbed on in post-production, Celine explains: "Haiti is full of contradictions Dr. Alan. These dancers for instance. They don't bleed and they don't burn". On her way out Marielle has rum blown in her face by a *houngan* and subsequently returns possessed by Erzulie, Vodou Goddess of Love. In the meantime Dargent Peytraud's arrival has given Alan a chilling psychedelic flashback. "He plays at being a *bokor*" Celine explains, "he is the chief of the Tonton Macoute, Duvalier's secret police". "You have seen him somewhere perhaps?" he asks. "Yeah, someplace," Alan responds. "Be careful my friend. In Haiti there are secrets we keep even from ourselves," Celine warns.

After having inquired into the story of Christophe Durand amongst his local community and family, Marielle and Alan eventually find him in the graveyard. Christophe explains that he was made into a *zombi* by a powder "that goes through the skin, and to the soul". When Alan asks Celine to help him find the secrets of the *zombi* powder he refuses, telling both the *blanc* and Marielle that if they blunder into it his people will get hurt. "The world should know what is happening here", Marielle replies. "What I'm after is going to save too many lives" Alan adds magnanimously, "I'm not going to back off". Celine gives them the name of Louis Mozart (the Marcel Pierre character) who drives a hard bargain for his *zombi* powder. Showing him a *canari* (the

---

Mentor, whom she was trying to photograph, which in turn evokes Seabrook's description of the "blind, staring eyes" of the *zombis* of La Gonâve (which Hurston was familiar with):

> Finally the doctor forcibly uncovered her and held her so I could take her face. And the sight was dreadful. That blank face with the dead eyes. The eyelids were white all around the eyes as if they had been burned with acid [...] There was nothing that you could say to her or get from her except by looking at her, and the sight of this wreckage was too much to endure for long (Hurston 195).

jar in which a *zombi*'s soul is kept) in his club, Mozart tells Alan that "It gives you power. You send it into people's dreams". "Whose soul is that?" Alan asks. "This place's previous owner" Mozart replies. Alan, as usual, seems to miss the joke.

Later Alan asks Marielle about her involvement with Vodou. She repeats some of the basic facts about the religion contained in Davis's book as the scene merges with footage of a candle-lit Madonna (Our Lady of Mount Carmel) being carried through the ruins of the Sans Souci palace by a procession of torch-bearing pilgrims, perhaps the most aesthetically striking and memorable sequences of the film, and the one for which the crew got into the most trouble while in Haiti. Sleeping with the pilgrims in candle-lit forests around the sacred Saut D'Eau waterfall, where a miraculous apparition of the Virgin had appeared during the U.S. occupation, Alan is visited in his dreams first by a serpent and then by Christophe who is carrying a tiny, squeaking corpse-bride who pulls her jaw open to release a snake that leaps on to Alan's face. As in the Amazonian trip, he awakes from the nightmare wrestling with the invisible spirit animal. Overwhelmed by the mystique of Saut D'Eau, of which there are some beautiful location shots, Dr. Alan and Dr. Duchamp retire to a cave above the waterfall to slake their passions in what has to be the lowest "high-point" in the film. The slow-motion, white-out climax of the love-scene cuts into a shot of a jeep racing through the Haitian countryside to the sound of a British radio newscaster announcing the immanent downfall of the Duvalier government. Back in Port-au-Prince the bins are on fire and the Tonton Macoute are arresting people everywhere. But Alan can't stop thinking about Christophe, the *zombi*. Why would people do such a thing, he asks Marielle? He was nobody important, she explains, just a simple schoolteacher, "but he wasn't afraid to speak out for freedom... for the people".[46] When Marielle explains why Christophe was turned into a *zombi* her words seem to be spoken in a different voice and we do not see her face. "He was very much admired," the *other* voice says, "that's why they made him what he is. Instead of inspiring courage, now he only inspires fear".

---

46 This is very different from Clairvius Narcisse, who according to Davis, was no freedom fighter. Narcisse it seems had violated several of the Bizango prohibitions, often fighting with his own family, neglecting several sired children and seeking to take land rightly belonging to other family members.

Alan is unceremoniously taken from the car by the Baron Samedi-Macoute to meet Captain Peytraud for the first time. In the Captain's office Alan opens a coffin shaped box resting in a window ledge next to a bust of Jean-Jacques Dessalines. It is filled with surgical-looking torture equipment. On arriving in the room Peytraud asks Alan, as Herard Simon had asked Davis at Beauvoir's compound, what he was doing in Haiti. Alan claims, unconvincingly, to be a tourist. "Yes, happy happy happy island people! Then why visit an insane asylum?" "I'm an anthropologist. It's a tax write-off. I hope you're not with the IRS?" Alan replies. Having claimed not to know anything about Christophe Durand, Peytraud points out that Alan is a poor liar. Alan repeats that he is a tourist and asks if he can go. Peytraud circles the *blanc* menacingly. "This country lives on the edge Dr. Alan. One weakness in the wrong place and over it goes right back into slavery again, just like with the French. The United States would like anarchy here I'm sure. Well this is not Grenada Dr. Allen. I'm here now! There are people like me who'll make sure that doesn't happen".[47] As we hear the sound of prisoners screaming from adjoining rooms, Alan is allowed to leave.

BLACK TERROR/WHITE HOPE

> The "paper tiger" hero, James Bond, offering the whites a triumphant image of themselves, is saying what many whites want desperately to be reaffirmed: I am still the White Man, lord of the land, licensed to kill, and the world is still an empire at my feet. James Bond feeds on that secret little anxiety, the psychological backlash, felt in some degree by most whites alive.
>
> - Eldridge Cleaver *Soul on Ice* (1969)[48]

Although Craven's film has more in common with *Live and Let Die* than *The Comedians*, the director seems to have re-interpreted

---

47 A reference to the U.S. invasion of the Caribbean island of Grenada in 1983 after a coup by the People's Revolutionary Army.

48 Cleaver 80

Davis's seemingly sincere admiration for Vodou, and his desire to correct popular distortions of the religion, as a humanitarian call to arms against the horrors of Duvalierism, something Davis carefully avoided doing. In this sense the film grafts Greene's explicitly anti-Duvalier sentiments on to the most sensational stories of Voodoo-horror during their presidencies. There is no account of the details of Papa Doc's torture methods in Davis's book, and the Bizango, as we have seen, are portrayed there as heroic defenders of Haiti's national independence and proud Maroon traditions. Nor is he ever threatened with zombification, or any other form of violence, himself. In Craven's version of events the Bizango, by inference, are explicitly associated with the Tonton Macoute and the worst excesses of the Duvalier regimes. Dr. Alan is eventually punished for his meddling by being turned into a *zombi* himself. Arrested by the Macoutes Alan finds himself strapped naked to a coffin-shaped chair in one of Peytraud's torture chambers. Blasting it with gas from an unlit acetylene torch, Peytraud compliments Alan on his pretty face. "The girls must like it," he says, clicking the fire steel in front of it. Does he likes his "pretty white face," Peytraud asks? Bleeding from the leather strap around his neck, Alan replies defiantly "Yeah. I like it!" "I like it too," Peytraud replies, igniting the acetylene torch and lighting his cigar with it. "I'll leave the face". Promising that he will be on the next plane, Alan tries to use his status as a U.S. citizen as a last minute plea. "I don't see the ambassador here, do you?" "I'm in medical research. There's a lot of money in it. There's plenty for you". "I don't want money," he responds. "Yeah? What do you want?" he asks. "I want to hear you *scream!*" The scenario is archetypical Fleming, but Alan is no 007, his naked, quivering terror palpably contrasted with Peytraud's icy authority. The lead Macoute hands Peytraud a twelve-inch nail as the others tighten the straps around Alan's arms and legs. "OK. You want to hear me scream, I'll scream". And he does. "Again!" Peytraud demands. He screams again, louder still. "Not good enough!" Peytraud tells him. Then, with a loud, metallic clink, he drives the nail through Alan's exposed nether regions. The doctor's scream echoes through an empty corridor of the police station hung with portraits of Papa and Baby Doc.

By now Craven's film has significantly parted ways with Davis's book, though not from accounts of the brutality of the Duvalier regime depicted by Abbott, Greene, Diederich and Burt and others. Although Davis's accounts of attending a Bizango ceremony certainly showed evidence of hostility towards the presence of outsiders, the real-life ethnobotanist was never imprisoned or tortured by the Macoutes. As with the re-casting of Clairvius Narcisse as a reluctant freedom fighter, Herard Simon is transformed into a Macoute torturer.[49] What is perhaps most interesting about the license taken with Davis's book is the way that, in the racial face-off between Captain Peytraud and Dr. Alan, it is the former whose morality, however cruel and unyielding, is depicted as purer in principle than the duplicitous scheming of a *blanc*, Biocorp errand boy pretending to be concerned about poor Haitian *zombis*.

Dumped from a truck in his bloody underpants the incapacitated doctor is embraced Pietà-like by his new "Guardian Angel" Marielle. After recuperating together for three days in a beach house (the wound inflicted by Peytraud "struck for fear not injury"), Allen is sufficiently "alive and intact" to continue his pursuit of the *zombi* recipe in ways relatively true to Davis's book. When asked by Mozart why he wants the *zombi* powder so badly he tells him that he wants to use the poison for good "to help people who are sick". Mozart finds this hilarious! He then entrusts Dr. Allen to tell the world about his botanical work in Haiti. There is something very apt about this scene in terms of Davis's overall project. Couldn't his selling the rights of *The Serpent and the Rainbow* to a Hollywood production company be a way of ensuring that his collaborators in Haiti would become "famous all over the world"? Bill Pullman's delivery of the lines, which he seems unable to believe himself, is once again entirely appropriate given the highly questionable nature of Davis's mission. By treating Davis's book as the basis for a sensationalist horror film, while at the same time trying to remain true to the author's virtuous intentions, Craven inadvertently exposes the duplicitous nature of the project as a whole.

During his stay at the beach house Dr. Alan is visited in his dreams by the corpse-bride strapped to the bow of a burning boat, who, after entering the cabin, transforms, to the sound of pan pipes, into his

---

49 Simon's involvement in torture and other forms of violence during the Duvalier era is not discussed by Davis. Whether or not he is the same Herard Simon who performed the reputed child sacrifice for the departing Duvaliers mentioned by Diebert remains a matter of speculation.

shamanic jaguar guide. Then, without warning, he has a psychedelic vision of himself being buried alive by Peytraud in a coffin filled with blood, before waking to find himself in bed with the decapitated corpse of Christophe's sister. Macoute paparazzi burst into the pastel-hued beach house and drag him away, along with Marielle, to the caves beneath the "dungeon of death". There Peytraud reveals himself to be a *bokor* who controls the souls "of those who were masters in the realms of the spirit", much as Murder Legendre had done in *White Zombie*. Dr. Alan is led handcuffed away at gunpoint to a waiting plane. There Mozart, disguised as a baggage-handler, gives him the powder they have made together on the condition that he lets the chemists in America know his name.

Back in Boston, seemingly fully recovered, Alan tests the samples on monkeys, as Leon Roizin had reputedly done in Davis's book. At a dinner party at Lehman's apartment Alan has to take some air. He tells Schoonbacher that he has to go back to Haiti to save Marielle. His mentor warns him against it. Cut to the caves beneath the dungeons in Port-au-Prince, where a Vodou ceremony is taking place.[50] At dinner in Cassedy's house Alan is asked by Mrs. Cassedy how it was that Christophe was able to speak after he was killed. As her husband answers, Alan's hand is touched by that of the corpse-bride before it disappears into his bowl. "Is something wrong with your soup?" Mrs. Cassedy asks, before directing her butler Albert to take his bowl away. "I've been having some stomach problems", Dr. Alan tells the table. Tapping her glass, Mrs. Cassedy stands up to make a toast to the homecoming hero. But before she can finish her speech she becomes possessed, takes a bite out of her wineglass and leaps across the table towards the doctor. Speaking in someone else's voice she tells him "You have been warned. You are going to die," before slashing him across the forehead with a steak knife and having a convulsive seizure.

Cut to the airport in Port-au-Prince where Alan is immediately arrested by what seem to be Tonton Macoutes but are in fact Celine and his people in disguise. Back at the *peristyle* the benevolent *houngan* prepares Alan for his forthcoming travails, drawing crosses of blood on his forehead and chest (as Maman Célie had done to William Seabrook to prepare him for his initiation). "Just remember", he tells Alan, "when the battle comes it will not be fought in the streets,

---

50 Craven depicts the ceremony as Bizango following the distinctive black and red ritual colours described by Davis.

it will be fought in your mind, in your soul". "These people," he continues, "Peytraud, Duvalier... they're not Haiti. They're mad dogs. The madness must stop". Meanwhile back in Peytraud's cave Mozart is ceremonially decapitated by Peytraud's red-sashed, sunglass-wearing Baron Samedi henchman. As Peytraud drinks his blood from a silver bowl, Celine collapses vomiting blood and a black scorpion crawls out of his mouth as a man blows yellow powder into Alan's face. After staggering through the streets in a delirium, Alan finally succumbs to the *zombi* powder and sees himself being pronounced dead in a Port-au-Prince hospital. There he is met by Captain Peytraud, who buries him along with a tarantula. Rescued by the *zombi* Christophe, who has heard his screams, Alan makes his way back to the cave where Marielle is about to be sacrificed. To the accompaniment of historical footage of Jean-Claude and Michèle Duvalier leaving Haiti, the British media reporter announces their imminent departure. As people take to the streets to celebrate and destroy the signs of Papa and Baby Doc, footage shot by Craven is intercut with actual television footage of Haitians doing the same thing in 1986. Meanwhile Marielle, wearing the colours of Our Lady of Mount Carmel, is made to kneel before Peytraud. But just as the Baron Samedi figure is about to behead her, the ceremony is disrupted by the "Liberté!" chanting crowds outside and the Bizango worshippers flee. "Where is your power now?" Marielle asks Peytraud, "the *lwa* themselves are having their vengeance".[51] Peytraud, now visibly greying, knocks her out as the Macoute headquarters are ransacked by the freedom-hungry mob. Thence ensues a mystical battle between Dr. Alan and Peytraud in which Alan is chased around the police station by the torture chair. The "*zombi astral*" of Celine, now controlled by Peytraud, tells Alan that "It is your work that caused this", before pulling his own head off and throwing it at the terror-stricken doctor. Revitalised by the released spirit of Celine and the absorption of his jaguar spirit guide, Alan finds the strength to knock Peytraud into his collection

---

51 Several commentators have noted how, with the popular crisis against the Duvaliers mounting in January 1986, Jean-Claude invited Max Beauvoir and eight other *houngans* and *mambos* to ask what the *lwa* thought about the situation. He was told that the spirits had wanted the Duvaliers to leave for over a year.

of *canari* jars, releasing the captive souls of the *zombis* in a *Raiders of the Lost Ark*-style moment of high horror-kitsch. In the final act of retribution Alan psychically straps the charred body of Peytraud to the torture chair and sends a nail into the same place Allen got his. The nightmare finally over, the rainbow-tinted vapours of the spirits of the emancipated dead flow into the celebrating, Coke-drinking crowds on the streets of the newly liberated capital.

THE WORLD MUST KNOW ABOUT THIS

By the time that Wes Craven's film was playing to cinema audiences around the world, Davis was cleansing himself of the media attention it attracted to him in Borneo, "a place wet with the innocence of birth". The mantle of presidential power in Haiti had been passed, as promised by Henri Namphy and the CNG, to the newly elected civilian President Leslie Manigat.[52] To the outside world it must have seemed that the good order of progressive liberal democracy had at last been restored to Haiti after the many dark decades of Duvalierism. Or, as Marielle Duchamp tells Dennis Alan at the end of his ordeal, "the nightmare [was] over". Oddly, like a menacing portent for the survival of "Duvalierism after Duvalier" (or, perhaps, a sequel: *The Serpent and the Rainbow II*), in the midst of the celebrating crowds into which the heroic lovers emerge from the "dungeon of death", a Tonton Macoute proudly carried aloft a portrait of Papa Doc. It is an uncannily emblematic sign of the actual situation in Haiti in which, despite the reforms attempted by the CNG, Duvalierism was still a powerful political force.

In November 1987, during the first attempt at elections, a number of Duvalierists publicly put themselves forward for office, despite being officially banned by an amendment to Article 291 of the constitution. The Namphy government, who many assumed to be bowing to U.S. pressure, proposed banning the candidates, and as a consequence a wave of anti-American sentiment swept through a country still bitter with the memory of occupation. When, finally, the electoral council

---

52 Davis, Wade 'Looking for Haitian Zombies' Lecture for IRIS Nights, Annenberg Space for Photography, February 14th, 2013. Craven's film would eventually gross around $20 million worldwide (Wooley 152).

officially announced the rejection of twelve Duvalierist candidates, violence broke out throughout the country. The army, attempting to remain neutral, initially refrained from intervening in the nightly terror and arson attacks against prospective opposition candidates and members of the Electoral Council and the open conflict between local communities and vigilante groups that had broken out on the streets of Port-au-Prince. The army eventually intervened but only to arrest and kill people suspected of being Leftist agitators.[53] In the small town of Marchand Dessalines in the Artibonite valley, a Canadian film crew, there to film a documentary about the emergent democracy in Haiti, had to hide in a Catholic presbytery while it was machine-gunned for forty-five minutes by Macoutes. As Michel-Rolph Trouillot put it, "By the end of its first year in office the CNG generously helped by the U.S. taxpayer's money, had openly gunned down more civilians than Jean-Claude Duvalier's government had done in fifteen years".[54] On the day of the election, emboldened by a night-long spree of violence, former Macoutes mowed down thirty civilians at polling stations, maiming hundreds more would-be voters. At 9 a.m. the elections were officially announced a failure and all U.S. economic aid was promptly curtailed. The election of January 1988 was, unsurprisingly, controlled almost entirely by the military. Within the year they were back in control.

The inclusion of a portrait of Papa Doc amongst the celebrating crowds at the end of *The Serpent and the Rainbow* is a deeply ambiguous sign. Was it an intentional decision by the director to add a cryptic pessimistic note to the otherwise happy ending or an opportunistic gesture made by a Macoute extra that the editors just happened to miss at the last minute? The question, no doubt, is academic. Its significance here is the light it casts on the peculiar function of what I have been calling the *chimerical optic* on Haiti manifest in mainstream Voodoo-horror. While obviously distorting the actualities of life in Haiti under Duvalierism in the interests of genre convention and box-office sales, *The Serpent and the Rainbow*, in both its book and film forms, did attempt, ostensibly at least, to tell a moral tale about Haiti and correct in some way the distortions of authentic Vodou brought about by depictions in previous books and films. But Craven's film was

---

53 Estimates of the number of deaths range from 39 to 200 (Abbott 357, Trouillot (1990) 223).

54 Trouillot (1990) 222

ultimately bound to fail in this regard because of the necessity internal to the genre of making supernatural evil (i.e. "bad" Vodou) the principle driver and ultimate concern of the narrative. This is what makes the superficial humanitarian gloss of the film so unconvincing, and Zakes Mokae's performance of Captain Peytraud the most impressive and memorable in the film. How Davis could have imagined it otherwise remains a matter of speculation. (Despite his dislike of the film, one of its producers, David Ladd remains a "good friend").[55] Like Seabrook, whose *The Magic Island* Davis's book is, in the end, much closer to in spirit than he would like us to think, the magnanimous ethnobotanist claimed to have been driven by the best of intentions to represent Vodou in a positive light. But unlike Seabrook, Davis seems less honest about the deeper motivations driving his project. It seems clear that Davis wrote *The Serpent and the Rainbow* to be a best-seller, cashing in on the new-found interest in Haitian *zombis* first brought to the attention of the world by a BBC news programme in 1981. And presumably he was not forced to sell the rights to a Hollywood production company with a machete to his throat. So what are we to make of his apparent dismay at what Craven did with his book? On the subject of selling books to Hollywood Davis has, in several public presentations, paraphrased Ernest Hemingway, who reputedly said that if it ever happens to an author, then they should "drive from Arizona to the California state line, throw the book over and go back to Tucson for a drink."[56]

In typical Hollywood fashion Craven's film reduced the plot of Davis's book to a struggle between the good, humanitarian Haitian doctors, Christian-Vodou *houngans*, Anglo-American medicine and "ordinary" Haitians, and the evil, Black, Duvalierist, Tonton Macoute and Bizango *zombi*-makers. In this way it not only conforms to the standard expectations of Hollywood blockbusters, but also to the genre of literature and cinema referred to here as Voodoo-horror, in which a heroic White male travels to the heart of darkness, defeats an evil witch doctor, rescues and wins the girl and, along the way, helps liberate the "happy, happy, happy island people" from the yoke of authoritarian servitude. It even includes a traditional climactic sacrifice party for

---

55 Lecture at the Annenberg Space for Photography February 14th (2013)

56 See his Lecture at the Annenberg Space for Photography February 14th (2013) and his interview with George Stroumboulopoulos, CBS February 5th 2013). Davis in fact left for Borneo when Craven's film came out.

good measure. It is, in this sense, exactly like the very films that Davis has accused of creating the image of Vodou as an "evil religion". As such Barbara Browning's denunciation of it as a racist and xenophobic film is understandable. But in the racial face-off between Dr. Alan and Captain Peytraud, the forces of darkness cast a cold light on the moral integrity of the White hero figure that no amount of schlock horror or *faux* romance can dispel. Ultimately Bill Pullman gives us an alternative version of the mythical self-portrait that Wade Davis sought to portray of himself, one that gives the lie to his reputedly altruistic intentions.[57]

As we have seen, throughout the 20th century representations of the folkloric Haitian *zombi*, Vodou possession, ritual sacrifice and "Black magic" have been used to evoke deep-seated cultural fantasies and fears about African atavism in the Americas, fears that simultaneously served to undermine international recognition of Haiti's role in the development of global modernity and to lend support for the imperial ambitions of the U.S. in the Caribbean. Davis, evidently aware of this history, has been at pains to point out that this is precisely *not* what he was intending to do. On the contrary, he would use his account of the "ethnobiology of the Haitian zombie" as a way to correct some of the most deprecatory distortions. At the same time his lack of attention to the political history of Haiti in the 20th century, his almost apologetic tone about Duvalierism, and his decision to discover the secrets of societies which, according to most popular and scholarly accounts, are not only directly associated with sorcery, cannibalism, zombification and human sacrifice in Haiti, but are also the object of widespread fear in rural Haiti amongst Haitians themselves, would seem in some ways to undermine that undertaking.[58] That is unless one sees the project as one set on "the very heart of voodoo darkness", to get at the deepest and most terrible secrets upon which the popular myths

---

57 In the talk given to The Annenberg Space for Photography Davis asked rhetorically "Why did we get this idea that Vodou was evil?" He answers that during the U.S. occupation "everyone above the rank of sergeant got a book contract" to write titles like *Cannibal Cousins*, *Black Bagdad* and *The Magic Island*, and it was the RKO movies of the '40s (*Night of the Living Dead*, *Zombies on Broadway*, *Zombies of the Stratosphere*, *The White Zombie Slave*) that gave Vodou this negative image.

58 See Hurston 199-217, Métraux 292-300.

are founded. This, I think, is the essence of Davis's mission in the final section of *The Serpent and the Rainbow*. It is odd therefore that no explicit mention is made in Craven's film of the Bizango secret society into which the author had himself initiated at the conclusion of his first book, and concluded his second with. That the distinctive red and black regalia of the sect, which peppers Davis's story, are present from the opening credits of Craven's film suggests that Peytraud is either a high functionary of such a society or a devout Duvalierist, as was, if rumours are to be believed, Herard Simon. Furthermore, despite the evident injustice done to the representation of Herard Simon in Davis's book, he *was* a leader of the Tonton Macoute, a *chef de section* and a man whose "body, lay ready to split, to release some great catastrophe of the human spirit", an apt metaphor for the explosive ending of Craven's film. It should be remembered too that Davis concluded both his books about Haitian *zombis* with intimations that the Bizango and the Tonton Macoute would continue to be the secret rulers of Haiti long after the departure of Baby Doc.

It is unlikely that we will ever know the exact nature of the pact Davis made with the Bizango, but whatever it was, it seems to have ensured that the sect would not be portrayed in a negative light, by either Davis or his good friends in Hollywood. That would have been an offense punishable by zombification, as Davis was well aware. Like Craven, Davis "sells" Vodou, not in the traditional, sensationalist mode of Voodoo-horror, but as a profound, mystical faith of universal significance, often accompanied by his own glossy, full-colour *National Geographic* photographs. His audiences may well be sensible, educated, politically correct, middle class and middle-aged rather than thrill-seeking teenagers, but sell it he does. In his frequent public appearances Davis creates a picture of Vodou as a religion of "ecstatic participatory democracy", where secret societies heroically defend the independence won during the revolution from foreign enemies. In a public lecture in 2013 Davis once again repeated the claim that Vodou is a "quintessentially democratic faith" in which "even the dead must be made to serve the living":

> to serve the living they must become manifest, to become manifest they must respond to the rhythm of the drums and the power of the chant, to come back from beneath the world of the invisibles, and momentarily displace the

soul of the living. So for that brief shining moment of spirit possession, human being and God become one and the same. That's why the Haitians will say to you "You white people go to church to speak about God. We dance in the temple and become God".[59]

Whatever we think about the peculiar notion of "Vodou democracy" promoted by Davis, an odd mix of *National Geographic* sentimentalism, New Age Gnostic Christianity and West Coast Kumabaya Environmentalism (with the Dead in service), it is difficult to credit the Bizango as heroes of Haitian democracy, untiringly resisting and checking the oppressive economic stranglehold and military objectives of the Mulatto elites. The facts of François Duvalier's actual rise to power ("often misrepresented in the Western press"), the use he made of the networks of Vodou worship and the role of the Bizango on maintaining his grip on them, are reduced to an uncomfortable footnote. Instead Davis seems to have struck a deal with the Bizango and his *zombi*-making *houngan* mentors that in return for the secrets of zombification he would present a positive image of them, their religion and their country to an otherwise woefully ill-informed outside world. By selling the rights of his book to Hollywood he ensured that the central characters of his story (Max and Rachel Beauvoir, Marcel Pierre and Herard Simon) and the Bizango secret societies would become "world famous". Despite the significant distortion that Craven's lens gives audiences of Davis's book, the Bizango, in the form of Captain Peytraud, *are* depicted as the heirs of the revolutionary struggle against imperialism and foreign interference in Haiti's affairs. But they are also depicted, as they are by Davis, as a fearful and violent sect capable of extreme acts of cruelty. Perhaps this is what most compelled Davis to hotfoot it to Borneo when the film was released.

Like the novels and films of the 1930s and '40s that Davis sought to distinguish his book from (but which it is, ultimately, a pseudo-scientific, *Reader's Digest* version of), Craven's film fits perfectly with the dominant ideological U.S. narrative of the importance of direct American involvement in Haitian society that has been a characteristic of such works since the 1920s. Its indirect political message supports the

59 Wade Davis 'Looking for Haitian Zombies' Lecture for IRIS Nights, Annenberg Space for Photography, February 14th 2013

necessity of international humanitarian aid to Haiti, the propagation of western civilising missions there, proxy economic influence (via the World Bank, IMF loans and structural adjustment programmes) and the eradication of the legacy of Duvalierism, Macoutism and "bad" Vodou. What both Davis's book and Craven's film leave us with is a fundamental question about the precise nature of the relationship between the Tonton Macoute, who Davis, following Laguerre, proposed were still ruling Haiti in 1988, and the Bizango, who Davis suggested were secretly ruling rural Haiti as of 1985.[60]

In a Canadian television interview with George Stroumboulopoulos in February 2013, Davis explained how his vocation as a storyteller was something he discovered by writing *The Serpent and the Rainbow*. He then tells a story about his car breaking down close to a Bizango *hounfo* in Haiti. As some local men were trying to help him fix it he became irritated by the way he was being hassled and gave one of the men a secret society handshake to show that he was not a *blanc* to be messed with. Flabbergasted that he would know such a thing, they invited him to the ceremony that was taking place at the nearby temple that same night. The ceremony began with a traditional invocation of Legba, then, at midnight, the drums changed tempo, a trumpet blew, a whip cracked and the order went out: "Soldiers of the Night Change Skins". Suddenly they all appeared dressed in black and red robes. At that point he was dragged across the *peristyle* and flung into a darkened room in which a tribunal of Bizango emperors and presidents presided. They tested what he knew of the initiation rites. It was both "too much and too little". Not knowing what to do he reached for a bottle of raw liquor that stood by the skull and candle at the base of the *poteau mitan*, poured it onto his hands, set it on fire with the light from the candle, and offered the handshake again. To his great relief everyone cracked up laughing.

---

60 Davis (1990) 290, Davis (1986) 255

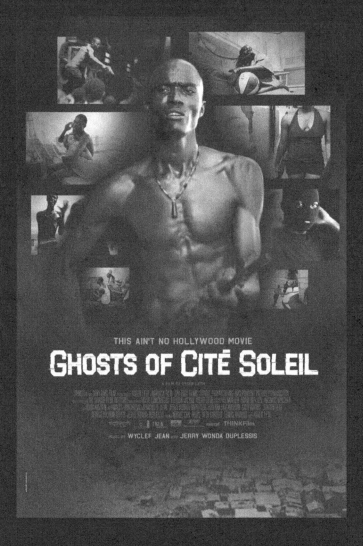

Ghosts of Cité Soleil, directed by Asger Leth, 2006

VII

GHOSTS OF CITÉ SOLEIL

LIVING PHANTOMS

Race, or the raced figure, particularly the figure of the
Black, occupies and enacts a kind of force-field, the
not/but-nothing-other-than human that maintains that
distinction while embodying the necessary danger of its
inevitable collapse. It is the very mark and location of the
non-categorical, of the outlaw that guarantees the law.
This is how the exemplary figure of abjection, exploitation,
pity and revulsion is also always the exemplary figure of
danger, threat and irreducible, unavoidable attraction.

- Fred Moten 'Black Kant (Pronounced Kan't)'.[1]

In December 2013 at an International conference about the cultural
legacy of the Haitian Revolution – *1804 and its Afterlives* – Martin
Munro, distinguished Professor of Francophone Caribbean Literature
and Culture at Florida State University, gave a paper called 'The
Revolution's Ghosts: Dessalines, The *Chimères* and Apocalyptic
Creolization'.[2] The *chimères* of the title was a reference to the gangs of

---

1 Lecture at the Kelly Writers House, University of Pennsylvania,
February 27, 2007

2 The conference was programmemed to coincide with the exhibition

young men from severely deprived neighbourhoods of Port-au-Prince who, during the final years of President Jean-Bertrand Aristide's second term in office (2001-2004), were widely identified as his unofficial private army, defending him against anyone seen to be a pressing threat to his hold on power. Munro described the *chimères* as apocalyptic figures, grotesque, nihilistic refigurations of the Creolized anti-hero Dessalines. The general thrust of Munro's thesis was that Jean-Jacques Dessalines' Creolization by historians had obscured the pronounced African character of his identity, the consequences of which could somehow be discerned in the figure of the *chimères*. Munro took his lead from Deborah Jenson's 2012 article 'Jean-Jacques Dessalines and the African character of the Haitian Revolution' in which she questioned the standard historiography that Dessalines was "literally Creole" but "performatively and ideologically African". If Dessalines was taken as a slave from Africa to Haiti, where he used his knowledge of African social groups for the revolution, he would represent, Munro argued, "a critical suppressed link, if an endlessly oblique one, in our understanding of how these experiences informed African revolutionary agency in colonial Saint-Domingue". The African Dessalines would be a much simpler character than the Creole Dessalines, Munro claimed, that "endlessly complex and contradictory entity... a chameleon that comes into being through metamorphosis... a kind of shape-shifter of unverifiable origins and contradictory motivations, unknowable and ambiguous, a kind of ghost, even as he lived."

Munro's apocalyptic reference comes from one of his three textual sources, Lyonel Trouillot's 2004 novel *Bicentenaire* which, like his second reference, the 2006 feature film *Ghosts of Cité Soleil*, tells a story about two brothers, in this case Lucien, the student, and his younger brother Little Joe, the *chimère*. Little Joe recalls for Munro the illiterate

---

Kalfou: Haiti, Art and Vodou curated by Alex Farquharson & Leah Gordon at Nottingham Contemporary gallery between 19th October 2012 and 6th January 2013. Munro is the author of *Shaping and Reshaping the Caribbean: The Work of Aimé Césaire and René Depestre* (2000), *Exile and Post-1946 Haitian Literature: Alexis, Depestre, Ollivier, Laferrière, Danticat* (2007), *Different Drummers: Rhythm and Race in the Americas* (2010) and co-editor of *Reinterpreting the Haitian Revolution and its Cultural Aftershocks* (2006) and *Echoes of the Haitian Revolution* (2008).

tyrant Jean-Jacques Dessalines, "the most unregenerate of Haitian leaders and the unsettling antithesis to the rational Toussaint". Like Dessalines, having retained "the memory of the mysteries", Little Joe practices Vodou (the Creolized religion) placing on his bed a red neckerchief, a pin, three leaves of artemisia and an image of Saint Jacques le Majeur, before setting off for battle. Munro's inference seemed to be that the so-called *chimères* were living phantoms of Dessalines, semi-mythical monsters, only part human, aware that they were not fully-alive, "existing somewhere between life and death, existence and oblivion", and that the practice of Vodou marked them as quintessentially Creole beings. Although Munro did not refer to Dessalines' Africanness in racial terms, his literary configuration of the *chimères* conforms to a construction of Blackness as a self-negating concept of disagreeable semi-humanness upon which an essentially paradoxical ontology of the properly human has been grounded since Kant.[3]

The term *chimères* derives from the French word for the mythical fire-breathing monster of Greek mythology, part lion, part goat and part snake. Generally referring to a fantastical monster or a phantasm, the word was traditionally used by Haitian elites as a class slur against poor and socially disenfranchised people who were deemed to be morally beneath contempt. By the time of Aristide's first election to president in 1991 the term had come to refer to an armed bandit or violent, slum-dwelling criminal. Canadian journalist and anti-war activist Richard Sanders has identified the term as part of a linguistic arsenal used by the Haitian and mainstream international media at the time of the coup against Aristide to prepare the general public for the cognitive dissonance that would arise with the growing awareness of the elite's fiscal and electoral complicity in war crimes.[4] *Chimères*

---

3 See Moten 'Black Kant (Pronounced Kan't)'. In 'On the Use of Teleological Principles in Philosophy' Immanuel Kant defines race as "a *radical* peculiarity that announces a common descent – along with several such persistently transmitted characters not admissible only to the same genus of animal but instead to the same line of descent" (Kant in Bernasconi (2001) 40). The apocalyptic motif is not without relevance here for the association it makes with "Blackness" as an irreversible deviation from the higher purposes of the species.

4 Richard Sanders 'Epithets without Borders' *Press for Conversion!* No.63,

was the aspersion of choice used by all those opposed to President Aristide to describe his loyal but impoverished supporters in the poor neighbourhoods of Port-au-Prince during the 2004 coup. The term was used in statements by Haiti's former military, the armed rebels, police, judges, businessmen, journalists and other anti-Aristide proponents of regime change, as a rhetorical device to defame-by-association Aristide and the Lavalas movement.

Derived from the Haitian word for "cleansing flood", "torrent" or "avalanche", *Operation Lavalas* was created by Aristide in 1990 during the run-up to the 1991 general election. Inspired by the ideology and politics of Liberation Theology, the movement was designed to politically mobilise the poorest segments of Haitian society, involve them in the democratising process, and to uproot and cleanse the country of all traces of Duvalierism. Lavalas only became a political party – the OPL (Organisation of People in Struggle), and later the *Organisation Politique Lavalas*, after the first military coup against Aristide in 1991.[5] It was at this time that the word *chimère* began to be used by elite-owned Haitian media and their foreign counterparts, Haiti's corporate-backed politicians, their Canadian, French and U.S. mentors, anti-Aristide NGOs in Haiti, and their government-funded partners abroad. Sanders quotes an interview with Haitian human rights lawyer and activist Mario Joseph who said that, after the departure of Aristide in 2004, the process of legal accusation had been reduced to name calling, and the word *chimère* was being used like a death sentence.

Given the highly contested and politically charged nature of the term then, it was surprising to hear a respected professor of Caribbean literature discussing this hybrid Creolized subject so matter-of-factly. Given that the name was not something chosen by the people to whom it became attached, it seemed strange that he would speak of those identified by the term as *subjects*. Those who *were* questioned about the label publicly generally rejected it as an invention used by their

---

Nov 2008. Sanders relates *chimères* to similar names like "gook" or "slant" used during the Vietnam war to dehumanise and vilify members of the Viet Cong.

5 See Hallward (2007) and Dupuy (2007). In 1996 Aristide broke with the OPL and formed the political organisation *Fanmi Lavalas* (Lavalas Family).

enemies to vilify them in the wider society. So what kind of entity was agency being conferred upon here, the actual individuals identified as *chimères*, or the phantasmatic figure of mythical speech and popular reproach? By bringing the two together, as if the people labelled *chimères* actually were *chimères*, Munro's proposition repeated, in a very direct way, the structure of negative designation that had already been used to label people made ready for eradication during what came to be a veritable War against Ghosts in the immediate aftermath of the coup. Moreover any *subject* assumed to be a kind of living phantom by one who is, presumably, not such a thing, places the burden of phantasmatic quasi-human otherness on to those named as such.

In his lecture 'Black Kant (Pronounced Kan't)' from 2007 Fred Moten proposes, following Foucault, that the current War on Terror is an off-shoot of the endless task of policing race (or Blackness) in its metaphysical, internal, self-differentiating sense. The War on Ghosts waged by the FLRN, PNH, U.S., French and U.N. forces in the immediate aftermath of the coup would seem to conform to this exterminatory logic. From this perspective the question of who gets to speak of others as if they were phantoms or monsters is more than mere academic or theoretical pedantry, it points to a definite correlation between political, literary and social fictions, and the actual people made fit for annihilation by them. If *chimères* designates a subject it is precisely one that has been predefined as exterminable.

CONVERSION OF THE CANNIBAL ARMY

President Aristide was ousted by a military *coup d'état* on February 29th, 2004. The circumstances surrounding his ousting continue to be the subject of divided and bitter debate.[6] The group formally responsible for the coup was the National Revolutionary Front for the

---

6 For two very different overviews of the Aristide era and the circumstances surrounding his ousting see Michael Deibert's *Notes from the Last Testament: The Struggle for Haiti* (2005) and Peter Hallward's *Damming the Flood: Haiti, Aristide, and the Politics of Containment* (2007). Nicolas Rossier's documentary *Aristide and the Endless Revolution* (2005) also represents opinion from both sides of the international political debate about the coup.

Liberation of Haiti (FLRN), a paramilitary alliance of two groups: an armed anti-government gang from the Artibonite region called the Cannibal Army, and former soldiers of the Haitian army that Aristide had disbanded when he was returned to power in 1994 (after a previous coup in 1991). The Cannibal Army grew out of the Popular Organisation for the Development of Raboteau – a poor slum in Gonaïves – during the uprisings against Jean-Claude Duvalier in the 1980s. It was one of the first armed gangs to be identified as *chimères*. Once they had turned against Aristide they re-named themselves rebels, a term also used positively by the right-wing and conservative press at the time, and identified *chimères* as their principle enemies. Its leader, Amiot "Cubain" Métayer, a former Aristide supporter, had been implicated in violence against the Convergence Démocratique (an anti-Lavalas political party created by the International Republican Institute (IRI) in 2000, and backed by Haitian business interests) in 2001, during a coup attempt against Aristide. He was subsequently arrested, in order, it has been claimed, to placate the OAS (Organisation of American States) whose criticism of the Aristide regime had led to the freezing of $500 million in foreign aid. It was his arrest that first turned Métayer against Aristide. Once freed from jail he reputedly donned the red sash of Ogoun and called for an uprising against the president.[7] Métayer died in 2003 under mysterious circumstances; his body was found after a night away from his home in Raboteau, showing signs of terrible torture, having had his eyes, heart and liver removed. Although popularly many Haitians believed Aristide was responsible for Métayer's death, the main suspect for the murder was Odenel Paul, an old friend of Métayer who had served in Aristide's Interior Ministry, and who, having left with Métayer the night before his death, disappeared immediately afterwards and was never seen again. According to Hallward, no one has ever confessed to, or been charged with, the murder, and his death remains "one of the biggest mysteries in the entire coup sequence".[8] In *Ghosts of Cité Soleil*, Buteur Métayer, Amiot's brother, who subsequently became leader of the Cannibal Army, explains that since Lavalas killed his brother, now they were against Lavalas.

In February 2004 the Cannibal Army were joined by twenty

7 See the Clara James article 'The Raboteau Revolt'.

8 Hallward 204

former soldiers led by Louis-Jodel Chamblain, former chief of the CIA-funded and trained Front for the Advancement and Progress of Haiti (FRAPH) which had murdered hundreds of Aristide supporters in the 1990s. *Chimère*s was the word used by the FLRN to describe their adversaries in the campaign and to justify their actions to foreign media.[9] A former Tonton Macoute, Chamblain was a sergeant in Henri Namphy's military government that took power from Jean-Claude Duvalier in 1986. He reputedly led the paramilitary groups that murdered voters during the 1987 election and was part of the first attempted coup against Aristide in 1990. In reaction pro-Aristide mobs killed his pregnant wife in the suburbs of Delmas. Described by Deibert as the public face of the FRAPH death-squads, Chamblain had been implicated in numerous atrocities and was convicted in absentia for the 1993 murder of Haitian businessman, pro-democracy advocate and Aristide supporter Antoine Izméry, and for his role in the Raboteau massacre of 1994, in which at least six pro-Aristide residents were murdered by soldiers and paramilitaries.[10]

Asger Leth and Milos Loncarevic's 2006 pseudo-documentary *Ghosts of Cité Soleil* – a primary text for Munro's Apocalyptic Creolization thesis – was shot in Haiti during the coup of February 2004.[11] Produced with support from the Danish Film Institute and Leth's father, the controversial and respected Danish film-maker Jørgen Leth (who has lived in Haiti since the early 1980s), *Ghosts of Cité Soleil* tells the story of two brothers from the slums of Cité Soleil, home to some of Aristide's most loyal supporters and one of the poorest neighbourhoods in Port-au-Prince.[12] It is also a thinly veiled work of anti-Aristide propaganda, posturing as a sensationally gritty

---

9 For examples of the use of the term *chimère* by paramilitary organisations in the 2004 coup see Jeb Sprague's *Paramilitarism and the Assault on Democracy in Haiti* (2012).

10 Deibert 397, Hallward 123. According to Human Rights Watch FRAPH were involved in the killing of at least 4,000 people (Sprague 9).

11 The other two were Charles Najman's 2004 documentary film *Haïti: La Fin des Chimères?* and Lyonel Trouillot's 2004 novel *Bicentenaire*.

12 Inspired by Graham Greene's *The Comedians* Jørgen Leth went to Haiti in 1981 to make a film in a country "in real crisis". The product was the fictional *Haiti Express* which tells the story of a foreign journalist's descent into an existential, obsessive and erotic abyss in Port-au-Prince.

and hard-hitting docu-drama, that has probably done more than any other work of popular culture to promote the *chimère* myth to an international audience.

THE CREATION OF AN OCCULT CRIMINAL MACHINE

Located between Toussaint Louverture International Airport, the former grounds of the Haitian American Sugar Complex (HASCO) and Fort Dimanche, Cité Soleil is a notorious slum district in the Delmas area of Port-au-Prince. First developed to house the families of workers at the HASCO factory in 1958, in 1966, after a fire in La Saline, a slum on the southern side of Fort Dimanche, 1,197 new homes were built, and the area was first named Cité Simone, after Simone Duvalier, Papa Doc's wife. By the 1970s it had grown significantly, its population swelled by a squatter community that had come to the area looking for employment in the newly developed Export Processing Zone. The migration of the rural poor to the slums of Port-au-Prince in the 1980s was largely a consequence of the disastrous agricultural policies of the Duvaliers, USAID programmes, the eradication of the Creole pig, and the creation of an internationally owned sweat-shop manufacturing economy based in the capital. Cité Simone was renamed Cité Soleil (Sunshine City) after the ousting of the Duvaliers in 1986. By 2004 it had an estimated 200,000–300,000 residents.

Ghosts of Cité Soleil opens with a series of moody, monochromatic shots of a verdant Haitian panorama, a mountain at dusk, a deserted coastline and a distant shot of Port-au-Prince in the mountain's shadow. It gives the viewers a potted history of the first Black Republic in three stacatto sentences. In 2004, the text tells us, with demonstrations in the streets and rebels closing in, President Aristide and his Lavalas party enlisted the support of armed gangs from the slum of Cité Soleil. "These gangs are known as the Chimeres. This is the story of two brothers, Chimeres leaders in Cité Soleil – described by the UN as the most dangerous place on earth".

The brothers in question, as we soon learn, were Winston Jean-Bart (aka Haitian 2pac) and James Petit-Frere (aka Bily), who had attended President Aristide's Fanmi Selavi institute for Street Children in the 1990s. Bily's mother was a community activist killed during the first coup against Aristide in 1991, his father killed by the anti-Aristide FRAPH death squads in 1993. After the incarceration of 2pac in 2001, Bily had become the chief of his brother's gang in District 19 of Cité Soleil.[13] 2pac, who at the time of filming had recently been sprung from prison, appears in the opening sequence asking the camera how his life is going to be.[14] "Lord knows", he says, as the soundtrack begins to play a melancholy hip-hop tune over shots of the run-down streets and shanty-towns of Cité Soleil. The soundtrack is accompanied by intercut images of Vodouists dancing at a Guede ceremony, 2pac smoking a blunt, loading a revolver and pointing it at the camera. Super-imposed over an aerial shot of Cité Soleil, the film title cuts to a car driving through one of its avenues, its horn being blasted to clear the crowds, its passengers brandishing semi-automatic rifles, as a gangster-rap track plays (one of several produced by Haitian-American rapper Wyclef Jean, co-producer of the film). Labouring the sensationalist tag-line theme of "the most dangerous place on earth", a title over the aerial shot reads: "Haiti is a two hour flight from Miami Beach, Florida".

Throughout the film grainy stock-footage of news reports, seemingly filmed from a monitor, is intercut with original footage shot by the film-makers. Their own footage also seems to have been put through filters that give it a grainy, high-contrast and distinctive dichromatic sepia and blue quality. The first use of stock footage shows President Aristide, speaking from the presidential podium, telling an audience that "Unity Creates Strength". In a pattern that runs throughout the film the found-footage is immediately followed by an American newscaster, presumably fictional, commenting on the political situation in Haiti. Although much of the news footage seems to be found material, the voice-over (like the English newscaster voice in *The Serpent and the Rainbow*) seems to have been added in post-production to add an air of formal authenticity to the film. The *faux* newscaster explains that, three years into his second term, now

---

13 See Michael Deibert's blog post 'Ghosts, Bandits and Cité Soleil' (May 19th, 2007).

14 Deibert 170. 2pac had been sprung from prison a month before the filming. According to Deibert the jailbreak had been staged by the Aristide government to coincide with the bicentenary celebrations of the founding of the republic in 1804 (Deibert 380).

Aristide's Lavalas government is in "big trouble". Echoing the final scenes of Wes Craven's film, *Ghosts* cuts to crowds in the streets of the capital carrying signs written in English and chanting "Freedom or Death! Aristide to Prison! *Chimères* to School!" Like the image of François Duvalier being carried by a Macoute at the end of *Serpent and the Rainbow*, this tiny, seemingly unimportant detail potentially tells us a great deal about the off-screen politics in which *Ghosts* is implicated. As Peter Hallward, author of *Damming the Flood: Haiti, Aristide, and the Politics of Containment* (2007) has shown, the English-language signs did not go unnoticed by the Haitian press at the time. A journalist for *Haiti Progrès* noted that the protests seemed to have been prearranged to make their meanings easily readable for CNN and other international news crews.[15]

One of Aristide's main political opponents at the time was Andy Apaid, a Haitian-based businessman and leader of the Group of 184, an alliance of individuals and organisations united in opposition to Aristide and his Lavalas government, with close ties to the U.S.-based International Republican Institute (IRI), an organisation responsible for training the opposition to Aristide from 1994 to 2003. An American-Haitian citizen of Syrian and Lebanese descent, Apaid was the founder and owner of Tele-Haiti, Haiti's largest cable television company – footage from which was given to the film-makers – and was one of the richest men living in Haiti at the time. Apaid's father, André Apaid Sr., a strong supporter of Jean-Claude Duvalier and founder of Alpha Industries, the biggest sweatshop operator in Haiti, had backed the junta that ousted Aristide between 1991 and 1994.[16] Apaid was also a leading figure in the 2003 campaign to stop Aristide doubling the minimum wage in Haiti. According to Michael Deibert, the Group of 184 organised a rally in Cité Soleil in July 2003 that was attacked by Aristide supporters, and the stock footage accompanying this early sequence of *Ghosts* is presumably from this rally.[17] As Hallward notes, Apaid's main factory was on the edge of Cité Soleil.[18]

---

15 Hallward 193

16 See Richard Sanders 'The G184's Powerbrokers – Apaid and Boulos: Owners of the Fourth Estate; Leaders of the Fifth Column'.

17 Deibert 346-7

18 Hallward 289-90

In Leth's film the newscaster explains that attacks on anti-government protesters have been made by armed gangs called *chimères*, and that members of these gangs say that the government pays them to intimidate dissenters. The film then cuts to a brief section of an interview with Apaid – identified simply as "Political Opposition" – who explains how bullets had been fired at his house. The newscaster repeats Apaid's claims that the Aristide government had trampled on Haitians' human rights by arresting government critics and paying armed thugs to beat up marchers, a claim, as we will see, that formed the basis for international condemnations of Aristide's government at the time. Apaid explains, presumably to the film-makers, though this is unclear due to the grainy filter added to the shots, that "the capacity of people that Mr. Aristide controls is very, very strong".

The creation of an historical association between Jean-Bertrand Aristide and François Duvalier seems to have been popularised by Aristide's political opposition during the 1990s, the implication being that the *chimères* were the new Macoute, and that Aristide had at his disposal an army of loyal and violent slum-dwellers who needed to be vanquished by the militias in order to create political security for foreign investors in Haiti. The inference was also made by Christopher Kovats-Bernat, an ethnographer who spent many years living amongst the street children of Port-au-Prince, and who was familiar with the Lavalas orphanage, Lafanmi Selavi, at which several of the so-called *chimères* were educated and politicised. Kovats-Bernat claimed that, by 1999, Lafanmi Selavi had become little more than a *"machin pwopogann politik"* (political propaganda machine) and that Aristide had created a palace militia who "in their cult loyalty to Aristide [...] are comparable to Duvalier's *Tonton Makoute"*.[19] In a particularly bizarre sequence mid way through the film we see Apaid, shot in an oddly strobing, bleached-out light, with a high-pitched digital noise and ambient drone in the background, telling a story about how one day when Aristide went to Cité Soleil he asked the chief of police Christine Jeune to shake hands with the chief of the *chimères* in front of the television cameras and press. She had told Aristide that the constitution was clear, there cannot be parallel armed people. "Ask these people to disarm then I will shake their hands", she told the president. Aristide insisted again, but again she refused. A week later she was found on a road raped and

19 Kovats-Bernat 158, 162-163

killed. This was a message from Aristide, Apaid suggests, to say, "I have put in place an occult criminal machine to help me control the formal institutions".[20]

Charles Henri Baker, vice-president of the Association of Haitian Industries, sweatshop industrialist, a member of the wealthy Haitian Mulatto elite and the Group of 184, brother-in-law of Andy Apaid and owner of several factories in Cité Soleil, appears in the film supporting Apaid's accusations.[21] Identified, like his brother-in-law, simply as "Political Opposition", Baker tells the camera that Aristide stole the elections in 2000, and that his Lavalas terrorists were killing people throughout the country. "Mr. Aristide is running the country by decree", Baker claims. We see shots of a wheelchair-bound protester being treated for head-wounds with other protesters as Baker continues, "after the attack on the universities, after the attack on our own groups, after attacks on the hospital the other day, we cannot negotiate with

---

20 According to Michael Deibert, Aristide visited Cité Soleil in January 1995 towards the end of his first term in office in order to try and calm tensions that had broken out between demonstrators protesting for increased wages, the UN and the Haitian police force (PNH). In a meeting attended by the police, local residents and members of a criminal gang called the Red Army, PNH officer Marie Christine Jeune objected to the president's attempt to create a working relationship between the police and the gangs. Unlike Apaid, Deibert does not accuse Aristide of direct involvement in the murder of Jeune however, and Apaid's designation of the Red Army as *chimères* is symptomatic of the strategy of generating a retrospective myth of Aristide's creation of an "occult criminal machine". The claim would mean that Aristide began creating the *chimères* after one year in office (as Alex Dupuy has also suggested) out of gangs loyal to the military rather than to Lavalas. According to Jeb Sprague, author of *Paramilitarism and the Assault on Democracy in Haiti* (2012), the so-called Red Army was in fact pro-FAd'H (Forces Armé d'Haiti) which had been disbanded by Aristide in 1995 and had subsequently terrorised Lavalas supporters in Cité Soleil in the mid '90s (Deibert 50, Sprague 375 n142).

21 Apaid and Baker have been accused of paying Thomas "Labanye" Robinson, a gang-leader from Cité Soleil, to kill Lavalas supporters, stir up conflict between the gangs controlling Cité Soleil and divide the base of Lavalas support there (Hallward 201, 289, Sprague 255). 2pac would eventually be killed by Labanye in September 2004.

Mr. Aristide".[22] Apaid is then seen explaining to reporters that Aristide had ordered the police to crush their demonstration. The scene fades out to snapshots of the man from the wheelchair lying on the ground with a bullet wound in his head.

Although *Ghosts of Cité Soleil*'s essential selling point is the ghosts of its title, the characters depicted in the film have a much more ambivalent relationship to the term, and rarely do they refer to themselves as such. As 2pac puts it: "Now they make us hot. They give us the name *chimères* and make everybody scared of us somehow". It is not made clear who precisely 2pac is referring to as "they". But the film then cuts to footage of Aristide, the voice-over telling us that "President Aristide denies the allegation", confusing 2pac's claim that the name *chimères* is given to them by others and Apaid's claim that Aristide is using the *chimères* as his personal army. We see Aristide explaining that the nation is in a "learning process of building a state of law". "How could we let thugs, gangs – moving ahead with weapons in their hands?" he asks. Cut to two young boys in the back of a car, one carrying a rifle and the other singing "We're with the big boss. Nobody can hurt us now". 2pac, who is driving, explains to the camera, whose operator we never meet, that he has been given the car by the mayor's department. The intimation of the edit is clear: Aristide's denial that he and the Lavalas party were arming the gangs was false, and that he is in fact the creator and controller of the *chimères*.

However, later in the film, 2pac explains his sense of betrayal by Aristide, and that, while in prison serving a sentence for an attempted kidnapping, reputedly ordered by the president, he had decided that when he went back to Cité Soleil he would fight *against* Aristide, but with music rather than guns (hence his nascent rap career and the involvement of Wyclef Jean in the film). So by his own admission, regardless of who created the term, and was using it for what ends, 2pac did *not* identify as one of Aristide's *chimères*. In a later sequence however we see 2pac and his soldiers donning black t-shirts and baseball caps, cutting eye-holes out of black face masks, over which

---

22 As Nicolas Rossier's film *Aristide and the Endless Revolution* shows, the Group of 184 used questions about the March 2000 senatorial elections as a reason to reject Aristide's presidential victory in November that year (with 92% of the vote), to block any negotiations with the Aristide government and therefore to make a political crisis inevitable.

"ARISTIDE'S CHIMERES" is written. Fully decked-out, a group of armed young men are driven away on the back of a pick-up truck to confront the rebels. Once again, the intimation is clear: these gangs are armed and directed by President Aristide to fight on his behalf against the forces who are planning to overthrow him, regardless of who or what they claim they are fighting for or against.

Throughout the film Bily retains his loyalty to the beleaguered president, at one point explaining that Aristide is the only person in power who has done anything for the poor people of Port-au-Prince. In one sequence Lele – Éleanore "Lele" Senlis, who ran the largest international NGO outpost in Cité Soleil from June 2003-2004, and who, as we will see, plays a central role in the drama that unfolds in *Ghosts* – asks Bily and 2pac whether they want to fight to the end for Aristide.[23] Bily responds by asking if she thinks the insurgents will leave him alone now and stop calling him a *chimère*? "I stop I die," he says, "anything I do I die".[24] Again, a central character identified as a *chimères* leader throughout the film, refutes the term as something made up to discredit the young men of Cité Soleil, and to condemn them to imminent annihilation. In fact, only one of the gang members in the film openly identifies as a *chimère*. It is Gabriel, one of 2pac's soldiers, who, while waiting for medical treatment in a clinic, explains to Lele that his aunt is always upset because he is a *chimère*. "We're all mean," he says, "if you do something to me, I can do the same thing to you". He brags that he cannot die because God is protecting him, as he pulls from his pocket a red scarf. "That's from your Vodou priestess?" Lele asks. "With this I can't die," he responds, flexing the cloth and snapping it before returning it to his pocket. It is the only moment in the film where the *chimères* are identified with the *Lwa*, and by Vodouistic association, with Dessalines, who himself identified with the red-sashed African warrior spirit Ogoun (an association central to Munro's understanding of the *chimères* as an expression of Apocalyptic Creolization).

---

23 Hallward 169

24 This is one of two passages in the film where the brothers associate being identified as a *chimère* with an impending death-sentence.

DANGEROUS LIAISONS

After the shooting of Ghana, one of 2pac's soldiers, by Bily during the food distribution scene, Lele is seen driving towards Cité Soleil to collect Ghana and to take him to hospital. Speaking directly to the camera she explains that, when she told Bily it was too dangerous for her to go to Cité Soleil, he had said, "Lele, I love you. I gave orders. Everybody knows your car. You are safe. You can come." After Ghana is taken to hospital and the bullet removed, Bily is shown naked except for his trunks, showering in his yard. The film then cuts to 2pac explaining how much Bily likes Lele. Lele is then seen giving Bily money and telling him not to spend it on girls. "I need money to eat, not for girls" he responds, "I need it to live... I give money to the people, not to girls". We then hear an excerpt from Lele's journal, accompanied by images of Bily visiting a Vodou *mambo*: "He says never mind if you don't want to be my girlfriend. One day I will be very rich and I will buy you an airplane. I have to say he's very good at convincing people. Bily says he can absolutely guarantee my security in the area. I honestly admire Bily more than 2pac. I think in his heart he wants to do good for Cité Soleil".

Later Gabriel threatens to kill Bily with an M-14 rifle. Having dramatically disarmed him after a tense standoff, Bily, 2pac and the rest of the men leave in a pick-up truck to confront the rebels in the capital. During the confrontation Gabriel is shot in the neck and dies and 2pac has to arrange Gabriel's funeral. The power has been cut in the neighbourhood so 2pac and Lele go looking for a generator. They find one and the party begins. Lele and 2pac drink beer and dance, 2pac and his soldiers waving their guns in the air. The next morning a shaky camera films 2pac bathing naked, just as we had seen Bily earlier. 2pac smiles at the camera, which cuts to a close up of Lele staring at him from behind a curtain in his shack. In the next scene we see Lele in bed with 2pac as he boasts "Yeah, that's me and my girlfriend, Nigga!" At first Lele seems to be hiding her face but when 2pac asks her to please give him a kiss, she does. "Black and white, Nigga. We love each other for real," 2pac boasts, as the telltale sound of Wyclef's bitter-sweet guitar comes in on the soundtrack.

The scene of Lele looking at 2pac showering is a pivotal moment in the film. It suggests, for the first time, that the film-makers had the intention to dramatise the sexual relationship between Lele and 2pac in the midst of an intensely fraught political and inter-personal situation, not only within Port-au-Prince as a whole, but especially between the two brothers at the centre of the film, whose relationship was becoming increasingly acrimonious after the shooting and death of Gabriel. The shot/counter shots and eye-line matches, characteristic of Hollywood continuity editing rather than documentary film, seem jarringly out of place in what would otherwise be a relatively conventional documentary (with an incongruous and saccharine, celebrity hip-hop twist). It is a knowing moment of traditional film language that introduces the idea of cinematic artifice into the otherwise broadly journalistic narrative. That it does this at a moment when a White European woman is staring at a naked, Black male body, seems deliberately structured to raise unsettling questions about voyeurism, sexuality, race and power, that thus far have had no ostensible significance in the film. These themes are given further significance by the earlier suggestion that Lele was giving Bily money. What significance it has for the overall narrative remains oblique and unrepeated, except for a brief shot towards the end of the film where Lele fondles 2pac's gun as he counts money on his bed. Both shots introduce an explicitly amorous and fetishistic dimension to the film whose dissonance relative to the over-arching narrative is unsettling. The repetition of the earlier shot of Bily bathing, which was shown directly before his attraction to Lele was announced by 2pac, retrospectively serves the romantic sub-plot and plays on the mutual exchangeability of the two men's bodies in the eyes of a foreign aid worker. From this moment on the audience is made uncomfortably aware of the director's extra-documentary motivations. No longer a documentary in the widest sense, it becomes a constructed drama about an international aid worker's amorous encounters with real-life *chimères,* framed in terms of the structural conventions of a docu-drama.[25]

---

25 I am not proposing here that anything resembling a "pure" documentary film exists in fact. I am referring to the conventions associated with different kinds of film language that are often combined by film-makers. Asger Leth's father Jørgen Leth has played specifically with these conventions in several films, not least *Interference* ('Haiti Express') from 1983.

Neither Leth nor Loncarevic (cameraman and co-director) are ever seen or heard during the film. But the fact that this scene had to be staged and re-constructed in postproduction suggests that this dimension of the narrative was cinematically constructed, even if the affair may have been genuine.[26] It is difficult to imagine why the directors would introduce this presumed artifice in such an obvious and disruptive way, except perhaps in the interests of box office appeal (i.e. adding a sexual-romantic subplot to the already harrowing and sensational narrative). It is also perplexing why Lele would choose to perform this role in the midst of a very real and potentially violent situation between the two brothers. Not only is her role as an aid worker compromised by the act, but her role in the film too. At what point did she decide to take on an acting role? Was this scripted in advance, or did it happen spontaneously? How much of the rest of the film, by inference, might have been scripted and staged too? And what intention motivated the two directors to put these sequences in the film?

These are all very interesting questions, and there is a long tradition of experimental film and mainstream film-making designed to challenge our expectations about fiction and fact in documentary, that this moment could be compared to. The dissonance stems from the function of this particular mode of artifice within a film that seems, ostensibly, to be telling a broadly political story about the lives of people struggling against the odds for survival during a civil war. The scene is made more troubling by the one which follows, where Lele meets with an exuberant Bily, who is clearly very happy to see the woman he has announced his affections for. Lele explains that she has something important to tell him. "Since not long, since a few days, I have some guy", she says, slapping him gently on the shoulder, "and the guy's your brother". Bily laughs unconvincingly. "You're joking", he says. "No, I'm not joking". Bily tries to laugh it off at first but then appears to be quite upset.[27]

---

26 Colleagues who were in Haiti at the time of the coup have suggested that Lele and the silent cameraman Loncarevic were lovers at the time of the filming, and that Asger Leth was never himself in Cité Soleil. Instead Leth procured the footage made by Loncarevic while the former was working for a Danish news crew in Haiti.

27 It is of course possible that this sequence was scripted and that the

In the analysis of Bily as a representative the *chimère* ethos, Martin Munro discussed at some length their curious ethical foundation, specifically Bily's paradoxical plea, expressed in Charles Najman's documentary *Häiti, la fin des Chimères* (2004), for the necessity of a police substation in Cité Soleil, and his holding the government to account for its lack of ethics. No mention is made however of the curious ethical decisions and intentions of the makers of *Ghosts of Cité Soleil*, who chose to perpetuate popular myths about the *chimères*, myths challenged by the two central characters in the film. The moral burden and ethical ambiguity of being-a-*chimère* is placed entirely on the individuals exploited by the film-makers as such, despite the fact that, with the exception of young Gabriel, none of them identify with the term imposed by their foreign film-maker friends. The power of the myth is presumably too seductive and exotic for international cinema audiences, appealing as it does to well established stereotypical images of Haiti as a macabre land of ghouls, monsters, apocalyptic violence and salacious inter-racial encounters. But the chimerical nature of Lele, part actress, part aid worker and divisive paramour of the brothers is not mentioned by Munro, nor that of Wyclef Jean, co-producer of the film, producer of the soundtrack, and would-be saviour of Haitian 2pac and his doomed, rapping soldiers, or the film-makers themselves, of whom we hear and see nothing during the film.

While visiting Bily for the last time in Cité Soleil in January 2004, Michael Deibert, noting the tension that seemed to have built up between the brothers, described a "curious set of foreign hangers-on, a pair of drug-addled European twenty-somethings, one of whom, a woman working with an NGO in Cité Soleil, had taken to negotiating exorbitant fees on behalf of the boys in order to take timorous *blan* journalists down to see real live 'Chimeres'". Presumably the pair in question were Lele and her cameraman companion Loncarevic.[28]

EVERY DOOR IS CLOSED

Cut to blue-grey monochrome of a street in Port-au-Prince on February

---

entire Lele-Billy-2pac love-triangle sub-plot was constructed by the central characters and the film-makers to add a romantic dimension to the film.

28 Deibert 384

29th, 2004, the day of the coup against Aristide. The camera enters Aristide's ransacked residence as the voice-over explains that Aristide had been forced into exile and left the capital at dawn. 2pac tells the camera that he is happy that Aristide has left, as another hip-hop track begins and we see a young woman carrying the M-14 rifle back to 2pac's place. "Guy Philippe and Louis-Jodel Chamblain received a hero's welcome from thousands of jubilant Haitians", the newscaster reports, as the rebel leaders and several dozen armed fighters triumphantly drive through Port-au-Prince. Chamblain explains to the camera that he has no problem with the police or with the people. "We have problems with the *chimères* and the chiefs of the *chimères*", he says, "who are crazy, and have done nothing for the country or the people". Guy Philippe, the newscaster tells us, will now move to disarm and neutralise the *chimères* in the slums of Port-au-Prince. Cut to Lele on the phone to 2pac telling him that Philippe will be going first to La Saline then to Cité Soleil. She encourages him to speak to the rebels and negotiate with them before they attack.[29]

The day after Aristide's departure from Port-au-Prince in 2000, U.S. and French troops arrived in the capital to secure the streets. In the film crowds are shown shouting "No more *chimères*! *Chimères* are nothing but trouble", as they pull down the billboard images of Aristide, as they had pulled down the images of Papa and Baby Doc in *The Serpent and the Rainbow*. The crowds are fired upon by Aristide supporters, and a journalist is killed. Cut to Andy Apaid saying that the guns should be taken from the gangs and that, if they continued to fight, they would be "against the wall". Lele organises a "peace call" between Guy Philippe and Bily who explains to the "rebel leader" that the chiefs of Cité Soleil don't want any more violence. They can guarantee a stop to the violence and will lay down their weapons. He's not worried about being attacked, Bily tells Philippe, only about his people. "We're ready for war" he tells him, "if it's about stopping the violence and for everyone to live in peace and have jobs". The line is cut. Lele tries to convince a defiant Bily that the gangs should give up all their weapons. In the next shot she is sitting on 2pac's lap who is explaining that he doesn't want his people to die. On the day of

---

29 How and why Lele would have direct contact with the rebels and be in the position to arrange a "peace-call" at the time remains a matter of speculation.

the scheduled disarmament, international troops and Haitian police arrive in Cité Soleil to gather their weapons. Shots of Bily and his wife playing with their baby and daughter cut to what appears to be a kind of pop video of Bily and friends playing basketball in slow motion as helicopters fly over the city.

U.S. and French troops, the newsreader's voice tells us, have begun patrolling the streets of Cité Soleil, going from house to house in search of wanted gang leaders and their remaining guns. When 2pac returns to his section of Cité Soleil he finds that Robinson "Labanye" Thomas, one of the section chiefs, has betrayed other leaders to the military.[30] As they drive back into Soleil 19, the area under 2pac's control, there is trouble. It seems Labanye has come to take over the area. Lele asks 2pac why he is angry with his brother. It's because Bily gave his gun to his soldier 50 Cent, he tells her. Cut to Lele on a bed in a hotel room with 2pac who is telling 50 Cent to hide his gun. If he gives it to Bily, 2pac will not be his friend anymore. He's going to put a bullet in Bily's ass, he says as he strokes Lele's hair. "I don't have a brother any more". Cut back to Bily with Lele: "If 2pac was not my brother I'd have killed him already". Back on the hotel balcony at night 2pac explains that he could kill his brother now if he wanted to, or that Bily could have him killed and pretend that it wasn't him. "It's like that Lele", he says, "we're Haitian man". Next we see 2pac and 50 Cent discussing whether it is best to kill Bily or let him be chief and get killed by one of the other gang leaders. Cut to Lele on the phone telling 2pac that the police want to make an example of him before the UN arrive. 2pac ponders how he will escape Haiti: "Like Wyclef says, when the doors close, you find another one open. But it's not true. I find the doors closed, I can't find another open. Every door is closed".

Eventually Bily is arrested by the police and 2pac tries to work out what to do. But there is nothing to do but make war, he concludes. He rests his head on his hand and cries. Back in the hotel he explains that, "In front of the Americans, they [the military and police] say they're going to arrest you. If the Americans aren't there, they're going to kill you. That's the big problem in Haiti since the beginning of Aristide. When Aristide came back he didn't want to sit with the Macoute. He

---

30 As already noted, Robinson "Labanye" Thomas was reputedly paid by Andy Apaid and Charles Baker to divide the gangs in Cité Soleil (Hallward 201, 289, Sprague 255, Diebert 430).

made us Lavalas kill Macoute. And now the Convergence comes back, they're going to kill Lavalas. It's always like that. When Convergence goes, Lavalas comes. It's gonna keep killing, killing. Come on! Haiti will never be changed". Shots of Lele back in Cité Soleil admiring 2pac's gun on his bed as he counts his money. Lele helps 2pac pack his bags in her hotel room and then kisses him goodbye as he gets on a bus to take him out of Port-au-Prince. The film loops back to the opening scene where 2pac reflected on how his life was going to be, ending with the image of a bus heading into the mountains and captions that read: "2pac made it out of Haiti in 2004. When his brother was released from prison 2pac decided to go back and be with him. 2pac was shot by Labanye on the 30th of September 2004. He died in Cité Soleil". The film fades to black and we read that Lele is now living in Paris, Bily has disappeared presumed dead, a new president was elected in 2006 and "the *Chimères* are still thriving in Cité Soleil".[31]

CHIMERICAL OPTICS

In his book *The Prophet and Power: Jean Bertrand Aristide, the International Community and Haiti* (2007) Alex Dupuy is reasonably sympathetic and supportive of the early Lavalas movement, its political goals and the obstacles it had to contend with. The tone changes however in the chapter dealing with the 2000-2004 period – 'The Prophet Checkmated' – where Dupuy puts forward the claim that Aristide began emulating the practices of Papa Doc in 1999 by using armed gangs against his political opponents, "chimerizing" the Lavalas party and betraying his mass base.[32] He traces the creation of the *chimères* as an extra-legal political instrument to 1995, when Aristide disbanded the Haitian army and a new Haitian police force was created with the help of the U.S., France and Canada: "Aristide understood the need to control that force and put his trusted allies in control," he wrote. Dupuy notes that many acts of violence occurred between 1999 and the election of 2000, including the killing of the

---

31 "Thriving" is quite an incredible word to use here, given the terrible circumstances that the gangs were living in before the coup, a situation that became even worse afterwards.

32 Dupuy (2007) 143-147. The term "chimerizing" is Hallward's.

renowned radio journalist Jean Dominique, the implication being that these were committed by *chimères* on Aristide's orders.[33] Shortly after the Jean Dominique murder investigation began, opponents of Aristide implicated him in a cover-up. In support of his case for Aristide's control of the *Chimères,* Dupuy cites an article written by the French journalist Jean-Michel Caroit for *Le Monde* on November 5, 2003 – 'Haiti, la Lois des milices' – which proposed that the directors of the police liaised directly with the gangs and supplied them with arms.[34]

As Hallward has pointed out, the impartiality of Caroit and *Le Monde* at the time was compromised to say the least. Long before Aristide's re-election in 2002 Caroit had begun to identify the Lavalas administration's revival of Duvalierist Macoutism. President Aristide had recently demanded from France repayment of the reparations that the former slave-holding nation had extorted by force from Haiti in 1825, the amount calculated in contemporary terms at $21 billion. The demand seems to have been a significant factor in his defamation as a tyrant and madman by the French press at the

---

33 The murder of Jean Dominique continues to be one of the unsolved deaths in the coup era. Hallward has suggested that his murder served the interests of Aristide's opposition who wanted to ban him from all media airways. Dominique played an influential role in the campaign against Jean-Claude Duvalier in the 1980s and *for* Aristide in the 1990s. Although he had become critical of the party after 1994, "Everyone knew that he was [...] a supporter of Lavalas" (Hallward 110). The investigation into his murder has allegedly been plagued by inconsistencies. One of the chief murder suspects, Danny Toussaint, owner of a well-known gun store in Port-au-Prince, was elected senator, granting him immunity from prosecution. No one has yet been prosecuted for Dominique's murder (Sprague 97).

34 Dupuy (2007) 144. The claim that Aristide created the *chimères* was repeated by Ian Thomson in the 2003 version of his Haiti travelogue *Bonjour Blanc: A Journey Through Haiti* (Thomson 358-9). He also accuses Aristide's "personal enforcers" of being directly involved in the cocaine smuggling trade. The theme is also present in Raoul Peck's film *Moloc Tropical* (2009) a thinly veiled allegory of Aristide during his last months in office.

time.[35] That Dupuy attempted to substantiate allegations made about Aristide and the creation of the *chimères* in 1995 on the strength of an article in a French newspaper written by a French journalist in 2003, undermines his case. But for Dupuy, whether or not Aristide had a personal role in creating and directing the *chimères* was immaterial.[36] He cites Clive Thomas, author of *The Rise of the Authoritarian State in Peripheral Societies* (1984), who argued that authoritarian regimes in the Caribbean often made use of armed civilian groups to do the government's dirty work without giving them official sanction or status, an accusation levelled at François Duvalier, as we have seen, in his use of the so-called *Cagoulards* and later the Macoute. "This allows such governments or rulers to deny responsibility for the operation of these groups, thereby avoiding official investigations and allowing the groups to operate with impunity".[37] This is precisely how Aristide would use the *chimères*, Dupuy asserts. It is remarkable that a scholar who is otherwise so thorough academically could make such an assertion on little more than abstract political theory and the unsupported claims of two journalists writing almost a decade after the tried and tested authoritarian instrument had allegedly been put in place.[38]

Dupuy's version of events conforms surprisingly well to that of the Group of 184 and Roger Noriega, U.S. Assistant Secretary of State for Western Hemisphere Affairs for the Bush administration, during the time of the coup. In *Aristide and the Endless Revolution*, Noriega

---

35 This idea was also promoted by the CIA. CIA agent Brian Latell testified to the U.S. congress in 1993 that Aristide was "a psychotic manic depressive with proven homicidal tendencies" (Hallward 44).

36 For a critique of Dupuy's book, and in particular the case made against Aristide and the *chimerization* of Lavalas, see Hallward 'Aristide and the Violence of Democracy: Review of Alex Dupuy's 'The Prophet and the Power: Jean-Bertrand Aristide, The International Community and Haiti'' *Haiti Liberté*, July 2007.

37 Thomas 91

38 One of these was Jean-Michel Caroit, whose objectivity, as we have seen, has been called into question by Hallward. The other was Anne Fuller, who, in a *Haitian Times* article from 19-25 November 2003 remarked that armed gangs were carrying out their criminal activity "with impunity" as long as they helped the police and their political leaders (Dupuy (2007) 145).

accuses Aristide of wilfully misgoverning Haiti, undermining the rule of law, denying political opponents the opportunity to contribute and participate peacefully in the government and loosing a whirlwind of violence on the country. When asked if he had any evidence supporting these allegations Noriega said:

> We know his record. I indicated to you that at least half a dozen prominent killings of political opponents took place, hit squads operating out of the national palace using weapons – we have the ballistic information that proves this – that were out of the inventory of the palace security unit, which was directly accountable to him, his key security aides are implicated in these political murders. So we think that's the way the man operated. And in recent weeks we see his supporters threatening to behead people and indeed people are beheaded. Are we witnesses to this? No. But I think we can draw certain conclusions about who is wielding this kind of political violence.

Noriega's reference to alleged beheadings of opponents after Aristide's exile brings us uncomfortably close to what looks suspiciously like a black ops operation created by supporters of the CIA-backed Group of 184, the so-called Operation Baghdad, reputedly initiated by the *chimères* after Aristide's departure to win back control of Cité Soleil and other bases of Lavalas support.[39] Rumours about such a sinister operation on the part of Aristide's grass-roots supporters would be used to warrant more extreme measures against them in the months that followed.

One of Wade Davis's favourite words to describe the miraculous feats of those in a state of spirit possession was their ability to perform otherwise harmful and life-threatening acts with *impunity*.[40] It was a word that came to the fore under Duvalierism to describe acts of

---

39 See Nik Barry Shaw 'Exposing the Big Lie of "Operation Baghdad"' *Press for Conversion! magazine*, Issue #63 (November 2008).

40 In *The Serpent and the Rainbow* Davis describes a woman carrying burning coal in her mouth for three minutes "with impunity" (50) and Macandal moving about Saint-Domingue "with the impunity of a god garnering favours and awakening the zeal of the people" (197).

violence committed by the Macoute against the Haitian population. During Jean-Bertrand Aristide's second term in office the word would once again be used to describe the actions of the so-called *chimères* who, like their Macoute predecessors, were purportedly allowed to operate with impunity.[41] In the foreign media discourse of special powers in Haiti there are then two distinct meanings of the word: one miraculous, mystical and Vodou-inspired, the other extra-legal, political and moral. In *Ghosts of Cité Soleil* there are none of the stereotypical and sensationalist Voodoo-horror tropes that have characterised popular, foreign representations of Haitian society and culture discussed so far. And there are only three explicit references to Vodou in the entire film: Bily's visit to a Vodou priestess, 2pac's nihilistic rejection of the religion and Gabriel, 2pac's soldier, who believed himself protected by the red sash of Ogun. There is no mention of zombies, wanga charms or ritual sacrifice (human or otherwise), and no reference to possession trance.[42] But the very figure of the *chimères,* from which *Ghosts* takes its name, has implicitly spectral, monstrous and violent associations that tend towards supernatural and inhuman meanings. When these meanings are situated in what we might call, following Michel-Rolph Trouillot, the "exceptionalist myth" of Haitian power-relations, the quasi-mythical *chimères* were clearly used by anti-Lavalas Haitian power brokers and foreign journalists to perpetuate the well-established idea that certain sections of Haitian society were subject to mysterious psychological forces beyond their control, that could make them act without reason, rationality or restraint. The figure of the *chimère* then, like those other remotely controlled agents-without-autonomy – the zombie, robot, slave and somnambulist – represents a *"kind of"* being, part-animal, part-machine, part-human, "existing somewhere between life and death, existence and oblivion" (Munro), mysteriously created by the mad genius of a fanatical, charismatic and haunted despot like the "endlessly oblique", "endlessly complex" and "unregenerate shape-shifter": the Creole Dessalines (Munro). In this

---

41 Dupuy (2007) 145

42 There are two more subtle inclusions of Vodou elements, one of which does make a reference to possession: a short clip of a Guede ceremony during the opening scenes and an apparently possessed woman prostrate on the road, breathing heavily and then dancing with her breast exposed at Gabriel's funeral.

sense the construction and perpetuation of the myth of the *chimères* brings together two distinct strands from the historical demonization of Haitian life and culture by outside observers since the revolution: that of basket-case Voodoo-Dictator, and occult-driven, ultra-violent and quasi-human (apocalyptic) insurrectionary.[43]

The extent to which 2pac, Bily and their soldiers were *actually* subject to the will of Aristide is an issue that *Ghosts of Cité Soleil* does address, if tangentially. Both Bily and 2pac reflect on their loyalty to the president in several scenes. 2pac's loyalties are to himself, his soldiers and his section of Cité Soleil. He explicitly rejects Aristide for betraying him personally, ridiculing his brother's loyalty to the president and the Lavalas movement that had "fucked with his head". Scoffing at Bily's belief in the power of Vodou, 2pac sys: "Fuck Vodou, Man. Fuck God. Fuck Vodou, brother... Fuck everybody, man. Believe me. I believe in my own finger." He flexes his trigger finger in front of the lens. "I believe in that baby, that!" Bily, on the other-hand, is dedicated to Aristide, and is willing to die to keep him in office. But this is not an irrational or unconscious impulse. It is rather one based on his respect for Aristide as the only Haitian leader in recent history to try to do good for the poorest and most vulnerable people in the country. Despite the evident disagreements about Aristide amongst the gang leaders represented in *Ghosts,* the opening lines of the film state emphatically that Aristide and his Lavalas Party had "enlisted the support of armed gangs from the slum of Cité Soleil" who were "known as the Chimeres". Although the statement has validity in terms of what is known about Aristide's second term in office, and the historical use of the derogatory epithet by the Haitian elites before then, by framing the narrative in this way *Ghosts* lends credibility to the

---

43 The term basket case, which was first used to describe U.S. soldiers returning from the First World War in baskets after losing their limbs, started to be used to describe the disastrous agricultural policies of former colonial nations and failing European states in the late 1960s and early 1970s. By extension it came to be personally associated with the psychology of the leaders of those countries. The term was first used in relation to Haiti in the 1980s when Jean-Claude Duvalier's agricultural policies and associated human rights record started to be the object of critical international analysis (see Lars Schoultz *Human Rights and United States Policy Towards Latin America* (1981)).

claims made by Andy Apaid and Charles Baker later in the film, and endorsed by Alex Dupuy. To underline this message Bily and 2pac are identified throughout the film as "Chimere Leaders" and their gangs as "Aristide's Chimeres". In so doing *Ghosts of Cité Soleil* explicitly reinforces the story promoted by the Convergence Démocratique, the Group of 184 and their international and NGO allies that Aristide had personally created, directed and armed a private army of living ghosts to maintain his sinister hold on power. In this sense the film endorses the myth that Aristide was secretly the new Duvalier, concealing his truly tyrannical nature behind the benign mask of a former Salesian priest, much as Papa Doc had done behind the image of a kindly country doctor, and that the *chimères* were the new Macoutes.

The extent to which Aristide was directly supporting the anti-opposition violence of the gangs in Cité Soleil, La Saline and other impoverished neighbourhoods, and personally responsible for attacks on the opposition, are recurrent questions in debates about the political legitimacy of his presidency and the justification for the coup. Deibert and Clara James argue strongly that he *was* directly responsible for the actions of the armed gangs, as do some of the gang members themselves. Hallward and Sprague take a more sympathetic view that, given the military opposition mounting against him, and their track record for extreme violence against his supporters, Aristide allowed the gangs to arm themselves in defence of his presidency, the Lavalas mission and the communities they represented. But whether or not Aristide actually created the *chimères* as a private and clandestine security force and army is a question whose answer lies well beyond the scope of this chapter. What seems to be clear however is that the term *chimère* was a cultural slur in Haiti before it came to be associated explicitly with Aristide and the gangs who were loyal to him in the slums of Port-au-Prince and other towns. The journalistic and scholarly sources consulted here suggest that this association was consolidated between 1996 and 2001. It was at this time that Aristide broke with the OPL (Organisation du Peuple en Lutte) and created his own Fanmi Lavalas political party that won several seats in the Haitian senate in 1997, leading to a parliamentary deadlock. When Fanmi Lavalas won landslide victories in legislative and local elections in May 2000, opponents of Aristide formed the U.S. backed Convergence Démocratique that would eventually become the Group of 184. This group led the political opposition to Aristide after his election to president in November 2000 (with 92% of the vote). It was around this time that the association of Aristide with the so-called *chimères* was promoted by representatives of the Group of 184, some of whose leading figures, such as Andy Apaid and Charles Baker, had a powerful influence on the national and international media apparatus.

By the time of *Ghosts of Cité Soleil* the association was sufficiently consolidated that few reviewers and commentators on the film considered it necessary to question it. In his review for *Variety* in September 2006, Todd McCarthy pre-empts Munro's configuration of the phantasmic *Chimères* as "already dead given their typically brief lifespans", an idea underlined by the revelation at the end of *Ghosts of Cité Soleil* that 2pac had been shot and killed by Labanye and that Bily was missing, presumed dead. In his review of the film for *Salon* magazine in June 2007 Andrew O'Hehir described Leth as taking "no overt position on the contentious issue of Aristide and his unfinished Haitian Revolution". One somewhat extreme exception to the rule was Charlie Hinton's May 2007 review for the *Haitian Action Committee*, which likened the film to Leni Riefenstahl's 1935 Nazi propaganda film *Triumph of the Will* in its depiction of the leaders of the coup as heroes. Hinton also claims that, according to documentary film-maker Kevin Pina, the more foreign journalists paid Bily and Tupac for their stories the more outlandish became their claims. But Michael Deibert, who knew the brothers personally, strongly renounces these charges.[44] What seems uncontestable from the various sources cited here is that leading figures of the Group of 184 supported the former *chimères* of the Cannibal Army once they turned against Aristide, and that they paid the gang leader Robinson "Labanye" Thomas to cause divisions between the gangs in Cité Soleil, a task which ultimately led to the murder of 2pac.[45]

Through the chimerical optic of works like *Ghosts of Cité Soleil*, actual people labelled by the term *chimères* have been made to coincide with mythical fantasies about them in ways that occlude the structural and political dimensions of the literary, televisual and cinematic media through which they are depicted. In this way Munro's literary analysis

---

44 Deibert 'Ghosts, Bandits and Cité Soleil', May 16, 2007.

45 Deibert claims that 2pac was eventually killed in September 2004 by police working in collusion with Labanye (Deibert 'Ghosts, Bandits and Cité Soleil', May 16, 2007).

of these living ghosts, like the film he takes as a primary source, has discomforting parallels with the explicitly repressive function the term was generated to serve. More cynically one could argue that *Ghosts of Cité Soleil* was itself part of the propaganda machine designed to defame Aristide and to ready his poor supporters for violent military suppression. Munro's decision to speak about the *chimères* at a conference dedicated to *1804 and its Afterlives* clearly played on the theme of "ghosts" of the Haitian Revolution and the founding of the Haitian Republic by Dessalines in 1804. That Aristide had been planning a national celebration of the Declaration of Independence the year he was ousted from office, and his demand for $21 billion in reparations from the French to coincide with the bicentenary celebrations, suggests a context in which the so-called *chimères* could conceivably be imagined as an echo of the apocalyptic revolutionary armies he understands Dessalines to have led. But this is not how they portray themselves. It is clearly the spectral and monstrous associations of the word *chimères* that allows a mythical and phantasmatic reading to be made of the people identified by a political and class slur central to the propaganda campaign against Aristide and the Lavolas movement as a whole, one that made the young men labelled by it ready for extermination by the paramilitaries, police and international peace keeping forces of the UN. The assumed apocalyptic nihilism of the so-called *chimères* is not that of hybrid beings living in the ambiguous space between life and death, but that of young men forced by extreme circumstances to fight, often to the death, for causes whose meanings had been lost.

The 'Happy Man', *A Voodoo Possession*, directed by Walter Boholst, 2014

VIII

NIGHTMARES IN A DAMAGED BRAIN

METAPHYSICAL MALADIES

One of the most controversial films banned during the Video Nasty controversy of the 1980s was Romano Scavolini's *Nightmares in a Damaged Brain*, a 1981 slasher film that tells the story of George Tatum, a recently released mental patient whose recurring nightmares about a childhood trauma compel him to murder his ex-wife, three children and their babysitter with an axe. It transpires that George had brutally murdered his own father and his lover when, as a child, he had found them having kinky sex in the family home. The idea that a traumatic event in one's childhood could compel a person to repeat it later in life has been a generic plot structure in horror films since the ideas of psychoanalysis were absorbed into mainstream popular culture in the 1940s. It is a fundamental theme in psychoanalysis, most famously formulated as "repetition compulsion" by Sigmund Freud in his *Beyond the Pleasure Principle* of 1920, an essay in which he attempted to account, in psychoanalytical terms, for a range of unconscious, repetitive behaviours encountered in the clinical setting, most notably the tendency of soldiers returning from the front after WWI to re-live their traumatic experiences in dreams.[1] Unsatisfied with his earlier theory that all fantasies, however distressing to those obsessed with or plagued by them, were ultimately the expressions of

---

1 The notion of a "compulsion to repeat" was first outlined by Freud in his 1914 essay 'Remembering, Repeating and Working Through'.

unfulfilled wishes, Freud concluded that there must be another force at work at the level of the human organism that sought to reduce all bodily stimulus and excitation to zero, and to return it to the state of inorganic matter. This force he named the "death drive", or Thanatos, after the Greek God of Death, twin brother of Hypnos, God of Sleep, an "entropic", countervailing tendency to the original regulator of all psychological life (the so-called "pleasure principle", personified by Eros) that expressed itself as an instinct for destruction directed towards the external world. By the time of *Nightmare*'s release in 1981 Freud's theory of death-driven, repetition-compulsion had become a normative touchstone of psychoanalytically-informed psychotherapy that had been reformulated by the DSM-III (Diagnostic and Statistical Manual of Mental Disorders) as Post-Traumatic Stress Disorder (PTSD), largely in response to the therapeutic treatment of soldiers returning from the Vietnam War in the 1970s. Films like Scavolini's deliberately compounded theories about PTSD with fears about representations of violence in the mass media as the potential cause of emotional trauma in themselves, in a kind of auto-traumatising recursive loop that particularly troubled censors in the U.K. at the time.[2]

As we have seen, when the *zombi* migrated into cinema it quickly took on the characteristics of that other archetypal *agent-without-autonomy*, the somnambulist, who, in sinister, criminal mode, could be made to perform acts that the waking personality would find morally reprehensible. It was a story that had precedents in those colonial commentators who had witnessed the bizarre, "Vaudoux" ceremonies of Saint-Domingue, obscurely intuiting the nascent eruption of anti-colonial violence they intimated in their fascinating and repellent ritual forms. From the earliest hypnosis-themed films, which drew directly from the speculations of clinical hypnotherapy, it was suggested that a second "dissociated" personality could be created in an individual as a consequence of some kind of extreme shock or trauma, and that historical accounts of demonic possession, such as those assumed to be still happening in "remote parts of the world", could be explained in terms of similar psychological mechanisms. The tragedy of primitive culture was that once its obscurest regions were illuminated by science, the rites and rituals that bound the archaic community together would be lost to the ineluctable forces of an homogenising,

---

2 A video distributor at the time, refusing the censor's demand to cut the film, served 18 months in jail.

universal modernity. Such theories had themselves emerged from a century of debates that attempted to account for the underlying causes of irrational and seemingly unconscious individual and group behaviour, like those theorised by Le Bon, Charcot, Janet and many others at the turn of the 20th century. A century earlier, at the time of the Haitian Revolution, these debates had a distinctly racial character based on assumptions about African peoples' erroneous reasoning about the causes of natural and supernatural phenomena, the so-called "primitive mentality" that recurred in the form of "survivals" in modern culture. It was in eager pursuit of such primitive archaisms that William Seabrook ventured to Haiti in 1927 while his Surrealist fellow-travellers in Paris revelled in whatever "black practices" could still be enjoyed in the modern metropolis, abandoning themselves to "the great shadow of the outside". And like those people compelled to unconsciously repeat the traumatic events of their past - fetishists, primitivists, animists, spiritualists, hysterics and psychotics (whatever their race) - they were assumed unable to properly distinguish, as matters of fact actual from imaginary events, the products of their imaginations from the effects of physiological and material processes. This tendency towards "delusion", so celebrated by the heroes and heroines of the *sousrealist* avant-gardes, was to become perhaps *the* defining characteristic of those deemed to be beyond the bounds of reason and the civilising and curative reach of either modernity or psychotherapy.

From the first intimations of Voodoo-horror in *White Zombie*, to its nuanced treatment in *I Walked with a Zombie* and its parodic re-formulation in films like *Dr. Terror's House of Horrors*, ambiguous associations between tales of African-derived Vodou sorcery and the categories of modern psychopathology have been a characteristic of the genre. From the 1920s onwards researchers into Haitian Vodou also discussed the relationship between the distinctive features of the religion with categories of contemporary clinical psychology like mythomania, epileptic seizures, paraphrenia, traumatic neurosis and dissociative personality disorder, the phenomena of possession trance being the object of particular fascination and academic attention by both inside and outside observers. Some, like Arthur C. Holly, proposed supernatural and metaphysical explanations for the phenomena, founded on the history of world religions and their esoteric lores; others, like J. C. Dorsainvil, tended towards hereditary and psychopathological explanations, seeing ritual possession as a kind of racial anachronism; while others still, notably Louis Mars and Rémy Bastien, took a socio-cultural perspective that combined both positions.[3]

By the 1970s film critics had begun to draw hypothetical correlations between the visceral shocks contained in extreme gore and slasher films and the repressed and unresolved substrates of massive historical trauma, a formula whose roots can be traced to Romero's *Night of the Living Dead*, the film that split the Zombie Complex into two distinct branches from 1968 onwards, at the height of a wave of anti-war and anti-imperialist sentiments in the "developed" world. From such a perspective the exceptional characteristics of Vodou worship, reported by ethnographers since the 1930s, could be understood as complex and multilayered cultural responses that had evolved amongst former African slaves over several centuries in response to their relentless subjugation by various forms of colonial governance: a highly ritualised reaction-formation on the part of those most brutalised by it, to the historical trauma of plantation slavery, its post-revolutionary legacy and the moral and existential paradoxes of compulsory Christianity. And is this not what the dead men working in the cane fields of HASCO in the 1920s also communicated – however mutely, through the blind,

---

3 Perhaps the most interesting contemporary commentator on this issue is Willy Apollon, author of *Le vaudou: Un espace pour les "voix"* (1976), and a Lacanian psychoanalyst who argues that the "voices" of the possessed are unable to pass through the form of writing without being reduced to signification, and hence interpretation and the limiting impasse of orthography. "The difficulty proper to the drive to subvert history in the field of the Vodou society or brotherhood [*confrérie*]", he writes "is derived from the historic political domination of the peasant masses, which compels them to invest the imaginary with cultural figures who substitute themselves for the economic and social structures that serve to order the relationship between the powers that be and the class struggle that lies at the heart of social conflict" (see 'The Crisis of Possession' (1999)). From this perspective the *lwa* are mediating agents between external and internal power struggles specific to the culture and history of Haiti. For Apollon, the possession of a *hounsi*, *mambo* or *houngan* by a *lwa*, far from being a threat to the colonial order, is in effect a form of theatrical, social control that circumscribes the capacity for revolutionary unleashing of unbound drives in a kind of ritualised, post-colonial pantomime.

unseeing eyes that stared into Seabrook's – to a modern world that had still not fully reconciled itself to the all-too-inhuman foundations of its cherished ideals of "Freedom", "Progress", "Individual Liberty" and "Autonomy"?

As I have argued throughout, at the traumatic historical kernel of the zombie's two future paths it is possible to discern, on the one hand, the inhuman violence of the plantation slavery system, informing the tradition of zombies as living-dead, monsters of misfortune, subject to the will of sinister external agents; and, on the other, the revolutionary response to that prolonged subjugation by the slaves of Saint-Domingue, culminating in the spectacular image of a massive "Black" insurrection of liberated (in)humanity. In both cases, the state of zombiedom is a hyberbolic reaction to the violent reduction of human beings to the status of mere things whose life can be terminated with impunity by their overlords and masters. But whether the motivating spirit of the zombie is imagined as a *bokor*, supernatural entity, a *lwa*, the Spirit of Liberty, "demon of the demos", an hereditary or historical psychopathology or an evolutionary rupture in the species-being, the theme of "possession" remains a constant speculative question: what makes them do what they do if it is not "themselves"?

The crucial moment of *transition* between living human and living-dead, flesh-eating zombie echoes the moment in traditional horror films when a person becomes possessed by a demon or a spirit of the dead. In this moment the individual, with its unique memories, loyalties, knowledge and values, the human we recognise as like ourselves, is replaced by *another being*, devoid of the restraining virtues or moral constraints of the host. Simply put, in scenes of zombic-transition and spirit possession, the good-old former self is uncannily superseded by a terrible and sinister *Other*. In the case of the flesh-eating zombie it is the *generic* spirit of the restless and ravenous dead that irreversibly overtakes the hitherto human. In spirit possession, on the other hand, it is a *super-singular* entity which *temporarily* takes control of its vehicle, driving it to perform acts that, in its proper *self-possessed* state, it would be normally unable to do or be morally repelled by. From this perspective the super-singular individuated agency of the demonic and the generic animalistic agency of the inhuman-undead share common features, especially for those humans on the other side of the divide. In *World War Z*, for instance, Gerry Lane watches a young man transition from human to zombie as his daughter's speaking doll counts down the arrival of the number twelve train. By the time it has counted up to twelve, "the train is in the station!" Typically the moment, like that of demonic possession, is depicted by the blind, staring eyes of the newly (dis)possessed, just before they fling themselves onto the nearest passerby.

The contemporary cinematic pre-occupation with the moment of possession-transition therefore brings the two separate strands of the Zombie Complex back into spectacular alignment. It is the pivotal moment where the *other within* is on the verge of superseding and replacing the subject it has come to inhabit. So common a trope has it become in horror cinema that one might call it one of the medium's great fascinators, capturing as it does, something of cinema's own inherent function: to summon in the viewer that sense of *the outside being on the inside*. As many commentators have noted, since the birth of cinema, the processes of cinematic fascination have more commonly generated feelings of idolisation and passionate erotic attachment to those immortal others we call stars. But it has been horror's special vocation, as Noel Carrol has shown, to stage an encounter with the categorically interstitial, monstrous boundary upsetters that Bataille would associate with the unhinged, ignoble, abject and sinister dimension of the sacred: the absolutely inassimilable Other.

A VOODOO POSSESSION?

> I was wondering about our yesterdays,
> and digging through the rubble
> and to say, at least somebody went
> to a hell of a lot of trouble
> to make sure that when we looked things up
> we wouldn't fare too well
> and come up with totally unreliable
> pictures of ourselves.

- Gil Scott Heron 'Black History – The World' (1982)

"You know the past can only haunt you if you let it."

- Bree to Aiden in *A Voodoo Possession* (2014)

In January 2014, almost four years to-the-day of the earthquake that devastated Haiti in 2010, a run-of-the-mill, low-budget horror film was released on DVD that, like so many in the genre, garnered next to no attention in the mainstream media and little more on the underground horror scene. An excruciatingly sentimental Voodoo-horror psychodrama, *A Voodoo Possession* tells the story of a down-on-his-luck and out-of-work American banker called Aiden Chase, who is convinced to go to Haiti by his TV journalist girlfriend Bree, to search for his estranged brother Cody, who had disappeared after setting up a charity hospital there to treat victims of the disaster. In the opening scene we are told by a television newscaster (Bree) that Cody Chase had disappeared in Haiti with thousands of dollars of earthquake relief money, a reference presumably to the by-then widely known fact that most of the billions of dollars of aid money raised for Haiti never arrived there, but were instead diverted to the American companies and NGOs who were awarded the contracts for a re-construction that mostly never happened. The actor who plays the missing doctor, David Thomas Jenkins, seems to have been cast to resemble Sean Penn, the Hollywood actor with a volatile reputation, who set up the J/P Haitian Relief Organisation in the aftermath of the earthquake and personally managed a 50,000 person camp there.[4] The newscaster asks rhetorically if Cody Chase had reverted to the ways of his chequered past, or whether the "darker forces of Haiti, filled with corruption, and violence and gangs got the best of a man just trying to turn his life around". "Only Haiti knows", she concludes.

The film's director Walter Boholst had already made a genre-typical zombie short called *D-volution* in 2011, in which a man, presumably in the midst of a zombie apocalypse, grapples with the agonising dilemma of having to kill his infected partner. The mini-drama frames one of the crucial moments of the apocalyptic zombie genre, when one of *us* is about to become one of *them,* and, for a shining moment, we have a chance to *terminate* the now slavering and frothing monstrosity before it *de-terminates* us. So great is the distance today between the apocalyptic flesh-eating zombie and its Haitian folkloric ancestors that it is unlikely popular audiences would make any association between Boholst's two films, the flesh-eating zombie, "voodoo" curses and demonic possession merely regarded as generic horror tropes that directors have mixed at will since the 1930s. But the issue of the zombie's readiness for extermination, though different in both cases, remains a shared characteristic of both. On the borderline between the living and the transitioning dead in flesh-eating zombie films, the difference between the proper and fully human, and the abject, inhuman monstrosity is endlessly re-enacted. But unlike the moment of spirit possession, transition into a flesh-eating zombie is an *irreversible* process that confronts the living with an absolute ultimatum: to kill it or be killed. In this sense it operates at the hard end of the human condition in pure survival (or species war) mode. In *D-volution* the transitioning female is momentarily brought back to sentient consciousness when she recognises the wedding ring on her partner's finger, a sign of her human attachment to the rites and rituals of modern, Christian kinship structures. It is a moment of moral ambiguity when the question of whether or not she is, or will become, a zombie fluctuates between two absolutely opposed states of being. And it is precisely because she momentarily slips back into her remembered, human "self" that her partner seizes the moment to blow her brains out. In *A Voodoo Possession* the spirit of the flesh-eating zombie is replaced by a

---

4 Penn was made Ambassador-at-Large for Haiti by President Martelly in January 2012.

sequence of blood-thirsty demonic entities all seeking to eat the souls of the various protagonists, whose morally compromised pasts form an interconnected labyrinth of traumagenic fantasy-production they all try to escape. It exploits many of the generic traits of earlier Voodoo-horror films, including a nail-fetish doll made from chicken entrails and a sacrifice ceremony that exceeds the 1941 *King of the Zombies* for sheer absurdity. Yveline Montasee, the hospital's director, like the Cathy Tyson character in *The Serpent and the Rainbow,* speaks with an improbable Creole-accented English as she shows the American news team around the semi-derelict institution, explaining that in Haitian culture mental illness is "highly stigmatised" and that the village where the hospital is located has "many secrets". In the dismal, barely lit corridors they encounter a compulsively rocking, clapping and fidgeting patient, and another, so violent that he has to be bound with chains, who leaps at the visitors babbling incoherent gibberish. Montase explains to the news crew that, because they are in a mental hospital with very few staff, some of the patients *have* to be restrained. The scene is an echo of one in *The Serpent and the Rainbow,* where Dr. Duchamp, when asked about the need to have patients manacled in the Port-au-Prince mental hospital, explains "Five hundred patients, three doctors, fifteen nurses, a week's supply of Thorazine: Handcuffs are the only thing in Haiti Duvalier makes sure Haiti has enough of". The inference, carried over from the earlier film to the current one, is that the insanity of the patients and the violence of their treatment are both peculiarly mired in the history and culture of this mysterious island, a place full of secrets that the locals keep "even from themselves". As such the "repressed secrets" of Vodou are made to coincide precisely with the repressed traumas of emotionally troubled and guilt-ridden Americans in search of answers for their spiritual woes in the gloomy labyrinth of an imaginary Haitian mental hospital.

Aiden, who has been popping Benazone [sic] for five years to stop himself jumping off a bridge in his sleep, finds video footage recorded when his brother was working with Happy Man, the babbling patient in chains. In a file labelled "Re: Voodoo Research" Cody explains to the camera, that in this particular entry of "Project Resurrection", they will be exploring Vodou's role in seizures associated with autoscopy in central lobe epilepsy.[5] Happy Man, it transpires, like

---

5 Autoscopy refers to the experience of an individual that they are

Christophe in *The Serpent and the Rainbow*, was a school principal who, during the earthquake, had seen many of his students die. Cody, assuming that he could not cope with the guilt, had diagnosed him with Post-Traumatic Stress Disorder. Like the stereotypical Baron Samedi figure from *Live and Let Die*, Happy Man is always laughing and, in his delirium, he has taken to drawing Vodou symbols on the walls of his cell. When Cody suggests bringing in the Vodou priest Papa J. from the local village to help analyse the drawings, he is told by the hospital administrator, Billy Kross, that "the Vodou in this place is off the deep end, even for Haiti. I don't like swimming in the deep end". "The fact that the village is a magnet for black magic" Cody suggests, "could be a Godsend". The villagers believe that the patients are not sick, Billy explains, but possessed by Vodou spirits. In entry twelve of Project Resurrection we see Billy Kross giving an elementary class in "Vodou 101" to Immanuel, the invisible cameraperson, illustrated by three cartoon images of Vodou deities: Enzulie [sic] Dantor ("Goddess of Romance and Jealousy"), Baron Samedi ("God of Death") and Kalfu ("Guardian of the entrance to the Spirit World"). He explains that the different Vodou groups worship differently, and that the local villagers and Papa J, believe that the spirits reside in *La Fe Vodou*, where the gods keep their possessed souls. Billy then explains that the Bizango - a "black magic secret society of sorcerers who use Vodou to serve the more evil and violent spirits" - were rumoured to have been kidnapping patients from the hospital for human sacrifices. The file freezes menacingly on the image of Kalfu, keeper of the Voodoo-horror-psychopathology crossroads since *I Walked with a Zombie*.

A Vodou priest called Jean Drouillard, Papa J's assistant, arrives

---

experiencing the environment from outside their body. The association of Vodou possession with epilepsy has been made by researchers working out of universities in Florida. In 'Epilepsy and Religious Experiences: Voodoo Possession' E. Carrazana *et al* discussed five cases of Vodou possession associated with epileptic seizures that had come to their attention in Florida hospitals. The article notes that personal ailments experienced by individuals in Haiti are traditionally attributed to the intervention of a *lwa*. In the five cases discussed seizures were variously attributed to possession by the *lwa* Ogu, Marinette-bwa-cheche, Melle Charlotte and spirits of the dead.

unexpectedly just as Aiden had given up hope of speaking to anyone about what had happened to his brother. When Drouillard advises him that he and his team should leave the village, Aiden asks if he is trying to scare them away with his "voodoo bullshit". "Aah! Stupid Americans" Drouillard sighs, "Voodoo is a world religion. Over four hundred years old. It's a mélange of African traditions and European Christianity. You should not reject what you do not understand. You should not fear the people of Haiti, you should fear its spirits. What happens to all of us in life is the will of the Spirits. They must be honoured in ceremony and ritual. If the Spirits are satisfied with their offerings they will bring good fortune". "And if they're not satisfied?" Aiden asks, "What do they bring?" "Punishment", Drouillard replies. "By whom? The Spirits... or the Bizango?" Aiden asks. As Drouillard stands up to leave, Aiden stops him. He shows him the video he has of Cody performing experiments on the patients, which convinces Drouillard to stay. He explains that Papa J also disappeared the same time as Cody and that he had been looking for him too, until now.

In the last remaining videos we see Cody describing numerous paranormal phenomena occurring in Happy Man's room: floating chairs, bleeding walls and bloody hand prints appearing on the walls. Happy Man has now been tied to the wall by Billy Kross who insists that Vodou is not the answer. "I am trying to use it to save them!' Cody shouts, "They believe they're cursed. They have to confront that curse in their own minds." "What do you know about being cursed?" Kross asks. "Everything", Cody replies, "We all have our demons Kross, even you... What would you give to be rid of that thing that haunts you the most?" "Anything", Kross says. "So would they", Cody replies, as Happy Man cackles in the corner. Then, as Aiden puts his hand to the screen of the tablet to touch the image of his brother's hand, he finds himself transported to his childhood basement, now full of polythene sheets smeared with blood, where his brother Cody warns him that someone is coming for him. "Who is coming for me?" he asks. "The Tormentor", Cody replies. Aiden turns to see a shadow retreating behind him and when he turns back to Cody he has been replaced by Happy Man, who lunges at him, jolting him back into reality.

Back in the hospital with Drouillard Aiden explains what just happened to him, noting that in the dream he was standing on a *vévé* shown in the video. The *houngan* consults his notebook, finds a match for the image on the screen, and explains that it is a *vévé* for Kalfu.

He concludes that the spirits must be using his memories to draw the two brothers together. To find out why, they consult the spirit that is possessing Happy Man. Later that night they perform a ceremony to make contact with the spirit. Drouillard explains that the spirit likes the taste of warm, fresh blood, and that sometimes it possesses people in order to continue its quest for more. Happy Man is brought to stand in the centre of the room. After having chopped the head off a chicken and poured its blood into a bowl, Drouillard holds it over Happy Man's head. As the other patients in the hospital become audibly agitated, Happy Man begins to writhe and convulse spasmodically on the floor before suddenly getting to his feet. He now has the telltale blind, staring eyes of the possessed. Drouillard, himself in trance, announces the arrival of Lenglessou, spirit of vengeance, and explains that Cody's soul is trapped with an evil sorcerer, who must be found in order to free him.[6] Happy Man draws a white cross on his face and babbles something in an incomprehensible language. "If you rescue him from the dungeon, I will let you go in peace", Drouillard translates, "but if you do not, you will pay homage to me for eternity". Happy Man than grabs a machete, impales Montase's hand with it, slashes the solitary drummer across the face and grabs Bree, as the remaining members of the news team are plunged into the parallel reality in which Cody's soul is trapped.

FEEDING DEMONS HUNGRY FOR BLOOD

The scene of Happy Man being possessed by Lenglessou brings together two archetypical stereotypes of Voodoo-horror which, as we have seen, have correlations in the foundation myth of Haitian independence as re-imagined by Haitian nationalists, Romantic French abolitionists and a generation of writers who lived through a foreign occupation that was widely regarded as essentially racist and neo-colonial in character: spirit possession and blood sacrifice. The latter continues to be one of the most fascinating and damning aspects of Vodou rites

---

6 Linglessu, or Lenglessou Bassin Sang (Bucket of Blood), is, according to Simpson, a violent and dangerous *lwa*, associated with the Petro rite, who is known to eat glass. According to Métraux, Linglessu is also a Freemason (Métraux 157).

for outside observers, most examples of Voodoo-horror intimating its horrible, sanguinary powers at the dark heart of the religion, and often assuming human sacrifice to be its ultimate expression. In *A Voodoo Possession* the religion is framed as one in which the *lwa*'s demand for blood sacrifice is an ever-escalating one that drives *serviteurs* to ever greater levels of blood letting, believing, in their deluded way, that this will redeem them of the sins of their fathers. From this perspective the "Blood Pact with Satan" version of Bois Caïman promulgated by contemporary Evangelical Christians, and popularised shortly after the 2010 earthquake by Pat Robinson, is echoed in a third-rate horror film from four years later in ways that perpetuate the idea that Haiti is cursed by the spirits its people worship. Seen through the chimerical optic of *A Voodoo Possession*, especially as it has been re-framed by writers like Reginald Crosley and others promulgating the Jean Vixamar-Legrande and Simbi-Makaya hypotheses, the Bois Caïman ceremony can look like a rite of blood sacrifice through which the violent African *lwa* of war and insurrection were summoned into the bodies of the revolutionary *serviteurs*, and the revolution a sanguinary expression of the mystical and insatiable appetites of savage Black gods, incarnated in fanatical slave armies. In the case of Happy Man the particular spirit is a bloodthirsty *lwa* called Lenglessou Bassin Sang (Lenglessou 'Bucket of Blood') associated in Haitian Vodou, like those reputedly summoned at Bois Caïman, with the Petro rite. Although Happy Man is not a cannibal, when possessed by Lenglessou he takes on a character much closer to the flesh-eating zombies that departed ways with their folkloric ancestor several decades earlier. But the awful exoticism of archaic blood sacrifice that, partly as a consequence of William Seabrook's stories about "Phantom Haiti" in the 1930s, seems to carry with it an echo of the bloody glories of the Haitian Revolution is re-configured as an act of mystical and massively de-personalised social potlatch. And the sadistic fantasies of revolutionary Surrealists would probably not see a great difference between the two kinds of being – cadaverous zombie-slave and insurrectionary flesh-eater – both horribly inhuman and mentally deranged in their own abject and bloodthirsty ways. So although there is no direct reference to slavery or the Haitian Revolution in either *A Voodoo Possession* or recent apocalyptic zombie films like *World War Z*, from the perspective of *Undead Uprising*, which is, in many ways, a perspective drawn directly from Bataille, both films refer, in genealogical terms, to traditional representations of unthinkable human monstrosity whose images the historical home of Vodou has been tarred with since colonial times. In this sense the tradition of Voodoo-horror that culminates in the flesh-eating zombie apocalypse re-stages in spectacular hyperbolic form the imaginings of Bataille on the eve of a war that promised to deliver even greater violence, loss and suffering on an even greater scale than the one Europe was still reeling from. Bataille's response to horror on such a massive scale was to stare into the face of the immense night of "human nature", as Hegel had done a century before when Napoleon, the great hero of Universal History, who had attempted to re-institute slavery to Haiti at any "human" price, rode into Jena, like the World Spirit on horseback.

In the final scenes of *A Voodoo Possession*, having travelled through the convoluted, interwoven labyrinth of the American film crew's guilt-ridden childhood memories – where they were stalked by a gibbering, machete-wielding Happy Man-Lenglessou – and having discovered that Cody, Aiden and Bree had some unresolved interpersonal issues through the intra-dimensional mediation of a Go Crocs poster, we learn that as a child Cody had been sexually abused by their stepfather Bob. Cody and Aiden had poisoned him and Aiden finished him off with a spade, just as their mom came in from the store. Cody had blamed Aiden for the murder and their mother, riddled with guilt, had chopped up his body and buried the parts in the basement. In one of the most embarrassing scenes in the film, Aiden, trapped in "Voodoo Hell", explains how his mother had hypnotised the boys into making them forget their memories. As he does so a Black woman in a white dress and headscarf shakes some odd-looking rattles in front of a television-set tuned to white noise, as Aiden, his childhood self, Cody and Bree stare blankly into space. Their mother, unable to cope, had killed herself by falling from a ladder onto a knife and the spirit of her guilt had returned in the form of The Tormentor to plague the brothers' dreams. Aiden Chase's journey into the repressed memories of his brother's sexual abuse and subsequent patricide are mediated through a narrative that uses post-earthquake Haiti and a "Voodoo 101" version of the religion as the flimsiest of pretexts to stage one of the most stereotypical Voodoo-horror narratives yet brought to film.

INTIMATIONS OF A PHANTOM HAITI (REVISITED)

Haiti, that dysfunctional, barbaric, undemocratic, and undemocratizable Haiti fatally prone to ever-renewed disasters, is a fantasy. It remains and returns endlessly, however, because this site has the misfortune of constituting an essential fantasy of Haiti's big Other: the fantasy [of] an eminently democratic, developed, and civilised nation. Haiti is the fantasy projection, the negative kernel of the real that so effectively sustains North American misunderstanding and disavowal [of itself]... Haiti is the impossible truth, the inadmissible real, of North Atlantic democratic self-identity.

- Nick Nesbitt, 'Haiti, the Monstrous Anomaly' (2013)

It's easy to fear the things we don't understand. We just need to understand it.

- Cody Chase, "The Vanishing Doctor" in *A Voodoo Possession*

I have been very aware while writing this book that to characterise contemporary zombie narratives as rooted in the history of Haiti was to risk repeating the pattern of Haitian exceptionalism that has been a great political and cultural burden on the nation since independence. I hope I have managed to counter that tendency by giving a more sober account of the republic's two-hundred-year history than that garnered from the chimerical optics of Voodoo-horror. In an attempt to correct the distortions and stereotypes they exploit and perpetuate, I have re-contextualised the Haiti of Voodoo-horror and zombie fantasies with the realities of the actual country at the time those representations were playing to audiences elsewhere. But as I suggested in the preface the "real" Haiti beyond the sensational distortions is still an "imaginary" one, the product of a different kind of discourse, more academic, trustworthy and respectable perhaps, but no less "immaterial" for that.

In her introduction to *Infectious Rhythm* – 'Haiti is Here/Haiti is not Here' – Barbara Browning evokes an idea of Haiti as both a concrete geographical place and an imaginary site of colonial fantasy for Americans and Europeans. Her title intimates the peculiar blending of popular fantasy and social fact that has often characterised representations of Haiti in popular culture and the sense that, whether we have been there or not, many of us carry a fantastical image of the country in our minds constructed from fragments drawn from a range of popular sources. The Haiti of which Browning writes, therefore, is simultaneously a *real* Haiti as it exists in actuality, and a *phantom* Haiti that exists primarily in the narratives and discourses that have represented it, and the imaginations of those who encounter them. These two Haitis are inseparable for Browning, asserting as she does, that Haiti has been shaped in dramatic and very real ways by the (mis)representations that have been made of it, particularly those which circulate in the powerful nations which have the greatest ideological investment in Haiti's past, present and future. And even in the most seemingly sober-minded of academic contexts the references to the real Haiti flow seamlessly into its most parodic, sinister and exotic misrepresentations.

What makes *A Voodoo Possession* such an appropriate film to close *Undead Uprising*, is the very fact that the Haiti it depicts, while making a direct reference to a real disaster that brought the country to international attention four years earlier, does so in ways that tell us nothing about the country, the ongoing suffering of those affected by the earthquake, the reasons why so many people died, the cholera epidemic subsequently introduced by UN troops that has killed over 8,000 people since 2010, the country's heroic history of struggle for independence after centuries of slavery, the consequences of two military occupations and the debacle of an international earthquake relief effort in which billions of dollars pledged for re-construction were redirected into the bank accounts of American contractors, the salaries of the CEOs of International NGOs, fleets of SUVs to drive their volunteer workers around the country and 5,000 American troops sent there to "secure the disaster".[7] Instead Haiti is used, in the most

---

7 In 2011 Gail McGovern, President and CEO of American Red Cross, boasted of having raised almost $500 million of relief money for Haiti since the earthquake a year earlier, in what was, at the time, one of the most successful fundraising campaigns in history. The charity claims that 90 cents of every dollar went to Haiti but an investigation by NPR and

trivial of ways, to stage a Voodoo-horror psychodrama about the sibling rivalry between two American brothers that blatantly exploits not only the most stereotypical and macabre elements of Vodou lore, but also the suffering of hundreds of thousands of Haitians directly affected by the earthquake, either through injury, loss of homes or the death of loved ones and relatives. Moreover it unintentionally perpetuates Evangelical Christian narratives about Haiti, imported from the United States, that came to the fore in the immediate aftermath of the earthquake that framed the Bois Caïman ceremony as a "Blood Pact with Satan" that had been the source of Haiti's woes ever since. Ironically, given its reception by serious scholars of Vodou at the time, and its lack of serious critical attention since then, compared to a film like *A Voodoo Possession*, Seabrook's *The Magic Island* reads like a masterpiece of responsible scholarship that still tells us more about the realities of Haiti than any of the Voodoo-horror films or sensationalist travelogues that followed in its wake.

Characteristically, in the popular fictions that followed Seabrook, the actual practice of Vodou is represented in a caricatured form that tells us next to nothing about its subtleties, complexities and spiritual values for practicing *Vodouisants*. In them it is used almost exclusively to express mysterious supernatural forces and popular beliefs that have become characteristic of Haiti's "exceptional" image to the outside world. The chimerical optics of Voodoo-horror, when analysed from the perspectives introduced at the beginning of the book, do enable a story to be told about Haiti's post-colonial history and the centrality of the categories of race, class and religion therein. But they do not do this alone. For the historical background to come into clearer focus one

---

ProPublica in 2015 discovered that only a fraction had actually been spent in Haiti, and claims on the charity's website that it had created 130,000 new homes were refuted by evidence that by June 2015 only 6 permanent new houses had been built. The 130,000 figure, it turns out, was the amount of people who went to a seminar about how to fix up their own homes and receive temporary shelters. As with many of the NGOs that rushed into Haiti in the aftermath of the earthquake, most of the senior project managers and international volunteers for the Red Cross spoke neither French nor Creole. See Laura Sullivan, 'In Search of the Red Cross's $500 million in Haiti Relief' NPR June 3rd, 2015.

must re-frame them in the historical contexts in which they were made. Or, in the words of the Hegelian-Marxist philosopher and theorist of the postmodern, Fredric Jameson, we must "always historicize" them. What seems clear from the examples discussed here is a remarkable continuity of stereotypical tropes in the representation of Vodou that have been present since Moreau De Saint-Méry's history of Saint-Domingue of 1789. One could feasibly call this pattern a conspiratorial continuum, implicitly or explicitly designed to morally undermine the image of Haiti to the outside world, as several Haitian and non-Haitian intellectuals over the centuries have convincingly argued. But what has also become evident is that indigenous attempts to counter foreign misrepresentations of Haiti and the culture of Vodou have at times backfired, lending fresh fuel to those who would condemn the country to irredeemable barbarism, such as the Evangelical Christian movements, discussed by Elizabeth McAlister, who have re-defined the Bois Caïman ceremony as a compact with Satan that has doomed the nation to endless calamity, in ways that echo Spenser St. John over a century before. It is an idea perpetuated by films like *A Voodoo Possession* in which middle-class Americans travel to Haiti to do good for its suffering poor, only to encounter a culture of blood-thirsty demons who have more power over Haitian minds than "western knowledge and medicine", as Yveline Montase, the director of the NGO hospital, puts it in the film.

To the extent that a distorted history of Vodou, informed by Voodoo-horror and its chimerical optics, continues to perpetuate sensationalistic and macabre images of the life and culture of Haiti and its peoples, it is still implicated in creating an image of Haiti to the outside world of a land mired in "primitive superstition" and irredeemable moral corruption. Like so many of the examples discussed here, *A Voodoo Possession* pits a resilient White, American male, a romantically involved female counterpart, and a sympathetic Haitian native, against the dark forces of Vodou, in order to perform an act of redemptive moral heroism. As such it is in keeping with a paternalistic U.S. ideology which has historically depicted Haitian Vodou as a barbaric and primitive religion. But beyond exploiting these generic sensationalistic tropes to mask the magnitude of the suffering of people in post-earthquake Haiti and the failure of the American government, despite its stated best intentions to do so, to ameliorate that suffering, a film like *A Voodoo Possession* is unlikely to have a significant impact on U.S. foreign policy decisions towards Haiti or the life of the people who live there. Certainly, as Dorsainvil, Herskovits, Price-Mars and others argued in the 1920s and '30s, and many others have since then, Haiti has been served badly by such representations, and the examples of Voodoo-horror and zombie films I have looked at here have done nothing to reverse that trend. But beyond perpetuating generic fantasies about a country that their audiences would be hard pushed to find on a map, most of the films and books discussed here can be given short shrift in terms of the historical and political realities of Haiti.

Critical commentators on contemporary apocalyptic zombie narratives, like Gerry Canavan, Patrick Mahoney and Jason Wallin, remind us that the logics of slavery, assimilation and extermination that characterised the patterns of European colonial expansion and the colonial phase of mercantile capitalism did not suddenly come to an end with Revolutionary Republicanism, the Universal Declaration of Human Rights or the abolition of slavery. According to the definition of Article 2 of the 1948 Convention of the Prevention and Punishment of the Crime of Genocide, between the publication of *The Magic Island* and the release of *World War Z*, the world witnessed some of the greatest genocides in history. Over the last century tens of millions of human beings, marked by their ethnic, linguistic, religious or racial difference, were subject to the "zombic logic" of quarantine, reduction to slavery and extermination.

Unlike *A Voodoo Possession*, films like *The Comedians*, *The Serpent and the Rainbow* and *Ghosts of Cité Soleil*, which purport to give an "insider's" view of the country, are more complicated cases, bringing us towards a murkier dimension of outside representations of Haiti that are closely tied to the real politics of the country and the covert manipulation of national and international media that could conceivably be understood as a form of contemporary "Black Ops". From Ian Fleming's *Live and Let Die* to *Ghosts of Cité Soleil*, nefarious political and economic interests, both inside and outside of Haiti, have sought to manipulate popular misconceptions about the country and its religion for covert propagandistic purposes. This complex play of endogenous and exogenous representations of Haiti seems to have emerged most markedly during the Duvalier era when the myth and reality of the "Voodoo Dictator" and his "Zombie Nation" became muddied by the play of cold war politics and covert intelligence operations, used at times to support the regime in its fight against communism, and at others to undermine it as a regional economic and human rights "Basket Case". That this occurred at the height of cold war conspiracy theories, when the control and manipulation of international public opinion through the use of popular culture and mass media became the object of widespread awareness, helps us frame the war of claims and counter-claims about the extent of the political use of Vodou in Haiti by Duvalier and his detractors. But since then it has been harder to clearly separate "black propaganda" from reactionary anti-Black and anti-communist politics in Haiti, a difference, long fought over inside Haiti herself, which finds its philosophical limit case in the legendary dialectical synthesis of Masters and Slaves that retrospectively put the revolutionary and world-changing Black Republic at the forefront of modern History, while simultaneously marking it, in the eyes of incredulous White imperialists, as a site of unspeakable revolutionary horror and immanent, race-bound catastrophe.

BIBLIOGRAPHY

Abbott, Elizabeth *Haiti: The Duvaliers and their Legacy* (1991) Robert Hale: London

Ackerman, Hans-W. and Gauthier, Jeanine 'The Ways and Nature of the Zombi' *The Journal of American Folklore*, Vol. 104, No 212 (Autumn 1991) 466-494

Ades, Dawn and Baker, Simon *Undercover Surrealism: Georges Bataille and DOCUMENTS* (2006) Hayward Gallery/MIT Press: London/Cambridge

Agamben, Giorgio *Homo Sacer: Sovereign Power and Bare Life* (1998)Stanford University Press: Stanford

Agamben, Giorgio *The Open: Man and Animal* (2004) Stanford University Press: Stanford

Andriopoulos, Stefan *Possessed: Hypnotic Crimes, Corporate Fiction and the Invention of Cinema* (2008) University of Chicago Press: Chicago, Illinois

Apollon, Willy *Le vaudou: Un espace pour les "voix"* (1976) Editions Galilee: Paris

Apollon, Willy 'Vodou: The Crisis of Possession' (1999) Translated by Peter Canning and Tracy McNulty, University of Southern California: Los Angeles

Archer-Straw, Petrine *Negrophilia: Avant-Garde Paris and Black Culture in the 1920s* (2000) Thames and Hudson: London

Aristide, Jean Bertrand 'Umoya Wamagama (The Spirit of the Worlds)', PhD thesis in African Languages from the department of Literature and Philosophy, University of South Africa, November 2006

Auguste, Max (*et al*) *Graham Greene Démasqué (Graham Greene Finally Exposed)* (1968) Bulletin du departement des affaires étrangèrs, republique d'Haiti, Imprimerie Theodore: Port-au-Prince

Bansak, Edmund G. *Fearing the Dark: The Val Lewton Career* (1995)McFarland and Company: Jefferson, North Carolina

BIBLIOGRAPHY

Barlow, Geoffrey and Hill, Alison (eds) *Video Violence and Children* (1985) Hodder Arnold H&S: London

Barnes, Sandra T. *Africa's Ogun: Old World and New* (1997) Indiana University Press: Bloomington and Indianapolis

Barnett, Stuart *Hegel After Derrida* (1998) Routledge: London

Bastien, Rémy and Courlander, Harold *Religion and Politics in Haiti* (1966) Institute for Cross-Cultural Research: Washington D.C.

Bataille, Georges *Visions of Excess: Selected Writings 1927-39* (1985) Manchester University Press: Manchester

Bataille, Georges *Writings on Laughter, Sacrifice, Nietzsche, Unknowing October 36* (1986) MIT Press: Cambridge, Massachusetts

Bataille, Georges *The Accursed Share: An Essay on General Economy: Volume I* (1988) Zone Books: New York

Bataille, Georges *The Accursed Share: An Essay on General Economy: Volumes II and III* (1993) Zone Books: New York

Bataille, Georges and Strauss, Jonathan *On Bataille* (1990) Yale University Press: Yale

Bataille, Georges *The Tears of Eros* (1989) City Lights: San Francisco

Bataille, Georges *Theory of Religion* (1992) Zone Books: New York

Bataille, Georges and Leiris, Michel *Correspondence* (2008) Seagull Books: Calcutta, London, New York

Bellegarde, Dantès *Histoire du peuple haïtien 1492-1952* (1953) Port-Au Prince

Benedicty-Kokken, Alessandra *Spirit Possession in French, Haitian, and Vodou Thought: An Intellectual History* (2015) Lexington Books: Lanham, Boulder, New York, London

Bernasconi, Robert 'Hegel at the Court of the Ashanti' in *Hegel After Derrida* (1998) Stuart Barnett (ed), Routledge: London

Bernasconi, Robert (ed) *Race* (2001) Blackwell: Malden, Massachusetts

Bird-David, Nurit '"Animism" Revisited – Personhood, Environment and Relational Epistemology' *Current Anthropology*, Vol. 40, Supplement, February 1999

Black, David *The Plague Years: A Chronicle of AIDS, the Epidemic of Our Time* (1986) Picador/Pan: London

Blessebois, Pierre-Corneille *Le zombi du grand-Pérou ou La comtesse de Cocagne* (1797/1862) Academic Press: Paris

Bogousslavsky, Julien, Walusinski, Olivier and Veyrunes, Denis 'Crime, Hysteria and *Belle Époque* Hypnotism: The Path Traced by Jean Martin Charcot and Georges Gilles de la Tourrette' *European Neurology* 62: (2009) 193-199

Boldt-Irons, Leslie Anne (ed) *On Bataille: Critical Essays* (1995) State University of New York Press: Albany

Boluk, Stephanie and Lenz, Wylie *Generation Zombie: Essays on the Living Dead in Modern Culture* (2011) McFarland and Company Inc: Jefferson North Carolina

Bonetto, Sandra 'Race and Racism in Hegel - An Analysis' *Minerva – An Internet Journal of Philosophy* 10 (2006): 35-64

Bonsal, Stephen *The American Mediterranean* (1913) Moffat, Yard and Company: New York

Booth, William 'Voodoo Science' *Science*, New Series, Vol. 240, No 4850 (April 15, 1988) 274-277

Bourguignon, Erika 'The Persistence of Folk Belief: Some Notes on Cannibalism and Zombis in Haiti' *The Journal of American Folklore* Vol. 72, No 283 (January - March, 1959) 36-46

BIBLIOGRAPHY

Bourguignon, Erika (ed) *Religion, Altered States of Consciousness and Social Change* (1973) Ohio State University Press: Columbus

Brennan, Michael G. *Graham Greene: Fictions, Faith and Authorship* (2010) Continuum Books: London/New York

Browning, Barbara *Infectious Rhythm: Metaphors of Contagion and the Spread of African Culture* (1998) Routledge: London/New York

Buck-Morss, Susan *Hegel, Haiti and Universal History* (2009) University of Pittsburgh Press: Pittsburgh, Pennsylvania

Burke, John *Dr. Terror's House of Horrors* (1965) Pan Books: London

Calder Williams, Evan *Combined and Uneven Apocalypse* (2011) Zero Books: Ropley, U.K.

Canavan, Gerry 'Fighting a war you've already lost: Zombies and zombis in *Firefly, Serenity and Dollhouse*' *Science Fiction Film and Television*, Vol.4, Issue 2, (Autumn 2011), 173-203

Canini, Mikko (ed) *The Domination of Fear* (2010) Rodopi: Amsterdam/New York

Carroll, Noël *The Philosophy of Horror: or Paradoxes of the Heart* (1990) Routledge: New York and London

Castle, Terry 'Phantasmagoria; Spectral Technology and the Metaphorics of Modern Reverie' *Critical Enquiry* 15 (1988) 6-61

Césaire, Aimé *Toussaint Louverture: La Révolution Française et le problème colonial* (1962) Présence Africaine: Paris

Chancellor, Henry *James Bond: The Man and his World* (2005) John Murray: London

Comte de Chastenet de Puységur, Antoine Hyacinthe, 'Discours pronounce dans la société de l'Harmonie établie au Cap-Français (Haïti), pour des réceptions, en 1784' in *L'Hermés: Journal du Magnetisme Animal* Volume 3, Paris (1828)

Christie, Deborah and Lauro, Sarah Juliet (eds) *Better Off Dead: The Evolution of the Zombie as Post-Human* (2011) Fordham University Press: New York

Clarck-Taoua, Phyllis 'In Search of New Skin: Michel Leiris *L'Afrique Fantôme'* *Cahiers d'études africaines*, n167 (2002/3), 479-498

Clarke, Vévé A. *The Legend of Maya Deren Vol. 1* (1988) Anthology Film Archives: New York

Cleaver, Eldridge *Soul on Ice* (1969) Jonathan Cape: London

Comaroff, Jean and Comaroff, John L. 'Alien-Nation: Zombies, Immigrants, and Millennial Capitalism' *The South Atlantic Quarterly* Vol. 101, Issue 4 (March 2003), 779-805

Cosentino, Donald J. (ed) *In Extremis: Death and Life in 21st Century Haitian Art* (2012) University of California: Los Angeles

Courlander, Harold *Haiti Singing* (1939) University of North Carolina Press: Chapel Hill

Courlander, Harold *The Drum and the Hoe: Life and Lore of the Haitian People* (1960) University of California Press: Berkeley and Los Angeles

Crabtree, Adam *From Mesmer to Freud Magnetic Sleep and the Roots of Psychological Healing* (1993) Yale University Press: New Haven/London

Craige, John Houston *Black Bagdad* (1933) Minton, Balch & Company: New York

Craige, John Houston *Cannibal Cousins* (1935) Stanley Paul & Company: London

Crosley, Reginald *The Vodou Quantum Leap: Alternate Realities, Power and Mysticism* (2000) Llewellyn Publications: St. Paul, Minnesota

Darnton, Robert *Mesmerism and the End of the Enlightenment in France* (1968) Harvard University Press: Cambridge, Massachusetts and London

BIBLIOGRAPHY

Dash, J. Michael *Haiti and the United States: National Stereotypes and the Literary Imagination* (1997) MacMillan Press: London

Dash, Michael J *The Other America: Caribbean Literature in a New World Context* (1998) University of Virginia Press: Charlottesville and London

Davies, Owen *Grimoires: A History of Magic Books* (2009) Oxford University Press: Oxford

Davis, Beale *The Goat Without Horns* (1925) Brentano's: New York

Davis, Erik *Techgnosis: Myth, Magic and Mysticism in the Age of Information* (1999) Serpent's Tail: London

Davis, Wade *The Serpent and the Rainbow* (1986) Collins: London

Davis, Wade *Passage of Darkness: The Ethnobiology of the Haitian Zombie* (1988) University of North Carolina Press: Chapel Hill, North Carolina

Dayan, Joan *Haiti, History and the Gods* (1998) University of California Press: Berkeley and Los Angeles, California

Deleuze, Gilles and Guattari, Felix *Anti-Oedipus: Capitalism and Schizophrenia* (1983) Continuum Books: London/New York

Dépestre, René 'Hello and Goodbye to Negritude' *Africa in Latin America : Essays on History, Culture, and Socialization* (1984) Manuel Moreno Fraginals (ed), 251-72 New York: Holmes & Meier

Denis, Lorimer and Duvalier, François 'L'évolution stadiale du Vodou: Introduction à l'étude comparée des données historico-culturelles de la culture populaire et des origines ethniques du peuple haïtien' *Bulletin du Bureau d'Ethnologie*, 3 (1944) 9-32

Deren, Maya *Divine Horsemen: Voodoo Gods of Haiti* (1953/1970) Chelsea House: New York

Desmangles, Leslie G. *The Faces of the Gods – Vodou and Roman Catholicism in Haiti* (1992) University of North Carolina Press: Chapel Hill and London

Dick, Bernard F. *Radical Innocence: A Critical Study of the Hollywood Ten* (1989) University Press of Kentucky: Lexington

Deibert, Michael *Notes from the Last Testament: The Struggle for Haiti* (2005) Seven Stories Press: London, Melbourne, New York, Toronto

Diederich, Bernard and Burt, Al *Papa Doc: The Truth About Haiti Today* (1969) McGraw Hill: New York

Diederich, Bernard *The Murderers Among Us: History of Repression and Rebellion in Haiti Under Dr. François Duvalier, 1962–1971* (2011) Markus Wiener: Princeton

Diederich, Bernard *Seeds of Fiction: Graham Greene's Adventures in Haiti and Central America, 1954–1983* (2012) Peter Owen Publishing: London

Dorsainvil, J. C. *Vodou et névrose* (1931) La Presse: Port-au-Prince, Haiti

Dubois, Laurent 'The Citizen's Trance: The Haitian Revolution and the Motor of History' *Magic and Modernity: Interfaces of Revelation and Concealment* (2003) Birgit Meyer, Peter Pels (eds) Stanford University Press: Stanford

Dubois, Laurent *Avengers of the New World: The Story of the Haitian Revolution* (2004) Harvard University Press: Cambridge, Massachusetts

Dunham, Katherine *Island Possessed* (1969) University of Chicago Press: Chicago

Dupuy, Alex *Haiti in the World Economy: Class, Race and Underdevelopment since 1700* (1989) Westview Press: Boulder, Colorado

Dupuy, Alex *The Prophet and Power: Jean-Bertrand Aristide, the International Community and Haiti* (2007) Rowman and Littlefield: Lanham, Boulder, New York, Toronto and Plymouth, U.K.

Ellen, Roy 'Fetishism' *Man*, Vol. 23, No 2 (June, 1988) 213-235

BIBLIOGRAPHY

Ellenberger, Henri F. *The Discovery of the Unconscious: The History and Evolution of Dynamic Psychiatry* (1970) Basic Books: New York

Elmer, Simon *The Colour of the Sacred: Georges Bataille and the Image of Sacrifice* (2012) Self-published

Engels, Frederick *Dialectics of Nature* (1941) Lawrence and Wishart: London

Fanon, Frantz *Black Skin, White Masks* (1988) Pluto Press: London

Fay, Jennifer 'Dead Subjectivity: *White Zombie*, Black Baghdad' *CR: The New Centennial Review*, Vol. 8, Number 1, Spring 2008

Fermor, Patrick Leigh *The Traveller's Tree: A Journey Through the Caribbean Islands* (1950) Penguin: London

Filan, Kenaz *The Haitian Vodou Handbook: Protocols for Riding with the Lwa* (2007) Destiny Books: Rochester, Vermont

Firmin, Joseph Anténor *The Equality of Human Races (Positivist Anthropology)* (2002) University of Illinois Press: Illinois

Fisher, Sybille *Modernity Disavowed: Haiti and the Cultures of Slavery in the Age of Revolution* (2004) Duke University Press: Durham and London

Fisher, Sybille 'Haiti: Fantasies of Bare Life' *Small Axe*, Number 23 Vol. 11 Number 2, June 2007

Fleming, Ian *Live and Let Die* (1954) Pan Books: London

Fluehr-Lobban, Carolyn 'Anténor Firmin and Haiti's Contribution to Anthropology' *Gradhiva 1* 2005, 95-108,

Forsythe, David P. *Human Rights and US Foreign Policy: Congress Reconsidered* (1989) University Presses of Florida: Gainesville

Foucault, Michel *"Society Must be Defended" Lectures at the Collège de France 1975-76* (1997) Picador: New York

Fouchard, Jean *The Haitian Maroons: Liberty or Death* (1981) Edward W. Blyden Press: New York

Fournier, Arthur M. *The Zombie Curse – A Doctor's 25 Year Journey into the Heart of the AIDS Epidemic in Haiti* (2006) John Henry Press: NW Washington, D.C.

Gabriel, Markus and Žižek, Slavoj *Mythology, Madness, and Laughter: Subjectivity in German Idealism* (2009) Continuum Books: London/New York

Gauld, Alan *A History of Hypnotism* (1992) Cambridge University Press: Cambridge

Geggus, David Patrick *Haitian Revolutionary Studies* (2002) Indiana University Press: Bloomington

Geggus, Davic Patrick and Fiering, Norman (eds), *The World of the Haitian Revolution* (2009) Indiana University Press: Bloomington

Goldschmidt, Henry and McAlister, Elizabeth (eds) *Race, Nation and Religion in the Americas* (2004) Oxford University Press: Oxford

Goodman, Felicitas D. *How About Demons? Possession and Exorcism in the Modern World* (1988) Indiana University Press: Bloomington and Indianapolis

Greenfield, William R. 'Night of the Living Dead II: Slow Encephalopathies and AIDS: Do Necromantic Zombiists Transmit Virus HTLV-III/LAV During Voodooistic Rituals?' *JAMA Journal of the American Medical Association*, Vol. 256, no 16, October 24/31, 1986

Greenlee, Sam *The Spook Who Sat by the Door* (1969) Allison and Busby: London

Greene, Graham *The Comedians* (1966) Penguin Books: London

BIBLIOGRAPHY

Greene, Richard and Mohammad, K. Silem (eds) *The Undead and Philosophy: Chicken Soup for the Soulless* (2006) Open Court: Chicago and La Salle, Illinois

Hall, Robert Burnett 'The Société Congo of the Ile à Gonave' *American Anthropologist* 31 (1929) 685-700

Hallward, Peter *Damming the Flood: Haiti, Aristide, and the Politics of Containment* (2007) Verso: London/New York

Harper, Stephen 'Zombies, Malls, and the Consumerism Debate: George Romero's Dawn of the Dead' *Americana: The Journal of American Popular Culture (1900-present)*, Vol. 1, Issue 2, Fall 2002

Hegel, G. W. F. *The Philosophy of History* (1956) Dover: New York

Hegel, G. W. F. *Phenomenology of Spirit* (1977) Oxford University Press: Oxford

Heinl, Robert Debs and Heinl, Nancy Gordon *Written in Blood: The Story of the Haitian People 1492-1995* (2005) University Press of America: Maryland

Herskovits, Melville J. *Life in a Haitian Valley* (1964) Octagon Books: New York

Hoffmann, Leon Francois 'Representations of the Haitian Revolution in French Literature' *The World of the Haitian Revolution* (2009) (eds) Geggus, David Patrick and Fiering, Norman, Indiana University Press: Bloomington

Holly, Arthur C. *Les daïmons du culte voudo* (1918) Port-au-Prince

Holly, Arthur C. *Dra-Po: étude ésotérique de Égrégore africain, traditionnel, social et national de Haiti* (1928) Nemours Telhomme: Port-au-Prince

Holly, James Theodore *A vindication of the capacity of the Negro race for self government, and civilized progress, as demonstrated by historical events of the Haytian revolution: and the subsequent acts of that people since their national independence* (1857) AfricaAmerican Printing Company: New Jersey

Hurbon, Laënnec *Voodoo: Truth and Fantasy* (1995) Thames and Hudson: London

Hurbon, Laënnec 'American Fantasy and Haitian Vodou' *Sacred Arts of Haitian Vodou* (1995) UCLA Fowler Museum of Cultural History: Los Angeles

Hurston, Zora Neale *Tell My Horse: Voodoo and Life in Haiti and Jamaica* (2009) Harper Perennial Modern Classics: New York

Jagodzinski, Jan (ed) *Psychoanalysing Cinema: A Productive Encounter with Lacan, Deleuze and Zizek* (2012) Palgrave Macmillan: New York

James, C. L. R. *The Black Jacobins: Touissant L'Ouverture and the San Domingo Revolution* (1980) Allison and Busby: London

Johnson, Paul Christopher 'Secretism and the Apotheosis of Duvalier' *Journal of the American Academy of Religion*, Vol. 4, Issue 2, 2006, 420-445

Jorgenson, Carl 'Blacks in the ''60s: A Centennial Reprise' *Social Text*, No 9/10, The '60s without Apology (Spring - Summer, 1984), 313-317

Joseph, Celucien 'The Rhetoric of Prayer: Dutty Boukman, the Discourse of "Freedom from Below," and the Politics of God' *Journal of Race, Ethnicity and Religion*, Vol. 2, Issue 9, June 2011

Kirk, Robert 'Sentience and Behaviour' *Mind, New Series,* Vol. 83, no 329, 1974, 43-60

Kirk, Robert and Squires, Roger 'Zombies v Materialists' *Proceedings of the Aristotelian Society, Supplementary Volumes* Vol. 48, 1974, 135-163

Kittler, Friedrich *Gramophone, Film, Typewriter* (1999) Stanford University Press: Stanford

Kovats-Bernat, J. Christopher *Sleeping Rough in Port-au-Prince: An Ethnography of Street Children and Violence in Haiti* (2006) University of Florida Press: Gainesville

Kracauer, Siegfried *From Caligari to Hitler: A Psychological History of the German Film* (1947/2004) Princeton University Press: New Jersey

BIBLIOGRAPHY

Krauss, Rosalind *The Originality of the Avant-Garde and Other Modernist Myths* (1985) MIT Press: Cambridge

Lacan, Jacques *Écrits: A Selection* (1977) Tavistock: London

Laguerre, Michel *Voodoo and Politics in Haiti* (1989) St. Martin's Press: New York

Larsen, Lars Bang 'Zombies of Immaterial Labor: The Modern Monster and the Death of Death' *e-flux Journal* 15, April 2010

Law, Robin 'La cérémonie du Bois Caïman et le "pacte de sang" dahoméen' *L'Insurrection des esclaves de saint-Domingue* Maryse Villard (trans), *22-2 auot 1791* (2000) Editions Karthala: Paris

Lawless, Robert *Haiti's Bad Press* (1992) Shenkman Books: Rochester, Vermont

Lawtoo, Nidesh 'Bataille and the Birth of the Subject' *Angelaki*, 16:2 2011, 73-88

Lawtoo, Nidesh *The Phantom of the Ego: Modernism and the Mimetic Unconscious* (2013) Michigan State University Press: East Lansing Michigan

Le Bon, Gustave *The Crowd – A Study of the Popular Mind* (2001) Batoche Books: Kitchener, Ontario

Le Bon, Gustave *The Psychology of Peoples* (1898) Macmillan: New York

Léger, Jacques Nicolas *Haiti: Her History and Her Detractors* (1907) The Neale Publishing Company: Washington

Leiris, Michel 'L'Ile Magique' (1929) *Documents* Vol. 6

Leiris, Michel 'Sacrifice d'un taureau' (2005) *Gradhiva* Vol. 1, 233-242

Lepetit, Patrick *The Esoteric Secrets of Surrealism: Origins, Magic, and Secret Societies* (2014) Inner Traditions: Rochester, Vermont

Lévy-Bruhl, Lucien *The 'Soul' of the Primitive* (1965) George Allen and Unwin: London

Lewis, Wyndham, *Paleface: The Philosophy of the Melting Pot* (1972) Gordon Press: New York

Lewis, Wyndham *The Art of Being Ruled* (1989) Black Sparrow Press: Santa Rosa

Loederer, Richard A *Voodoo Fire in Haiti* (1937) The Mayflower Press: Plymouth, U.K.

Lowenstein, Adam *Shocking Representation: Historical Trauma, National Cinema, and the Modern Horror Film* (2005) Columbia University Press: New York

Lycett, Andrew *Ian Fleming* (1996) Phoenix: London

MacCormack, Patricia *Cinesexuality* (2008) Ashgate: Aldershot

Mackay, Robin and Avanessian, Armen *#Accelerate: the Accelerationist Reader* (2014) Urbanomic: Falmouth, U.K.

Magloire, Gérarde 'Haitian-ness, Frenchness and History: Historicizing the French Component of Haitian National Identity' *Pouvoires Dans La Caraïbe: Revue Du CRPLC*, Spécial (1998)

Magloire, Gérarde and Yelvington, Kevin A. 'Haiti and the anthropological imagination' *Gradhiva*, 1, 2005, 127-152

Magloire-Danton, Gérarde 'Anténor Firmin and Jean Price-Mars: Revolution, Memory, Humanism' *Small Axe 92*, 2005, 150-170

Mars, Louis P. 'The Story of Zombi in Haiti' *Man*, Vol. 45, 1945, 38-40

Marx, Karl *Capital: A Critique of Political Economy 'Volume One* (1976) Penguin Books: London

Matheson, Richard *I Am Legend* (1954/2001) Gollancz: London

BIBLIOGRAPHY

Mbembe, Achille *On the Postcolony* (2001) University of California Press: Berkeley, Los Angeles

Mbembe, Achille 'Necropolitics' *Public Culture* 15(1), 2003, 11-40

McAlister, Elizabeth 'A Sorcerer's Bottle: The Visual Art of Magic in Haiti' in *Sacred Arts of Haitian Vodou* (1995) Donald J. Cosentino (ed), UCLA Fowler Museum of Cultural History: Los Angeles

McAlister, Elizabeth, 'Slaves, Cannibals, and Infected Hyper-Whites: The Race and Religion of Zombies', Wesleyan University, Division II Faculty Publications, Social Sciences, Paper 115, January 2012

McAlister, Elizabeth 'From Slave Revolt to a Blood Pact with Satan: The Evangelical Rewriting of Haitian History' in Polyné (2013)

McClellan III, James E. *Colonialism and Science – Saint Domingue in the Old Regime* (1992) John Hopkins University Press: London

McLuhan, Marshall *Understanding Media: The Extensions of Man* (1964) McGraw-Hill: New York, Toronto, London

McLuhan, Marshall 'The Playboy Interview: Marshall McLuhan' *Playboy*, March 1969

Meyer, Birgit and Pels, Peter *Magic and Modernity: Interfaces of Revelation and Concealment* (2003): Stanford University Press: California

Métraux, Alfred *Voodoo in Haiti* (1972) Schocken: New York

Midelfort, H. C. Erik *Exorcism and Enlightenment: Johann Joseph Gassner and the Demons of Eighteenth-Century Germany* (2005) Yale University Press: New Haven

Moreau de Saint-Méry, Médéric Louis-Elie *Description topographique, physique, civile, politique et historique de la partie française de l'isle Saint- Domingue* (1797-8) Callow Hill Streets (Philadelphia) Librarie Dupont (Paris) and Hamburg

Moreau de Saint-Méry, Médéric Louis-Elie *A Civilisation that Perished – The Last Years of White Colonial Rule in Haiti* Translated, Abridged and Edited by Ivor D. Spencer (1985) University of America Press: Lanham, Maryland

Moreman, Christopher M. and Rushton, Cory James (eds) *Race, Oppression and the Zombie: Essays on Cross-Cultural Appropriations of the Caribbean Tradition* (2011) MacFarland & Co: Jefferson, North Carolina

Moten, Fred *In The Break – The Aesthetics of the Black Radical Tradition* (2003) University of Minnesota Press: Minnesota

Moten, Fred 'Black Kant (Pronounced Kan't)' Lecture given at Kelly Writer's House, University of Pennsylvania, February 27 2007

Muir, John Kenneth *Wes Craven: The Art of Horror* (1998) MacFarland: Jefferson

Munro, Martin *Different Drummers: Rhythm and Race in the Americas* (2010) University of California Press: Berkeley and Los Angeles

Münsterberg, Hugo *The Photoplay: A Psychological Study* (1916) D. Appleton and Company: New York and London

Nemerov, Alexander *Icons of Grief: Val Lewton's Home Front Pictures* (2005) University of California Press: Los Angleles

Nesbitt, Nick *Universal Emancipation: The Haitian Revolution and the Radical Enlightenment* (2008) University of Virginia Press: Charlottesville and London

Newell, William W. 'Voodoo Worship and Child Sacrifice in Hayti' *The Journal of American Folklore*, Vol. 1, No 1 (April - June, 1888), 6-30

Nicholls, David *From Dessalines to Duvalier: Race, Colour and National Independence in Haiti* (1979) Cambridge University Press: Cambridge

BIBLIOGRAPHY

Olmos, Margarite Fernández and Paravisini-Gebert, Lizabeth (eds) *Sacred Possessions: Vodou, Santeria, Obeah, and the Caribbean* (2000) Rutgers University Press: New Brunswick, New Jersey and London

Oesterreich, T. K. *Possession: Demoniacal and Other among Primitive Races, in Antiquity, The Middle Ages, and Modern Times* (1930) Kegan, Paul, Trench, Trubner and Co. London

Paffenroth, Kim *Gospel of the Living Dead: George Romero's Visions of Hell on Earth* (2006) Baylor University Press: Waco, Texas

Palmié, Stephan *Wizards and Scientists – Explorations in Afro-Cuban Modernity & Tradition* (2002) Duke University Press: Durham

Palmié, Stephan 'Thinking with *Ngangas*: Reflections on Embodiment and the Limits of "Objectively Necessary Appearances"' *Comparative Studies in Society and History*, October 2006, Volume 48, Issue 4, 852-886

Parsons, Elsie Clews 'Spirit Cult in Hayti' *Journal de la Société des américanistes*, Volume 20, 1928, 157-179

Patterson, Kathy Davis 'Echoes of Dracula: Racial Politics and the Failure of Segregated Spaces in Richard Matheson's *I Am Legend*', *Journal of Dracula Studies* 7 2005

Patterson, Orlando *Slavery and Social Death – A Comparative Study* (1982) Harvard University Press: Cambridge, Massachusetts and London, England

Paravisini-Gebert, Lizabeth 'Women Possessed: Eroticism and Exoticism in the Representation of Woman as Zombie' *Sacred Possessions: Vodou, Santeria, Obeah and the Caribbean* (1997) New Brunswick: Rutgers University Press

Pellett, Gail 'Ti Legliz: Liberation Theology in Haiti' *New Age Magazine* July/August, 1986

Petit-M., La Martine *Vers un Nouvel Écho D'Haiti* (2011) Xlibiris

Pettinger, Alasdair 'From Vaudoux to Voodoo' *Forum of Modern Language Studies*, Vol. 40, No 4, 2004, 415-425

Pick, Daniel *Svengali's Web: The Alien Encounter in Modern Culture* (2000) Yale University Press: New Haven and London

Pietz, William 'The Problem of the Fetish, I' *RES: Anthropology and Aesthetics* No 9 (Spring), 1985, 5-17

Pietz, William 'The Problem of the Fetish, II' *RES: Anthropology and Aesthetics* No 13 (Spring), 1987, 23-45

Pietz, William 'The Problem of the Fetish, IIIa' *RES: Anthropology and Aesthetics* No 16 (Spring), 1988, 105-124

Piguenard, Jean Baptise *Zoflora; or, The Generous Negro Girl: A Colonial Story* (1804) Lackington, Allen and Co: London

Platt, Meredith *Storming the Gates of Bedlam: How Dr. Nathan Kline Transformed the Treatment of Mental Illness* (2012) DePew: Dumont, New Jersey

Polyné, Millery *The Idea of Haiti: Rethinking Crisis and Development* (2013) University of Minnesota Press: Minneapolis/London

Price-Mars, Jean *So Spoke the Uncle* (1983) Three Continents Press: Washington D.C.

Price-Mars, Jean *Une étape de L'évolution Haïtienne: Études de socio-psychologie* (1929) La Presse: Port-au-Prince

Ramsey, Kate 'That Old Black Magic: Seeing Haiti Through the Wall of Voodoo' *The Village Voice* September 27, 1994, 29

Ramsey, Kate 'Prohibition, Persecution, Performance: Anthropology and the Penalization of Vodou in mid-20th century' *Gradhiva 1* 2005, 165-169

Ramsey, Kate *The Spirits and the Law: Vodou and Power in Haiti* (2011) University of Chicago Press: London and Chicago

BIBLIOGRAPHY

Reed, Ishmael *Mumbo Jumbo* (1996) Scribner: New York

Renda, Mary *Taking Haiti: Military Occupation and the Culture of US Imperialism 1915-1940* (2001) University of North Carolina Press: Chapel Hill

Rey, Terry 'Kongolese Catholic Influences on Haitian Popular Catholicism: A Sociohistorical Exploration' *Central Africans and Cultural Transformations in the American Diaspora* (2002) Cambridge University Press: Cambridge/New York

Rhodes, Gary D. *White Zombie – Anatomy of a Horror Film* (2001) McFarland: North Carolina

Richardson, Michael *Refusal of the Shadow: Surrealism and the Caribbean* (1996) Verso: London/New York

Richman, Karen E. *Migration and Vodou* (2005) University of Florida Press: Gainesville

Rigaud, Milo *La Tradition Voudoo et Le Voudoo Haïten (son Temple, ses Mystères, sa Magie)* (1953) Édition Niclaus: Paris

Rigaud, Milo, *Ve-Ve: Diagrammes Rituels Du Voudou* (1974) French and European Publications Inc.: New York

Robinson, Cedric J. *Black Marxism: The Making of the Black Radical Tradition* (2000) University of North Carolina Press: Chapel Hill and London

Romero, George A. *Interviews* (2011) University Press of Mississippi: Mississippi

Schmidt, Hans *The United States Occupation of Haiti, 1915-1934* (1995) Rutgers University Press: New Brunswick, New Jersey

Schoultz, Lars H*uman Rights and United States Policy Towards Latin America* (1981) Princeton University Press: Princeton, New Jersey

Schwartz, Timothy T. *Travesty in Haiti: A True Account of Christian Missions, Orphanages, Fraud, Food Aid and Drug Trafficking* (2012) Booksurge Press: North Charleston, South Carolina

Sconce, Jeffrey *Haunted Media: Electronic Presence from Telegraphy to Television* (2000) Duke University Press: Durham and London

Seabrook, William B. *Adventures in Arabia: Among the Bedouins, Druses, Whirling Dervishes and Yezidee Devil-Worshippers* (1928) George Harrap & Company: London, Bombay, Sydney

Seabrook, William B. *The Magic Island* (1929) Harcourt Brace and Company: New York

Seabrook, William B. *Jungle Ways* (1931) George Harrap & Company: London, Bombay, Sydney

Seabrook, William B. *Witchcraft: Its Power in the World Today* (1940) Harcourt, Brace and Company: New York

Seabrook, William B. *No Hiding Place: An Autobiography* (1942) J. B. Lippincott Company

Senn, Bryan *Drums of Terror: Voodoo in the Cinema* (1998) Midnight Marquee Press: Baltimore, Maryland

Shannon, Magdaline W. *Jean Price-Mars, the Haitian Elite and the American Occupation 1915-1935* (1996) MacMillan Press: Basingstoke

Shaviro, Steven *The Cinematic Body* (1993) University of Minnesota Press: Minneapolis, Minnesota

Sherry, Norman *The Life of Graham Greene – Volume Three: 1955-1991* (2005) Pimlico: London

Sidis, Boris *The Psychology of Suggestion: A Research into the Subconscious Nature of Man and Society* (1919) Appleton and Company: New York

BIBLIOGRAPHY

Simpson, George Eaton 'The Vodun Service in Northern Haiti' *American Anthropologist* Vol. 42, no 2, April 1940

Simpson, George Eaton 'The Belief System of Haitian Vodun' *American Anthropologist*, Vol. 47, No 1, January - March 1945

Skal, David J. *The Monster Show: A Cultural History of Horror* (1993) Faber and Faber: New York

Smith, Matthew J. *Red and Black in Haiti: Radicalism, Conflict and Political Change, 1934-1957* (2009) University of North Carolina Press: Chapel Hill

Sprague, Jeb *Paramilitarism and the Assault on Democracy in Haiti* (2012) Monthly Review Press: New York

St. John, Spenser *Hayti or The Black Republic* (1889) Scribner & Welford: New York

Stocking Jr, George W 'Animism in Theory and Practice: E B Tylor's Unpublished "Notes on Spiritualism"' *Man*, New Series, Vol. 6, No 1 (Mar, 1971) 88-104

Stratton, Jon 'Zombie trouble: Zombie texts, Bare Life and Displaced People' *European Journal of Cultural Studies* 14, 2011, 265

Surya, Michel *Georges Bataille: An Intellectual Biography* (2002) Verso: London and New York

Swanson, Lucy 'Zombie Nation? The Horde, Social Uprisings and National Narratives' *Cincinnati Romance Review* 34, Fall 2012, 13-33

Thomas, Clive *The Rise of the Authoritarian State in Peripheral Societies* (1984) Monthly Review Press: New York

Thomson, Ian *Bonjour Blanc: A Journey Through Haiti* (2003) Vintage Books: London

Thornton, John K. '"I am the Subject of the King of Congo": African Political Ideology and the Haitian Revolution', *Journal of World History* 4 No 2, 1993, 181-214

Thylefors, Markel '"Our Government is in Bwa Kayiman:" A Vodou Ceremony in 1791 and its Contemporary Significations' *Stockholm Review of Latin American Studies*, 4, March 2009, 73-84

Tiqqun *This is Not a Programme* (2011) Semiotext(e): Los Angeles

Trouillot, Michel-Rolph *Haiti: State Against Nation – The Origins and Legacy of Duvalierism* (1990) Monthly Review Press: New York

Trouillot, Michel-Rolph 'The Odd and the Ordinary: Haiti, the Caribbean and the World', *Cimarron 2*, no 3, Winter 1990, 3-12

Trouillot, Michel-Rolph 'Haiti's Nightmare and the Lessons of History' *NACLA Report on the Americas*, Vol. XXVII, January-February 1994, 46-53

Trouillot, Michel-Rolph, *Silencing the Past: Power and the Production of History* (1995) Beacon Press: Boston

Wallin, Jason 'Living... Again: The Revolutionary Cine-Sign of Zombie Life' in Jagodinski, Jan (ed) *Psychoanalyzing Cinema: A Productive Encounter with Lacan, Deleuze and Žižek* (2012) Palgrave Macmillan: New York

Walmsley, D. M. *Anton Mesmer* (1967) Robert Hale: London

Weaver, Karol K. *Medical Revolutionaries: The Enslaved Healers of Eighteenth Century Saint Domingue* (2006) University of Illinois Press: Urbana and Chicago

White, Ashli *Encountering Revolution: Haiti and the Making of the Early Republic* (2010): John Hopkins University Press: Baltimore

Williams, Tony *The Cinema of George A. Romero: Knight of the Living Dead* (2003) Wallflower Press: London

Wirkus, Faustin and Dudley, Taney *The White King of La Gonave* (1931) Doubleday: New York

BIBLIOGRAPHY

Wooley, John *Wes Craven: The Man and His Nightmares* (2011) John Wiley & Sons: Hoboken, New Jersey

Worth, Robert F. *'Nigger Heaven* and the Harlem Renaissance' *African American Review*, Vol. 29, No 3, Autumn 1995, 461-473

Worthington, Marjorie *The Strange World of Willie Seabrook* (1966) Harcourt, Brace and World, Inc: New York

Zieger, Susan 'The Case of William Seabrook: *Documents*, Haiti and the Working Dead' *Modernism/modernity*, Vol. 19, No 4, November 2012, 737-754

Žižek, Slavoj *The Parallax View* (2006) MIT Press: Massachusetts

TELEVISION DOCUMENTARIES

'Haiti: Papa Doc and His People' Ralph Renick, *FYI (For Your Information)*, Channel 4, WTVJ-Miami, 1966

'Papa Doc: The Black Sheep' *Whicker's World*, Yorkshire Television, 1969

ARTICLES

Adams, David 'Aristide's last days' *Tampa Bay Times*, February 28, 2006

Barry-Shaw, Nik 'Exposing the Big Lie of "Operation Baghdad"' *Press for Conversion!* magazine, Issue #63, November 2008

Biberman, Herbert 'We Never Say Nigger in Front of Them', *The New York Times*, January 19, 1969

Biodrowski, Steve 'Wes Craven on Dreaming Up Nightmares' *Cinefantastique*, October 15, 2008

Boyd, William 'The Secret Persuaders' *The Guardian*, Saturday August 19, 2006

Canby, Vincent 'Slaves' Opens at the DeMille: Militancy Depicts Life in Antebellum South Dionne Warwick Plays Mistress in Debut' *The New York Times*, July 3, 1969

Carrazana, E. *et al* 'Epilepsy and Religious Experiences: Voodoo Possession' *Epilepsia* 40 (2) 239-241, 1999

Caulfield, Catherine 'The Chemistry of the Living Dead' *New Scientist*, December 15, 1983

Curnutte, Rick 'There's No Magic: A Conversation With George A. Romero' *The Film Journal*, October 2004

Dash, Mike 'The Trial that Gave Vodou a Bad Name', *Smithsonian.com*, May 29, 2013 (accessed November 17, 2012)

Deibert, Michael 'Ghosts, Bandits and Cité Soleil', Michael Deibert Blogspot, May 16, 2007 (accessed March 23, 2015)

Ebert, Roger 'Just Another Horror Movie - Or Is It?' *Chicago Sun Times*, January 5, 1969

Hallward, Peter 'Aristide and the Violence of Democracy: Review of Alex Dupuy's "The Prophet and Power: Jean-Bertrand Aristide, The International Community and Haiti" *Haiti Liberté*, July 2007

Harrison, Lawrence 'Haiti and the Voodoo Curse', *The Wall Street Journal*, February 5, 2010

Hinton, Charlie '*Ghosts of Cité Soleil*: Don't Believe the Hype' *Haiti Action Committee*, May 2007

James, Clara 'The Raboteau Revolt' *Z Magazine Online*, Vol. 15 No 12, December 2002

McManus, John T. 'Walking Dead in Angkor' *The New York Times*, May 24, 1936

McCarthy, Todd 'Review of Ghosts of Cité Soleil' *Variety*, September 27, 2006

BIBLIOGRAPHY

O'Hehir, Andrew '"Ghosts of Cité Soleil": Brothers at war, over politics and a woman' *Salon*, June 28th, 2007

Russell, Candice 'Bone Chilling look at Good, Bad of Voodoo' *Sun Sentinel*, February 9, 1988

Sanders, Richard 'Epithets without Borders' *Press for Conversion!* Issue #63, November 2008

Sanders, Richard 'The G184's Powerbrokers – Apaid and Boulos: Owners of the Fourth Estate; Leaders of the Fifth Column' *Press for Conversion!* Issue #61, September 2007

Scott, A. O. 'Hip Hop Gangsters on an Isle of Chaos' *The New York Times*, June 27, 2007

Shaw, Christopher 'What Zombies can teach us about Climate Change' *New Left Project*, March 28 2013

Sullivan, Laura 'In Search of the Red Cross's $500 million in Haiti Relief' NPR, June 3, 2015

Tapper, Jake 'The Witch Doctor is in: Max Beauvoir ran voodoo's biggest attraction in Haiti, but he's having trouble summoning the spirits to Northwest DC' *Washington City Paper*, June 26, 1998

Taylor, Eric J. 'Legalizing Voodoo: Haiti Officially Recognises Vodoun as a Religion' *Rutgers Journal of Law and Religion*, New Developments 69

Thomas, Kevin 'Good, Evil Clash in "Serpent and Rainbow"' *Los Angeles Times*, February 5, 1988

Weiner, Tim "'93 Report By CIA Tied Haiti Agent to Slaying' *The New York Times*, October 13, 1996

Williams, Tony 'White Zombie, Haitian Horror' *Jump Cut* No 28, 18-20, 1983

Worthington, Rogers 'Repressive Haiti Group Says It Can Be A Loyal Opposition' *Chicago Tribune*, November 6, 1994

Young, Tim 'Red Cross Chief Executive Outlines Haiti Relief' *The National Press Club*, January 12, 2011

Zaborowski, H. ed *Natural Moral Law in Contemporary Society* (2010).

INTERVIEWS AND PUBLIC PRESENTATIONS

Craven, Wes Public talk at the Aero Theatre, Santa Monica, February 21, 2010 http://www.dailymotion.com/video/xcccju_wes-craven-the-serpent-and-the-rain_shortfilms

Davis, Wade 'On Haitian Zombies' Interview with CBC's Peter Gzowski, January 25, 1986 http://www.cba.ca/entry/wade-davis-on-haitian-zombies

Davis, Wade 'Dreams from Endangered Cultures' TED Talk: http://www.ted.com/talks/wade_davis_on_endangered_cultures?language=en

Davis, Wade Interview with George Stroumboulopouloss, CBS February 5, 2013 http://www.cbc.ca/strombo/videos/wade-davis-1

Davis, Wade 'Looking for Haitian Zombies' Lecture for IRIS Nights, Annenberg Space for Photography, February 14, 2013 https://www.youtube.com/watch?v=qGq2Bj3FGpc

FILMOGRAPHY

The Criminal Hypnotist (1909) D. W. Griffith
Der Andere (The Other) (1913) Max Mack
The Cabinet of Dr. Caligari (1920) Robert Wiene
Dr. Mabuse the Gambler (1922) Fritz Lang
White Zombie (1932) Victor Halperin
The Ghoul (1933) T. Hayes Hunter
Chloe: Love is Calling You (1934) Marshall Neilan
Drums O' Voodoo (1934) Arthur Hoerl

BIBLIOGRAPHY

Ouanga (1935) George Terwilliger

Revolt of the Zombies (1936) Victor Halperin

The Devil's Daughter (1939) George Terwilliger

King of the Zombies (1941) Jean Yarbrough

Revenge of the Zombies (1943) Steve Sekely

I Walked with a Zombie (1943) Jacques Tourneur

Zombies on Broadway (1945) Gordon Dines/Gordon M. Douglas

Lydia Bailey (1952) Jean Negulesco

The Last Man on Earth (1964) Ubaldo Ragona/Sidney Salkow

Dr. Terror's House of Horrors (1965) Freddie Francis

The Comedians (1967) Peter Glenville

Night of the Living Dead (1968) George A. Romero

Isle of the Snake People (1971) Juan Ibáñez

Live and Let Die (1973) Guy Hamilton

Sugar Hill (1974) Paul Maslansky

Dawn of the Dead (1978) George A. Romero

Zombi 2 (1979) Lucio Fulci

Day of the Dead (1985) George A. Romero

The Return of the Living Dead (1985) Dan O'Bannon

The Serpent and the Rainbow (1988) Wes Craven

Voodoo and the Church in Haiti (1988) Bob Richards

The American Nightmare (2000) Adam Simon

28 Days Later (2002) Danny Boyle

Haïti: la fin des chimères? (2004) Charles Najman

Shaun of the Dead (2004) Edgar Wright

Aristide and the Endless Revolution (2005) Nicolas Rossier

Land of the Dead (2005) George A. Romero

Ghosts of Cité Soleil (2006) Asger Leth and Milos Loncarevic

Diary of the Dead (2007) George A. Romero

Moloch Tropical (2009) Raoul Peck

D-volution (2011) Walter Boholst

The Seduced Human (2012) Truls Lie

Assistance Mortelle ('Fatal Assistance') (2013) Raoul Peck

Birth of the Living Dead (2013) Rob Kuhns

World War Z (2013) Marc Forster

Doc of the Dead (2014) Alexandre O. Phillipe

A Voodoo Possession (2014) Walter Boholst

INDEX

INDEX

ACKNOWLEDGEMENTS

Special thanks to Leah Gordon, who first invited me to speak about Voodoo Terror and without whose friendship and support this book would never have been written, and to LeGrace Benson for her constant encouragement and patient guidance in the ways of Haitian scholarship. Thanks to Sam Iya and John Russell for reading the early drafts and staying interested; to Simon O'Sullivan for his unbroken confidence in the project; and to Stephanie Moran, for being such an attentive and supportive proof-reader. Finally, unreserved thanks to Mark Pilkington and Jamie Sutcliffe at Strange Attractor, with whom it has been an unbroken pleasure to work.

Ayibobo!

JOHN CUSSANS

John Cussans is an artist, writer and educator based in London. His writing has been published in numerous collections and journals, and he has exhibited widely since his first solo exhibition, Buried Alive, at the Cabinet gallery in London in 1994. After completing his doctoral thesis on Georges Bataille and the video nasty controversy in 1995, he developed a collaborative artistic research practice culminating in a number of projects including: The Bughouse (a tribute to Philip K. Dick 2000-2003), The Free School in a New Dark Age (2010–2013) and DRUGG (Diagram Research, Use and Generation Group 2012-2016). Since 2009 he has been involved with the Ghetto Biennale in Port-au-Prince, Haiti, and is currently working on a Leverhulme–funded research project, The Skullcracker Suite, investigating processes of cultural decolonisation in British Columbia. He is a departmental lecturer and MFA course leader at the Ruskin School of Art, Oxford. Haiti, and is currently working on a Leverhulme–funded research project, The Skullcracker Suite, investigating processes of cultural decolonisation in British Columbia. He is a departmental lecturer and MFA course leader at the Ruskin School of Art, Oxford.

Printed in the United States
by Baker & Taylor Publisher Services